# From Empire to Revolution

*Sir James Wright and
the Price of Loyalty in Georgia*

GREG BROOKING

*The University of Georgia Press*
ATHENS

Publication of this book was supported, in part,
by the Kenneth Coleman Series in Georgia History and Culture

© 2024 by the University of Georgia Press
Athens, Georgia 30602
www.ugapress.org
All rights reserved
Set in 10.5/13.5 Adobe Caslon Pro Regular
by Kaelin Chappell Broaddus

Most University of Georgia Press titles are
available from popular e-book vendors.

Printed digitally

Library of Congress Cataloging-in-Publication Data
Names: Brooking, Greg, author.
Title: From empire to revolution : Sir James Wright and the price of loyalty in
Georgia / Greg Brooking.
Description: Athens : The University of Georgia Press, 2024. | Series: Early
American places | Includes bibliographical references and index.
Identifiers: LCCN 2023043116 (print) | LCCN 2023043117 (ebook) |
ISBN 9780820365947 (hardback) | ISBN 9780820365930 (paperback) |
ISBN 9780820365954 (epub) | ISBN 9780820365961 (pdf)
Subjects: LCSH: Wright, James, Sir, 1716–1785. | Governors—Georgia—
Biography. | American loyalists—Georgia—Biography. | Georgia—Politics and
government—To 1775. | Georgia—Politics and government—1775–1865. |
Great Britain—Colonies—America—Administration.
Classification: LCC F289.W75 B76 2024 (print) | LCC f289.w75 (ebook)
LC record available at https://lccn.loc.gov/2023043116
LC ebook record available at https://lccn.loc.gov/2023043117

*For my wife, Adrienne,*
*my children, Alex, Gabby, and Michael,*
*and my parents, Gerri and Roger.*
*I love you all!*

# CONTENTS

# ACKNOWLEDGMENTS

I am a parent and a high school teacher, and I firmly believe in the wisdom that "it takes a village" to raise a child. It also takes a village to write a book, and I am indebted to far too many villagers to thank in the following pages. Please do not take offense if I have omitted you, for it arose simply from my well-known forgetfulness. For that, I apologize.

First and foremost, I must acknowledge the support of my family, who provided emotional support and far too often did without both material things and my presence while I journeyed to various places in search of James Wright. My wife Adrienne's sacrifices were numerous, but most importantly, she instilled in me the belief that I could and should complete this project. My children, Alex, Gabby, and Michael inspired me to achieve my dream of becoming an author. This book is truly for them. My parents, Gerri and Roger, imparted a love of books and history. My siblings, Tracy, Brian, and Meredith, have always loved and supported me. If not for family, this project would have never been started, much less completed.

My graduate school mentors and fellow students also played an invaluable role in shaping who I am as a historian and what this book has become. Georgia College's John Fair, Anne Bailey, and Lee Ann Caldwell embraced a middle-aged master's student with open arms, giving me sage advice and, in the case of Anne, the terrific opportunity of serving as the graduate student editor of the *Georgia Historical Quarterly*. My dissertation advisor at Georgia State University, Chuck Steffen, was the perfect mentor because he taught me to relax and not take my work too seriously. My dissertation committee, which included Wendy Venet, Jeff Young, and Jim Piecuch, never took themselves too seriously but kept me on track and focused. Jim has always been a dear friend and mentor who carefully read each chapter of this manuscript. Larry Grubbs, another professor at Georgia State, has been a true friend and research companion. I also want to acknowledge the emotional and intellectual support of my fellow students at Georgia State, especially Mark Fleszar, Casey Cater, Clif Stratton, and Lauren Moran.

Another group of graduate students whom I met at various conferences and research institutions also deserves mention. Michael Hattem is a dear friend and tireless supporter, and compatriot. In addition to reading much of this manuscript, he has provided tremendous encouragement throughout my academic career. Chris Pearl, Will Tatum, and Nichole George, whom I met at the David Library, made those long fellowships personally rewarding, as did the entire library staff. Josh Howard led me on numerous battlefield tours in South Carolina and has read much of this biography, providing encouragement and insight. Often traveling with us was Dan Tortora. His expertise informed much of my work on Native Americans.

Various archival and library staff made the arduous task of research much more bearable and fruitful. In addition to the kind folks at the David Library, the staff at the Georgia Historical Society, especially Stan Deaton, has gone above and beyond in assisting me for over a decade. Ellen Wilson and the Society of the Cincinnati staff made my fellowship smooth and beneficial, as did the staff at the Clements Library at the University of Michigan. Wade Dorsey and Brent Holcomb at the South Carolina State Archives answered questions and made suggestions with ease and kindness.

Another group has also provided research assistance and collegial friendship. Carol Berkin has been my most constant supporter during this project. She has critiqued many chapters and written important fellowship recommendations. Her assistance cannot be overstated. The late Robert C. Calhoon, the dean of Loyalist studies, was an early supporter of this biography, as was Todd Braisted of The On-Line Institute for Advanced Loyalist Studies. Thomas Hallock and Rick Hererra improved this project with their discerning comments and suggestions. Greg Urwin was a real cheerleader during this process. David Wilson provided a couple of important hard-to-find documents. Andrew Musselman of the famed Gray's Inn in London clarified a few important points about learning at the famed Inns of Court. Also from the United Kingdom, Ric Berman elucidated Wright's experiences as a Mason. Lastly, I extend my gratitude to Ean Parsons from the Manor House in Sedgefield, U.K., the former home of James Wright's father, for providing photos of the home for this volume.

Some very close friends helped in myriad ways. From my first high school history teacher, Kevin Dockrell, who inspired me to join this vital profession, to my two best friends from high school, Michael Cass and Doug Bush. Michael read the entire manuscript, which is better for it, and Doug was my constant study companion in high school. Another friend, Jim Jordan, has patiently prodded my progress with kind words and worldly advice. Also, the gang from the social studies department at North Springs High School in Atlanta afforded me time and space to write more frequently than I would have otherwise been afforded and, more importantly, always kept me laughing.

I owe a tremendous debt to the editorial staff at the University of Georgia Press: Nate Holly, Lea Johnson, and Mary Hill. Nate believed in the project from the beginning. He and Lea guided this first-time writer through the maze of publishing. I cannot imagine a better copyeditor than Mary Hill. Her appreciation for the book, eye for detail, and professionalism have made this a much better book.

Finally, aside from family is the group to whom I owe the most. Charles Baxley has led me on a dozen battlefield tours and hosted me during numerous historical conferences. His passion for the American Revolution spurred me to never give up on this project. His kindness can only be repaid by paying it forward. I hope to honor his generosity appropriately. Sandra Boling transcribed James Wright's will, an accomplishment that still boggles the mind. Farris Cadle aided with my understanding of the legal and real estate issues in colonial Georgia, and Robert "Bob" Davis never failed to pass along any research tidbit he encountered. Lastly, Ken Thomas and the late Mary Bondurant Warren likely matched my passion for learning about James Wright. Their interest preceded my own. Their encouragement for this project and knowledge about the inner workings of colonial Georgia and the imperial system, combined with Mary's transcriptions, have made this work possible.

Despite the dozens of villagers mentioned above and I am sure others I failed to acknowledge, all errors are my own.

# From Empire to Revolution

# "Sir James,
# You Are My Prisoner"

A special session of the rebel Council of Safety convened in Savannah, Georgia, on the chilly evening of 18 January 1776. Their meeting at Tondee's Tavern at the northwest corner of Broughton and Whitaker Streets focused on the recent arrival of two British men-of-war at Tybee Island. In this moment, Georgia's rebel Council of Safety resolved to plunge Britain's youngest colony deep into the maelstrom of rebellion by ordering the arrest of royal governor Sir James Wright and three loyal members of the Governor's Council. Disheartening for the governor was that his best friend's son, Joseph "Joe" Habersham, volunteered to execute these traitorous orders.[1] As Habersham organized his posse, the governor greeted several dinner guests at the governor's house, sometimes referred to as the Government House, on St. James's Square.[2] But this was no ordinary dinner party: it was a meeting of the highest-ranking provincial officials, and their discussion focused on the town's ever-growing mobocracy. While anxiously eating at Wright's mahogany dining table under the reassuring gaze of a portrait of King George II, the Loyalists were startled by a scuffle at the front door.[3]

Major Habersham barged into the dining room just a few seconds later and, with apparent grace and dignity, bowed to the assembled guests. He then marched to the head of the table. Placing his arm on Governor Wright's shoulder, he stated: "Sir James, you are my prisoner."[4] The Council of Safety soon reconvened and decided that each of those arrested should be permitted to return "to their respective homes upon their parole." But

Wright's parole had come with the additional guarantee that he maintain peace and keep at bay the "ships of war" in the harbor.[5]

The promised safety of parole seemed more dubious with each passing day. On more than one occasion, shots were fired into the governor's home.[6] Three weeks later, and fearing for his life, James Wright, Georgia's most popular and successful colonial governor, whose efforts doubled the colony's boundaries and enriched many a parvenu, secured his safety in the predawn hours of 11 February.[7] He told Lord George Germain, the secretary of state for the American Department, that he fled Savannah in the middle of the night "in order to avoid the rage and violence of the Rebels."[8] Patriotism to king and Crown had a steep price tag.

The story of James Wright is one about loyalty—loyalty to his family, his friends, his colonies, and his country. It is also the story of loss—the loss of his wife and three daughters, his status, his power, his wealth, and his home. Manuscript collections only reveal tantalizing bits of detail about his personal life, but his professional correspondence illuminates his career. He led a thoroughly imperial life and served two colonies and two kings from the 1730s through the mid-1780s. His family history reveals much about both Wright and the transatlantic opportunities available to those with a few well-placed connections. It also sheds light on how a man could rise and fall within that imperial system, as well as the lengths to which he might go to recoup his family's name and wealth.

The patriarch, Wright's grandfather, had reached the pinnacle of his profession and counted King James II among his sponsors. It is possible, in fact, that James Wright was named after the infamous king. This relationship, or, better yet, his loyalty to his sovereign, cost him first his freedom and then his life, as he died a political prisoner following the Glorious Revolution of 1688. James Wright's father then undertook the arduous task of resurrecting the family's name and modest fortune, a task that required a transatlantic relocation to the British Empire's periphery in Charleston, South Carolina, in 1725.[9] His appointment as colonial chief justice afforded him a position and salary sufficient to both invest in valuable Lowcountry lands and find appropriately affluent matches for his children. He proved so successful in augmenting the wealth he brought from England that by the time of his death more than a decade later, he could rest in peace in the knowledge that his children's future looked considerably more secure than the one bequeathed to him by his own father. But before we proceed, we must make a further examination of the lives of Wright's paternal forebears.[10]

## Sir Robert Wright,
## "Last of the Profligate Chief Justices"

James Wright's grandfather Sir Robert Wright, chief justice of the King's Bench, was born about 1634 in the North Sea town of Wangford, Suffolk.[11] He matriculated at Cambridge University's Gonville and Caius College in 1651 and gained admission to the famed Lincoln's Inn three years later before being called to the bar in 1661, even though he did not possess the keenest of minds and struggled to write his own legal opinions.[12]

Gregarious and personable, Wright married three times, each time to a woman who had more money and a higher social standing than he did.[13] These connections helped get him elected to Parliament and appointed to various and increasingly important governmental positions. But Wright always found trouble. His debauched lifestyle, coupled with an unsound moral compass, seemed a magnet for the authorities.[14] But his willingness to be the king's tool ultimately cost him his life. In 1687 and 1688 Wright became the centerpiece of two unrelated but important legal dramas, the latter, known as the Trial of the Seven Bishops, proving fatal.[15] Sir Robert Wright, as he was knighted at the beginning of the decade, thus died miserable, alone, and an utter outcast at Newgate Prison. Known as the "last of the profligate Chief Justices," he was said to have been fortunate that he had contemporaries such as George Jeffreys, Lord Chief Justice of the King's Bench, and Wright's father-in-law, William Scroggs, who considerably exceeded him in their atrocities. Had he run the same career in an age not more than ordinarily wicked, his name might have passed into a by-word, denoting all that is odious and detestable in a judge.[16]

## Robert Wright,
## "So Firm and Able a Judge"

James Wright's father, also named Robert Wright, was a twenty-three-year-old bachelor at the time of his father's death. He had been born in Norfolk in 1666.[17] He attended Eton College, Gaius College at Cambridge University, and the Middle Temple.[18] Like his father, Wright had been successful in securing affluent spouses, marrying Alice Johnson Pitt, the heiress of John Johnson and the widow of Baldwin Pitt, Esq., the same year his father died in Newgate Prison. Alice passed away in 1723 after thirty-four years of marriage.[19] It became apparent after her death that Robert had inherited his fa-

The Manor House in Sedgefield, County Durham, home of Robert Wright.
Photo courtesy of Ean Parsons.

ther's seedier traits. He fathered seven children out of wedlock and likely simultaneously sustained two households, one with Alice Pitt and the other
with Isabella Bulman, whom he married within a week of Alice's death.[20]

It is likely that this behavior compelled Wright to relocate his family to South Carolina, where he had been appointed colonial chief justice.
Wright's family would face no stigma in Charleston, and no one would
question the children's right to his inheritance.[21] Unlike his father, however,
Robert proved to be a very capable jurist.[22]

Charlestonian Elizabeth Hyrne witnessed the arrival of the Wright family in the spring of 1725. She observed a "gentleman of a large family." They
were, she wrote, a "very genteel people [of] good substance." Importantly,
"they have now 400 or 500 pounds in England at a place called" Sedgefield, near Newcastle. She even noted that Wright "has brought over a coach
[with] several servants in livery." The rumor mill pondered what had brought
the Wrights to Charleston. Hyrne acknowledged that "some say his father
was a judge in King James's reign" but that the family preferred to keep their
past private. In any event, she mused, the Wrights should make good settlers,
as the father had purchased a sizeable plantation on the Ashely River.[23]

Wright received his official appointment from South Carolina's Lords
Proprietors, but they were in a decade-long battle for colonial control, which

they lost. Wright consequently could not begin in his full official capacity until six years later.[24] He encountered resistance from the colonial Commons House of Assembly (usually referred to as the Assembly) prior to even taking office. Emblematic of South Carolinians' propensity to clash with authority, Assembly members took umbrage with Wright's lifetime appointment. But this dispute proved rather minor, and he would soon begin anew in America.[25]

But Wright was indeed his father's son, and his inflexibility and his Crowncentric and aristocratic worldview courted controversy throughout his tenure, traits that were also deeply ingrained in his son James. His view of the world often placed him at odds with a provincial Assembly that by the 1730s had entered a period of testing the British constitution and their role within it.[26] Their frustration with Wright's strong monarchical leanings resulted in their refusal to pay his full salary, claiming he "hath lately invaded and violated the known privileges of this house" by having the audacity to demand that the Assembly issue writs of habeas corpus when incarcerating citizens.[27]

Wright's salary dispute became such a concern that the acting governor, William Bull, tried to intercede on his behalf. With no apparent sense of irony, the slaveholding official declared in a statement to the legislature: "I take it for an allowed maxim both by the laws of God and man that the labourer is worthy of his hire. I therefore think it proper to remind you that the chief justice hath duly held the Supream Courts of Judicature for more than nine years past and hath received from the publick no more than £1,400 currency."[28] These rough lessons also provided an education for Wright's son, who would one day deal with similarly recalcitrant Assemblies. Despite these issues, Wright made his mark on the judicial branch. By the time he left office, the judiciary had attained its independence by refusing to yield to Assembly demands even at the literal cost of his financial stability.[29]

As the battles for colonial control raged, a yellow fever epidemic struck the Lowcountry in the fall of 1739. It claimed Robert Wright as one of its nearly two hundred victims on 12 October.[30] While Wright lay stricken and confined to his bed, likely with severe body aches, a high fever, and uncontrollable vomiting, a friend of his informed the Duke of Newcastle in London of the lamentable situation. "The Chief Justice of South Carolina is a very worthy gentleman," James Oglethorpe wrote, and "I hope he may long continue but as all men are mortal and he is sick of an illness which hath been fatal in Carolina," his fate seemed clear.[31]

Wright owned no fewer than ten thousand acres of land in various South Carolina counties.[32] According to historian George Rogers, future governor

Charles Pinckney's "great mansion" had been "designed to emulate, if not excel, the finest mansions of that day," including former "Chief Justice Robert Wright's home."[33] Aside from his £1,000 annual salary, of which Wright received intermittent portions, there are numerous records indicating the sale of sizeable tracts of land.[34] Wright also reaped huge profits from his plantations.[35]

The process of redeeming the family reputation, so tarnished in England, had begun in colonial South Carolina. Even though it would take decades, Robert Wright had begun the process. By the time of his death, his sons were well on their way to successful careers, and his daughters had been appropriately matched. Nineteenth-century South Carolina historian Edward McCrady observed, "It was fortunate for the liberty of the people that so firm and able a judge as Robert Wright . . . was on the bench."[36] The most notable of his seven children was his fourth son, James, who would become a man of real importance on both sides of the Atlantic and die a baronet in the years following the American Revolution.[37]

This book makes several historiographical interventions and contributions. In addition to engaging with the scant literature related to James Wright, this work affords special attention to four historiographical areas: revolutionary-era Loyalism, the frontier or backcountry, Native American relations, and, to a lesser degree, Lowcountry slavery.[38] Although artificially separated for this introduction, these fields are in fact inseparable. Anthropologist Sydney Mintz perfectly illustrated this point in 1996: "Lifeways of all the peoples we study are forever subject to influences from elsewhere, and are forever in flux. . . . They are historical products, processual products, such that most categories and continuum run the risk of immobilizing and misrepresenting them."[39] The very interconnectedness of these fields is what makes this project complex and intriguing.

## James Wright, Tortured by a Dual Patriotism

The scarce literature on James Wright has often focused on his life as a governor in crisis during the American Revolution and has neglected to examine his life outside of that context and the public realm.[40] This volume corrects that omission, discussing his ancestry, personal life, and entire career. Loyalists like James Wright were tortured by a dual patriotism. Wright once wrote that he "always studied to promote the prosperity of the province, and happiness and welfare of the people, as well as to discharge [my] duty to the Crown with integrity, and was fortunate enough to succeed in both, till the Spirit of Rebellion broke out."[41] This is the first work to minutely examine the career of a southern Loyalist, much less a Loyalist from Georgia, the often forgotten colony, but it owes a debt to previous Loyalist historians who provided an important context to Loyalism.[42] This work is also indebted to the historians who have examined American Loyalism from a multiethnic perspective.[43]

This historiography clearly illustrates that Loyalists were virtually indistinguishable from their rebel counterparts. Demographically, they fit comfortably into every economic, ethnic, and racial category we can devise to categorize humans.[44] Aside from royal governors and some imperial officials, both groups truly identified as Americans rather than Britons. Both groups admired and sought to emulate British culture. Both groups believed in the value of empire. Yet despite these similarities, the Loyalists opposed independence. Personal issues—social, economic, and local—figured much more prominently in the decision-making process for both groups than did political ideology.[45] For example, rebel intimidation pushed many Americans from a neutral position into the waiting arms of the Crown and Parliament. Moreover, family ties often but by no means always dictated a person's loyalty. Others were motivated by personal economic interests. Many simply feared change and felt more secure nestled in the British bosom. Still others could not comprehend that the rebellion could succeed. Of course, each of these motivations could be juxtaposed on their rebellious brethren.[46]

Perhaps most importantly for this work, I have relied upon the biographers' touch, and here I will mention them by name. It is my hope that the influence of Bernard Bailyn's monumentally important study of the life of Thomas Hutchinson, royal governor of the Province of Massachusetts Bay, can be seen throughout this book. The Hutchinson revealed through Bailyn's erudite and sensitive study is a man very much like James Wright. "I am quite certain," Bailyn wrote, that "the reasons for the ultimate failure of this otherwise successful and impressive politician ... [were] his calculatingly pragmatic approach to politics, his insensitivity to the moral ingredients of public life and to the beliefs and passions that grip people's minds, and his incapacity to respond to aspirations that transcend the ordinary boundaries of received knowledge, prudence, and common sense."[47] The quotation could apply just as aptly to James Wright. Also important among biographical studies have been the works of Andrew Walmsley, Ed Cashin, Carol Berkin, John Ferling, Sheila Skemp, Frank Lambert, and James Corbett David.[48]

The lives of revolutionary-era Loyalists have only recently become a fashionable topic of historical inquiry. Aside from a consistent interest maintained by genealogists, serious historical interest in Loyalists and Loyalism has been negligible until the past generation or so, but even then, studies of southern Loyalists have been almost nonexistent. Historian John Ferling opined that those occupying the top tiers in the colonial hierarchy made "decisions that impacted countless lives, determined the shape of the [American Revolution] and to some extent its length, and certainly were important to the outcome of the conflict." These well-heeled aristocrats, he argued, were ideological conduits to the citizenry, giving "voice and meaning to previously ill-defined or unarticulated aspirations."[49] But what of those Loyalist leaders, those men and women, white, Black, and "red," who held equally strong convictions and made innumerable consequential decisions? They too have often been neglected, simply cast as villains in American "patriot" historiography, because, as Thucydides once wrote, "the people made their recollection fit in with their sufferings."[50] "Patriots" who remained loyal to their king and country were confined to the status of secondary figures, traitorous scoundrels in the rich drama of the War of Independence. This is especially true of southern Loyalists, and this volume aims to address our understanding of these Loyalists.

## A New Order of Things

At the 1893 annual meeting of the American Historical Association, Frederick Jackson Turner delivered a monumental essay about the significance of the frontier in American history. Henceforth, any discussion of said frontier had to begin with Turner. In his opening remarks, he stated: "The existence of an area of free land, its continuous recession, and the advance of American settlement westward, explain American development."[51] That land meant opportunity, and as long as it was available, Americans could invent and reinvent themselves in the West. Native American poet laureate N. Scott Momaday described the frontier as a dream: "It is what people who have come here from the beginning of time have dreamed. It is a dream landscape to the Native American. It's full of sacred realities."[52] These statements aptly describe the juxtaposition of people settling the backcountry: some people wished to create a new dream, while others sought to perpetuate an existing one. This contrast was on full display during the career of James Wright in both South Carolina and Georgia and will play an important role in both his rise and his fall. This work prefers to interpret the backcountry as a zone with a defined territory and the presence of multiple cultures, as well as observable interactions between those cultures.[53] Most importantly, the backcountry was filled with contingency and agency. Its actors, in both their origins and their motivations, changed during Wright's career.[54] For the most part, James Wright held the common view of Native Americans during his life: they were savages in need of civilization. His view of backcountry whites was only marginally better. He referred to settlers as "a set of almost lawless white people who are a sort of borderers and often as bad if not worse than the Indians."[55]

Joshua Piker has argued that an examination of eighteenth-century Georgia "should begin with a basic fact: the Deep South was an ethnically diverse and economically fluid place" that was "neither [Indian] country nor European territory."[56] It was a fully contested middle ground in which all people, Native Americans included, were full-fledged actors in the drama unfolding in the American Southeast. But this is not to suggest that all actors possessed the same tools with which to shape their lives. White traders proved the most instrumental in defining European imperialism on the frontier, while men like Wright engaged them in a contest to mold the relationship between core and periphery. Native Americans were then left to carve out their own destiny within a less than unified imperial structure. More than specifically challenging Native American historiography, *From Empire to Revolution* employs it to tell the story of James Wright.[57]

## Domesticating Slavery

Although often at odds, backcountry leaders and the Lowcountry elite found common ground regarding slavery. Any discussion of slavery is multifaceted and complex. Unfortunately, aside from the jarring statistical data gleaned from James Wright's Loyalist claim, his official documentation for postwar compensation from the British government, he left precious few details about his eleven plantations and more than hundreds of enslaved humans. Despite the paucity of records, however, this book is conversant with the historiography of Lowcountry slavery.[58] It will also be the first volume to analyze as much as possible Wright's views upon slavery, his slaves, and his numerous plantations. He was in many ways quite typical of eighteenth-century enslavers: avaricious, acquisitive, and efficient. But Wright may have deviated in other ways from either the norm or the perceived norm of southern planters. But that story must wait for now.

Wright's story is deeply captivating. He enjoyed a comfortable existence on two continents, and he resided near and influenced those at the very pinnacle of power. He proved himself to be one of Britain's most able colonial governors and then, once that portion of the empire had been lost, one of the most ardent defenders of its Loyalist subjects. His story is certainly unique and merits attention on its own. More importantly, however, his story is emblematic of many colonial American stories of men and women who sacrificed all, for a variety of motivations, in the name of loyalty, order, and conservative eighteenth-century values. Averse to change and incapable of believing that the mother country plotted to enslave Americans, Wright often questioned the wisdom of the government's policy but firmly believed that reform must come from within the constitutional system.

James Wright lived in an emerging transatlantic world that linked people, goods, and cultures across several continents. As a man of the Atlantic he equally split the first two-thirds of his life between the cosmopolitan capitals of Great Britain and South Carolina. His background and dual identity afforded him the unique ability to understand the needs and desires of people on both sides of the Atlantic. Having a foot in two colonies and in England may have meant that Wright was a man with no home or, perhaps, with many homes: London, Charleston, and Savannah. Moreover, his family owned a long tradition of service to the Crown in both Britain and America. His desire to augment his family's status and fortune necessitated a certain degree of unquestioned loyalty to Crown and Parliament. It certainly required the fortitude to implement parliamentary legislation, odious or otherwise. Likewise, he assiduously acquired land and firmly entrenched himself among Georgia's burgeoning planter aristocracy. His desire to secure Georgia's economic future endeared him to the colony's local power brokers. Walking this political tightrope required great dexterity, and Wright truly endeavored to honorably serve both his country and his colony. "It has ever been my desire," he wrote to the Duke of Hillsborough, "to discharge my duty to the King & People with integrity, & to the utmost of my power."[59]

Born in London on 8 May 1716, Wright's father, Robert, moved the family to Charleston nine years later in expectation of his appointment as South Carolina's chief justice.[60] James Wright lived most of the next thirty-five years in that important colonial entrepôt. During this period he established himself as a full-fledged member of Charleston's planter elite. He also served as the colony's attorney general and agent to Great Britain.

Fully utilizing the station into which he was born, Wright embarked on a legal career at a very young age. Shortly thereafter he married Sarah Maidman in February 1742.[61] She bore him nine children before her death aboard the H.M.S. *Epreuve*, along with two daughters, when the ship was lost at sea in 1764.[62] In 1737 Wright became South Carolina's attorney general, a position he held, off and on, until becoming that colony's agent to London twenty years later.[63] After spending three years fulfilling his duties in London, he was appointed lieutenant governor of Georgia by the Crown, a temporary expedient until he could replace the popular but ill Henry Ellis, becoming the third and final royal governor of Georgia. A thorough eighteenth-century conservative, Wright believed government to be the purview of the independently wealthy, virtuous citizen.[64] Moreover, he possessed a comprehensive familiarity with the southern colonies and a keen understanding of the British imperial system. As governor, Wright, whom one historian termed "an aristocratic servant of the king," oversaw colonial Georgia's greatest era of economic and territorial expansion.[65] His tenure represented royal government at its most effective in no small part because of both his personal investment in the colony and his belief that local matters should be subordinated to imperial concerns.[66]

Wright believed that Georgia's future rested on agricultural expansion, which required peace with the Indians and a revision of the colony's land laws. He oversaw two massive cessions of Indian land (1763 and 1773) and worked diligently to maintain peaceful relations with the Native Americans. He also thought that treaty obligations applied to both parties, although guaranteeing colonial obedience proved quite difficult. Lastly and against significant opposition from some corners, Wright insisted that ceded land only be granted to settlers, not speculators.[67]

Chapter 1 highlights Wright's career from the early 1730s to his gubernatorial appointment in Georgia in 1760. His rise was steady and progressive, no doubt initially aided by his father's connections. Chapter 2 examines Wright's early years in office, especially notable for Native troubles and the conclusion of the French and Indian War. The next chapter illustrates Wright at his critical best, deftly navigating the Stamp Act crisis. The fourth chapter finds Wright traveling back to England to negotiate his second Native American land cession in a decade. Chapter 5 sees the war's beginning in New England and Wright fight for his political life in Georgia. The sixth chapter finds Wright actually fighting for his life and witnesses his capture and escape from Georgia's rebels. Chapter 7 examines Wright's influence upon Britain's southern strategy, his return to Georgia, and his role during the siege of Savannah. Chapter 8 explores the final years of the revolution and Wright's ultimate evacuation. The epilogue reviews Wright's final few years, tirelessly working to ensure compensation for Georgia's loyal subjects.

# CHAPTER 1

# The Making of an Aristocrat

At the cost of his life, James Wright's grandfather Sir Robert Wright loyally served as King James II's chief justice. James's father, also named Robert Wright, faithfully upheld the prerogative of King George II as chief justice of South Carolina. Both judges possessed significant, though occasionally squandered, fortunes, and the Wright family story reveals the integration of a once-important English family into the colonial economic and political power structure during their generational attempt to redeem both their name and their fortune. James Wright's father brought significant capital to Charleston in 1725 and augmented his wealth throughout his life through purchases of land and human beings, providing educations, dowries, and substantial inheritances to each of his children. James Wright and his siblings married well and consolidated their holdings. Acutely aware of his own ancestry, Wright followed in the path of both his father and grandfather, choosing a career in the legal field and holding a deep devotion to the English constitution as represented by Crown and Parliament. Like his father, he used his strong legal mind to climb the socioeconomic ladder.

Although Wright frequently appeared in legal documents and newspapers, a lack of documentary evidence makes a full accounting of his life and early career impossible to re-create. This is mostly true because much of his personal correspondence was destroyed at the beginning of the American Revolution.[1] Enough evidence exists, however, to construct a dependable and nuanced sketch of his long journey to the pinnacle of power in colonial America. From an early age, Wright occupied a central role in provincial Charleston—he was a church leader, Freemason, landholder, lawyer, attorney general, and, lastly, colonial agent to Great Britain.

## James Wright as Freemason

In the sweltering, sticky summer of 1737, James Graeme, master of Solomon's Freemason Lodge in Charleston, nominated his brother-in-law, twenty-one-year-old "James Wright, Esq.," to be senior warden of Solomon's Freemason Lodge.[2] Such appointments would become common for this precocious and well-connected young man, who would soon rise to serve as master of the lodge, provincial deputy grand master, and provincial grand master.[3] Lodge members like Wright were among the most socially and financially prominent men in Charleston, and his roles within the organization serve as a clear indication that the city's elite deemed him worthy of important leadership positions from a very early age.[4] Of course, his father's position as chief justice of South Carolina could have only helped pave the way for his entrance into elite society, but there is no denying that once there, Wright proved his merit.

Freemasonry had been founded in 1717 in London. In Charleston its membership was filled with leading merchants, lawyers, and planters dedicated to mutual fellowship and civic works. For example, Wright joined numerous other Masons in founding the Charleston Library Society.[5] Masons were generally led by "malleable young aristocrats who provided freemasonry with celebrity appeal, financial resources and political security," wrote historian Ric Berman. The organization promoted "Newtonian natural science and education" with roots deeply embedded in the religious and political uncertainties arising from the Glorious Revolution that had earlier forced Wright's grandfather into prison.[6] On a broader scale, however, English Freemasonry likely played a central role in developing and sustaining the British Empire, which Wright held so dear. One historian has argued that "Freemasonry was one institution that contributed to the development of [the] intra-cultural connections in the British Empire. By creating a global network that had both practical functions and ideological dimensions, freemasonry played a critical role in building, consolidating, and perpetuating the Empire." Moreover, and this is important to understanding the rise of James Wright, "belonging to the fraternity not only gave members access to an actual network of individuals and lodges that helped those who crossed the Atlantic in both directions; it also carried with it membership in an ideological network, a set of emotional and mental connections."[7]

Freemasonry was tailor-made for James Wright: he was a man of the empire to his very core, and his entire professional career saw him traveling from the imperial core in London to its periphery in Charleston and Savannah.[8]

Masons were quite active in Charleston society, and they had put on a play just a few months prior to Wright's elevation to senior warden. At the Queen Street theater, they staged the comedy *The Recruiting Officer*.[9] Written by Irish playwright George Farquhar in 1706, this play, which followed the sexual exploits and social follies of two soldiers, was one of the most popular of the century.[10] After the play, which was performed "to the satisfaction and entertainment of the whole audience," Wright and his fellow Masons returned to the "Lodge at Mr. Shepheard's" to continue the festivities.[11] It was no doubt in these moments that James Wright made business and professional connections that furthered his career and augmented his wealth. A couple of years later, the Masons celebrated the festival of St. John the Evangelist with the "firing of guns at sunrise from several ships in the harbor." At 9:00 that evening, Solomon's membership chose Wright as their provincial grand master.[12]

Wright maintained his membership in the lodge throughout his time in Charleston, and such high-level friendships and connections certainly helped him expand his law practice and find appropriate matches for his children.[13] He seems, however, to have ended his membership in the late 1750s or 1760s. It is likely that he left the organization because he considered it appropriate to maintain a healthy distance from the organization after he became royal governor, especially once the rising political differences surfaced following the passage of the Stamp Act in 1765.

## James Wright as Planter

Wright's maturation occurred at precisely the opportune moment to make the most of his many connections and advantages in the South Carolina Lowcountry. Nineteenth-century physician and historian Dr. David Ramsay claimed with perhaps a little hyperbole that "few [places] have at any time exhibited so striking an instance of public and private prosperity as appeared in South Carolina between the years 1725 and 1775."[14] Rice and enslaved people were at the heart of this rapid growth, and South Carolina enjoyed the highest per capita wealth among Britain's original thirteen colonies.[15]

The Wright family's arrival in Charleston coincided with the transition from proprietary to royal control of the colony, and the newly minted royal government gave rise to a new period of prosperity. James Wright understood that much of that prosperity was tied to the land and bound labor. He understood, as did George Washington, that while currency "will melt like snow before a hot sun . . . lands are permanent, rising fast in value."[16] South Carolina governor James Glen, whose family intermarried with Wright's, wrote that Lowcountry "land is really valuable as it is fit for rice, for indigo [because] it lyes near to creeks or rivers."[17] Indeed, Wright probably echoed the sentiments of his friend Henry Laurens, who desired little more than to "plant & cultivate my vine & my fig tree" and "sit quietly under them."[18] Of course, these men did not actually engage in the physical planting, nor did they possess the temperament to idly rest. Furthermore, these men could not just acquire a mere sufficiency. Acquisition was in their soul.

Incomplete records and the existence of multiple James Wrights in the greater Charleston area make it impossible to create a complete portrait of Wright's landholdings.[19] But cross-referencing land grants for "James Wright" with land grants for Wright's family members allows a reasonable accounting of his landholdings. He received dozens of land grants in South Carolina totaling over ten thousand acres and spread across multiple plantations in Craven and Granville Counties beginning in 1735. Lowcountry colonists inhabited a world, according to historian S. Max Edelson, "defined by movement across a landscape in the throes of change."[20] James Wright was one of those colonists who helped transform that landscape by cultivating plantations where a swampy wilderness once lay. Wright believed that this land would provide his economic security, and his thirst was never satiated. Men like him continued to devour land for the remainder of their lives, willing to chance almost everything—including their trade in deerskins and peaceful relations with Native Americans—to acquire more land and more bondspeople.[21]

Of this rapaciousness, surveyor Frederick George Mulcaster noted: "There is a certain something in the air . . . or some curs'd power . . . which actually turns the brain." It seized some "violently the moment they set foot on shore, others do not catch it till some days after their arrival, [and] even I with all my resolution could not stand it." Soon, Mulcaster found himself "most desperate" in this pursuit and found the malady so "incurable" that he promised to "tease [his friend] no more" lest he also "catch the infection."[22] Henry Laurens lamented that his own eight plantations were not enough: "I did not think I [ever] had too much land."[23] He was not alone, he complained, asserting that everyone was "anxious in the pursuit of his own" plantation.[24] James Wright was no less anxious, in large measure because he understood that the return for investment could be mighty. During the middle of the century, annual profits on Lowcountry rice and indigo plantations exceeded 20 percent.[25]

The period of Wright's most active planting coincided with a colony-wide surge in bound labor acquisition and agricultural production. South Carolina witnessed a 54 percent increase in rice exports, a 63 percent increase in indigo exports, and an astronomical 566 percent spike in slave imports, the largest rate of increase throughout the entire colonial period.[26] Comparing Wright's South Carolina landholdings, about which we have moderate confidence, with his Georgia possessions (525 enslaved humans dispersed across eleven plantations in 1776), of which we are certain, it is not unreasonable to conclude that he owned up to 200 bondsmen while he lived in South Carolina. Admittedly, this supposition only makes sense if Wright cleared and planted on much of this land, and doing this may have been a dubious proposition. The creation of a Lowcountry plantation during this period required significant investment in a workforce, which was only just becoming available. It also required civil engineers, which may or may not have been sufficiently available. The process could take some time, and Wright's early landholdings in South Carolina could have largely been used for their lumber. The likeliest scenario would be a combination of the above: Wright both established operational plantations and sold lumber.

Aside from the base accumulation of wealth, the acquisition of enslaved labor became concomitant with influence and power. In many ways, Wright's life mirrored that of any number of Lowcountry planters. These extremely ambitious parvenus exploited the power derived from landownership to obtain governmental and societal positions of leadership. They in turn used these positions of authority to both control local government and establish connections at the imperial center in London and further augment their personal wealth. Although a confident identification of these contacts is difficult to ascertain, it can be surmised that Wright's English heritage afforded him certain advantages in this burgeoning transatlantic world. In addition to these advantages, his determination to succeed ensured his status as a colonial leader and, ultimately, a member of South Carolina's and, later, Georgia's first planter elite.[27]

Almost without fail, Lowcountry residents with means like Wright purchased land with the sole purpose of stocking it with the enslaved, who then produced goods whose sale would afford the owner opportunities to purchase even more land and, consequently, more humans.[28] This ravenous desire was perfectly encapsulated by a future colleague of Wright's who maintained: "The Negro business is a great object with us, it is to the trade of this country, as the soul to the body, and without it no house can gain a proper stability, the planter will as far as in his power sacrifice everything to attain negroes."[29] Simply put, according to historian Emma Hart, South Carolinians like Wright "were willing to risk everything for the opportunity to improve their social and economic standing through purchasing a slave."[30]

Historian Timothy Lockley has argued that these planters "secured for themselves a new status symbol, the slave, and the new title of 'master,'" and the ownership of the enslaved quickly became a point of social distinction in an increasingly hierarchical Lowcountry. Enslaving others guaranteed a degree of acceptance among the highest ranks of society.[31] It is unclear when James Wright purchased his first human being, but the first extant bill of sale for Wright as a purchaser is dated 3 January 1749, when he purchased Jack from John Vaun, a Charleston carpenter, and, later that year, a young slave named Cesar. The "price of [their] pound of flesh" was £350 in South Carolina currency.[32] He was later involved in a flurry of slave acquisitions in 1754. In March he purchased nine humans from the estate of Joshua Wilkies before buying Cato, whose previous owner was a blacksmith named James Lingard.[33] At about this time Wright placed two newspaper advertisements, one seeking to recover a twenty-two-year-old runaway named Cupid, who was five feet, six inches tall, "very black, and [with a] smooth face [who] speaks very little English," and the other to hire an overseer for a rice plantation.[34] Wright transformed his burgeoning human portfolio into increased landownership, especially in and around the Dorchester area.[35] This was where his father and brothers established their Lowcountry plantation roots. His primary residence, however, was in the city of Charleston.

With no surviving letters to or from his overseers and only accounting references to his enslaved property, reconstructing James Wright the enslaver is even more problematic than untangling James Wright the landholder. Given that he eagerly acquired land and humans, it is likely that he held similar beliefs to many other Lowcountry planters of his day, paternalists who highly valued "family and status" and who adhered to a "strong code of honor," bound by "many sacred obligations to treat [these "family" members] with humanity at all times."[36]

Two of his closest friends exhibited such paternalistic tendencies: Henry Laurens and James Habersham. Historian Gregory Massey believed Laurens to be an "enlightened patriarch" who "exerted firm control over his slaves but also tried to mitigate the cruelty of an inhumane institution with respect for their humanity." In a letter to Georgian Lachlan McIntosh, Laurens expressed the patriarchal belief that a master must attend to the slaves'

well-being: "If [an overseer] makes less rice with more hands but treats my
Negroes with humanity I would rather him to be at their head, than submit
to the charge of one who should make twice as much rice and exercise any
degree of cruelty towards those poor creatures who look up to their master as their father, their guardian, & protector."[37] In another letter, Laurens
spoke against the breaking up of enslaved families, declaring he could not
"be deaf to their cries least [*sic*] a time should come when I should cry and
there shall be none to pity me."[38] Wright likely felt the same way, but the
only nonsuppositional evidence to truly support that statement is a 1764 letter in which James Habersham informed his agent in London that Wright
desired to clothe his enslaved better than most.[39] Augmenting this primary
document is the opinion of historian Betty Wood. "It was an exceptional
owner," she opined, "who sent to England for slave clothing and an even
more exceptional master who expressed concern for the physical comfort
of his slaves."[40] Of course, it is also possible, maybe even likely, that Wright
and Habersham were merely sensible businessmen seeking to purchase a
higher-quality fabric so that it would last longer and maybe ingratiate them
a bit in the eyes of their human property in order to produce better workers. Also, these reasons are not mutually exclusive.[41] Regardless, Wright enslaved hundreds of human beings, and their daily toil and sufferings must be
at the forefront of every discussion of his role in slavery. Sadly, the historical
record is mostly mute on this subject.

Slavery was the single most important factor to the flourishing
eighteenth-century Lowcountry economy. One study suggests that slaves
comprised about half of all personal wealth in colonial South Carolina, and
slave ownership was so desirable that 80 percent of all estates owned slaves,
including many with "low levels of wealth, such as small farmers."[42] While
historian William G. Bentley acknowledged that he was unsure if the recorded estates "represent a good cross-section of different levels of wealth,"
he found that 95 percent "of all small farmers held at least one slave and most
held between eight and nineteen."[43] James Habersham well understood that
it was his enslaved workers who made his plantation profitable; thus, even
though he viewed them as dependents, he was also dependent upon them,
especially when it came to their knowledge of rice cultivation. In the minds
of his contemporaries, Habersham (and Wright) exhibited something of a
more humane character concerning their human property—if one can pay
attention to such degrees concerning this peculiarly awful institution. But
they also "exercised absolute power over [their] slaves" even while taking "a

TABLE 1.1. James Wright's valuation of his enslaved

| Men | Women | Boys | Girls | Totals |
|---|---|---|---|---|
| 56 valued at £63 per (£3,528 total) | 65 valued at £48 per (£3,120 total) | 26 valued at £38 per (£988 total) | 18 valued at £36 per (£648 total) | 165 (£8,284 total) |

SOURCES: Sir James Wright, Loyalist claim, in *BGLC*. Additionally, there was a Jenny listed in Wright's son Alexander's claim. She had been valued at sixty-five pounds. Alexander Wright, Loyalist claim, in *BGLC*.

paternalistic attitude toward" them, thinking of them, but not quite treating them, as "family."[44]

There is still yet one more bit of information that might be revelatory of Wright's attitude toward his enslaved. He provided a caveat in his will and testament that stipulated a fifteen-pound annuity for his "black servant Jenny who is free" for her many years of "faithful services." Additionally, he desired that "some of [his executors or family] will employ her as a servant or endeavor to get her a place if she chooses to go."[45] Wright must have been Jenny's enslaver at some point, and there was a Jenny, valued at fifty pounds, on Wright's Laurel Grove plantation in 1776.[46] He identified Jenny as a servant, not a slave. When and how was Jenny manumitted? What was the nature of her relationship with Wright—could it have been like that of, for example, Sally Hemings's with Thomas Jefferson? Unfortunately, the historical record is silent on this matter.[47] Lastly, Wright sent his enslaved population to Jamaica at the end of the Revolutionary War. But he could not find any work for them in the now oversaturated market of the West Indies. His son informed him that "they can get no employment for their Negroes . . . who in short are rather a burthen than a profit."[48] And this, aside from the stark brutality of the number of human beings he enslaved and his consistent support for the institution as the province's chief executive, is essentially what the historical record says about Wright as an enslaver.[49]

Of course, such purchases of land and slaves (as seen in table 1.1) alone were insufficient to become a successful planter. One must also establish the plantation, which was time-consuming and costly, especially in the Low-country. Wright well understood that a failed plantation would be financially ruinous for his family. By midcentury, the startup costs would have been approximately £1,800 sterling, with much of that devoted to the labor pool.[50] Common wisdom asserted that a plantation could not successfully operate with fewer than forty slaves. Additionally, Wright would have to hire engineers and overseers to build and run the plantation.[51] And this he did.

He owned no fewer than two plantations in the Carolina Lowcountry and would seek more and more and more—he was never sated.

## James Wright as Lawyer

Although Wright was a prolific accumulator of land and "one of the best planters in the country," according to a contemporary, he considered the law to be his profession and had a lucrative practice for two decades.[52] He was among the 12 percent of colonial South Carolina attorneys who actively practiced law for at least twenty years, beginning in 1734 at the ripe age of eighteen.[53] His first such employment came after receiving a royal commission as remembrancer clerk of the pleas and estreats of the Court of Exchequer. One of the busiest colonial courts in the province, it heard cases concerning royal financial matters.[54] The newspaper's designation of Wright as "Esq." may also suggest that the youthful Wright was already fully acting as an attorney, but it could also refer to his social status. According to Samuel Johnson's *Dictionary of the English Language*, the term "esquire" referred to a "title of dignity, and next in degree below a knight," "younger sons of noblemen," or "a justice of the peace."[55]

Colonial South Carolina's entire legal community operated from Charleston because no courts existed beyond that town's borders during this period. Thus, Charleston became the hub of all legal activity and was the destination of all South Carolinians in need of legal advice. Attorneys with transatlantic connections earned the best salaries, and James Wright had deep and generational contacts in London. Beginning in the early 1730s, shortly after the Crown took control of the province, Charleston witnessed a tremendous economic boom. As one of the British Empire's most important peripheral entrepôts, Charleston was dominated by a planter and merchant oligarchy that heavily relied on attorneys to secure debt collection.[56]

Much of Wright's successful legal career was built on a foundation of elite legal training in London, or so the story goes. Virtually every biographical sketch of James Wright has maintained that he attended the famed Gray's Inn.[57] Located in the heart of London, the Inns of Court provided young affluent students with unfettered access to the political and economic center of the empire. Gray's Inn occupied Reginald de Gray's Portpoole manor house, across Fleet Street from the Middle Temple.[58] Even though it was the least well known (and respected) of the four inns, Gray's Inn was immortalized by alumnus and patron Francis Bacon, who lauded the gardens as providing the "greatest refreshment to the spirits of man."[59] Which refreshments, however, may be debated. In 1747 the inn had in fact been described as the destination of "'Beaus' or 'Whorers'" rather than of serious students, making it highly unlikely that James Wright would have deigned to enter through its doors, for he possessed an incredibly sober mindset.[60] For this reason alone, it is doubtful that Wright physically attended Gray's Inn, but if he did, it would have been for the primary purpose of making the necessary connections and earning sufficient credentials in order to be officially named South Carolina's attorney general.

Gray's Inn officially matriculated Wright for legal training on 14 August 1741, seven full years after the first reference to his practicing law at the age of eighteen.[61] He likely never attended the inn, as evidenced by his consistent case load from 1736 through 1757. Just two months after his admittance, Wright is listed in the *South Carolina Gazette* as a contact regarding the purchase of several Charleston lots.[62] A few months later he is identified as the sole legal contact in a debt collection case. In fact, the advertisement requires that those debtors put their "bonds and notes . . . into the *hands of James Wright*, Esq., Attorney at Law."[63] Many such advertisements consistently appeared in the Charleston papers until the late 1740s without significant gaps in time.[64]

Additionally, the *Gazette* announced Wright's wedding to Miss Sarah Maidman, "a young lady of great beauty, merit and fortune."[65] She was the daughter of Captain James Maidman, of an independent military company in Bermuda, and Martha Dolphin.[66] Captain Maidman died in Bermuda in 1728, and Sarah's mother then married Alexander Heron, a British army officer, in short order.[67] He served under General James Oglethorpe at Fort Frederica in Georgia during the 1730s and was later commander of British forces in that province, later serving in India.[68]

Casting more doubt on Wright's physical attendance at Gray's Inn is the fact that he is not listed in the pension records.[69] The only possible exception to this supposition might be an eighteen-month period from November 1746 to April 1748, in which Wright's name does not appear in the *South Carolina Gazette*. Even this seems unlikely, because he would have likely spent at least two months at sea, leaving little more than a year to study in London.[70] But here provincial legal records have their say, announcing Wright's appointment as attorney general in the spring of 1747.[71] Lastly, Gray's Inn never called Wright to the bar. This would not, however, been a requirement, because "London's policy of centralizing judicial systems encouraged the development of infant bars around the supreme courts at important commercial and administrative centers" like Charleston.[72] Moreover,

the inns typically called students "to the bar only for paying fees and producing a 'certificate of having dined a certain number of times in the hall of the
inn.'"[73] For the most part, then, prospective barristers would dine at the inn
occasionally, gathering contacts, studying those dull legal primers and tomes
on their own, and visiting Westminster Hall to see the practice of law in action. It was entirely possible for a student to "pay the fees and be admitted
on paper but then not appear in person . . . and [still] proceed to [be] call[ed]
to the Bar."[74]

Whether or not Wright physically attended Gray's Inn is of minor consequence. The fact that he had been admitted, however, is of importance.
The wealthiest colonial families often shipped their sons across the Atlantic to obtain a proper and "polished" education, especially in the law, which
by the mid-eighteenth century had become the preeminent English profession.[75] Prior to 1815 there were 236 American-born members of an Inn
of Court, Middle Temple being the most popular. In large measure because
of their wealth (as well as their desire to emulate the British gentry), South
Carolinians alone contributed one-third of these students, easily outdistanc-
ing all other colonies.[76] Many colonial elites, according to Member of Parliament Edmund Burke, "seem to have thought that there was an advantage
in being able to claim membership of an Inn . . . as a sort of qualification for
other things."[77] The *London Magazine* observed that "if a man is a clever fellow, [the legal profession] 'tis [a] sure step to an estate. 'Tis necessity that
has driven the practitioners of the law hither, from Europe, and other parts
of America, and I remember few that had not made it very well worth their
while."[78] Benjamin Franklin's son William was just one such American. His
biographer observed that William used his time at the Middle Temple "as a
springboard from which to launch his career," as did James Wright, with one
notable exception: Franklin was a colonial; Wright was not.[79] He was a native Briton with deep transatlantic connections.

Burke's reference to the prestige connected with such an affiliation cannot be overstated, especially because the actual legal training provided by
the inns was suspect and usually of an autodidactic nature. Students learned
their craft by "teach[ing] themselves, with the help of books and regular attendance in courts," by visiting the Houses of Parliament, and by forming
learning cooperatives.[80] The questionable education provided by the inns
became an increasingly important issue throughout the eighteenth century
as calls for "a more real and substantial knowledge" of the law reverberated throughout the empire, and Wright was among a small cadre of South
Carolinians who made the "practice of the law both lucrative and respect-

able."[81] The "instruction actually received at [the inns] was often thin on the ground," according to historian Julie Flavell, "but association with them gave one a definite social purchase."[82] With both his grandfather and father serving as jurists, Wright certainly received a practical legal education to go along with his hands-on training as a clerk and, quite likely, a legal apprenticeship.

Whatever his training, formal or informal, James Wright served as South Carolina's acting attorney general at the tender age of twenty-one, a full four years prior to his admittance to Gray's Inn.[83] Although additional details concerning this appointment are unavailable, it is likely that this was a temporary and purely local commission resulting from the inability of the current attorney general to fulfill his responsibilities. Moreover, it is probable that Wright's father, then serving as provincial chief justice, played some role in this assignment.[84] In any event, an Assembly House committee directed the lieutenant governor to pay Wright £250 for his services as attorney general.[85] Upon full consideration, however, the members of the House denied this request, as they were wont to do regarding the distribution of salaries. Much like his father (and other officials), Wright experienced incessant frustrations in collecting his salary from the provincial legislature.[86]

Fiscal disputes with the Assembly aside, Wright collected significant earnings as an attorney general.[87] From 1735 to 1757 (the years in which we know Wright served as either a temporary or a permanent attorney general), he earned a minimum of £5,123 (see table 1.2). But these fees only constituted a small portion of Wright's earnings, as these numbers omit earnings from his private practice, which was among the most lucrative in the province. In trying to estimate his wealth, we must also consider the estates of South Carolina's legal community. During the eighteenth century, 19 percent of the colony's lawyers possessed wealth in excess of £5,000 sterling. Their combined assets accounted for nearly 95 percent of the entire profession's wealth. Additionally, Wright was one of the 17 percent of attorneys who also enslaved one hundred or more humans. Wright's net worth was likely comparable to or exceeded these figures, as he was known to be a prolific lawyer.[88] To place this amount in perspective, economic historians John McCusker and Russell Menard estimate the average annual wealth per free white male in British America in 1774 to be £74, compared to a figure of £131 in the southern colonies.[89] Additionally, for example, Thomas Jefferson averaged £175 per annum in attorney's fees by the 1770s, approximately seven times the annual income of an urban tradesman.[90]

Anecdotal and financial aspects aside, records of two specific incidents

TABLE 1.2. Payments received by Wright for his services as attorney general

| Date range | Billed | Paid |
|---|---|---|
| 1736–1740 | £431 | £125 |
| 1741–1745 | £616 | £458 |
| 1746–1750 | £1,946 | £1,722 |
| 1751–1755 | £1,560 | £1,458 |
| 1756–1760 | £570 | £660 |
| TOTAL | £5,123 | £4,423 |

NOTE: Per extant records, no amounts were billed or collected for 1736, 1740–1742, 1747, and 1759–1760. Data may be incomplete, and billing and payments sometimes overlapped years. The Assembly incessantly determined that Wright overcharged the province for his fees, and it typically paid him less than he billed, though this became less common as time progressed. For these issues, see, for example, 12 January 1743, in *JCHA, 14 September 1742 to 27 January 1744*, 375, 377.

SOURCES: For Wright's billing and payments, see *JCHA, 10 November 1736 to 7 June 1739*, 282–283, 661; and *JCHA, 20 November 1755 to 6 July 1757*, 180.

provide some insight into Wright's legal acumen if not also his character. By the late 1750s, provincial authorities had grown increasingly alarmed about the rising number of Acadians now living in Charleston, most of whom were Catholic and destitute. Governor James Glen was "truly concern'd to see the inhabitants of this province so grievously burthen'd with subsisting the great number of Accadians now amongst us." He proposed to "have shipped off the single men" but was uncertain of the "legality of doing such an act." Accordingly, he concluded, "I thought it advisable to take the opinion of His Majesty's Attorney General [James Wright]," who advised him that such an action would indeed be both "illegal & unwarrantable."[91] In another case, revelatory of his character, Wright examined a petition of Benjamin Wall regarding a warrant for a land survey that mistakenly listed another man as the petitioner. Wright "immediately order[ed] the mistake to be rectified" and acknowledged that he was "sorry it has happned [*sic*]."[92] These examples and others illustrate that Wright was a man of "marked ability and character."[93]

Such traits kept his docket full, and the bulk of his legal responsibilities, whether as a private attorney or in his official capacity as attorney general, revolved around trade, real estate, and naval issues. In the mid-1740s, for example, he represented Berkeley County planter Elihu Baker, and, a decade later, he argued Stephen Miller's case in a real estate dispute.[94] He also represented one of South Carolina's leading merchants, James Crokatt.[95] The Commons House of Assembly urged Chief Justice Benjamin Whitaker to heed Wright's advice to prosecute "such persons as have erected buildings in front of the curtain line, contrary to the laws of the province."[96] A curtain line was a line on the bay used for defenses.[97] The following summer, 1744, the Board of Trade appointed Wright advocate for the Vice-Admiralty Court. In short order, the provincial Assembly requested that he bring a suit against a Mr. Comett for trading with "His Majesty's enemies" during King George's War.[98] The next year, Wright "libeled Captain [Edward] Morris, master of a merchant ship lying in Charleston harbor, for sending armed men aboard a vessel with a flag of truce for the purpose of taking by force deserters whom he suspected were on board. Wright charged that the action was contrary to the law of nations" and, in language reminiscent of his grandfather, "an affront to the peace and dignity of the king."[99] In 1749 Governor Glen sought Wright's advice concerning a piracy case.[100]

In sum, Wright practiced law in Charleston for more than two decades, trying more cases (471) than any other colonial South Carolinian prior to 1750.[101] He ranked in the top 15 percent of colonial South Carolina attorneys in cases tried before the Chancery Court, Vice-Admiralty Court, and Court of Common Pleas.[102] His success as an attorney can be attributed to his legal acumen, transatlantic connections, and relationships with members of both the merchant and planter elites. His merchant connections were unrivaled, with more than 40 percent of his clientele coming from the merchant class, while 15 percent came from the planter elite.[103] Lastly, his international network garnered him "the fattest fees" in the province.[104] Wright stood at the pinnacle of his profession and led the charge in bringing professionalism and respectability to the legal profession in South Carolina, for which the colony would reward him with a prestigious transatlantic position.

## James Wright as Lobbyist

The South Carolina Assembly convened during the first week of November 1756 to choose its new colonial agent, who would represent its interests in London. The colonial agent was always an important figure in the imperial power structure, and such appointments were crucial to both the colony and the agent. The Assembly's first choice was William Middleton, heir of the former governor and distant Wright relation through marriage, but he had no interest in serving. The Assembly and Governor's Council (the upper house) engaged in three weeks of hotly contested debate about which of them had the legal authority to fill the position. This issue once again thrust the Wright family into the tumult of the unremitting warfare between the members of the Assembly and whichever group they presently believed infringed upon their authority. Such squabbling over the appointment of agents was, however, commonplace by the middle of the eighteenth century, especially in the southern provinces.[105] As usual, the Assembly maintained that the appointment privilege was its sole prerogative. The Council disagreed, and while the two sides compromised with the selection of Wright, the Assembly gained the upper hand concerning future appointments.[106] So with less than full-throated support, James Wright became South Carolina's thirteenth and penultimate colonial agent. Lord Lyttelton (the governor's father) and Lord Halifax expressed their pleasure at the legislature for "making so regular and proper an appointment of an agent."[107] No evidence exists to illuminate Wright's motivations to return to his birthplace, but it is likely that he sought to be closer to the seat of power in hopes of gaining favor in London or receiving an important overseas appointment.

Wright quickly busied himself during the winter of 1756–57 with preparations for settling his personal and business affairs in South Carolina. He began to liquefy some assets to cover his London expenses or perhaps because he never planned to return to America. In February he advertised the sale of his Cedar Hill plantation, "pleasantly situated" on the Cooper River. Seven miles outside of Charleston proper, Cedar Hill was a 530-acre estate largely cleared and "fit for indigo and provisions, and . . . rice." The lot also included a "very good brick dwelling house" with a "neat garden and several convenient outhouses."[108] Four weeks later, Wright continued his liquidation, advertising his Goose Creek plantation, the Retreat, which bounded the properties of Joseph Wragg and James Michie. This Ashley River plantation, which consisted of 508 acres and included a "capital mansion house and all other houses, outhouses, and buildings," was sold to slave importer Samuel Brailsford for £6,300 in provincial currency.[109]

Later that spring and now fully in Wright's corner, the Lower House urged Wright to "speedily embark for England." He readily completed his preparations for the move by requesting, as required by law, that all those who had "demands upon him to come and receive satisfaction."[110] Finally, after months of assiduous planning, Wright finally embarked for Europe on 7 August 1757.[111] We know that his family did not join him. While Wright was in London, his wife, Sarah, placed an advertisement in the *Gazette*, announcing that Cato, "a middle sized black Fellow, [who] speaks very good English," had run away from Wright's Santee plantation, presumably near his previous enslaver's home.[112] Additionally, Mrs. Wright explained that a recently arrived Gambian "Negro man, named Titus, a tall well made fellow, and pretty black," had run away from their Wambaw plantation. She offered a twenty-five-pound reward for assistance in recovering the Wrights' human property and, interestingly, added that if either returned of his "own accord, within three months, [he] shall not receive any punishment."[113] The Reverend Johan Martin Bolzius identified why the Wrights offered such large rewards for their enslaved, calling those from "Gambia and Angolo" the "best Negroes."[114] We cannot positively ascertain the fates of Cato and Titus, but they were certainly of great value to Mrs. Wright, who actively sought their return a year later.[115] It is possible that one or both men were returned to the Wrights, as men of both names were itemized in James Wright's Loyalist claim following the American Revolution.[116]

The voyage across the Atlantic was incredibly difficult. "I got to Plymouth!" a relieved Wright informed South Carolina's governor, William Henry Lyttelton, on 7 November, "after a most exceptional bad passage" of nearly ninety days. This is a titillating blurb indeed and typical of Wright's correspondence: short and to the point. A three-month Atlantic crossing must have been harrowing, to say the least. A springtime passage in this era should have taken no longer than two months, and he surely struggled with malnourishment and likely feared for his very survival. But upon his arrival he wasted no time in assuming his duties and obtaining the proper certifications from both the Board of Trade and Plantations and the Admiralty Office. The ministry welcomed Wright and George Montagu-Dunk, 2nd Earl of Halifax, and Sir George Lyttelton "promised to assist me in my solicitations" as agent.[117] Successful agents needed such support because the complications of their varied responsibilities "were legion."[118]

Shortly after his arrival in London, Wright secured temporary quarters in the Conduit Street home of his cousin William Rugge before finding suitable accommodations of his own. There existed in London a vibrant and affluent community of South Carolinians consisting of members of the Laurens, Wright, Manning, Izard, Moultrie, and Lowndes families. No fewer than fifty South Carolina families lived in London's fashionable West End. These wealthy planters and merchants established tight-knit extended kinships in that area, and they were so numerous that a London entrepreneur opened a business on nearby Birchin Lane called the Carolina Coffee House.[119] Such coffee houses enabled Britons to stay abreast of imperial and maritime affairs, as they provided a variety of newspapers and brought people together to discuss the issues of the day.[120]

Wright's responsibilities for South Carolina were to secure favorable legislation, promote provincial trade interests, forward varied professional and personal correspondence, draft and present sundry petitions, and protest unfavorable regulations.[121] In short, he operated as a power broker, negotiating the slippery terrain of both imperial and provincial politics, with their often-competing worldviews. The successful navigation of imperial politics required him to negotiate a veritable labyrinth of offices and boards. For example, Wright first had to submit memorials or petitions to the secretary of state for the Southern Department, who often redirected him to the Privy Council, which then forwarded him to the Board of Trade, which then consulted legal counsel concerning the matter before often reversing the entire process until a decision had been made.[122]

Benjamin Franklin could attest to such bureaucratic rigamarole, describing the process as a "kind of labour in vain to attempt making impressions on such immovable objects; 'tis like writing on the sands in a windy day."[123] Similarly, Massachusetts agent William Bollan described navigating this tangled web as similar to negotiating with a "rope of sand."[124] Throughout this process, agents such as Wright had to constantly grease the wheels of government by proffering gratuities and bribes to anyone who could aid their cause. Bollan sardonically wrote that the "expenses necessarily attending the negotiation of business here are ... considerable."[125] South Carolinian Peter Manigault similarly observed that agents must possess sufficient "interest with people in power" in London to "keep fair with the ministry."[126]

For Wright's services, South Carolina paid him an annual salary of £200 plus expenses.[127] He also received a percentage of all funds he collected for the province from the ministry, typically around 2 percent, which often far exceeded his annual salary.[128] For example, Wright procured a parliamentary grant in 1759, and he charged the province £248 11s. as his rightful commission. But as he had no doubt learned at this point in his life, the South Carolina Assembly objected. It claimed that he had not promptly delivered the grant, even though he informed the members that he had great difficulties receiving the payment from the government. In fact, his frustrations were so high that he complained to Governor Lyttelton that he would never "depend on anything till I have it in my possession."[129]

James Wright spent much of his three-year tenure as colonial agent focusing on two recurring issues: colonial defense and trade. His actions were typically bound by the instructions he received from the provincial legislature, excepting scenarios in which timing did not permit transatlantic consultations, which was not infrequent.[130] These instructions, however, proved to be the bane of most colonial lobbyists, and Wright incessantly complained to both Governor Lyttelton and the Assembly about their neglect in submitting timely and clear instructions.[131] At one point, Lyttelton assured Wright that "your not hearing from the committee has not proceeded from any disapprobation of your conduct, but rather I believe from the confidence that you was acting properly for the interest of the province."[132] Wright was sensible to the duties of an imperialist with one foot planted in London and the other in the colonies—conscious of his duty to both his country and his province, and in that order. But this did not mean that he did not feverishly advocate for his colony.[133] His agency coincided with a critical period in the Seven Years' War, and by necessity, Wright spent much of his time lobbying for monies and military units for South Carolina's defense, primarily to ward off the Cherokees.[134] He submitted endless petitions seeking naval convoys to protect trade to and from the province and successfully pressed for thousands of pounds in gifts to influence Native Americans, even though he feared doing so may have overstepped his instructions. If so, he wrote, "it must be attributed to my zeal for the service of the province."[135] One of the first steps he took upon arriving in London was to submit a memorial "setting forth the defenceless condition of the province and praying for aid and relief." To buttress his claim, he attached a "plan of fortifications now carrying on at Charleston and an account of the cannon in the province." Just such a plea was also one of Wright's last before returning to America. Security measures would plague him throughout the remainder of his career.[136] Although the Board of Trade provided multiple grants to the colony, Wright continued to badger it for additional succor and provided a precise accounting of the specific military needs of the colony, even though he had been informed by Lord George Sackville that military supplies were now "very scarce."[137] Moreover, the ministry stated a preference for only garrisoning "great rivers and lakes," because it was too expensive to otherwise supply backcountry forts.[138] Wright was, however, engaged in much more than military matters.

Wright needed to be something of an expert concerning economic and financial issues, as colonial agents were expected to be knowledgeable of the wholesale prices of an interminable list of goods.[139] For decades, South Carolina had fought for the right to freely ship rice throughout Europe, Africa, and the Caribbean. Although the ministry recognized the benefit to the province, it was loath to grant the request because doing so would require transformative legislative measures at home. James Wright brought the issue up again in 1758, agitating for permission to directly transport rice to any European port of entry. Even though his entreaties seemed to fall on deaf ears at that moment, more liberal trading regulations were soon passed by Parlia-

ment.[140] Wright also proved to be willing to work with other agents to effect
the best outcome for the province, something that was uncommon at this
time. He and his Craven Street neighbor, Benjamin Franklin, worked on a
project to bring about a colonial post office, and in 1758 he enlisted the support of Virginia's agent, James Abercromby, to submit a joint application for
the right of importing bay salt into the southern colonies, a benefit already
granted to the northern provinces. Of this variety of salt, a London physician wrote: "For certain uses such as curing fish English white salt and rock
salt are not as good."[141] At the same time, Wright and Abercromby successfully opposed a salt monopoly enjoyed by New Jersey's governor, Lewis
Morris.[142]

The following February, Wright successfully secured the rejection of a
petition by a merchant who asked the Board of Trade for permission to exchange some number of enslaved from the French West Indies for indigo.
The board agreed with Wright that such a move would be "impolitick" and
threaten British mercantile interests in both the mother country and the
colonies.[143] In the early winter of 1759 Wright learned from his contacts that
the ministry was considering a reimbursement grant for the colonies and
immediately made himself a pest in the appropriate quarters, petitioning the
board for South Carolina's portion.[144] Endlessly preoccupied, James Wright
had now been in London for nearly two years, and still his family remained
in Charleston. But not for long.

Finally, after remaining in South Carolina waiting for her husband to establish himself in the metropole, Sarah Wright placed an ad in the *South
Carolina Gazette* offering the family's brick home in Dorchester for rent.[145]
This delay was likely the result of a few factors: first, Wright needed to determine if the move would be permanent; second, he needed to find permanent
lodgings for his large family; and third, Sarah needed to put their provincial
affairs in order, which was no small task. A few months later, she loaded her
eight children aboard H.M.S. *Penguin* and departed for London.[146]

Just nine months later, however, the Wrights' lives would change forever
as James Wright informed the South Carolina Assembly that he had just
"obtained the appointments of Lt. Governor of Georgia ... [and that] I expect to leave England towards the end of summer, [but that] I shall continue to serve the province as agent to the utmost of my power, to the day
I may leave London." He added that he hoped his "past services have been
agreeable to the province ... [as] I know that nothing was omitted that occurred to me as beneficial, nor any pains spared." Lastly, he could not resist
the temptation to insult the colonial Assembly before leaving South Caroli-

na's employ when he acknowledged that he could have been of even greater service if the Assembly had just provided more timely and detailed correspondence.[147] He really need not have worried about his job performance. In a lengthy letter, Governor Lyttelton extended his "many thanks for the attention you have been so good to pay to all such matters as I recommended to you & those of the province are due to you for your very active sollicitation." He added that procuring the needs of the colony during a time of war must prove even more difficult and that "the success of your applications in my opinion has been as great as could have been hoped for."[148] High praise indeed from a man with impeccable credentials and connections in London who quite likely expressed such admiration for Wright to his ministerial friends.

A great deal of one's success in the eighteenth-century British world rested on the ability to obtain patronage—support from a social superior. According to historian R. C. Simmons, "family and social connections . . . were prime considerations" for climbing the social ladder.[149] Gordon S. Wood described patronage as a "delicate [web] of paternalistic obligation inherent in a hierarchical society."[150] It is, according to political scientist Simona Piattoni, a strategy "for the acquisition, maintenance, and aggrandizement of political power, on the part of the patrons, and strategies for the protection and promotion of their interests, on the part of the clients."[151] In essence, then, patronage allowed one to avoid the odious label "stranger."[152]

Although a positive identification of Wright's patron may prove impossible, there are several prospects. Wright had many connections and friends in London. Lord Hillsborough was among a small group who signed a letter to Wright "your loving friends," a most unusual valediction for the times.[153] But the most likely is Georgia's founder, James Oglethorpe, who was a friend of Wright's father (see the introduction). Failing that, the likely frontrunner is either Governor William Henry Lyttelton or perhaps his father, Sir Thomas Lyttelton. In addition to his imperial associations, Governor Lyttelton possessed an intimate knowledge of Wright's history, ability, character, and aspirations. Moreover, he did not conceal his affection for Wright, promising him that he should freely seek the assistance of his family members then in London and that "it will always be a real pleasure to me to do any thing in my power to serve you."[154] Wright's father-in-law, Colonel Alexander Heron, may also have been his patron. Heron was a primary deputy to James Oglethorpe and quite well-connected in the British East India Company, having recently "brought home great treasures" from India.[155] A long-shot candidate would have been Lord John Monson, the president of the Board of Trade. The two families were related through their Wren heritage, and Monson seems to have procured for Wright his position as attorney general.[156] Lastly, there are other, less likely candidates, most notably, George Montagu-Dunk, 2nd Earl of Halifax.

The *South Carolina Gazette* reported in March 1760 that "the Hon. James Wright, Esq., Agent to solicit the affairs of this province in Great-Britain, is appointed Lieutenant-Governor of Georgia."[157] The appointment was the first step in making him governor, which would become official upon his arrival to Georgia.[158] An intriguing nugget was revealed in a letter William Knox wrote that month. He informed an anonymous recipient that Governor Ellis offered "to mention me for his successor," but Knox declined the offer for fear of being ill-equipped to handle such an important position, as well as "from the narrowness of my [financial] circumstances." The gubernatorial position was a far reach, but Knox solicited Ellis's assistance in being named Georgia's colonial agent.[159]

Since Ellis was still technically the governor of Georgia, Wright could not assume that position until he safely landed in Savannah and replaced Ellis. Samuel Urlsperger, a Lutheran minister and the leader of the Salzburgers, a German-speaking emigrant community in Georgia, expressed great optimism about Wright's appointment. He hoped "God [would] let this change redound to the good of the country."[160] Prior to Wright's departure, the Charleston aristocracy then residing in London's West End joined with numerous other "gentlemen concerned in the Carolina trade [and] gave a genteel entertainment [honoring him], at the King's-arms in Cornhill."[161] After settling his affairs yet one more time, Wright departed England and began the long voyage to Georgia, a province he had likely never visited, at least in any substantial way.[162]

By his early forties, then, James Wright had amassed a small personal fortune, rubbed elbows with some of the empire's most important figures, and accumulated numerous important provincial and imperial positions. He would soon face his most difficult opportunity to date as governor of Georgia. The youngest of Britain's thirteen colonies, Georgia was in 1760 still a "fledgling province" and somewhat of an afterthought in the minds of imperial officials. Wright's task would be to validate Georgia's existence by transforming it into a beneficial cog in Britain's mercantilist machine.

# CHAPTER 2

## A New Governor

### "A Very Ticklish Footing"

Throughout the spring and summer of 1758, colonists believed that roving bands of angry Cherokees had begun filtering into the Carolina and Georgia backcountry. Many concurred with South Carolina militia captain Paul Demere, who referred to these Natives as "horse thieves." Virginian William Byrd predicted that the frontier discord would force the Cherokees to soon "revolt from our interest."[1] However, most of these Cherokees were simply British allies returning home after serving with Brigadier General John Forbes in his campaign against the French. These Natives were upset at their treatment by the British both during the campaign and on their journey home. Backwoodsmen from Virginia to the Lowcountry sporadically attacked the Cherokees as they trekked home either because they were unsure of their loyalties or because they simply did not want the Indians on their frontier.[2] The Cherokees' kinsmen soon responded with raids on that frontier.

Georgia governor Henry Ellis had not yet ascertained the situation. The only thing that mattered to him in the moment was that these "gangs" had recently settled among the Creeks and then "robbed & murdered a whole family not 40 miles" from Savannah. The attacks, he added, were a consequence of Georgia's neglected condition, which saw the backcountry languishing in a "very unpleasant & hazardous situation." Georgia's second royal governor and a thoroughly connected imperialist, Ellis often complained about the home government's failure to adequately defend his prov-

ince, as would his successor, James Wright. In this instance, Ellis persuaded
the Creeks to punish the offenders. But this assurance was tenuous because
he knew he had no way to compel Creek compliance. Had they realized this,
he feared, such "crimes . . . would probably have been perpetrated daily."[3]
The real damage caused by the Creek attack, the departing Ellis wrote, was
the truly weak nature of provincial defenses. This, in turn, would discourage
"persons of real property" from migrating to Georgia.[4]

Historian Louis DeVorsey described colonial Georgia's frontier as a du-
ality. It was a space for both those who advanced and those who responded
to that advancement. It was an often aggressive and contested space of interaction between "the inventive and energetic Europeans and equally capable Indians."[5] It was home to a thriving trade that originated in Charleston, South Carolina, but in which Augusta, Georgia, became increasingly
important. Traders like Georgian Lachlan McGillivray established credit-
based relationships with both frontiersmen and Natives.[6] These relationships helped build Georgia's mercantilist credentials but often complicated
imperial governance of the frontier. As the number of traders grew, their
methods became more unscrupulous, escalating tensions with the Native
Americans.

Governor Ellis believed that Native tensions had recently escalated because of the unprincipled behavior of traders and squatters alike. Certainly,
those returning Cherokees were losing patience with the "opportunistic and
unlicensed traders" from the Southeast who plied the Cherokee people with
rum. Presbyterian missionary William Richardson complained that this was
to be lamented because the Natives generally behaved well "when sober."[7]
The Cherokees had sacrificed much to aid General Forbes. His request had
drawn them away during hunting season, and upon their return, the traders
preferred to exchange rum instead of more practical goods, which convinced
the Cherokees that the British "wanted to starve them."[8] Ellis joined with
Georgia's Assembly to ameliorate this situation by limiting trading to only
those with official licenses.[9] Controlling the traders, however, proved a dubious proposition, especially because he had no authority over the Carolina
traders who crisscrossed the Savannah River at their leisure.

While Ellis sought Creek assistance against the angry Cherokees, French
and Creek envoys secretly prodded the Cherokees into committing "many
horrid murders."[10] As South Carolina's colonial agent, James Wright believed the Cherokees to be a "set of dastardly wretches, the most so of any
of the Indian tribes." He hoped that Governor William Henry Lyttelton
would "endeavour to destroy their towns & seize upon their women & chil-

dren."[11] Lyttelton seemingly agreed and escalated the situation by holding all Cherokees responsible for the actions of a few. Alarming news continued to pour in from the backcountry. Maximilian Moore, who was half Cherokee, confirmed that a party of young Cherokee warriors had recently returned to the town of Settico with nearly two dozen white scalps and "put all our frontiers in sad confusion."[12]

The real concern among Georgians was that the Creek and Cherokee nations would unite, which they had already nominally done, and Governors Ellis and Lyttelton put their militia on full alert.[13] Ellis, in fact, went a step further, actively encouraging the Creeks to attack the Cherokees because a war with the latter "would be extremely costly to the province in more ways than financial."[14] This policy likely helped forestall an intense Cherokee war in Georgia, but it was ultimately the Creeks who provided the most immediate threat to Georgians.[15]

In May 1760 Creeks killed several traders near Augusta.[16] Aware of his inability to fully engage them militarily and sympathetic to their concerns, Ellis wisely accepted the advice of the Governor's Council "to suffer justice to give way to prudence and . . . prevent this colony from being involved in a war."[17] With limited options, he told William Pitt, secretary of state for the Southern Department, that only through his own "great management" of the Natives had he been able to keep them at bay. He added that Georgia would be unable to entice immigrants and grow its economy without adequate defenses, and these defenses were especially important because this most recent attack raised concerns of the possibility of a much larger assault.[18]

Henry Ellis had devoted three years of his life to Indian policy, and it wore on him deeply. In his final letter from Georgia, he again expressed frustration with the lack of ministerial support. "I cannot help expressing my surprize," he wrote, that Georgians "should be suffered so long to continue exposed as they are," especially because the colony remained "on a very ticklish footing with regard to the neighbouring Indians."[19] But it was Georgia's climate that "officially" drove him to write that "as my health continues in a very bad state . . . I am at length reduced to the necessity" of begging leave to return to England.[20] A friend encouraged him to stay, hoping that "your public spirit may get the better of your philosophy."[21] Fellow Georgian William Knox empathized with Ellis's dilemma. He divulged to a friend that he too longed for England because "neither the climate or [Georgia] are agreeable to me," mostly because it was not lucrative enough for royal officials.[22]

But Ellis really just hoped for a short return to England to recover his health, telling Lyttelton that his "private advisors encourage me to hope I shall have leave to go home without resigning the government here."[23] Such hopes were illusory, he was informed, because James Wright had already informed "his friends [in South Carolina] that he is to have the commission of Governor."[24] Ellis himself soon substantiated the fact, writing that he had learned that he in fact "did not obtain leave" and must resign his position. He bemoaned how quickly the ministry moved to replace him but quietly began liquidating his possessions.[25]

### "A Very Capable & Worthy Man"

The appointment of James Wright as Georgia's third royal governor would provide the province with a capable, honest, and sober administration led by an acquisitive and expansionistic leader.[26] He was intelligent, hardworking, and increasingly skilled in the political arts, and it would take no time for the planter and merchant classes to learn that he was their champion. Wright also had much in common with his predecessor. Both men were thoroughly British: Ellis hailed from Monaghan, Ireland, while Wright had been born in London. Both were middle-aged—in 1760 Ellis was thirty-nine, and Wright was forty-four. Both were bright, wealthy, and experienced. They were both capable men possessed of strong character, and they were thoroughly men of the empire, strong adherents of its mercantilist mantra. Ellis tended to believe that his role was to ensure Georgia's economic growth, the consequences of which would benefit the empire as a whole. Wright concurred but ultimately believed that Georgia's interests must be subordinated to those of Great Britain.

After another grueling Atlantic voyage, the Wrights arrived in Charleston on 7 September 1760. What should have been a moment for reflective joy, however, had become one of indescribable misery as the Wrights "lost [their infant daughter, Elizabeth] in the passage," a not uncommon occurrence of the day. Nearly 10 percent of all seagoing children died.[27] The infant "was privately interred" at St. Philip's on the southeastern corner of Broad and Meeting Streets.[28] One can only surmise that this tragedy deeply impacted Wright, a supposition supported not only by logic but also by his later correspondence, which portrays a deeply devoted father. He likely spent the next several weeks mourning and visiting with friends and family, especially his brothers Charles and Jermyn.

Wright also needed to settle his personal affairs, and after about a month in Charleston, the family set out for Savannah.[29] They reached their destination a week later and "in good health."[30] Reverend Samuel Urlsperger witnessed the celebration that followed Wright's commission, the largest such celebration in Georgia's three-decade history: "Yesterday about noon we heard heavy cannon fire from Savannah, which is presumably a sign that the new governor has announced his commission from the king."[31] Governor Ellis informed his superiors in London that Wright had indeed safely arrived and, moreover, "seems to be a very capable & worthy man" who would "conduct the affairs of this government in the best manner." He did, however, advise the board that Wright would need additional military support to protect the colony against the Native Americans, and he informed Wright of his plan to visit and persuade General Jeffery Amherst in New York to send more troops to Georgia.[32] The Georgia Assembly also praised Wright for his reputation for "integrity and uprightness joyned with solid sense and sound judgment," which would undoubtedly "make us a happy and flourishing people."[33] Georgians would always acknowledge Wright's integrity. For his part, Wright complimented the outgoing governor, acknowledging that Wright was "not insensible of the merit and abilities of that great gentleman."[34] Of course, such things are said during these occasions, but the Assembly's comments accurately reflected Wright's honesty and decency.

Several months before, the Georgia Assembly passed an act making 121 Barnard Street in St. James's Square (modern-day Telfair Square) the official residence of the royal governor.[35] The home, referred to as Government House, probably resembled the finer homes in the town, which is to say that it was a very nice home but not opulent. The house was likely two stories with a brick foundation and one or two piazzas, from which Wright would pen correspondence during the fairer months. Inside, the house consisted of a parlor, a dining room, a study, and three bedrooms, as well as a kitchen and a cellar. He decorated it with the best furnishings from London and Savannah.[36]

Wright owed his new position to an act of 31 October 1754, which finalized the transfer of Georgia from proprietary to royal colony.[37] This, of course, meant that Georgia's colonial governors, including James Wright, served as the official representatives of the king.[38] For his services as chief executive, Wright received an annual salary of £1,000, which he augmented with the collection of a variety of fees. These fees grew increasingly larger as the colony grew and by the revolution amounted to £300 per year, or about twenty-five years' wages for a skilled tradesman.[39] As they did with his position as colonial agent, Wright's responsibilities as governor were extensive. To bolster the monarchy's colonial prerogatives, Wright possessed signifi-

cant patronage in his early years, but less so as time passed. Patronage was
a way to include provincials and to in some part purchase their loyalty and
support. Massachusetts governor Francis Bernard understood patronage to
be the "chief weights in the royal scale which keep the balance of political
power in equilibration."[40] Wright held the power to appoint provincials to
official royal posts, to grant land, to pardon most crimes, and to remit fines
and forfeitures. As Jonathan Boucher penned at the end of the century, "In
the present state of human affairs . . . a man has, or has not, influence, only as
he has, or has not, the power of conferring favours." The power of bestowing
such largesse was connected to one's relationship with the Crown.[41] Additionally, Wright held two military positions. As the colony's commander in
chief, he was empowered to erect forts and declare martial law. As Georgia's
vice-admiral, he presided over cases involving violations of maritime law.[42]
But whom and what did he actually govern?

In the 1750s Georgia was most notable for its youth, its lack of wealth,
and its sparse population. Upon his arrival in 1757, Henry Ellis, the godson
of Lord Halifax, observed that "the people are so poor & so involved with
their neighbours of Carolina; that their utmost industry affords them but a
scanty subsistence & a small surplus that goes thither to pay their debts."
Moreover, he observed, "The publick buildings are in a ruinous condition.
The light house at the entrance of [the Savannah] River . . . is upon the point
of tumbling down."[43] Georgia would have been lucky to boast a dozen men
worth fifty pounds, and there were only about two hundred mostly wooden
structures and three brick houses in Savannah.[44]

Georgia's Trustees had sponsored a "utopian" society based on three practical ideas. First and foremost, they had a philanthropic mission in which
they desired to relieve Britain's worthy poor and debtors, though concern
for them soon disappeared following the issuance of the colonial charter in
April 1732. Second, they wanted Georgia to play a critical role in Britain's
growing Atlantic-based economy. Third, they envisioned Georgia as a buffer
zone for South Carolina, providing protection from Spanish Florida. Ultimately, they viewed their colony as a land of small farmers, and they provided
fifty-acre land grants for all free settlers. The Trustees wanted their colonists
to be hard-working, sober in all facets of their life, and self-reliant.[45]

Accordingly, the Trustees implemented three regulations that handicapped the possibility of financial success in the eighteenth-century Atlantic
world, at least according to Georgia's Malcontents, a group that vigorously
sought to introduce slavery into Georgia. First, they limited the amount of
land one person could legally own, thus proscribing plantations, so central

to the wealth of neighboring South Carolina. They also gave land to set-tlers rather than selling it to them, and the recipient of a grant was prohib-ited from selling it, thus limiting large accumulations of land. Additionally, they restricted inheritance to male heirs only, a medieval-era policy known as "tail-male." These policies effectively eliminated Georgia's land trade, the very resource it abundantly possessed. A second and related regulation for-bade slavery, a policy that many early Georgians feared would ensure their own poverty, especially as they looked to their Carolina neighbors. The ban had been grounded not in altruism or morality but along more prac-tical lines. The Trustees believed that the presence of an enslaved popula-tion would both diminish the white work ethic and threaten colonial safety during wartime. The third odious regulation so far as settlers were concerned forbade the import and consumption of rum and other hard liquors.[46] Thus, according to historian W. W. Abbot, "The Trustees did not establish a colony between 1733 and 1752: they failed to establish one."[47] Ultimately, though, Georgians, and not the Trustees, would decide the direction of the colony, and they fully repudiated that plan, choosing instead to adopt the Barba-dian plantation system, as had South Carolina in the preceding decades, be-cause, in the words of the Reverend George Whitefield, "Georgia never can or will be a flourishing province without Negroes."[48] In other words, Geor-gians chose the "capitalist exploitation of land, intensive labor [slavery], a highly stratified society, and the production of a staple commodity for ex-port."[49] Georgians, specifically, the Malcontents, had won their battle and helped bring about the end of Trustee Georgia in 1752.[50] Wright would be an ideal governor for a colony with such ambitions, and he approved of the incredibly harsh slave codes enacted in Georgia in the years preceding (and following) his arrival.[51]

Wright brought an array of skills to Georgia in 1760. He had a firm grasp of the mechanisms of colonial and imperial government, mercantil-ism, planting, and the law. Moreover, his relentless desire to succeed profes-sionally and personally was exactly what the colony needed upon his arrival. Historians are unanimous in their judgment of Wright. He was "ideally qualified" for his new position, much more so "than most of his fellow gov-ernors."[52] He was the only colonial governor of Georgia with any actual qualifications for his position, according to another.[53] All historians tended to agree that Wright was ideally suited for his position. Historian Rob-ert Calhoon wrote that Wright's "intimate knowledge of British adminis-tration and of colonial needs and conditions made him an unusually able Crown official. He was driven, however, not only by heady success and self-confidence but also by the dim apprehension that his position was precarious." This skillset would serve him well in tough times, for he was "equally at home with the landowning aristocracy of the Southern colonies as within the bureaucratic administration of the Empire."[54] He was also "intelligent, diligent, and politically savvy."[55] In a similar vein, he possessed "a steady and sound, and growing understanding of politics."[56] He was, according to Calhoon, "that rare kind of individual who rated his own abilities very highly and took himself utterly seriously but was at the same time neither vain nor self-deluded."[57]

Despite his significant qualifications and traits, Wright had never served in an executive position. He did, however, possess judicious reasoning and confidence from the very beginning. In one of his first letters to the Board of Trade, he exhibited the wisdom to delay the submission of his initial report until he had sufficiently grasped the complex situation in the province. But he struggled to find the requisite time for such bureaucratic concerns, because Native relations were pressing in from all corners.[58]

## "White People's Blood Should Be Spilled"

As Henry Ellis prepared to depart the province, he provided a forthright assessment of the state of public affairs in Georgia, describing them as being in "as good a situation, as could reasonably be expected" in light of worsening relations with the Indians.[59] According to Wright, the dire situation resulted from the artful way in which the French and Cherokees had infiltrated the Creek mindset, dividing them in their opinion between the "cool & sensible elderly [who] are for continuing at peace" and the "young people [who] are strongly excited."[60] This division would persist among Native Americans in the Lowcountry for the next two decades (or more). Furthermore, Wright echoed his predecessor, insisting that "this southern frontier [be placed] in a state of security, without which, in spite of every effort it must decline."[61] Just two days later, on 25 October, King George II died and was succeeded by his grandson, though Savannahians would not receive word until January.[62] Much of Wright's assessment was based on his concern that he could not rely on the militia, most of whom he suspected "would run away" if confronted.[63] When Wright first arrived in Georgia in October 1760, there were fewer than nine hundred militia and about two hundred Rangers, a full-time military force recruited from the militia.[64] They would have struggled to hold their own against the more than two thousand Creek gunmen.[65]

Foremost in Wright's mind must have been one of the recent "base [and] unmanly" attacks from the Lower Creek warriors from the town of Coweta in which they killed three children.[66] The Native situation was so dire that the new governor met with a group of Creeks—the tribe he viewed to be of the "most consequence to the province"—virtually every week in Savannah.[67] His grave concerns for the safety of the fledgling province arose from a meeting with Ellis when Wright arrived in Savannah, as well as his experiences in London trying to provide for South Carolina's frontier defenses. Wright brought to Savannah presents from London and utilized the occasion of his first speech as governor to address these concerns, paying special attention to the "one object which is very striking, and which requires our immediate attention; I mean the dangers of this province in general is exposed to from the Creek Indians."[68] He encouraged Georgians to join him in solidifying the province's defensive network. These types of issues would plague Georgia for most of the next twenty years, and the colony was fortunate in having for their governor a man with some experience in this arena.[69]

Throughout November 1760, Governor Wright met with nearly 150 Creeks in Savannah who desired a complete resumption of trade with the British, which had recently been curtailed. Georgia boasted a healthy commerce with the Creeks, and Wright wanted to continue this lucrative relationship, but on his terms.[70] South Carolinians expressed their approbation for Wright's measures, praising his "prudent and proper management, [which led] every one of [the Creeks], to all appearance, [to] ha[ve] gone away perfectly well satisfied, [and] giving the strongest assurances of their good dispositions."[71] But the Cherokees did not share this pacific spirit. Wright notified the Board of Trade that the Cherokees continued to incite the Creeks to wage war against the British, and he implored the commissioners to fund Georgia's defenses.[72] He soon begged officials to send immediate aid, but the British commander in chief in America, General Jeffery Amherst, shrugged off the request and suggested that British successes against the Cherokees farther north should convince Creeks of the propriety of behaving.[73] The great Creek chief Mortar hoped so, insisting that their young warriors would remain troublesome unless they also "received a hardy drubbing such as the Cherokees had."[74] Wright would fight some derivation of this battle with British civil and military leaders well into the 1780s.

Indian affairs dominated Wright's first early months (and years) on the job, and here one can see his modus operandi on vivid display. Although forced to learn diplomacy on the job, he became a direct communicator who avoided schemes and excessive flattery, preferring instead to find equitable solutions to the problems he encountered and delicately balancing the inter-

ests of merchants and traders with the need to maintain peaceful relations
with the Indians.[75] This approach earned him the respect of Native leaders,
and he responded to this current situation by warning the Creeks that ill behavior on their part would result in a similar fate that befell the Cherokees in
the Carolinas during the Anglo-Cherokee War: who "are now naked and in
want of every thing."[76] In January 1761 Tallapoosa, the Wolf King of Muck-
lassee, personally promised the governor that his nation desired friendly relations. He expressed a "good heart and esteem for the English" as well as the
hope that "the children of both people [could] grow up together."[77] Wright
then assured Georgia's legislature that "no measure in my power have [*sic*]
been omitted, [which] I thought might make a good impression on our
neighbours the Creek Indians." He added that although the colony had enjoyed several peaceful months, even stronger defenses were needed to ensure provincial prosperity. The Assembly thanked Wright for his "vigilant
and prudent measures" in securing peace during "this critical conjuncture,"
but, as members often did when it came to spending money, balked at further strengthening their defenses. The "heavy expenses we are obligd to lay
upon our constituents," they insisted, necessitated postponing the construction and repair of fortifications.[78] Such short-sighted action by the Assembly especially agitated Wright because he possessed little leverage in negotiating with the Indians, and "they well know we have no force to oppose
them."[79]

Frontier events during the summer illustrate both Wright's keen insight
into the Native American problem and his understanding of the colonists'
culpability in creating or exacerbating those problems. That July a backcountry trader had plied the young Creeks with "punch until they got drunk"
and insulted them, after which they murdered him and fled for Cherokee
country.[80] Fearful of negative trade consequences, several Creek headmen
apologized to Wright for the incident. It is important to understand that
the Creeks and Cherokees were "organized" as loose confederations, and individual towns could act autonomously. The Creek leaders promised that
the affair was "entirely against our wills and knowledge [and] it troubles us
much that any of the white people's blood should be spilled by us, but some
of our young people are mad and we cannot rule them." More to the point,
they added, "we hope you will not stop the trade or goods from coming
amongst us."[81] Even though he firmly believed the traders to be the primary
instigators of the conflict on the frontier, Wright saw in this episode an opportunity to exert some control and decided to chastise the Creeks. He uti-

lized the threat of the denial of trade as his best bargaining chip and disingenuously insisted that the trader was simply trying to supply goods when he was ambushed. Wright gained the upper hand by poignantly noting that the murder occurred after the Creeks promised that "they would never hurt a white man [and desired] to keep the path strait and white between us."[82] The Creeks would have understood that the word "white" was an expression of friendship and was a metaphor for harmony.[83] The governor then demanded satisfaction for this transgression, requiring the Creeks to execute the guilty individuals.[84]

Finding the "Indian trade running into great confusion," Wright would have agreed with military surgeon George Milligen who argued that traders turned Native respect for the British "into a general contempt and dislike."[85] General Thomas Gage concurred. In 1767 he informed a subordinate that "we must always expect quarrels between the Indians and the back inhabitants and in general we shall find the latter in fault."[86] In fact, Wright himself believed they were "not the honestest or soberest people . . . [and] I am beyond a doubt that almost every disturbance & injury that has happened from the Indians has in a great measure, if not totally proceeded from the great misconduct & abuses committed amongst them by traders & packhorsemen."[87] He agreed with his friend Henry Laurens, who believed colonial "avarice & misconduct" to be the cause of much of the frontier discord. Regardless, they both firmly believed that the Natives "must suffer most by a contest" with the British and their unlimited resources.[88] Exacerbating traders' general character defects, in Wright's estimation, was their sheer volume. He worried that there were far too many Indian traders in the backcountry, many of whom were the "very worst & most abandoned set of men." For their part, traders typically disdained colonial authorities. "Who or what is the governor," one queried a Creek leader. "He is no King for we white people have but one King but in this nation we obey none but the merchants that supply us with goods."[89] A recipe for frontier disaster indeed. A fellow colonial governor condescendingly wrote that if the Indian trade were to be deregulated, he was confident that "none but vagabons & runagadoes will go to trade among [the Natives]."[90] Nevertheless, Wright seized the opportunity to use Native dependence on British goods to coerce them.

In the absence of support from both British officials and colonial legislators, Governor Wright concluded that trade was to be his most important asset in ensuring good behavior from the Indians. Accordingly, he sought to restrict and regulate unfettered trading on the frontier to maintain a proper

balance between supply and demand. In this way, the Natives would always need supplies but never be so needy that violence might result.[91] With
this in mind, Wright deviated from Ellis's policy of cultivating relationships
with one trustworthy Creek from each town and shifted his focus to traders.
He devised a plan to grant licenses and specific territories to a set number
of traders, most notably, George Galphin and Lachlan McGillivray, whom
he considered to be "men of very considerable property & the best characters." He often believed the wealthy to possess the "best character."[92] Although his policy was sound and, if successful, would have eased tensions in
the backcountry, the settlers viewed it as an example of unwanted imperial
interference. Their complaints convinced the Board of Trade, which forced
Wright to abandon the plan despite his repeated assertions that free trade
with the Natives was incongruous with Georgia's particular circumstances.[93]
But many Lowcountry Georgians agreed with Wright's handling of Native
issues. William Knox communicated to his brother that the governor "continues to give great content. He is a realy honest man and acts with great
caution" and in concert with the Governor's Council. Knox added that "I am
upon the best terms with him."[94] This was an important acknowledgment,
because members of the Council represented Georgia's elite, and Wright
could make little impact without their support. According to historian Alan
Gallay, these men "possessed not only great wealth and political power but a
wide knowledge concerning the economic and political affairs of their colony and the Atlantic world." Along with Wright, these men controlled the
disbursement of public lands, work projects, and jobs, and they created a local patronage system that mimicked the system in England.[95]

By the winter of 1761, troubles with the Creeks seemed to have subsided
as Wright continued to earn their trust through his sensitive handling of the
various headmen and his careful administration of the traders. But this is not
to suggest that Wright himself created an environment that fostered positive
relations. Instead, he continued in his own way many of the efficacious policies implemented by Ellis. Additionally, the success of British arms against
the French and their Native allies provided ample motivation for the Creeks
to remain on friendly terms even if the French had not yet resigned themselves to defeat.

Several months earlier, a French privateer had landed at Tybee Island and,
according to Wright, "taken five of Mr. Thomas Tucker's negroes . . . [along
with] Mr. Edward Tucker and four of his negroes."[96] The tangible threat of
the French, who actively engaged the Native Americans from the Missis-

sippi eastward, combined with the risk to Georgians' human property, finally compelled the legislature to approve Wright's requests to improve provincial defenses, and construction began immediately on Fort King George in Darien, about sixty miles southwest of Savannah.[97] The governor also warned the Board of Trade of the variety of measures the French had undertaken to excite the Creeks into hostilities against the Georgians. The French also made incursions upon the Georgia coast, absconding with seven "Negroes . . . , of which two or three were good [river] pilots."[98] He again requested additional funds for defensive measures, including Indian gifts.[99]

In the meantime, though, Wright used his favorite tactic. He reminded tribal leaders that "we can pour in goods upon you like the floods of a great river when it overflows." But he made sure they knew that such largesse was conditional and that the path could be made dark and barren if they misbehaved.[100] This statement only rang partially true, because Wright struggled to control the traders, who ran great risks to trade with the Indians. According to Wright, the Creeks had been known to insinuate that if they "were to make war against us, they would get their goods on better terms."[101] While this was likely true in the short term, Creek leaders knew they could not rely on such a tactic in the long run. Wright was soon able to inform the Assembly that the Creeks now appeared "disposed to continue in friendship."[102] These assurances of goodwill, combined with similar messages from the Cherokees in the Carolinas, gave the governor the confidence to suggest that some public funds could be transferred from the defense budget to the general coffers. These monies could then be used to bolster provincial commerce. Thus, Wright's indefatigable exertions in securing Georgia's defenses and his earnest diplomatic efforts with the Native Americans were largely responsible for maintaining peace, albeit a tenuous one. Even King George III expressed his satisfaction with Wright's performance, specifically regarding provincial defenses, which rightly met with "his Majesty's approbation."[103]

Looking to effect a land cession or simply to assert British dominance, Wright called for a conference of leading Creek headmen, and in December 1762 the Gun Merchant, Okfuskee Captain, and Handsome Fellow visited Savannah. The Gun Merchant, who had never visited Savannah, well understood his nation's reliance on British trade and promised to keep his young warriors on the straight path. Wright described him as "a man of by far the greatest interest & influence of any Indian in the Nation."[104] Although Wright took an aggressive stance with these leaders, little of consequence

was accomplished aside from maintaining the status quo. He reminded the
Creeks of past treaties and expressed concern over the "frantic and rash behaviour of some of your young men." While he understood that such actions
had not been endorsed by the headmen, he feebly stated that "you know you
cannot do well without us, but we can do without you." He reminded them
of the agreement that the only proper response for such murders was an eye
for an eye. The Gun Merchant half-heartedly promised that the headmen
would attempt to enforce their treaty obligations but that the British decision to allow wayward Natives "to be in the settlements amongst the white
people was a great evil." This problem could only be ameliorated if the British prohibited freelance trading, which Wright had already attempted without success. Additionally, in private conversations away from the Council,
Wright learned that the Creeks had been upset that the Cherokees had obtained favorable trading rights following the Anglo-Cherokee War. Many
of the younger Creeks thought that perhaps they should instigate their own
war in search of better terms.[105]

Then in February 1763 an ominous cloud rose over the Southeast. The fiery Creek leader and bulwark of the French contingent of Creeks, the Mortar of Oakchoy, held a conference of his own. Creeks, Cherokees, and Choctaws all convened at Fort Toulouse, the French fort in modern-day central
Alabama. Lieutenant de Lanoue Bogard, the fort's commander, had stoked
Native unrest and dissatisfaction against the British, prompting many traders to flee to safer environs. The Mortar, whom General Gage called an "inveterate and troublesome enemy," held tremendous sway among the Upper
Creeks, "who ever since, threaten and treat our traders with insolence."[106]
But as he had promised Wright, the Gun Merchant meant to maintain cordial relations with the British, and he worked to ensure that his people remained pacific. In the end, the Mortar's conference merely resulted in an
official protest to Wright, complaining that British settlements above Augusta "had prevented [the Creeks] from being able to supply their women
and children with provisions." But as rumors began swirling throughout the
spring of 1763 that the French and Spanish had agreed to withdraw their
forces from North America, the Mortar grew more indignant, grousing to
Wright in a personal meeting that "whites appear to believe that the red
people have no lands . . . [and] intend to stop all their breaths by their settling all round them." He even suggested that the Creeks would not accept
territorial agreements made in Europe.[107] In June the Indian superintendent for the Southern Department, John Stuart, reported to London that
the Mortar and his allies were planning serious mischief.

## "Believe That the Red People
## Have No Lands"

Then came news from Europe. The Seven Years' War was coming to an end.[108] Georgians learned that the "ministry are intirely occupied in reducing the definitive treaty into order."[109] But concluding such a global war was no easy matter, and reports confirmed that "peace will not be proclaimed till after the expiration of hostilities in the East Indies, which term is not out till the 3d of May."[110] Word of the "definitive treaty" finally reached Savannah in late May, and Governor Wright had "no doubt of [Georgia] making great strides, & very soon becoming usefull to the Mother country."[111] Important, however, was the last clause: "usefull to the Mother country." This letter provides a nice summation of Wright's view of Georgia's and thus his own imperial role. He was an unabashed mercantilist, constantly and with single-minded purpose endeavoring to build Georgia's comparably infant agricultural, lumber, and naval stores industries while simultaneously working to expand Georgia's frontier and population to meet the needs of the imperial core.[112] In fact, as historian Kenneth Coleman correctly identified nearly fifty years ago, "this concept of empire and the colony's place in it is essential to any understanding of James Wright."[113]

Before long the battle for the frontier resumed, and in the summer of 1763 the Creeks killed two traders, and Creek leaders failed to deliver satisfaction. The nativistic Mortar now felt more claustrophobic than ever and began wreaking havoc over the backcountry, killing three more traders in October. He tried to persuade the Cherokees to join him in a war against the British. Although most Creek elders had little interest in declaring war, their young men followed the Mortar's lead, prompting Captain Allick, a Cussita elder, to send a messenger to Savannah reminding Wright of their friendship. As the French made their way to the Gulf of Mexico, the British determined to take control and clear the road for Georgia's expansion. This would require new treaties.[114]

Wright now shifted his energies from the daily maintenance of Indian peace to the establishment of long-term geographic settlement. Of course, the two issues were intertwined, and the ministry sought to maintain Native peace in part through the check of settler expansion via the Proclamation of 1763 and the stationing of troops in America. Both solutions angered most Americans, regardless of their political stripes.[115] For many colonists, the victory over France eliminated the need to continue to placate the Native Americans.

In June 1763 Wright received instructions from the Board of Trade to work closely with the new Indian superintendent, John Stuart, to secure a cession of Indian lands and bring the various southern tribes under British dominion.[116] Although Wright believed that Stuart often usurped the governor's authority, the two often agreed in their approach to Native relations.[117] According to South Carolina lieutenant governor William Bull, "All the Indians love [Stuart], and there will never be any uneasiness if he is there." Although Stuart had a fine Charleston mansion and enslaved approximately two hundred people, his sympathies largely rested with the Native Americans and his loyalty to the Crown.[118] The idea for the cession, however, was the brainchild of Wright's predecessor, Henry Ellis, and the sentiments in London were that this important initiative be treated with the utmost care. In fact, Ellis's goal was to reassure the tribes of the continuation of fair trade following the expulsion of the French and the Spanish. Moreover, the British were to forgive all past misdeeds as a measure of good faith as they transitioned to "a new order of things."[119]

From his vantage, however, Wright expressed doubts about the willingness of the Indians to even engage the British in such conversations, because their attitude of late had not been the "most cordial & friendly." Their "jealousies and suspicions . . . are really inconceivable," Wright wrote, as they interpreted every new settlement as a confirmation of French warnings about British intentions. Wright also noted that the Creeks understood what the Peace of Paris would mean for them. For them, the consequences would be an unmitigated disaster, because they had relied on their ability to play the Europeans against one another. In his words, they "now think the white people intend to take all their lands and throw away the old talks, and that it makes their hearts cross to see their lands taken without their liberty."[120] In fact, many Native Americans realized that the British had readily supplied them while the war with France remained in doubt, but the British "did not care how [they] treated us" once they conquered the French.[121]

Relations between Georgians and the Creeks were always in flux, but they now seemed especially tenuous. Wright reported in September that "three men have been killed" by a group of Creeks with long-established ties to the French.[122] Much of the blame for the renewed frontier violence must be firmly placed at the feet of the backcountry settlers, who constantly encroached on Native lands and took advantage of the Indians in trade. Put simply, the Mortar and other Creeks feared that the upcoming congress was to be a land grab.[123]

Amid this threatening environment, Wright set to work in helping John Stuart organize an Indian congress between the five southern nations (Creeks, Cherokees, Choctaws, Chickasaws, and Catawbas) and the other southern royal governors (Thomas Boone of South Carolina, Arthur Dobbs of North Carolina, and Francis Fauquier of Virginia).[124] Wright had been eager to reach a settlement with the Native tribes, and his role in coordinating the details between the superintendent, the governors, and the Native tribes was significant.[125] The logistics for such a congress were enormous, and much needed to be coordinated, not the least of which was the location of the congress.

The other governors hoped the meeting could take place in Charleston, and Wright acknowledged that although "accommodations would be better in Charles Town," it was best to meet in Augusta.[126] His arguments for meeting in the comparative backwoods of Augusta were simple. First, Charleston was currently struggling with a smallpox outbreak. Second, the tribes preferred the Georgia location.[127] Besides, he argued, Augusta "affords sufficient houses, plenty of provisions, and accommodations of every kind," even though the village had been hit by an earthquake just six weeks prior.[128] But the governors were not satisfied. Fauquier, who had been battling an illness for some time, and Dobbs, then seventy-four years old and in poor health, arrived at Charleston in early October and were not keen to travel again.[129]

After joining Stuart and Bull in Charleston, Fauquier and Dobbs first sought to provide for their own comfort. They lodged a formal complaint to Governor Wright concerning the "inconveniences attending a journey by land or water to Augusta," maintaining that aside from providing a more comfortable setting, Charleston would afford them the opportunity to better "check & control" Indian behavior.[130] Wright's response reached Charleston a week and a half later and revealed his deep concern about the Creeks. He needed them at the congress because their continued dissatisfaction could be catastrophic for Georgia. Although he conceded the governors' points, he noted that convincing the Creeks to proceed beyond Augusta would be a dubious proposition indeed. Furthermore, he admonished the governors that "the King's intentions would be more effectually executed at Augusta."[131] The Creeks likely feared traveling beyond Augusta because of the fate that befell the Cherokees in 1759, when some had been captured and held as hostages by the South Carolinians as a means of ensuring the good behavior of their countrymen.[132] In fact, to alleviate this concern, Wright wisely enlisted leading Augusta trader George Galphin, whom the Creeks trusted, to persuade them to attend the meeting, because without their participation, the congress could have accomplished little. Galphin served as Wright's private agent with the Native Americans.[133]

Meanwhile, nefarious reports about Native dispositions continued to swirl in Charleston, and the governors remained uncomfortable with a trek to the Georgia backcountry, especially because they were fearful of the Creeks.[134] "The Creek Indians," Henry Laurens noted, "have been intolerably insolent," a complaint Wright made to Amherst shortly thereafter.[135] Additional reports arrived in Charleston indicating that the Cherokees had not wanted to even go to Augusta, much less Charleston. They were apoplectic because two of their number had been murdered by the Creeks. Consequently, the governors expressed a concern with which Wright could surely empathize. "We are in great hopes," they wrote, "that the late acts committed by the Upper Creeks are not the acts of the nation in general."[136] Here, Wright decided to personally intervene and make the arduous five-day journey to Augusta to meet the Creeks "in case they will not proceed to Charles Town."[137] Escorted by Indian trader and fellow planter Lachlan McGillivray, the governor departed Savannah on 20 October amid great fanfare.[138] Here is an early example of Wright's willingness to both lead by example and thrust himself into the fray. He remained true to these character traits throughout his life.

The Charleston contingent forwarded Wright's letter to Stuart, who had arrived at Augusta on 11 October. They reminded the superintendent to remove "every umbrage that may have been taken by or given to the Creeks" and to convince all tribes to now meet at Dorchester, South Carolina, a compromise locale situated due north of Charleston but only slightly closer to Augusta.[139] Wright bitterly opposed the change, and the tribes refused to go one step beyond Augusta.[140] Again, logistics proved problematic. Stuart was in Augusta, Wright was traveling there from Savannah, and the other governors had comfortably convened in Charleston.

It often took days for letters to travel from one place to the other, and communication was delayed and disjointed. By now, Stuart fully understood that the congress would have to be held at Augusta. From there he informed Governor Boone that leaders from the Chickasaws and the Upper Creeks were already upset because no governors had yet arrived at the congress. One complained that "he had come punctually at the time and to the place of appointment and expected to have seen the governors[,] that it was their hunting season when they should have been in the woods providing for their families." He then accused the British of "speaking with two tongues."[141]

Alas, Stuart informed the governors that they needed to follow Wright's lead and make haste for Augusta, because it was only "with great difficulty" that he had prevailed upon the tribes to "wait here ten days." Stuart feared that unless the governors and gifts arrived soon, "a Creek war would immediately take place."[142] The fact, however, that any Creeks had arrived was great news for Wright and the other governors. Moreover, their being led by Emistisiguo of Little Tallassee was important, because he had always proved to be a British ally.

Accordingly, Boone, Dobbs, and Fauquier forwarded Stuart's letter to Wright and began their journey to Augusta on 18 October.[143] In the meantime, as messages crisscrossed the backroads of South Carolina and Georgia, Wright informed them that neither the Chickasaws nor the Creeks would cross the Savannah River and that he would continue his own multiple-day journey along the Savannah River to greet them.[144] Back in Augusta, the Indians were growing impatient, especially the ill-tempered Creeks. On 23 October, the day after Wright's arrival, Stuart wrote that the Creeks planned to leave soon, fearful that the British had laid a trap and sought revenge for the recent "murders committed by the Mortar." In fact, while the British refused to invite the Mortar because of these murders, they had no such plans. Ironically, Stuart also feared that the Mortar was conspiring to create a southern Indian confederacy to link with the forces under Pontiac, an Odawa leader from modern-day Illinois who organized a large pan-Indian revolt against the British.[145]

The four governors finally arrived at Augusta on 3 November, and the congress officially began two days later, with nearly nine hundred Indians present. This number included a surprising 287 Creeks, though most of the Upper Creek chiefs were absent. It turned out that several Creek leaders attended solely because they believed they were to "have received very sufficient presents." The rationale here was twofold: first, they wanted presents; second, they did not want their Native foes to "benefit at their expense." As the official host, Governor Wright opened the talks and informed tribal leaders that the governors and Stuart were in full accord. Wright's approach to this congress and to Native Americans in general was to favor diplomatic over martial solutions and to treat the Native Americans equitably, according to his understanding of their proper relationship to both the British people and the empire. He understood that Georgia lacked the military capacity to physically exert its will, and, like William Knox, he agreed that it would be "ridiculous to the highest degree to think of gaining [the influence of the Native Americans] by assuming a superiority over them."[146]

Superintendent Stuart followed Wright's introduction and disclosed the reasons for this "friendly" meeting. He expressed the "Great King's good disposition toward his red children." King George III, Stuart said, "wishes to extend the commerce of his subjects," as well as that of the Indians, and to live "in peace and brotherly friendship together." Furthermore, and this must have pleased the Creeks, all past offenses were to be forgiven, and current grievances were to be addressed.[147] The congress then adjourned until Monday.

Native leaders issued their formal individual responses on Monday and Tuesday. Their declarations revealed how desperately they wanted to nurture positive relations with colonial officials to maintain the constant flow of European goods. Chickasaw leader Paya Matta voiced his gratitude "for the services already done them" by the British and iterated that "he and his are few but faithful . . . [and] as good friends as if they sucked one breast. Altho his skin is not white," he wrote, "his heart is." Finally, he readily admitted what Wright had suggested months ago: that "he could not do without the white people." Despite the veracity of Wright's assertion, Paya Matta expressed concern about the number of "white men being among the Indians as traders," believing, as Wright did, that that fact itself was the cause of the disturbances. He also brought forth what had been a consistent source of tension in Anglo-Native relations: the inability of Native chiefs to control their younger warriors, who tended to be "outrageous and mischie[vous]" because of the unscrupulous behavior of the colonial traders.[148] Creek leaders followed, and their talk would not be as sanguine as that of the Chickasaws.

The typically defiant Creeks, though, had much to fear in the days leading up to the congress. First, they faced incursions on their lands from all corners. Virginians, North Carolinians, and especially Georgians in the Little River region north of Augusta slowly but surely had encroached upon Creek lands. Second, they understood that Wright still presented an "unrelenting focus" on the fact that no satisfaction had been given for the murders of eleven colonists a few years prior. Third, like the Chickasaws, the Creeks were generationally divided and unable to control their young warriors.[149] In their talks, however, they tended to focus on the behavior of the unscrupulous traders. Ocmulgee leader Telletcher suggested that the path should only remain open to those "traders that are peaceable." But traders were not the only problem. Sempoyaffi (a.k.a. Fool Harry) expressed grave concern about the effect of European rum on the young warriors, who foolishly traded their skins for it while forsaking repayment of their actual debts. Fool Harry went so far as to threaten white traders who continued to trade rum to the "young people" in his nation.[150]

Stepping up next, Cherokee spokesman the Prince of Chota notified the governors of his desire that the path "will always be straight." Attakullakulla, the Little Carpenter, then conveyed his goodwill and desire that Wright and the governors would forgive the "young men [who] have been rogues," and he promised that he would "endeavour it shall be no more repeated" so that their mutual children would "grow up in peace." In addition to echoing the peaceful intentions of the Chickasaws and Choctaws, the Cherokee leader also mirrored their desire for consistent and fair trade but complained about the prices and tactics of the backcountry traders. He then presented beads and promised "to keep clean his path." Likewise, the Prince of Chota "presented a pipe and some tobacco as a testimony of friendship between the Cherokees and the white people."[151]

Catawba chief Colonel Ayres echoed earlier complaints about the influx of white settlers, a problem Wright worked endlessly to ameliorate, with nominal success. Colonel Ayres complained that his lands were "spoilt [as] he had lost a great deal both by scarcity of buffalos and deer" due to white settler encroachment. He concluded, however, on a positive note and presented strings of white beads as "tokens of the friendship he professed for them all."[152]

The goodwill continued into the next day, when Captain Alleck and an unnamed Creek also articulated their desire that their "children will grow up without interruption." Captain Alleck promised to return "any Negro[,] horse[, and] cattle" to the British. Although led by a sizeable contingent of Lower Creeks, the Upper Creeks, many of whom were Francophiles, were largely absent. Their leaders did not trust British intentions. They believed the British sought to extort a land deal from them. The primary representative of the Upper Creeks had been the lesser chief Emistisiguo.[153] Finally, Cherokee leader Attakullakulla presented a string of beads and stated his wish that only "good traders . . . [and] not rioting fellows who commit disturbances" be allowed to open stores.[154]

Later that day, Stuart, Wright, and the other governors responded to each tribal spokesman. To Paya Matta, they acknowledged the repeated examples of his fidelity and assured him that this meeting had added "additional strength and brightness" to their "chain of friendship." To Captain Alleck, they promised to fully exert themselves in "putting a stop" to the ill behavior of the whites. To the Choctaws, they expressed their desire that "your whole nation will [continue] to embrace the offers of good will which we have made you" and that their bond will remain strong. To the Cherokees, they explained that "your towns [have] but lately [been] cleared from blood" and that trade, at least in Georgia and South Carolina, should continue to be strong. And, finally, to the Catawbas, they guaranteed that "our King and Father holds out his arms to receive and protect you from all your enemies and is very sensible of your constant love and friendship."[155] According to Governor Wright, however, this veritable lovefest occurred only after he and the others had plied the tribes with "rum, tobacco, and an extraordinary allowance of provisions" amounting to nearly £5,000.[156] Upon the satisfaction of all involved, a full treaty was agreed upon.

## "Cession My Lord Cost Me Some Pains"

In preliminary discussions prior to the congress, Wright and Stuart learned that the Creeks were willing to make a land cession in exchange for the forgiveness of past infractions. Even though Wright and Stuart had both assured the tribes that the British had no intention of taking their lands, they eagerly encouraged this train of thought.[157] In fact, Wright would later argue that such a cession had been his primary objective.[158] He informed George Montagu-Dunk, 2nd Earl of Halifax, that the "cession my Lord cost me some pains, as I saw it was absolutely necessary to obtain it." But he did acknowledge that "part of the lands [had] been granted" prior to his arrival, though never formally ceded.[159] This semantic twist may expose the possibility that the cession had largely been agreed upon prior to Wright's arrival. In fact, it is likely that such arrangements had been made prior to his arrival, thanks to the efforts of traders Lachlan McGillivray and George Galphin. Wright's role in this instance, and it was important, was his enlistment of these men to negotiate with the Creeks. Here, he relied upon a trusted colonial strategy in the South in which governors had long utilized respected traders to mediate disputes with Native tribes.[160]

In any event, the Creeks had likely been willing to make such a deal to simply ease the tension with the settlers, and much of the land ceded had been the same land that the colonists had already begun settling upon.[161] The cession itself added millions of acres between the Savannah and Ogeechee Rivers.[162] The two sides also agreed that Indian complaints of whites illegally trading or trespassing should be made directly to the colonial governors before action was taken, a move that would bypass Stuart. That said, even though he believed both parties should live up to their treaty obligations, Wright well understood that effectively policing such disruptive behavior was indeed a dubious proposition.[163] In a letter to Lord Halifax, the former president of the Board of Trade, Wright grumbled about his inability to control the people on the frontier because he possessed "no coercive power over traders."[164]

The tribes and governors also renewed the decades-old eye-for-an-eye provision concerning satisfaction for murders committed by either party. But it was the actual Creek cession that dominated Wright's correspondence that winter. He assured the Board of Trade that the deal "gives room for a great number of inhabitants," and he advised his superiors of the importance of taking great care in granting these lands. Rather than granting large tracts of land to single owners, Wright suggested something quite different, which would have serious long-term implications. "I humbly conceive," he argued, that the "middling sort of people, such as have families & a few negroes," would be the group most capable of enriching and strengthening the colony. It should be noted here that Wright held a quite different philosophy in the Lowcountry, where he freely granted himself and his friends significant swaths of plantation-worthy lands. By the time of the American Revolution, he and his friend Lieutenant Governor John Graham were the two largest landholders in the province.[165] He added that "if our Indian affairs continue quiet, I doubt not but I shall soon see the province in a most flourishing condition."[166] Wright understood that peace with the Indians was a prerequisite for Georgia's economic growth. So too did James Habersham, who noted that Georgians are "in general in a thriving situation" and are "in no more apprehension of danger from the savages, than you are in London."[167]

The caveat here is important. Indian affairs, be they related to trade or security—and those two cannot be separated—dominated these first three years of James Wright's governorship. More than anything, he proved himself capable of handling his new position with dexterity, patience, fairness, and common sense. He also proved to his superiors in London that he could be faithfully relied upon to further His Majesty's interests along the southern frontier. He confidently reported to General Jeffery Amherst that "we hope [the treaty] will be agreeable and demonstrate that nothing in our power has been omitted" in securing such an important concession.[168] Amherst's successor, General Thomas Gage, had been quite satisfied with the congress, "which finished much beyond his expectations," even though the "Cherokees and Chickasaws urge us to be cautious concerning Creek designs."[169] Many Indians, too, were satisfied, leaving Augusta at least with their trade goods, which proved to be more than what could be transported in one haul. According to John Stuart, they departed the congress "with all the marks of satisfaction and humour."[170]

As the congress closed, Wright had real reason to be proud. Historian John Juricek rightly believes that "Wright's [contribution] to the cession . . . [was] more important than that of any other British official," including Stuart.[171] But for Wright and the British, this congress would prove to be a double-edged sword. On the one hand, it was nothing short of a coup, especially coming on the heels of the French and Spanish withdrawal. It augmented the colony by 2,408,800 acres and would provide for relative peace into the next decade.[172] One historian opined that if all colonies had conducted Native diplomacy as successfully as Georgia, the government would likely have had no reason to proceed with the administrative changes that brought about the American Revolution. General Gage seemed to agree.[173] On the other hand, as historian Ed Cashin correctly observed, the congress was "a crucial watershed in the history of the southern frontier." The "seeds [of the rebellious spirit in Georgia] were sown" here, Cashin wrote, because Wright's successful opening of more land to backcountry settlers would soon pit those backwoodsmen against the Natives, whom they believed the British preferred.[174] But James Wright could not have known that, nor was he able to bask in the glow of the massive land cession for long. He soon found himself staring down the barrel of an imperial crisis that would forever change his life. Before that professional crisis, however, the governor would face another deeply painful personal trial.

# CHAPTER 3

# A Governor in Crisis

## "All Perished"

An ancient Middle Eastern geographer once described the Atlantic Ocean as the "green sea of darkness."[1] Famed author, lexicographer, and bon vivant Samuel Johnson once quipped that oceanic travel was akin to being tossed into jail but with the added prospect of being drowned.[2] Another Samuel Johnson—a Connecticut colonial agent named William Samuel Johnson—warned his daughter that "the fatigue & danger of the voyage is too great to engage in, merely for the sake of seeing it."[3] There was truth to Johnson's witticism, however, as 20 percent of eighteenth-century Atlantic voyages ended in disaster. Twenty percent! In mid-March, just two months after James Wright's son Robert had been admitted Trinity College, Cambridge, the *Georgia Gazette* reported news of a disaster concerning the governor's wife, Sarah, who had gone "aboard H.M.S. *Epreuve*, in order to go to England."[4] The poor battle-fatigued ship had had its struggles in the recent past. Less than a year before, it had struck Cockspur Point (near present-day Fort Pulaski), "filled and bilged, so that the people were obliged to quit her [the] next morning, and gave her [up] as entirely lost."[5] But Captain Peter Blake had the ship repaired, and it continued its Atlantic duties after "many expensive and fruitless attempts, and immense trouble."[6]

Governor Wright's nearly seventeen-year-old daughter joined her mother, both named Sarah, aboard this dilapidated vessel with the express purpose of traveling to England to marry Georgia's colonial agent, William Knox.[7] Shortly after Sarah and her daughter embarked on this voyage, Wright family friend James Habersham wrote to Sarah in London and assured her that her husband was well. "I do myself the pleasure," he wrote, "of visiting the governor very often, and next week, we propose going for a few days to regale ourselves with viewing the fertile swamps and delightful pine groves on the banks of the Great Ogeechee River." In other words, they were going to inspect their plantations. But according to Habersham, Wright missed his wife: "I must own there seems to be a vacuum in your house, and I can truly sympathize with the governor in his present tho' *temporary state of widowhood*."[8] That same day, Habersham sent a letter to William Knox suggesting that by the time this letter reached him, he would be "happ[ily] in the company of Ms. Wright . . . whose company and presence must make you . . . happy."[9]

Provided the route was direct and the weather predictable, the journey from Savannah to the coast of England should have taken between six and ten weeks.[10] A full four months after the *Epreuve* left the Lowcountry, a London newspaper published an extract of a letter from the British seaport town of Portsmouth that expressed great apprehension that the *Epreuve* "is lost, she not being heard of."[11] But despair quickly turned to elation when the same newspaper announced three days later that the vessel had "put into Cape Fear [in North Carolina] some time ago, dismasted, and is now on her passage home [to Savannah]."[12] Then nothing. Silent weeks turned into silent months, and still there was no word from the *Epreuve* until the *London Evening Post* reported in September 1764 that a correspondent from Portsmouth announced the arrival of a sloop of war that the writer hoped was the *Epreuve*.[13] It was not.

The vessel, in fact, had indeed been lost at sea.[14] Only the *Pennsylvania Gazette*, however, provided details concerning the *Epreuve*'s demise when it published a letter from Captain Jacob Lobb, captain of another ship. The captain recounted "a misfortune I lately met with" in which a "hard gust of wind, with smart rain chewed up all the sails . . . [and the mizzen sail] blew to pieces." The mainmast even had to be "cut away." Lastly, Captain Lobb provided the details that must have left Wright grief-stricken. He was "sorry to acquaint [Commander Archibald Kennedy that] the EPREUVE, Captain Blake, is lost, and all perished. Governor Wright's Lady and daughter were on board."[15]

In Savannah, as spring turned to summer and then to autumn, Wright had received no word from his wife, and he had not read the above accounts from London. In September he put worried pen to paper and inquired if the Board of Trade had received the letter he had sent via the *Epreuve*.[16] There is no record identifying when Wright learned of the tragedy, but a comparison of the dates of his letters to the board, letters from Georgians, and newspaper accounts suggests that it is likely he had learned the awful news by early October.[17]

No extant Wright letters reveal his reaction to this news, which unfolded at an agonizingly slow pace, but a few of his friends discussed these troubling days. Writing that October, James Habersham lamented, "Our present tranquility is greatly alloyed by the (I fear) loss of our worthy governors lady and two daughters. What a stroke is this to the poor gentleman."[18] Here, Habersham added a twist to the story. In March the *Georgia Gazette* mentioned that the *Epreuve* only transported Wright's wife and daughter, but Habersham stated that Wright lost two daughters. The Reverend Bartholomew Zouberbuhler confirmed this. In December he wrote that "unhappily this vessel is lost with all the people that were on board among which was our Governor's Lady and 2 daughters—a family of undissembled goodness and in all respects most exemplary—especially in their attendance on divine worship. The fortitude with which the Governor bears so complicated a calamity is really admirable."[19]

Wright was by all accounts deeply devoted to his family, and he had now lost three children and his wife in the span of four years. The loss of his wife affected him so profoundly that he never remarried, even though he was middle-aged, with seven minor children. Habersham also revealed a little about Sarah Wright herself, who apparently more than adequately filled the roles of an eighteenth-century wife: "There are few such good wives, tender mothers, and affectionate friends remaining! But we must repine, least we charge God foolishly." But Wright responded to this tragedy with characteristic stolidity. "You would be surprised," Habersham wrote, "and pleased to see how magnanimous the governor behaves." Wright's friend concluded his letter on a personal note, writing that the governor "appears to have a friendship for and a confidence in me and therefore I have been as much with him as possible, and I really feel so much with him and for him that I almost forget I have any concerns of my own to attend to."[20] Habersham had also recently lost his own wife and found comfort in his relationship with Governor Wright. Their mutual loss strengthened their bond, and Habersham made plans to temporarily move in with Wright.[21] Another letter, written by a close friend a year later, revealed the depth of Wright's sufferings. Former South Carolina governor William Henry Lyttelton wrote to the man who was supposed to have been Wright's son-in-law: "I have heard very lately of poor Governor Wright who was then in pretty good health, but his spirits have never recovered from the severe shock of that unhappy event which affected you also so deeply."[22]

In the spring of 1765, as the imperial crisis began to unfold, the *Georgia Gazette* printed a poem about the loss of the *Epreuve* that certainly echoed Wright's own sentiments:

> A wat[e]ry *trial* may a fiery trial prove,
> ........................
>   The greatest suff'rer, overwhelm'd with grief
> ..........................
> And thinks no sorrow equal to his own;
> His sorrows such as will no comforts bear,
> Unwip'd away by oceans briny tears,
> ..................
>   Yet still the great, the glorious Lord of all, In all he does is still
>   supremely just,
> ....................
> Nor sends us woes for which he knows no cure,
> ........................
> With comforts equal knows to sooth the mind.
> ........................
> And when emerg'd from trouble's stormy sea,
> Stand calm and pleas'd before the God of all.
>   *There* all the good shall meet, and never part no more.[23]

Although William Knox seems to have left no personal account of this tragedy, the breadth of his grief greatly distressed Governor Lyttelton, who tried to console his friend "upon the melancholy event which has been so just a cause of affliction to you."[24] Thus it was, amid this deeply felt personal tragedy, that James Wright set sail on his most difficult professional voyage, at least to date.

### "No Stamps, No Riot Act!"

In the early spring of 1763 a correspondent in Boston received some distressing news from a friend in London. It seemed that Parliament was considering a measure that, "if carried into execution, will in its consequences greatly affect the colonies." The revenues, the writer added, would help offset the debt incurred during the Seven Years' War and "will be levied . . . and arise on a stamp duty."[25] The *Georgia Gazette* confirmed these rumors a full year later.[26] Even then, the news seemed to elicit no immediate response from Georgians, as the issue did not resurface for quite some time. Of course, in that moment, they had much good news with which to distract themselves, including the successful conclusion of the war and the nearly simultaneous agreement for a substantial Native American land cession.

In April 1764, reeling from the immense debt incurred during the recent war and eager to regain control of its imperial possessions, Parliament passed the Sugar Act and announced its intention also to consider a colonial stamp act.[27] At the onset of the ensuing crisis, Georgians were content with their relationship within the empire. Governor Wright helped engineer significant economic, territorial, and demographic growth during his years in the colony. Additionally, helping to ease its transition from a "fledgling province" to a viable colony was an annual parliamentary stipend. Georgians had great confidence in their governor, thinking of him as a "very agreeable humane kind gentleman" and an able administrator.[28] Perhaps more importantly, Wright and the Assembly congratulated each other for the "remarkable unanimity" with which they collaborated.[29] Even though they cooperated on most economic issues, the Sugar Act and Stamp Act troubles would forever alter their relationship, even if few realized it at the time.

While many Georgians enjoyed their newfound prosperity, colonists elsewhere were quick and organized in expressing their displeasure with the new legislation. The General Assembly of the Province of the Massachusetts Bay swiftly dispatched a circular letter that summer encouraging its sister assemblies to "unite in the most serious remonstrance" against both the Sugar Act and the proposed Stamp Act.[30] It took Georgia's Assembly seven months to react to the circular with any conviction. Legislators instructed William Knox, the colony's agent in London and the man who was to have been Wright's son-in-law, to "make proper application for redress" of the Sugar Act.[31] Almost concurrently, across the Atlantic, the king signed the Stamp Act into law on 22 March 1765. The new measure required all legal documents, newspapers, pamphlets, broadsides, leases, bills of sale, bonds, insurance policies, and ship's clearances to be produced on official stamped paper.

The Georgia Assembly objected, arguing not that Parliament had no right to tax them but that the stamp duty would place an unbearable financial burden upon them. They also questioned the notion of virtual representation, a somewhat fanciful concept that had been practiced in Britain for some time. It was a theory that each member of Parliament represented all of Britain and not simply his own local constituency.[32] The Assembly then urged Knox to join with the other colonial agents in protesting the stamp measure.[33] Although James Wright believed the stamp duty to be poorly conceived, he could not fathom the Assembly questioning parliamentary sovereignty. For him, there simply was no middle ground. Either the colonies were dependent upon the mother country, or they were themselves sovereign. "Authority and subordination," he wrote, must always exist in a civilized society.[34] Decades of legal study and practice supplemented his inherent respect for authority and his belief in the sanctity of the law. He, in fact, was as firm in his conviction that the rule of law must be upheld as was King George III, who wrote that "no consideration could bring me to swerve" from this conviction.[35]

That summer the Massachusetts House of Representatives again led the colonial resistance. This time, however, its members dispatched a circular letter that called for the colonies to send delegates to a congress in New York.[36] The Georgia legislature was not in session when the letter arrived, but Assembly Speaker Alexander Wylly requested that Governor Wright call the legislature into session so members could answer the request. He quickly refused. The speaker then usurped Wright's prerogative and directly summoned representatives to Savannah. Sixteen of the twenty-five soon arrived, but since the Assembly was not officially in session, Wylly demurred, not wishing to push the issue any further. Georgia refrained from sending delegates. Not willing to fully yield, however, Wylly informed the Massachusetts legislature that Georgia's Assembly would endorse the resolutions made by the congress in New York.[37]

Also not wishing to press the issue, James Wright wisely chose to not confront Wylly about his unprecedented infringement upon royal authority. Did Wright's silence indicate tacit approval of the peaceful legislative protest? Perhaps so. His close friend, South Carolina governor William Henry Lyttelton, thought it laughable that the ministry believed the colonists would comply with the stamp measure.[38] Although Wright had been surprised by colonial reaction, t he most assuredly agreed with Lyttelton's suggestion that the measure was ill-advised, and he could accept the pursuit of legal and constitutional recourse.[39] Additionally, the dogmatic Wright would have been unable to hold his tongue if he had been terribly opposed to Wylly's breach. Even had he determined that silence was the prudent course of action, he most assuredly would have aired his frustration with his superiors in London, which he did not.

On 1 August the *Georgia Gazette* reported the fiery parliamentary exchange between former president of the Board of Trade Charles Townshend and Seven Years' War veteran and Whig leader Isaac Barre. In a debate over the Stamp Act, Townshend rose in the House of Commons and questioned how "those children of our planting, nourished by our indulgence, until they are grown up to a good degree of strength and opulence, and protected by our arms . . . [could] grudge to contribute their mite to relieve us from the heavy load of national expence." Barre defiantly sprang to his feet and exclaimed, "NO! Your oppression planted them in America!"[40] Thus Georgians were primed for a reaction when portions of Knox's anonymously published pamphlet appeared in the newspaper later that month. It did not then take long before Georgians learned the identity of the author of the pamphlet, and they reacted with predictable anger.[41]

Back in London, agent William Knox opted not to robustly present the Assembly's protest memorials as instructed. A memorial is typically a statement identifying the legislature's opinion, desire, or intent. Instead, he authored a pamphlet aggressively defending Parliament's right of taxation.[42] Governor Wright received a copy of Knox's pamphlet in July but tried to suppress its publication. Knox's behavior infuriated Wright. Their mutual friend, James Habersham, wrote that the treatise "would not suit our present meridian."[43] His instincts proved correct, and he bluntly informed Knox: "I think not one of your friends can justify your making that publication . . . [and] I am sure your particular friend [Wright] does not approve of it, and very heartily wishes it had never appeared."[44] Wright's attempt to suppress Knox's pamphlet failed, however, and his friend would not escape the consequences of choosing Crown over colony. He would not be the last.

But that's not the whole story. Knox maintained that his pamphlet was simply a public justification of his refusal to align with other agents who questioned parliamentary supremacy. Moreover, he did not desert his constituents, pointing out that practical situations existed that provided "cogent reasons for a peculiar tenderness to be observed in laying taxes upon the colonies."[45] Moreover, Knox officially opposed the Stamp Act, but not because Parliament lacked the authority to tax the colonists directly. Rather, he deemed the legislation to be impractical.

Even though many Georgians felt betrayed by Knox, their opposition to the Stamp Act remained relatively muted that fall, and Wright confidently reported that all was well in Georgia.[46] But that changed after the *Georgia Gazette* published a flurry of evocative accounts from the northern papers reporting the hanging of stamp agent effigies from the Carolinas to Massachusetts. Those dispatches included news that must have caused Wright additional concern, as they described the destruction of property belonging to colonial officials such as Massachusetts lieutenant governor Thomas Hutchinson.[47] Early in October 1765, the convening of the Stamp Act Congress in New York emboldened Georgia's Liberty Boys, a group whose name first appeared in the 7 November 1765 issue of the *Georgia Gazette*.[48] Georgia's Sons of Liberty caused Wright endless grief.

Also echoing the calls of liberty, even during these early days of the crisis, were perhaps some of Georgia's enslaved population. In early 1765 Olaudah Equiano had been beaten senseless by a Georgia enslaver. He recalled that Lowcountry treatment of the enslaved was more barbaric than it was in the West Indies; indeed, it was the worst of all slave societies he had endured.[49] That November, in between Lowcountry "visits" by Equiano, a group of enslaved men, women, and children fled to a swamp on the north side of the Savannah River and "committed several robberies and depredations."[50] The group sustained themselves in the marshes by plundering nearby plantations and even inhabited a small "town" surrounded by swamps. They proved determined to seize their freedom and managed to maintain that freedom for several years, despite the significant two-pound reward for their capture. Over the next several years, the Assembly, in fact, sent multiple militia detachments as well as bands of Indians to hunt these people down, seemingly without success.[51]

Meanwhile, Georgians customarily celebrated the accession of George III on 25 October, but the 1765 celebration aggravated the increasingly cantankerous mood in the colony. The festivities included alcohol and parades and an especially excited atmosphere along the wharf in Savannah. With the heightened tensions regarding parliamentary taxation, some members of this raucous crowd paraded effigies of the yet-to-be-named stamp distributor through Savannah's busy streets. Especially worrisome for Wright was that the burning of the distributor's effigy occurred "amidst the acclamations of a great concourse of people of all ranks and denominations."[52] Just a few days later, several inebriated sailors assembled on the anniversary of Guy Fawkes Day and constructed a scaffold, upon which they placed an effigy of the stamp distributor. They proceeded to traipse through the town, chanting "no stamps, no riot act!" and placed the effigy in front of Machenry's Tavern, about four blocks east of Wright's home.[53] Although the spirit of those participants seemed innocent enough and no property had been damaged, the Liberty Boys made their point in a direct message to the distributor, whoever he might be, that they found his position and the legislation to be quite loathsome.[54]

## "The Phrenzy of an Unthinking Multitude"

The Stamp Act had been scheduled to take effect on 1 November, but in Georgia there were neither stamps nor distributor. Governor Wright was frustrated that he had not yet received "one scrape of a pen" about the odious legislation.[55] This fact, however, did not reduce the tension along Savannah's wharf. The Liberty Boys, or, as Wright called them, "the sons of licentiousness," made their presence fully known throughout the late fall.[56] Concerned that the governor was hiding both the stamps and the distributor, the Liberty Boys audaciously threatened to murder five of Savannah's leading citizens, accusing them of being involved with the dreaded stamps and warning them of the "fatal consequences" surrounding such involvement.

Hyperbole? Perhaps, but semantics mattered little to those involved. In response to the threat from "The Townsmen," George Baillie, Simon Munro, and Thomas Moodie all publicly denied their involvement with the stamps.[57] Baillie's denial had been deceitful, as he later testified that the governor had asked him to take the stamps "under his direction." Moreover, his brother John testified that George had assisted in "protecting the distributor of the stamps . . . [and had] privately conveyed" him to the house of their father, Robert, in the country.[58] The fourth man threatened, Denys Rolle, a member of Parliament, simply returned to England posthaste. The last man targeted was the well-respected Habersham, who simply ignored the threat. Governor Wright had now had enough, and he offered the substantial reward of fifty pounds for the identity of those involved in the threats. Even the Assembly balked at the violent threat, at least publicly, and unanimously agreed to pay the reward in the hopes of showing its "detestation and just abhorrence of such malignant" behavior.[59] Wright then ordered the Rangers and officers from various outposts to return, bringing the total force in Savannah to fifty-six privates and eight officers.[60]

As Savannah began to take on the aspect of a militarized zone, the Assembly discussed the documents recently arrived from the Stamp Act Congress in New York, a convention of Americans who opposed the Stamp Act and coordinated the American response to the legislation. Up to this point, the Assembly had never directly questioned the legality of the act so much as questioned its wisdom and Parliament's disregard for the Assembly's own authority. But the mood was changing, and Wylly directed that the proceedings from New York be published in the *Georgia Gazette*.[61] The full record of the Stamp Act proceedings, however, was not laid before the Assembly for another month, nearly four weeks after the act was supposedly set to be implemented. After much philosophical jostling, the lower house voted to fully endorse the work of the congress in New York.[62] In short, and as a preface of things to come, Assembly members still acknowledged their allegiance to the Crown but defended their own "inherent rights and liberties," namely, the concept of no taxation without representation.[63]

Meanwhile, Wright and his Council made three important decisions that placated the merchants and shipmasters in the harbor. They agreed to close the land office, suspend the courts, and keep the ports open.[64] Fearful of such maneuvering, the Liberty Boys held a meeting at Machenry's Tavern to determine the "properest measures to be taken at this very alarming and critical juncture." They unanimously decided they should run any risk to force the immediate resignation of the stamp master upon his arrival.[65] As Wright's concerns grew, he reported that the radicals "began to have private cabals [and] many had signed an association, opposing the distribution of the Stamp't papers."[66]

No matter his feelings about the legislation, Wright simply did not have the temperament to accept such lawlessness, even if he believed that the cause of the Sons of Liberty was just. Tensions continued to rise with the news that an Englishman named George Angus had been appointed distributor.[67] The increased excitement pushed Wright to complain to the Board of Trade that "too much of the rebellious spirit in the northern colonies has already shewn itself here," and Georgians have been for "many months past stimulated by letters" sent from the other colonies, especially South Carolina.[68] He then issued a proclamation forbidding "all riots, routs, and tumultuous assemblies" and threatened that violators would be punished to the "utmost rigour of the law."[69] He also made plans to protect the stamp agent upon his arrival.[70] During these difficult days, Habersham wrote that he and Wright were "upon the most friendly and intimate terms, and most of my vacant hours are spent with him."[71] Moreover, the two men had formed an incredible bond in five years, sharing similar interests, political beliefs, and personal griefs. In fact, Wright later wrote that Habersham had "behaved extremely well towards the support of government & authority [and] taken great pains to assist" during the Stamp Act crisis.[72] With a stamp agent named and stamps surely en route, the Assembly ended William Knox's employment as colonial agent.[73] Rather than come to the aid of his friend, Wright proffered Richard Cumberland as a suitable replacement, calling him a "gentleman perfectly conversant in the business of an agent [and] well known and respected at the several offices" in London.[74]

The Governor's Council, however, of which Knox had formerly been a member, refused to abandon him and instead communicated their appreciation for his performance, leading to a deeper breach between the two houses, which would widen in the ensuing years. It had likely been the recent uptick in violent confrontations that had spurred the Council to the defense of its former member. Habersham had written Knox that he had recently been "waylaid in the night and threatened to have my house pulled down" for his suspected ministerial tendencies. "How dreadful it is," he lamented, "to have one's person and property under the dominion of the mob."[75] For his part, Knox appreciated the Council's backing, writing that it gave him "the highest satisfaction to have the approbation of those whose opinion is to be influenced neither by the frowns of power nor by the more despicable menacies of a deluded and artfully instigated populace."[76] Members of the Commons House then asked Charles Garth, an MP and South Carolina's agent, to submit their petitions and memorials and, in a move asserting their legislative independence, voted to pay him fifty pounds.[77] He also remained Georgia's de facto agent, against Wright's wishes, until the completion of Knox's term.[78]

William Knox had straddled the fence during the Stamp Act crisis. He privately asserted the need for a refashioning of imperial laws to provide colonial governors with greater control over legislatures, and he publicly maintained Parliament's right of taxation. On the other hand, he candidly acknowledged that colonial legislatures possessed certain rights and privileges, and he advocated for those in respect to parliamentary taxation.[79] He said there existed "cogent reasons for a peculiar tenderness to be observed in laying taxes upon the colonies" and that standard procedures "should be relaxed on behalf of subjects in America."[80]

As Georgians anxiously awaited the arrival of the stamps, Governor Wright observed with great concern the "spirit of faction and sedition" that now existed in the colony.[81] The Sons of Liberty had, in fact, abused and insulted him. Worse yet, he complained to his superiors in London, "I have very nearly seen the power & authority . . . vest[ed] in me, wrested out of my hands, a matter my Lords too cutting for a good subject & servant to bear." He never shied away from utilizing hyperbole with his superiors in London, but this situation was different. He fully understood that his hold on power had indeed become tenuous, and this left him apoplectic. He simply could not fathom a world in which this could be the case, and he fully exerted himself in preventing the "mobs from daring to attempt to obstruct the due course of law."[82] Habersham confirmed this. "We are here in the utmost confusion," he wrote, "and our honest governor, who will not submit an inch to the phrenzy of an unthinking multitude, is laboring night and day to prevent the worst consequences."[83] And the stamps had not even arrived.

## "We Are Almost in Arms, One against Another"

Wright at long last received a copy of the Stamp Act "in a private way" in mid- to late November, and, predictably, he toed the imperial line. Regardless of his personal feelings about the legislation and paying no heed to the unruly behavior of the Liberty Boys, he determined to uphold the law at all costs. He immediately "thought it his indispensable duty to take" the required oaths, which he did on 22 November.[84] He then announced the closure of the port effective 30 November, assuring the Board of Trade that its commands "will ever be most punctually obeyed by me."[85] The stamps arrived the next day, although without a distributor. Wright and his Council considered the appointment of a temporary distributor but voted five to four against such a measure.[86] A revelatory letter written by James Habersham affords an understanding of Wright's own sentiments that November. Habersham described the Stamp Act as "ill advised" and "very burthensome," but he believed law and order must be maintained and could not understand how rejecting the stamps could have "the least efficacy towards obtaining a repeal of [the act]." Regardless of the accuracy of his prediction, the political climate in Savannah was heating up, and those who "dare[d] to deliver his free sentiments," Habersham wrote, "is threatened to be mobbed" by those who "miscall themselves the Sons of Liberty." Lastly, Habersham announced his intention to remain silent until the "popular clamour and passion subsides [because] I have no doubt of being thought a *real son of Liberty*."[87] As their mutual friend William Knox wrote, those crying for "liberty and privileges" will always "be the favourites of the populace," while those comfortable in their rights "expose themselves to calumny"; thus, "cool thinking men" who prefer to stay above the fray "withdraw themselves from the tumult."[88] Knox may have been correct, but such a view could only be made by the privileged few.

A skilled executive, James Wright was learning when to hold firm and when to concede, and his actions during the Stamp Act crisis were masterly. As the confrontation mounted, Wright convinced the town's mer-

chants to request Council permission to employ someone to act as temporary agent until the official agent's arrival so as to not retard commerce.[89]
Unlike Habersham, though, Wright did not have the luxury of silence, and
his actions frustrated the Liberty Boys, who grumbled that he acted "with
the haughtiness of a Nero." They intended to respond in kind.[90]

Following the arrival of the stamps, publisher James Johnston announced
that he was "under the necessity of putting a stop to the publication" of the
*Georgia Gazette*. Although he would publish one more issue, he suspended
operations until the end of May 1766.[91] But while in operation, the *Gazette*
published an incredible eighty-nine articles about the Stamp Act, only thirteen of which presented what might now be considered the Loyalist perspective. The primary reason behind this imbalance toward the more radical elements in Georgia was economic in nature, according to historian S.
F. Roach Jr.[92] Johnston's newspaper and bookstore were only modestly successful, and he simply "could not afford" to toe the ministerial line, despite
his Tory predilections.

The sentiments of the town's population, however, did not exactly align
with the ratio of support shown in the *Gazette*, even though many thought
the act imprudent. The merchants favored repeal of the Stamp Act but generally through the constitutional methods of peaceful protest and petition. Concerned that their goods might spoil while languishing in the harbor, however, the merchants joined with several shipmasters and petitioned
Wright to let the loaded vessels sail. His Council advised him in the negative
and even suggested that he not appoint a temporary stamp distributor.[93] But
pressure from the merchants mounted, and practical considerations compelled the Council to change course two days later. They now urged Wright
to designate a stamp master should an applicant come forth.[94]

Many merchants began to support distribution of the stamps, which infuriated the Liberty Boys. The *Pennsylvania Gazette* reported two months later
that the self-interest of "some of [Georgia's] merchants (finding their interest
concerned) . . . have even endeavoured to suppress the spirit of liberty."[95] The
merchants, according to historians Edmund Morgan and Helen Morgan,
"were willing to play the role which those of North Carolina had disdained,
and they earned the hatred and contempt of the other colonists for this betrayal of American unity."[96] Charleston's radical leader, Christopher Gadsden, chided Georgians for being "out-cunninged" and "so easily deluded and
bullied" by their governor.[97] Heady talk, to be sure, and it was emblematic of
the aggressive strategy employed by the radicals in the 1760s and beyond. Sa-

vannahians, however, were divided on this issue. On the one hand, the Liberty Boys were working overtime to keep the province enflamed, increasing conservative fears that "we are almost in arms, one against another."[98] On the other hand, many wanted to maintain the traditional order of things. Several gentlemen visited Wright the day after Georgia's ports officially closed. They assured him that they never had any intention "to harm the stamps."[99] Wright accepted their assurances and changed his plan to store the stamps at the guardhouse; instead, he sent them to the warehouse under the care of the commissary. This appeared to settle things down.[100]

The perceived betrayal by the merchants, however, invigorated and drove the Liberty Boys into action. In early January 1766 they gathered en masse in the center of town and "marched to the governor's gate."[101] Ranger captains John Milledge and John Powell, whom Wright had ordered to town back in November, informed him that approximately two hundred Liberty Boys were assembling near the wharf and had, in Wright's words, "declared they were determined to go to the fort & break open the store & take out and destroy the stamped papers."[102] Desiring to head off a potential disaster, Wright armed himself and ordered the officers to get their men and meet him at the guardhouse. A raucous crowd soon approached the guardhouse with drums beating.

Wright hurried from his home two short blocks away and thrust himself directly into the crowd, demanding to know their business. They asked him if he intended to appoint a distributor. He chastised them, insisting that this was no "manner to wait upon the governor," but since no one had applied, the position remained vacant. Moreover, Wright assured them that they would soon realize that "he was a friend to liberty, while their measures were destructive of it." The disgruntled but mollified crowd dispersed, promising to return if Wright acted in a way contrary to their liberty. After the crowd broke up that night, Wright and the remaining Rangers patrolled the town until well after dark, with the governor returning to his home after 9:00 p.m. To preserve at least a semblance of order, Wright maintained a minimum of forty men on duty every night and patrolled Savannah's streets alongside the soldiers, because without such measures, he was "confident [the stamps] would have been destroyed."[103] Anxieties ran so high in the ensuing days that the governor slept in his clothes and with his musket for days on end.[104]

Wright received word shortly before noon on the morning of 3 January that George Angus, the stamp distributor, had arrived from England and was waiting at Tybee Island. Having already made arrangements that he be the first to learn of the stamp master's arrival, the governor quickly dispatched the Rangers to escort Angus safely and quietly to Wright's home on St. James's Square. His forethought may have saved Angus's life and at the very least lessened the likelihood of riotous behavior. Angus was spirited away to the country "to avoid the resentment of the people." But he had seen enough and left Georgia at the end of March, never to return.[105]

Wright reopened the ports at Savannah and Sunbury on 7 January 1766 after an informal detente was reached between the Liberty Boys and the town's merchants, with the latter agreeing to only apply for stamps required for shipping and the former promising to offer no objections to the duties performed by customs officials.[106] The vessels currently waiting to depart purchased the stamped paper and sailed, making Governor Wright the only governor among the thirteen colonies that later revolted to successfully issue the stamped paper. Wright had outmaneuvered the Liberty Boys, protecting the stamps and the distributor, and the confidence of the Liberty Boys waned. The *Pennsylvania Journal and Weekly Advertiser* declared that "any opposition will now be fruitless, as those yet hearty on the cause of liberty, are but few in numbers."[107] But the pendulum had not come to a rest.

Although an uneasy calm descended over Savannah, news of Angus's arrival had filtered into the backcountry. Rumors then made their way back to Savannah that some rabble rousers from South Carolina had enflamed the frontier and were now marching toward Savannah.[108] Wright confirmed that some "incendiaries from Charlestown came full fraught with sedition and rebellion, and have . . . inflamed the people to such a degree that they were again assembling" in large numbers.[109] Finding himself "in a most uncomfortable situation," Wright "found it necessary to be under arms myself for some time."[110] A disdain for authority seemed to exist in the DNA of colonial South Carolinians. They had been a thorn in the side of Wright's father, the provincial chief justice, and in Wright's own side during his years as attorney general and colonial agent. Now they incessantly endeavored to spread that trait to their neighboring colonists. William Knox had once complained that "no King can govern nor God can please [the] sordid legislators of Carolina."[111]

### "The Reins of Government Nearly Hoisted out of My Hands"

By now Wright feared for both his government and his life. To Henry Seymour Conway, the secretary of state for the Southern Department, Wright wrote that he had the "greatest mortification to see the reins of government nearly hoisted out of my hands."[112] He then decided to expend some of his hard-earned political capital and reach out to "many of the most sensible & dispassionate people" beyond Savannah, urging them to help ease the rising tempers in the backcountry. His efforts bore fruit, and he was assured by the frontier leaders that "they never will appear in arms again, or oppose his Majesties authority."[113] He reported to his superiors that his "weight & credit was sufficient to check & prevent all commotions & disturbances in the country."[114] Although his efforts were productive, he still struggled to maintain the fragile peace, finding "a much greater spirit of rebellion than he had thought possible."[115] But in this ever-changing climate, Wright had been too sanguine about his ability to keep the radicals at bay, learning that the Liberty Boys planned to shoot him if he contravened their wishes. Habersham, in fact, had been warned not to leave his home on Johnson Square.[116] The threats had so frightened him that he determined "to take shelter" in the governor's home, where at least one sentry was stationed.[117]

Wright now confronted a pivotal moment in the Stamp Act crisis, and his actions in the next few days would determine control of the city. He decided to send the stamped paper to Fort George on Cockspur Island, just south of the town, but he did not simply relocate the paper; he sent most of his Rangers with it, leaving the town virtually defenseless. His bold move left James Habersham to fear the "fatal consequences" of the upcoming days, noting that his "flesh trembles" for the future. With good reason. According to Wright, a "knot of rebellious turbulent spirits" lurked around Savannah's streets, and another group planned to enter the city, surround his home, and "extort a promise from [him] that no papers should be issued till his Majesty's pleasure be known on the petitions sent to London." Wright wisely refused to call out the militia out of fear that "I should have armed more against me than for me."[118] Regardless of the "repeated threats & insults," he assured his superiors, "I will firmly persevere to the utmost of my power, in the faithful discharge of my duty." He did, however, want to make the Board of Trade aware of the sufferings of those loyal to the Crown: those who "are firm in their opposition to the present seditious spirit . . . [now] have a very uncomfortable time of it."[119]

Seemingly on cue, Captain Robert Fanshawe returned onboard the H.M.S. *Speedwell* on 2 February and "promised me the assistance of twenty men . . . if the villains should come to town." In addition to these men, "several gentlemen and others" also came to the governor's aid. Although he was now confident that he had convinced many of those angry backcountry inhabitants to disperse, a couple hundred still moved inexorably toward

Savannah, angry at Wright. Those firebreathers finally arrived in Savannah two days later, loaded with flags, guns, and drums, but by then, Wright had fully secured the city with "near 100 men that I could command & depend upon."[120]

It was not only South Carolina's Sons of Liberty who infuriated Governor Wright. He felt abandoned by the royal executive in neighboring South Carolina. According to Wright, Lieutenant Governor William Bull, the acting governor of that province since 1764, caved to popular pressure and opened that colony's ports under the pretense that he had no stamped paper. One Charlestonian in fact called Bull a "damd fool" for failing to exert royal authority.[121] Wright insisted that Bull did have the papers but had stored them at Fort Johnson. Wright had risked everything while his compatriot in South Carolina yielded. "I am continually perplexed & kept in hot water not only by the seditious spirit of the people," Wright groused, "but by the conduct of those in authority" elsewhere.[122] As it turned out, Bull did not have the stamps, but the incident confirmed in Wright's mind the mischievous impact of South Carolina's radicals.

Then suddenly came the news in May of the Stamp Act's repeal.[123] Wright now felt abandoned by the Board of Trade in much the same way he felt betrayed by Bull. As the crisis subsided, however, Wright continued the fight for Georgia's political soul by trying to convince colonial leaders that all mob action, for whatever reason, was injurious to their cause, and it must be curbed for the colony to continue to grow. Predictably, he reached out to Georgia's elder statesmen rather than trying to bridge the gap with the younger generation, who bore most of the responsibility for the recent troubles. Meanwhile, the Assembly reconvened in July and congratulated him on the official announcement of the legislation's revocation. The governor and legislature also praised themselves for navigating the crisis in such a way as to avoid the destruction of property in the colony, which had plagued many other provinces. Although most Georgians reveled in their comparative civility as well as their successful lobbying efforts, Wright feared that his zealous enforcement of the Stamp Act would cost him his position in Georgia. It very well might.

Several Liberty Boys had recently "been very industrious in propagating a report," Wright said, "that my conduct in endeavouring to enforce the Stamp Act, was disagreeable & disapproved of [in London], and therefore a Lieut. Governor is coming over and that I am to be superseded."[124] He became apoplectic at the prospect of losing because he had won. It would be months before he received a reply, but in the interim, he continued to try and restore proper order in the province. He remained unconvinced that all was well in Georgia, even though the Assembly twice expressed its "fealty" and "loyalty to our King." At the end of the summer, he persisted in expressing the prescient concern that "republican spirits [would] rather cherish those ideas, than recede from them."[125]

As this new reality set in, Wright received an important communication from the board. In September William Petty, 2nd Earl of Shelburne, secretary of state for the southern department, promised Wright that rumors about his dismissal had no factual foundation. In fact, Shelburne wrote, the king was pleased with his "conduct during the disturbance" and "has had [no] thoughts of sending you any letters of recall."[126] A London paper corroborated this: "Notwithstanding so many reports [that] have been inserted in all the papers relative to the change of a certain American governor [Wright], it is now said, his conduct has not been disapproved of on this side of the water."[127] However, the phrase "it is *now* said" seems to indicate that the board had had issue with Wright's conduct. Additionally, Shelburne chided the governor for his conduct, reminding him that it was his duty "to conduct [himself] as not to create groundless jealousies or suggest suspicion that [he was] capable of [restraining] with ill will or wishing to restrain the just & decent exercise of that liberty which belongs to the people."[128] Here we can see the predicament in which colonial governors found themselves. They were to simultaneously enforce parliamentary legislation while not offending the easily offended, a no-win situation indeed.

While Shelburne reproached Wright for the way in which he successfully implemented the Stamp Act in Georgia, George Grenville, chancellor of the exchequer, encouraged the king to "bestow some mark of favor upon those governors and officers in America who had suffered by their loyalty."[129] Yet James Wright received a rebuke for being the only governor who, in his own words, "had influence enough to prevent [the Assembly's] even attempting to make any resolves as to the rights and privileges claimed by the [A]mericans, and also any applications relative to the non execution of the Stamp Act."[130] Wright sent a frustrated and forceful response to the board detailing how he envisaged his role in the colony during the first half of the decade. "I am perfectly sensible," he wrote, "how essential the prerogatives of the Crown are to government, & that I cannot be too vigilant in observing, or too firm in resisting . . . any encroachment on them." He added with only slight exaggeration that he always practiced "mildness & moderation" in such moments. This was a pretty accurate self-reflection, certainly in terms of his actions, if not in his letters. He closed his letter with a foreboding warning: "Your Lordship has not been pleased to hint what may be deemed the *just* and *decent* liberty of the people and w[hi]ch I'm afraid will be a difficult matter to settle [because] what may be judged so in Great Britain will not in America."[131] To Wright, the Board of Trade seemed to have little actual idea of the situation in America, despite his repeated attempts to explain the temper of the people.

## "Faithful Servant of the Crown"

In that light, Wright thought dubious Shelburne's hope that Parliament's "equity & lenity ... [had] made those just impressions" on its subjects and that "there are at present no marks remaining of that ill temper which has so much prevailed."[132] But he did sense after the repeal that there was a general mood of gratitude and a desire for a return to normalcy in Georgia, although he warned the ministry that "there are many who still retain the late avowed sentiments and strange ideas of liberty & insist" that only their representatives could directly tax them.[133]

Such a concept was foreign to Wright, for he was conservative to his core and believed governance to be the purview of the elite few. From a policy standpoint, he found the Stamp Act's repeal to be horrifically shortsighted, a sign of imperial weakness, and a portent of doom. He grieved that Parliament had shown the colonists "extraordinary lenity and indulgence," especially because many people retained "strange ideas of liberty."[134] That indulgence caused him the greatest discomfort, and he believed that only strength and vigor would allow Britain to maintain its North American empire. Massachusetts governor Thomas Hutchinson concurred, arguing that failure to enforce the virtually unenforceable measure would erode colonial confidence in the Board of Trade.[135]

While the king and the ministry may have taken issue with the sternness with which Wright negotiated these troubling times, there was much of which to be proud. In the early stages of the crisis, scientist and naturalist John Bartram journeyed through Georgia and noted in his journal that Governor Wright was "universally respected by all the inhabitants [of Georgia and] they can hardly say enough in his praise."[136] James Habersham agreed, writing toward the end of the impasse that "our governor has behaved with unusual firmness & spirit" and "has on this critical occasion behaved like himself, I mean like a man of honor and a faithful servant of the Crown."[137] Even the typically confrontational Commons House seemed to be in step with Governor Wright's actions throughout much of the crisis and does not seem to have exchanged any oppositional correspondence during the entire period.

Wright confirmed his own popularity, at least among those who mattered to him, in a letter to the Board of Trade: "I have the great pleasure to find that many of the *better* sort of people begin to see that my firmness in the discharge of my duty to his Majesty, and perseverance in my endeavors to convince & set them right on this occasion, will redound to the interest and happiness of the province & people in general."[138] Historian Pauline Maier agreed: "One of the first communities to organize Sons of Liberty was Savannah, Georgia, where, ironically, the Sons were the most successfully divided and dispirited" by Governor Wright.[139]

The governor's unequaled success in distributing stamps as well as minimizing civic disruption lay in his preparation, which afforded him the opportunity to generally seize the initiative. He believed his successes would have been multiplied had he not been handicapped by the absence of more troops. In fact, this is a complaint that he would consistently lodge from his arrival in Georgia in 1760 through his final expulsion in the summer of 1782. He emerged from the Stamp Act crisis more bold and more confident in his interactions both with the board and with his fellow Georgians. But his frustration with the board's handling of the conflict and its treatment of him made a lasting impression. As historian W. W. Abbot observed, "There is not a scrap of evidence that Wright at any time before 1765 overtly questioned any decision of the Board of Trade; after 1765 he disagreed with these gentlemen often."[140] In fact, he harbored an air of impatience and possessed a habit of being uncompromising, which only hardened after 1765.

But ultimately, Wright had exhausted most of his political capital during this crisis and had become, to many Georgians, a symbol of imperial authority rather than the representative of their interests. The crisis forced Georgians to pay closer attention to their connection with Britain and to no longer simply take for granted that what was good for the empire was good for Georgia. More than anything, this idea took root in the Georgia Assembly, where two factions emerged. One faction identified themselves as defenders of colonial rights. They insisted that both Wright and Parliament had to operate within certain limits. The other supported Wright, the rule of law, and traditional conservative British values.

James Wright believed the stamp duty to be poorly conceived. "Authority and subordination," he wrote, "must always exist in a civilized society."[141] Decades of legal study and practice supplemented his inherent respect for authority and his belief in the sanctity of the law. Not only was

James Wright the only one of the original thirteen mainland governors to not "yield to the torrent of popular fury," he was the only one to "enforce the law in one instance," and he did so in the face of widespread popular opposition and the threat of physical attack.[142] It was, according to historian Jack Greene, "Wright's careful supervision" of the stamp crisis that "prevented [the colonial Assembly] from attaining the power acquired by lower houses elsewhere."[143] In spite of these successes, however, he paid a steep price and "at the hazard of my life," he said.[144] First, his growing confidence resulted in increasingly less flexibility in future quarrels with the Assembly. Second, he clearly identified himself as a Crown man first and a Georgian second. Third, the entire affair exacted a significant personal toll, which engendered in him a desire for a safer and perhaps more lucrative locale. Fourth, he lost some of the precious political capital he had built over the years. Lastly, the Liberty Boys had learned that Parliament lacked the fortitude to enforce its legislation. Wright learned this as well, and he foresaw the ramifications of this, confiding to the Board of Trade: "After the people in a country have been inflamed to the highest degree, it's not to be supposed or expected that all heats & party spirits can subside at once . . . and this province is not without some violent republican spirits, full of rancor against the government & Parliament, and still fix't in their strange mistaken ideas of liberty, and that no power can tax or restrain them &c but themselves."[145] Nearly ten years to the day, he presciently predicted the independence movement, observing that such "republican spirits" would positively "rather cherish those ideas, than recede from them."[146]

# CHAPTER 4

# A Governor and
# Colony on the Move

In the decade following the tumult caused by the Stamp Act, James Wright experienced an incredibly wide range of emotions. His position in Georgia and within the imperial bureaucracy had been solidified. Georgia witnessed a relatively tranquil period that was abruptly interrupted by disturbances related to the Townshend Duties, a 1767 act that taxed goods imported to America. All the while, Governor Wright had to negotiate frontier troubles. His successful land deal in 1763 created perhaps as many problems as it solved, and his solution was to call for an additional cession of Native lands. Moreover, it appears he hoped to parlay that bounty into a new, more prestigious imperial position. But the ministry and fate had other plans for him. They returned him to Georgia just in time for the Boston Tea Party and the onset of an imperial crisis that Britain struggled to navigate.

Several months removed from the Stamp Act crisis, Wright sat down to provide a "sketch of affairs" in Georgia relative to his five years in the province. According to Wright, Georgia's population stood at about ninety-five hundred when he arrived in November 1760. Of that total, whites comprised about two-thirds. Now, Wright wrote, the white population had increased to ninety-nine hundred out of a population close to eighteen thousand. This, however, was a decrease in the percentage of the overall white population, a situation that presaged what historian Peter Wood called the "Black Majority," which had occurred earlier in the century in South Carolina. In 1760 Georgia exported four hundred barrels of rice, compared to more than ten thousand five years later, Wright's report continued. In 1761 forty-two "sail of vessels" had been loaded on Georgia's wharves, whereas in 1765 that number had nearly quadrupled. The colony still lacked manufactures of any consequence, however, and its "whole strength & attention is employed in planting rice, indigo, corn & pease, & a small quantity of wheat & rye, in making pitch, tar, turpentine, shingles & staves, in sawing lumber, scantlings, & boards of every kind, and in raising stocks of cattle, mules, horses and hogs and next year he hopes some essays will be made toward planting & making hemp."[1] In essence, then, Georgia had become exactly what mercantilism required of it.

In addition to his description of this rapidly expanding economy, Governor Wright observed in his report that "the people in general are well disposed except a few Republican spirits, who endeavour to inculcate independency, and keep up jealousies & ill blood." In the same vein, he mentioned his surprise that the spirit of "sedition & almost rebellion [should have] then appeared even in this infant colony." But Wright may have misunderstood the nature of the revolt when he said that Georgians only rose in defiance when they had been "spirited on by their northern neighbours, who never let them rest nor gave them time to cool."[2] He also had more issues to deal with than the purely political. The frontier issues of the first years of his tenure continued apace in the latter half of the 1760s.

## "Generally the Worst Kind of People"

In the winter of 1766, an endlessly frustrated James Wright complained to William Petty, 2nd Earl of Shelburne and secretary of state for the Southern Department: "I think it very necessary to acquaint your Lordship that I am apprehensive of some disturbance & mischief gathering & breaking out amongst the Indians, indeed I have long expected this would be the consequence" of the ill-conceived royal proclamation of 1763. In addition to confining colonists east of the Appalachian Mountains, the edict undermined the authority of the colonial governors by ordering them to grant licenses to any colonist who desired to trade with the Native Americans. The primary difficulties, according to Wright, arising from such legislation were that the Indians were "over stock't with goods" by an infestation of "white Indians," those small traders and packhorsemen, whom Wright derided as "generally the worst kind of people." The abundance of goods and increasing interaction with these traders led to "insolence, wantonness, & mischief" from the Natives. This economic imbalance, Wright argued, had led to innumerable "irregularities & abuses committed by the traders," which in turn would likely occasion a never-ending cycle of violence and retribution. Wright had submitted similar warnings in previous years: "The Indian trade [is] running into great confusion, numbers of people [are] applying for licenses, and 3 or 4 persons were trading in one & the same town, which was productive of almost continual disputes & quarrels between the traders & the Indians. By so many persons trading in one town, the Indians [have become] over supplied with goods, which I conceive to be a bad policy." Georgia's Assembly even encouraged Wright to "remonstrate in the strongest terms possible" the need to regulate traders.[3]

Moreover, the proclamation's prohibition of settlements west of the Appalachians resulted in hundreds of settlers migrating to Georgia's frontier. Although many were yeoman farmers, squatters were also common. This last group, according to James Habersham, "have no settled habitation and live by hunting and plundering the industrious settlers."[4] Moreover, this new group of frontiersmen differed from their predecessors. They neither liked nor wanted to engage in commerce with the Natives. They feared and hated them and wanted their lands. The British policy that allowed the Natives free access to Augusta was bound to cause friction.[5]

Historian Alan Gallay has argued that if the other provinces "had conducted Indian policy as successfully as Georgia, the Crown might not have had reason or excuse" to issue the proclamation.[6] Gallay's assessment was spot on. In 1767 Shelburne informed Wright that "His Majesty approves entirely of your sentiments in regards to the Indians & wishes that that same attention had been paid to maintain peace among them by the governor of West Florida," who had since been recalled.[7] Governor Wright had maintained the peace initiated by Henry Ellis by continuing the former's policy of minimizing settler and trader misconduct. In this light, then, Wright's frustration with the Board of Trade is understandable. As the consequences of the proclamation unfolded over the next decade, it became clear that it substantially and forever altered Georgia's relationship with both the Native Americans and the new immigrants. The increasingly frequent backcountry troubles stemmed from both the proclamation and Wright's Native land cession of the same year and placed Georgia on a dangerous path by the mid-1770s.

As Wright predicted, the Georgia backcountry erupted in sporadic yet unending lawlessness and bloodshed. The frontier settlers around Augusta sent a petition to the governor in July 1767 "complaining of great plunder and depredations committed on their stock of horses and cattle by a party of Creek Indians." After the latest theft, a group of angry and obstinate settlers pursued several Creeks to demand the return of their horses. After coming upon a much larger body of Indians than they expected, however, the settlers determined to lie in wait in the hopes of capturing some of the horses at night, but "one of [the Indians' dogs] yelpt which alarmed" the Creeks and elicited "their war hoop." A cacophony of musket fire soon sent the colonists scurrying off. The colonists, "terrified at the thoughts of loosing [*sic*] our stock and very possibly our lives," implored the governor for assistance lest their settlement be forced "to break up."[8] They also petitioned General Thomas Gage, commander-in-chief of the British army in North America, complaining that the "inconsistency of [the Indians'] behaviour and the consequences that may attend it has given us no little uneasiness."[9]

In early August, Governor Wright dispatched a missive to the Creek leaders in northeast Georgia. Even though the governor viewed the Indians through an eighteenth-century racist prism, he firmly believed in the value of honoring treaty obligations. He reminded them of their obligation under the 1763 treaty to "prevent any of your people from giving any disturbance," and if "any damage be done" to the English, "satisfaction shall be made for the same" to the injured party. In fact, Wright wrote, "I know perfectly well that I have taken the utmost care and pains that all the white people should conform" to the treaty, and "I have always been ready to do you full justice" when the colonists violated their obligations. Yet while he had earnestly attempted to maintain white compliance with all agreements, Wright knew that his wishes and frontier behavior rarely coincided. Both illicit and well-intentioned traders flocked to the region following the Augusta Congress of 1763, and this influx caused no shortage of confrontation and conflict. Even so, Wright proceeded to recommend that the Creeks not "suffer any of your people to settle on the Oconee River" or anywhere "near the white people." Essentially, then, he wished for a significant geographical "no-man's land" separating the less disciplined members of both races.[10]

The surplus of Indian traders along the colonial frontier was not the only reason, however, for the increased hostilities between the Indians and colonists. A rapid and insufficiently regulated population explosion throughout the first decade of Governor Wright's tenure also exacerbated the already tenuous relationship between the two groups. Although southern tribes lived in distinct and separate spheres from their backcountry counterparts, Native and Euro-American worlds often intersected through an economic "frontier exchange."[11] These meetings increasingly led to conflict as the white population grew. James Wright found the interplay between these two groups to be all too frequent and excessively violent, requiring him to construct a virtual barrier to prevent such closeness. These interactions "only gradually became dangerous," according to historian Joshua Piker, and "cannot be attributed solely to an onrushing horde of colonists," as these pioneers also encountered explorers like Native Americans making their way southeastward. The ensuing frontier exchange nearly ensured conflict as the two new arrivals competed for resources and land with the Natives currently residing there. Thus "the region itself was . . . complicated, conflicted, and frequently [engaged in] violent relationships . . . with new and alarming consequences," even though the framework for "enduring, mutually beneficial relationships" existed.[12]

During this middle third of the century, the colony's population increased by 144 percent to 23,375 by 1770. Although the number of white Georgians increased by over 100 percent, the income potential of slavery lay at the heart of this phenomenal growth, and the number of enslaved increased by nearly 300 percent. Indeed, Wright's own personal wealth heavily relied upon the labor of the enslaved. At the outset of the American Revolution, he owned 25,578 acres and enslaved 523 human beings. Historian Betty Wood has suggested that only 6 percent of all enslavers held more than fifty people in bondage.[13] As governor, however, Wright tried to discourage such accumulations, at least in the backcountry. He assiduously promoted white settlement beyond Savannah's environs because increased habitation guaranteed better frontier security, but only if those settlers were small landowners, because plantation owners tended to be absentee. Wright sought to discourage this and populate the backcountry with only the "better sort of people"— those pioneers who simply aspired to live on and cultivate the land.[14]

Wright believed he could accomplish this type of settlement by restricting the size of land grants to "100 acres to the master or head of the family and 50 acres for the wife, child & each slave."[15] In addition to trying to limit Native-colonial interactions, Wright feared that the enslaved would find common cause with the Native Americans in the backcountry. He outlined his plan for "populating the colony" to the Board of Trade and insisted that only smaller land grants be distributed to "the middling sort of people, such as have families, & [only] a few negroes."[16] Wright reasoned that purchasers of land "will of course be something better than the common sort of back country people, and . . . will naturally be more industrious and better disposed to protect it."[17] The process of establishing a formal "no-man's land" and augmenting the frontier population with the "better sort" of white settlers took nearly a decade, but the forthcoming New Purchase of 1773 would add 2,116,298 acres of "very fine land" to the province's terri-

TABLE 4.1. Georgia's colonial population

| Year | Total | White | Black |
|------|-------|-------|-------|
| 1750 | 5,200 | 4,200 | 1,000 |
| 1760 | 9,578 | 6,000 | 3,578 |
| 1765 | 11,300 | 6,800 | 4,500 |
| 1770 | 23,375 | 12,750 | 10,625 |
| 1773 | 33,000 | 18,000 | 15,000 |
| 1780 | 56,071 | 35,240 | 20,831 |

SOURCES: John McCusker, ed., "Colonial Statistics," in *Historical Statistics of the United States: Earliest Times to the Present*, ed. Susan B. Carter et al. (Cambridge, 2006), 5:651–653; Wright to Dartmouth, 20 December 1773, in CO, 5/663. "I suppose the number of white men, women, and children in the whole province may be 18,000 and upwards, and the number of blacks is computed at 15,000." See also James Martin Grant, "Legislative Factions in Georgia, 1754–1798: A Socio-political Study" (PhD diss., University of Georgia, 1975), 2.

tory.[18] Lord Adam Gordon visited Georgia in the 1760s and was certain that "Georgia will become one of the richest, and most considerable provinces in British America, and that in a very few years, provided peace continues."[19] History proved Gordon correct. No province could match Georgia's rapid economic growth in the colonial era.[20] But the story of James Wright and the New Purchase takes us back to 1763.

## "Jealousies & Ill Blood"

Wright felt certain in 1763 that Georgia would soon become a "most flourishing" colony because recent conditions "seem extremely well calculated to make these southern colonies become considerable & beneficial" to Great Britain.[21] Idealism soon gave way to the stark reality that all was not quiet on this western front. In ceding the lands they deemed most likely to have been trespassed upon, the Creeks hoped to eliminate frontier turmoil. Younger and less trusting Indians, however, viewed the cession as an English "land grab" that confirmed in their minds previous French warnings concerning British designs.[22] In January 1764 Wright informed his superiors in London that his worst fears had come to fruition. In likely retaliation for the Creek cession, "fourteen people," he cried, "have been murdered . . . by some runagate [*sic*] Creek Indians" along the Georgia–South Carolina border.[23] Gage responded to Wright's concerns with a somewhat dismissive statement: "I am willing to believe the storm will blow over."[24] He did, however, post a guard in Augusta "purely at the desire of Governor Wright."[25] Though the details were murky, the situation threatened to precipitate a full-blown con-

flagration in the backcountry, which could be devastating for the nascent
province. "If there should be a war," Wright wrote, "this province will certainly stand in great need of assistance, for my Lords if an handfull of Indians at the northward have been able to massacre so many people & so
greatly to distress those populous & opulent countries Pensilvania, New Jersey &c., where there are also a great number of His Majesties troops, what
may or may not be the fate of Georgia?"[26] To prevent such a calamity, Governor Wright initiated a dialogue with South Carolina governor Thomas
Boone, Indian superintendent John Stuart, and a number of Creek leaders.
Stuart issued a formal protest to the Creeks, who all promised satisfaction.[27]

Wright's initial suggestion to Stuart was that trade should be suspended
with the Creeks only if they refused to give satisfaction for their malfea-
sance.[28] Boone proved much less patient, having grown tired of repeated
"talks & expostulations."[29] Governor Wright, however, was keenly aware
of his limited bargaining position, because he possessed "no [real] coercive
power over the traders" or Indians.[30] Besides, Wright knew that this was no
time for bluster. "Its [sic] a matter that I apprehend ought not to be too hastily done," he advised Boone, "for it is very probable it may bring on a war," for
which Georgia "is nearest, weakest & most exposed to their ravage."[31] General Gage agreed with Wright. He feared that aggressive demands "would
be look't upon as a declaration of war." Instead of pressing trade restrictions,
however, Gage urged Wright and Stuart to incite intertribal tensions in the
hopes that a British alliance with the Creeks' Native rivals would set them
straight.[32] Furthermore, Gage acknowledged that Wright's "present situation certainly requires great circumspection, & artfull management & from
your experience and abilities, I trust you will be able to extricate your province out of its present difficulties."[33]

While Wright pondered his options, he urged Georgia's legislature to
better enforce the existing measures designed to regulate frontier trade and
squatting. He explained his reasoning to the Board of Trade that spring,
emphasizing Georgia's unique circumstances. "I [am] clearly convinced," he
wrote, "that most of our broils with & insults received [from the Creeks]
have been occasioned by the persons trading with the Indians, & other vag-
abonds who have neither property nor habitation."[34] It is important to note
his continued frustration with the traders and his distaste for the lower
classes. Creek headmen confirmed trader misconduct, complaining that the
colonists had violated the treaty made at Augusta. "We have long been silent," Creek leader Emistisiguo bemoaned, but "a white man Robt. Sallit
has run out of this nation & occasioned much disturbances." Oakchoy King

echoed these sentiments, insisting that "many of these disturbances is owing to white men, who are very guilty . . . who are very impudent & occasions uneasiness." He added: "Our forefathers lived in perfect friendship with you. They had room to hunt, to kill game[,] to supply their wants. . . . We desire nothing else, & we hope you'll not encroach upon our lands; as hunting is our only dependence."[35] By the late summer of 1764, it appeared that Governor Wright's patience had indeed paid off, and he could report to his superiors that the frontier violence had subsided.[36] General Gage expressed his "great satisfaction that my sentiments on the situation of the Indian affairs coincided so entirely with your own, and it appears already that by not being too hasty and precipitate, you have avoided an Indian War."[37]

Despite the recent calm in the backcountry, Wright keenly understood that the present situation likely offered only a temporary respite. He again implored the Board of Trade in late August to regulate the Indian trade, because, in his estimation, traders "are not the honestest or soberest people, and I found they were in general undermining one another, and in order to get the greatest share of the trade, *each endeavoured to make the Indians believe that the other cheated them*, which raised jealousies & ill blood amongst them all, & disorders were frequently committed."[38] Additionally, Wright worked with the legislature to improve Georgia's backcountry defenses. He requested British captain James Mark Prévost, whose widow would later marry Aaron Burr, to send a force to Augusta, and he asked the Assembly to make much-needed repairs to Fort Augusta, but they demurred, as they usually did. Ultimately, the Assembly's refusal to adequately supply the garrison, coupled with the Board of Trade's reluctance to do so, led to a significant reduction in the garrison.[39]

At the end of August, the Upper Creek leader, the Mortar, extended an olive branch to Governor Wright. For years, the Mortar had, according to Wright, been "our greatest & most active enemy."[40] He freely acknowledged "the many outrages & hostilities that I have committed against the English, during my attachment to the French interest, but am now extremely sorry for it, & humbly beg forgiveness." He presented the governor with a white bird's wing and a string of white beads with the hope that "the great old path between Augusta and the Nation may be kept white [peaceful] & clean, and that they may be supplied with goods &c by that path, as they want to know no other."[41] This last statement is critical and confirmed Wright's fear of the glut of traders now roaming the backcountry. The "old path" referred to the path that Governors Ellis and Wright had worked hard to ensure remained relatively free of traders and squatters. The Proclamation of 1763, however, opened the floodgates, filling the path with rapacious and unscrupulous traders. Wright's response resounded with paternalism:

> [I] am very glad that the great being, and master of breath has opened your eyes and that you now see & are convinced that the English are your real & best friends, and that the French only instigated you against the English to involve you in misery and ruin. . . . And this is what I have been endeavouring to convince all your people of . . . and that it was & is your true interest to be good friends with, & hold fast by the great King & his English subjects, in him you will always find a father, & a friend to supply all your wants, but he will expect a gratefull return, and that you protect his white children.[42]

Governor Wright then returned to his favorite stratagem: dangling trade goods as a means of ensuring Native compliance on the frontier. He promised the Creek chief that he would encourage the traders to utilize the "old path," but only if their safety could be guaranteed. General Gage appreciated Wright's efforts on this front, writing that he was pleased that "this most inveterate and troublesome enemy [the Mortar] is at length inclined to peace."[43] Wright soon informed the board that "the storm did blow over." And just in case the board failed to understand that it was Wright's restraint that had, at least for now, won the day, he posited that had Governor Boone's proposal for a complete termination of trade been followed, he was "firmly persuaded we should have had a war with the Creek Indians."[44]

Furthermore, Wright suggested that the royal governors, and not Superintendent Stuart, must possess final authority concerning Indian affairs, because "lodging the supreme political power, in any other hands . . . may be attended with embarrasing [sic] & bad consequences."[45] Thus, with a growing sense of self-confidence, if not conceit, Wright emphasized his worth to the empire. Lord Hillsborough joined General Gage in recognizing Wright's value: "Nothing can be more pleasing to us, than to find, that the savage hostilities of the Indians . . . have ceased; and that they are at present in a state of perfect peace & tranquility."[46] For his part, Stuart argued that the governors understood neither the frontier nor the Indians, and by the fall of 1768, Wright was about ready to fully absolve himself of the responsibility of controlling the Indian trade.[47]

With the matter at least temporarily settled, Governor Wright and the legislature turned their attention to boosting the colony's population. In March 1766 the governor signed into law "An Act for Encouraging Settlers to Come into This Province." The act enticed prospective settlers to form townships containing at least forty Protestant families. The enticements included free survey and registration of the town and a ten-year exemption from provincial taxes, excepting those on the enslaved. Wright and the legislature wished for the settlers to form a geographically compact settlement of mostly nonslaveholding families who would be able to alter the ratio of white to nonwhite backcountry inhabitants while at the same time augmenting the region's defenses. The bill provided for the establishment of a new township whose land, survey, and registration would be provided for at public expense as soon as no fewer than forty Protestant families, consisting of at least one man and one woman, provided a sufficient testimony verifying their solid character.[48] Wright believed that only families of "good character" could adequately augment Georgia's militia, strengthen its frontier defenses, and support its growing economy in addition to lessening the negative effects of the backcountry "Crackers," as Wright referred to them.

Two groups utilized the prospects of this legislation to establish settlements. The first group to arrive was led by a sect of the Society of Friends from Orange County, North Carolina, who established a new home near Little River just north and west of Augusta. The Quakers named their settlement Wrightsborough in honor of the governor. Hardworking and frugal—settler traits most admired by Wright—the Quakers were politically conservative and tended toward positive relations with the Native Americans. On the eve of the Revolution, their population topped six hundred, and they had amassed some thirty thousand acres in the region.[49] William Bartram described the region as a plain with forests, swamps, and savannas with a rich and deep soil.[50]

The second group to take advantage of the 1766 legislation moved into an area along the Ogeechee River just to the southwest of Augusta. Wright decided to call the settlement Queensborough, and it came to be known as the "Irish Settlement."[51] These Scotch-Irish dwellers had been overburdened by taxes in Ireland and sought a new life in Georgia. By 1774 their numbers exceeded nine hundred. Unlike the pacific Quakers of Wrightsborough, the Queensborough settlers were consistently at odds with the Creeks. Indian trader George Galphin predicted that their behavior would be the cause of the next frontier conflagration.[52] He was right.

### "They Are Nicknamed Crackers"

All in all, Wright's attempts to attract settlers were successful, though it's impossible to ascertain how many people would have found their way to the region regardless of government enticements. Georgia's population had increased steadily and significantly during Wright's tenure. By 1770 he reported a population of eleven thousand whites, with roughly one-third capable of militia service. That number jumped to eighteen thousand within a few years (along with fifteen thousand Blacks). By 1776 Georgia's population totaled nearly fifty thousand, including the enslaved and free Blacks. Historian Kenneth Coleman has suggested that approximately half of the white population were English, a third were Scotch-Irish, and the remaining sixth were German. Additionally, he calculated about one hundred Jews in Savannah.[53] Unfortunately for those settlers, the king repealed the law offering incentives to settlers, which Wright believed "would have been attended with very salutary consequences." Believing the legislation to be in accord with similar laws in other colonies, Wright pleaded for an explanation so that he could better guide the legislature in the future.[54] As it was, his plan to fortify the frontier and minimize the impact of the backcountry Crackers failed to realize its full potential. The somewhat modest augmentation of the white population in this region would lead to increased points of contact and friction.[55] Captain Gavin Cochrane, who commanded Fort Augusta, vividly described these Crackers in a letter to the Board of Trade:

> The practice of horse stealing is very common [in Augusta], which is very scandalous, owing to a lawless set of rascals who often come here. They are nicknamed Crackers and bring their peltry to sell.... [They] are too apt to occasion discontent amongst the Indians by grossly imposing on them.... [They get their name] from being boasters ... [and] often change their places of abode ... [and] get merchants by degrees to trust them with more and more goods to trade with the Indians and at first make returns till they have established some credit, then leave those that trusted them in the lurch.... [Worse yet, they] delight in cruelty.[56]

George Washington would have agreed with Cochrane's commentary, referring to Crackers as "a parcel of Barbarian's."[57] Historian Delma Presley has described these Georgia Crackers as "an unbeloved invader. He was an outsider, a herdsman, a squatter, a hunter, and an Indian fighter." These lower-class inhabitants were a "restless, land-hungry, and hardy folk" who "generally reflected some of the strengths and weaknesses" of Scots Lowlanders.[58] Historian Edward Cashin accurately observed that if "given the choice between Indians and Crackers, Wright and other royal officials seemed to prefer the Indians."[59] Wright, in fact, claimed this group of "lawless white people" to be "as bad if not worse than the Indians."[60] General Gage insisted to

Lieutenant Colonel Lewis Fuser that "we must always expect quarrels between the Indians and the back inhabitants and in general we shall find the latter at fault."[61]

Wright later admitted that perhaps the Native Americans could do what he could not: restrain the frontiersmen. He believed that Indian attacks on the backcountry inhabitants were not especially worrisome because perhaps they could "keep a sett of people within bounds whom no law can restrain."[62] One Georgian described "these crackers [as] very troublesome . . . driving off gangs of horses and cattel to Virginia and committing other enormities," including causing disturbances with the Native Americans.[63] Understanding this viewpoint requires little imagination. On 29 August 1767 East Florida governor James Grant informed Gage that some backcountry inhabitants had burned an Indian village of fifteen families as satisfaction for livestock theft, though an unconvinced Grant suggested that "it is likely that the horses were carried off by some of their brother crackers."[64] Gage notified Shelburne that "a banditti hovering about the frontier" had burned the Creek village of Oconee in the center of the province and added that Governor Wright was very apprehensive that "this rash step in the people might produce very bad consequences."[65] Wright was by nature the very picture of caution and prudence, and he always ruminated carefully before determining a course of action. In fact, rather than recognizing that either the imperial policy of placing whites on the Native border or his own granting of lands forty miles beyond the border might be the cause of this friction, Wright blamed these problems on "a set of almost lawless white people who are a sort of borderers and often as bad if not worse than the Indians."[66] Superintendent Stuart predicted that such a close boundary "will expose us to perpetual broils. The inhabitants of those countries . . . and the Indians live in perpetual jealousy and dread of each other, so their rooted hatred for each other is reciprocal."[67] Worse yet, especially for the Creeks, General Gage rejected their request for reparations for their losses, stating: "It is highly unreasonable that the Crown should be put to an expense for the unruly proceedings of every lawless banditti upon the frontiers."[68] This statement suggests that the government had come to expect a general disorder on the edges of civilization, which underscored the rationale behind the proclamation line. Ultimately, Wright assuaged the Creeks by supplying them with a keg of rum per burned dwelling.[69]

A Creek elder named White Lieutenant told James Seagrove, Indian agent, that the Okfuskees had a "friendly disposition towards our brothers and friends the white people of Georgia" but that they were endlessly

flummoxed by the contradictory messages from colonial officials and traders. Creek leader Emistisiguo was also confused, writing to Wright: "When
there was but one path it was peaceable but not so now, for there are too
many paths, and that these things and the confusion in the trade have been
the cause and foundation of all the evils, and which cannot be removed if
the trade is carried on as it has been of late." The Natives typically blamed
the traders, especially because they falsely claimed to speak for the government.[70] Wright agreed.

In theory, Gage's decision not to compensate the Indians may have
seemed wise. But as was often the case, British policies were woefully short-
sighted. Decisions such as these, Wright cannily understood, "have been extremely mistaken, and [the Board of Trade] will probably be convinced of it
when it is too late."[71] But Gage patronized Wright: "I wish the policy lately
adopted for North America had been more agreeable to your own sentiments . . . tho I am confident of your endeavours as well as of your abilities to
keep every thing quiet in your own province, and to manage the Indian trade
to the best advantage."[72] Whether Gage was confident of Wright's abilities
or hopeful is hard to know, but Wright's task was made all the more difficult
by the steady flow of immigrants.

Many of these "banditti" flooded into the Georgia backcountry from Virginia and the Carolinas, but the Indians often simply referred to them as
"Virginia people," and they loathed them for constantly stirring up a great
deal of trouble in the backcountry.[73] Creek leader Captain Alleck lamented
that "before these Virginia men came to settle in the back country the white
men and red men lived like brothers . . . but these Virginians are very bad
people, they pay no regard to your laws."[74] Although Captain Alleck was being hyperbolic or selective in his memory, his real point was the destructive
consequences of these new settlers.

Tallachea of Ocmulgee agreed. When the Creeks threatened to burn
settlers' homes for encroaching on Creek lands, those rowdy frontiersmen
vowed they would retaliate by burning Governor Wright's home "over his
head."Tallachea smartly wondered: "If the governor cannot keep these Virginia people under how can we keep our people under?"[75] Consequently, as
historian Patrick Griffin incompletely opined, "colonial authorities stood by
as the West descended into violence."[76] Perhaps he should have stated that
the Board of Trade "stood by," even though that is not altogether as accurate, as the board had no solutions and left colonial authorities to their own
devices. Although the backcountry devolved into the situation described by
Griffin, colonial officials such as Wright, Stuart, and Habersham did not

stand idly by, allowing frontiersmen to settle on Indian lands. They each expended great energy in trying to prevent what may have been unavoidable.
Gage perfectly encapsulated the problem in a prophetic missive to Stuart:
"The frontier people of most of our provinces are not to be limited by any
bounds."[77] Gage would submit similar missives in the coming years. They,
too, would fall on deaf ears.

This tension, however, was not solely a matter of interracial conflict between the colonists and the Indians. The Indians themselves were incessantly in conflict with one another. It was just such tensions in 1766 and 1767
that likely distracted the Creeks from expressing their dissatisfaction with
the colonists more forcefully. "Our Indian affairs my Lords continue quiet
& easy," Wright informed the board in February 1767, "but this I attribute
to a kind of war, that has for some time subsisted between the Creeks &
Chactaws. . . . And in my opinion it is this favourable & lucky circumstance
alone that has saved us from being embroiled with them."[78] Lucky or not,
the comparative frontier harmony served Georgia well, as Governor Wright
reported to the board at the end of 1768: "The province is in a very flourishing state, & that we are making rapid progress towards becoming opulent
and considerable."[79]

In the spring of 1769 Wright's sixth child, Alexander, married the wealthy
heiress Elizabeth "Betsy" Izard.[80] Just three months later, with provincial affairs "quite tranquil," Governor Wright sought permission to return to London to see his eldest son, James Jr. The younger James had been in London
since the fall of 1760 obtaining "a regular education at Eton and Cambridge,
and is now preparing himself for Westminster Hall." The father ardently desired to "assist him in entering upon the great scene of action and setting out
properly in life, [which] is a duty . . . to him as well as for my own satisfaction." Governor Wright requested a twelve-month leave to begin no sooner
than June 1770, provided the situation in Georgia then permitted his absence. If the board granted his request, Wright suggested James Habersham
as the interim governor. Habersham was not only Wright's closest friend but
also "a firm friend to government, and a very worthy honest man . . . [whose]
abilities [are] sufficient to fill up a short vacancy or absence."[81] What Wright
did not state at the time, at least to Hillsborough, was that he did not intend
to return to Georgia.

In his lengthy Loyalist claim following the American Revolution, Wright
admitted that he did "not mean to go out again" to Georgia following this
leave of absence, but because of the "desire of ministry he went out a second
time."[82] Moreover, he placed Habersham in charge of selling his property.

At one point during his absence, his friend informed him that it would not be possible to sell his "Coach and Charriot" because they "wou'd be treated as a burlesque" in a public sale.[83] Wright likely sought a government position in London or a more lucrative gubernatorial appointment in the West Indies or New York.

Shortly after word of the so-called Boston Massacre reached Savannah and as Governor Wright prepared to return to London, the ongoing dispute between the Creeks and Choctaws finally started to abate, which may or may not have been good news for Georgians. Gage informed the Board of Trade that Stuart was actively involved in the negotiations but had been hampered by the Crackers, "who have endangered the publick tranquility lately, by a very unwarrantable and licentious conduct towards the Creeks." Additionally, his dialogue was hindered by the lack of bureaucratic institutions with which to engage, because Native tribes were nominally led by populist leaders. Stuart added that, as usual, Governor Wright was taking appropriate "steps to punish some of the ringleaders."[84] For his part, Wright stated with incredible overconfidence on 20 July 1770 that he had "put an end to all disputes between Indians and back-settlers." But with a sense of foreboding, he acknowledged the receipt of "intelligence that Creek chiefs have gone to Mobile to ratify peace with the Choctaws, which makes it probable they will pick a quarrel with us." He added that "making peace between Creeks and Choctaws is making war between Indians and us."[85] Consequently, he decided to delay his return to England until the following spring. Wright always put his country's needs before his own, and he viewed Georgia's best interests to be in England's best interests.

In the meantime, he implored the Assembly again to pass legislation to better regulate Indian affairs by "restraining our back settlers."[86] The Assembly responded that while they were in perfect accord with the governor's sentiments, they feared that such a measure would be of limited value if Georgia's neighboring provinces did not also pass such a bill. In any event, the representatives expressed their deep gratitude for Wright's "unwearied endeavours in promoting the welfare of this very thriving province."[87] Platitudes aside, they still refused to pass the needed legislation.

The dearth of provincial leadership in such matters, coupled with the home government's frugality and lack of interest, proved remarkably frustrating for Wright as he tried to maintain frontier peace, which must have seemed a fool's errand, given these constraints. Most infuriating, though, was the legislature's "continue[d] disregard [for] the King's recommendation to enact laws for preventing any improper intercourse between the inhabitants . . . and the neighbouring savages." He added, "I shall always lament their being attended with fatal accidents, but the blame must fall upon those who neglect to apply the remedy."[88] However, he was again forced into just such a fool's errand following the murder of two white settlers in August. According to Wright, the Creeks "in cool blood, and without any cause or reason whatever, barbarously murdered" these men near Wrightsborough.[89] Even though he must have known that the Creeks' actions had not been without provocation, he tinged much of his official correspondence with such accusations in the hopes that he could compel the board to provide relief. In the meantime, however, Governor Wright demanded satisfaction from the Cowetas and any other Creek groups that may have been involved. Samuel Thomas, Superintendent Stuart's Creek interpreter, stated that several Indian dwellings had been burned, but it was unclear which begat which.[90]

In December an angry Wright expressed doubt that the Creeks would give satisfaction for these murders and noted that his patience was wearing thin: "It is high time those wretches should know that they shall not be suffered to murder His Majesty's subjects." However, as both the governor and even the Indians knew, without support from the board, Wright possessed no coercive power.[91] Provincial law also provided Wright with an additional obstacle. "It is one part of our law that no man can be punished," Wright wrote, "until he is found guilty of the crime or offence that he is accused of by a jury of 12 men," and procuring such a verdict was dubious indeed.[92] Although his friend Lord Hillsborough was sympathetic to Wright's predicament, he only offered general advice.[93] In early 1771 he wrote: "I think that the best security we can have on the part of the savages . . . is that of their good will and affection towards us, which ought to be cultivated."[94]

## "Greatly Distress If Not Totally Ruin That Most Flourishing Province"

In the meantime, a chain of events transpired along South Carolina's northern border that would alter Georgia forever. In October 1770 at the Lochaber (South Carolina) Congress, Indian trader and colonial official Edward Wilkinson persuaded the Cherokees in the region to cede nearly two hundred thousand acres of land in exchange for the forgiveness of a debt of £8,000. He then sought Crown approval of this private cession, by which he would either recoup his £8,000 through the proceeds from selling the land or be given free use of the land for a decade.[95]

Although Stuart blocked this scheme, other southeastern traders eagerly followed Wilkinson's lead, endeavoring to acquire Indian land under the same pretenses.[96] In Georgia, however, such private "purchases" had been outlawed.[97] Although Wright opposed a private sale, he viewed Wilkinson's scheme as a "favourable opportunity" and "a very good precedent" for obtaining a public cession for Georgia.[98] Two months later, in December, a number of Augusta merchants informed James Habersham, president of the Governor's Council, that the Cherokees "were willing to give up a body of land on Savannah River in lieu of all debts contracted by them since ... 1761."[99] But Cherokee leader Judd's Friend (Ustenaka) recalled the exchange differently. He insisted that the traders initiated the conversation.[100] Superintendent Stuart supported this version, insisting that backcountry traders and merchants had instigated the talks and were actively deceptive in their dealings with both the Indians and Wright.[101]

But the governor was so eager to strike a deal that he again presented an entirely different portrait of the frontier situation to his superiors in London. In an approximately fourteen-thousand-word memorial, including enclosures, the governor outlined his rationale for an additional Native land cession, the second such major cession of his tenure. He had convinced himself that cessions would be just the tonic to remedy the frontier's ills. For years he had complained that the Crackers stirred up trouble in the backcountry; moreover, it was their conduct and not the Indians' that had been to blame for most trouble in the region. Now, however, after years of blaming the Crackers and traders for all the backcountry ills, he went out of his way to place the responsibility for frontier disruptions squarely on the Indians' shoulders. Self-interest now replaced honest analysis, and Wright believed the best way to gain support for this cession was to maximize the threat posed by the Natives, because this would emphasize the need for a greater geographic barrier between the settlers and the various tribes.

Wright both lauded colonial "settlements" and "improvements" upon the land and impugned the Indians' poor behavior in his memorial to Hillsborough. The "lurking" Natives, he wrote, persistently "rob and plunder" and "sometimes murder" Georgians without provocation. They often acted in "cool blood," causing "His Majesty's good subjects [to] live in constant fear." Moreover, Wright wrote, "it is out of the power of the province" to compel proper behavior from the Natives because "they well know that there is not a single soldier" in Georgia, "nor has [there] been since April 1767." The Indians knew full well, Wright insisted with another hyperbolic flourish, that they "can whenever they please, greatly distress if not totally ruin that most flourishing province." It was not until deep into his memorial that Wright acknowledged the traders' culpability, and he did so while also taking a subtle swipe at the home government for what he believed to be their ill-conceived Proclamation of 1763. He wrote that the influx of traders and lack of regulations to restrain their impulses had led to "mischievous wantonness and insolence" by the Natives and "frauds and abuses" by the traders.[102]

Regardless of culpability, Wright insisted it had become "absolutely necessary that some steps be speedily taken to support His Majestys honour and authority," although doing so "by force of arms, tho probably the most honourable way . . . may be wished to avoid." His first suggestion was one that he had made many times before: limiting the number of traders. He argued that this would ensure that the "Indians are supplied with goods sparingly, or otherwise according to their conduct and behaviour . . . [because] an over supply of goods makes them wanton, insolent and ripe for every kind of mischief." But achieving this goal would be problematic at best. He again reminded the board of the ill effects of the Proclamation of 1763, because it made management of the frontier "impossible," as it was now flooded with traders who "are rather the worst sort of people, and commit every kind of fraud and abuse towards the Indians, [which] disposes them to resent it by robbing and murdering." Thus, Wright begged, the board must assert its authority and control the Indian trade once and for all. He even suggested that a monopoly be granted to one or two traders, because "it seems better that an inconvenience of that sort should be submitted to for a few years" than to simply allow frontier violence to continue unabated.[103]

Having clearly and thoroughly laid the problem before the Board of Trade, Wright now proffered his solution. The Cherokees sought to relieve their heavy debt to the merchants and traders by ceding millions of acres of land. A tremendous opportunity had presented itself, the governor wrote. A "very considerable body of land," containing some of the "richest and best quality soil and very fit" for cash crops of all varieties, could be acquired. Doing the math for the board, he supposed, at worst, that the cession would net the Crown two and a half million acres. He proposed that the land be "sold in small tracts . . . not exceeding 1,000 acres to one person or family," with an additional fifty acres for each settler, white or Black, they bring along. If sold at six pence per acre, the New Purchase, as it was called, would net £62,500 in addition to quit rents and taxes. This would more than erase the Cherokee debt, which was estimated at £45,000. Wright hoped to use the surplus to augment frontier defenses by raising a troop of Rangers and building additional forts.[104] He concluded that the ceded lands could "accommodate 10,000 families of 5 in each family," leading to a minimum of ten thousand additional militiamen, which would provide for the region "intire security against the Indians without . . . putting Great Britain to any expence." These figures seem overly optimistic, but if they were accurate, then Georgia's fortunes would take a dramatic leap forward. Failure to complete this transaction, Wright maintained, would likely lead to another "rupture with the Indians," in which case "Georgia would certainly be ruined."[105] William Legge, 2nd Earl of Dartmouth and secretary of state for the American colonies, believed Wright's plans for the settlement of these lands would prove difficult, but he was confident that, "thro' your zeal and activity, it would not fail of producing the many and great advantages which you stated."[106]

Ensuring that "no persons should have" any of these lands except those "who purchase" them would ensure that the settlers would be "something better than the common sort," Wright argued. These people would be "industrious and better disposed to protect" the land. He also insisted that "great numbers of very well disposed and industrious white people are now ready to remove" to Georgia. He then suggested that the board exempt them from quit rents for ten years and taxes for up to seven years. With the groundwork laid, Wright asked that instructions be sent to Superintendent Stuart to call for a "Congress of the Creek and Cherokee Indians at Augusta." As part of the call, Stuart should announce that those with "demands on any of the said Indians should liquidate and prove the reality of their debts" and that commissioners be appointed to "better [conduct and manage] this matter." To bolster the importance of his memorial, the governor submitted eight lengthy enclosures.[107]

The first enclosure made clear that the Cherokees had requested Wright's assistance in obtaining the cession. It also included a promise from the Cherokees either to convince the Creeks to surrender their portion of the lands in question or to provide the Crown with additional acres elsewhere. The second through fourth enclosures provided additional confirmation that "it was with the unanimous consent of [Cherokee] young men & warriors" that the lands mentioned would be ceded. In the fifth enclosure, Governor Wright assured the Cherokees that he was "very soon going to England where the great King lives [and] I will take care your case shall be properly represented." The sixth enclosure was a transcription of a lengthy talk between the Upper Creeks and Wright in which they addressed frontier disturbances. They insisted that they remained steadfast in their desire "to keep their path . . . white and clean," even though some "mad young people [remain] amongst us." Having said that, the Creeks complained to Wright—

whom they called "an old and a sensible man"—that the traders continued to violate the parameters set forth at the Augusta Congress of 1763.[108]

Wright responded to the Creeks in the seventh enclosure. He confirmed his desire to also "keep the path straight and white" but said that "in some things they were mistaken." Specifically, and he must have known this to be false, Wright stated that it was the Creeks and not the settlers who had caused the recent disturbances, and if the Creeks would simply "take care to observe the talks and treatys they may depend on being supplied with plenty of ammunition and goods." Finally, the eighth enclosure included details of a meeting of Cherokee leaders and their traders. The traders informed Wright that they believed the cession to be the only way for the Indians to extricate themselves from their extensive debt. Moreover, and maybe more to the point, the traders themselves needed this relief because the merchants had cut off their credit.[109]

The specific events leading up to Wright's memorial had begun to unfold in February 1771, when the Cherokees tried to cede to their traders a significant tract of land.[110] Superintendent Stuart informed the Cherokees that their cession was not allowed for two reasons. First, the government forbade private purchases of Native lands. Second, the Creeks claimed part of the ceded lands by right of conquest.[111] The Cherokees, however, paid no heed to Stuart's protest, maintaining their freedom to sell land to whomever they chose, especially because the British had proved themselves incapable of upholding their obligations to keep settlers off Indian lands.[112]

In early May the Cherokees assured Governor Wright that if "any part of this land should be claim'd by the Creek Indians we will use all our endeavours to get them to join with us in consenting to give up their claims." If such efforts were unsuccessful, the Cherokees promised to "make up the full quantity" of lands elsewhere. Moreover, with Wright's prompting, they officially solicited his assistance in "laying ... our desire before the Great King."[113] He responded to their request a few weeks later and pledged to personally submit their request, "as I am very soon going to England," provided they were able to convince the Creeks to also surrender their lands in question.[114] This would be no easy task, however, as leader Emistisiguo, chief of the Creek town Little Tallassies, opposed the cession of land. "It is most certain our nation is much in debt," he said, but "[we] intend to discharge [these] debts with skins & don't mean to give up [our] lands at all as the skins is the produce of the land."[115] Rarely deterred, Wright likely persuaded the Cherokees to reach out to the Creeks and offer a cancellation of their debts, too. He also attempted to improve upon Georgia's haul by extending the cession to include lands between the Oconee and Ogeechee Rivers. Although not valued by the Cherokees, these lands held great value to the Creeks, who used them for hunting.[116] With plans in hand, the governor prepared to return to Britain.

### "The Dignity of a Baronet"

With his family in tow, James Wright departed Georgia on 10 July 1771, en route to London via Charleston, with two principal aims: to see to his eldest son's affairs and to secure royal approval for a second, even larger, land cession. Georgians bid Wright farewell "with several volleys from Sir Patrick Houstoun's light infantry as well as a discharge from the cannon."[117] Wright's close friend and council president, James Habersham, who would serve as the interim governor, informed the Board of Trade that Wright had "acquitted himself with great uprightness and honor in his administration of this government, [and] I have no doubt of his receiving distinguishing marks of the Royal favour."[118] As interim governor, Habersham learned that executive leadership in colonial America was no easy position. He later told Wright that he wished he could "acquit ... [himself], in ... [his] public capacity, as honourably and uprightly" as Wright had.[119] In Charleston, Wright visited with family and friends. He also gathered various communications that needed to be delivered to both officials and private citizens in London. After about a week, South Carolinians honored Wright with "several affectionate and respectful addresses."[120]

The voyage aboard H.M.S. *Governor Wright* was smooth and lasted only five weeks. But this was Wright's first transatlantic voyage since his wife and daughters were lost at sea, and those painful memories, coupled with the inherent difficulties of oceanic travel, must have caused Wright no small amount of anxiety. One traveler described "the horrors of despair [that] prey on my mind" when preparing to recross the Atlantic.[121] The passengers disembarked at Portsmouth on 18 August, and Wright wasted no time in pursuing his official plans.[122] The journey to London took three days, and he personally met with the king and his ministers to discuss the advantages that the cession offered both Georgians and the empire.[123] In short, Wright consolidated these advantages to two: economics and defense. He argued that although Georgia was a "very flourishing province," its population remained scattered. These new lands would both augment and condense the colony's population. The enhanced population would in turn solidify Georgia's frontier defenses and strengthen the colonial and imperial economies. The lands to be ceded, he promised, would be "of the richest and best quality and very fit" for any number of cash crops.[124] The king and his ministers warmly received Wright's thoughtful and thorough petition. Additionally, many Londoners also viewed the proposed cession in a favorable light.

Shortly after arriving, the governor sat for a portrait by the renowned artist Andrea Soldi, whom Henry Clinton had sat for the previous decade. The vibrant likeness depicts a physically fit, stern, attentive, and robust man. His attire illustrates a man who adored elegant fashion and possessed the wealth to indulge that fancy. His hair is stylishly coifed. Wright also made sure to include a document from colonial Georgia in his portrait, ever connecting him to the colony with which he identified himself and his status. In November Georgia's London merchants held a "genteel entertainment" at the London Tavern in Wright's honor.[125] This positive reception from both public and private persons only furthered Wright's growing sense of confidence. One friend observed that the governor "hinted to me with a very kind smile his hopes of success."[126] Georgia's colonial agent, Benjamin Franklin, also expressed high hopes that the matter would soon "be brought to a favourable conclusion."[127] Acting Governor James Habersham hoped for both a favorable and a speedy conclusion to this business, complaining to Wright that white Georgians, numerous and eager to settle the backcountry, were losing patience with the Indians.[128]

During their two-year stay in England, Wright and his children lived in a fashionable district in northwest London. Their residence on Berners Street, near Oxford Street and Tottenham Court Road, was right in the middle of a neighborhood dominated by South Carolinian planters, such as the Laurenses, Middletons, and Izards. As was their custom, the Wright family lived in great comfort, as evidenced by the advertisement placed in preparation for the return to America, which offered "all the rich household furniture, &c. of his Excellency Sir James Wright, Bart., Governor of Georgia, at his late dwelling-house in Berners-Street, Oxford-Road, consisting of crimson Damask, Cotton, Morine [a sturdy wool or cotton fabric], and other furniture in beds and window curtains, goose-feather beds, Girandoles, carpets, &c."[129]

Writing from Westminster in December, Henry Laurens conveyed to Habersham that the governor "did me the honour to call here yesterday, and John [Laurens's son] and I are to dine with him to morrow in Berners Street. The Governor is well," he added, "and as alive as ever I saw him in his junior days. His thoughts seem to be all employed in the service of Georgia."[130] In this moment in time, these men shared dinner and conversation and no

doubt rejoiced in a decades-long friendship, which would soon be torn asun-
der by the flames of rebellion. James Habersham later told Wright that "the
people of this province are greatly obliged to you for the pain you have
taken to serve them."[131] Habersham well knew the difficulties of serving the
province. He had in fact grown tired of the work required while serving in
Wright's stead. "You seem surprized," he said to Wright, "that I should complain of being so much hurryed with business. . . . You had been practised in
the usual business . . . and every thing was plain and easy to you. It is not so
with me. . . . [C]onscious of my falling very far short of your abilities, I act,
in every step I take with doubt and fear."[132] Even worse than the workload,
Habersham now suffered from "a fresh attack of the gout in his left arm" and
often had to rely on the assistance of a son to write his correspondence.[133]

Wright officially delivered his memorial to the Board of Trade on Thurs-
day, 12 December 1771, and it was ordered to be officially "taken into consideration" the following Wednesday. He attended that session as well, and
although he answered questions relevant to Georgia, a discussion of the
proposed land cession was inexplicably "put off to another opportunity."[134]
The matter then sat quietly for several months until some notable London
merchants with Georgia connections submitted a memorial in support of
Wright's proposal at the end of March 1772.[135]

At about this time, Wright became gravely ill at his home on Berners
Street. One newspaper reported that "Governor Wright has had a severe attack lately; an inflammation upon his liver was his disease, and we were once
in great fear of a mortification. He is now, thank God, in a recovering way,
but his earnestness for the good of Georgia, will not allow him to take that
respite from business, which the state of his health requires. The first day we
thought him out of danger, he dictated a letter to Lord Hillsborough, that
there might be no delay in the determination of the Cherokee land business."[136] James Habersham also expressed concerns about Wright's "late severe illness."[137] Based on the date of Habersham's letter, Wright could have
been sick as late as early May. But by the end of June he was on the mend. "It
gives me great pleasure," Habersham soon wrote, to learn "that [you are] recovering from [your] late dangerous illness."[138] The scare perhaps prompted
Habersham to express his true feelings about the governor to James Wright
Jr. "I am extremely glad to find . . . that the Governor was perfectly recovered
from his late dangerous illness," he wrote. "My friendship for him obliges me
to wish him every degree of happiness, and to do all in my power to promote
it, . . . I most sincerely rejoice with you, that his health is reinstated."[139]

Concomitantly, London's *General Evening Post* reported news of great consequence for Georgia: "Governor Wright, of Georgia, we hear, has resigned that employment, and is to be succeeded by Governor Shirley, of the Bahamas."[140] The rumor made its way across the Atlantic. Savannah minister John Joachim Zubly even mentioned Wright's resignation in his diary and added an important tidbit: "At supper Revd [Haddon] Smith related that Govr Wright was made one of the Lords of Trade & Govr Shirley [is] to succeed him."[141] Perhaps Wright's recent illness forced a discussion of a career change, but neither the *General Evening Post* nor Smith provided further details or sources about this topic.

Finally in November, nearly one year after Wright formally presented his proposal, the Board of Trade officially considered Wright's memorial. Whereas Hillsborough had thus far ignored Wright's proposal, his replacement, William Legge, 2nd Earl of Dartmouth, drafted a formal representation to the king endorsing the plan to purchase land from the Cherokees and the Creeks, sell it to the settlers, and then use the proceeds to pay the Indians' debts to the white traders.[142] Governor Wright's detailed and cogent analysis of Georgia's needs and utility to the empire, along with his tireless efforts while in London, made a deep impression upon the king and his ministry. On 5 December 1772 the king entertained Wright at St. James's Palace, where he "has been pleased to grant the dignity of a Baronet of Great Britain unto James Wright, Esq., Governor of His Majesty's province of Georgia, in America."[143] Was this honor bestowed as an inducement to get Wright to return to Georgia? Perhaps. In any event, it was quite the honor, and it seemed that James Wright had finally redeemed his family's name following his grandfather's imprisonment and death at Newgate Prison at the conclusion of the seventeenth century.[144]

Wright's labors in both Savannah and London earned him the plaudits of both provincial and imperial leaders. The Assembly praised his efforts regarding the cession, which was "of the utmost importance to us [and] we are indebted to you."[145] Although Wright's home in Savannah had fallen into disrepair during his absence, the Assembly voted to inspect and make all necessary repairs as a symbol of gratitude for his efforts. The legislature also debated whether to greet Wright upon "his arrival at the landing place, to congratulate him on his safe return." The divided Assembly voted in the affirmative by a margin of seventeen to eight.[146] With or without the Assembly's unanimous consent, the town discharged the guns to "congratulate [Wright] on his safe arrival [with] the whole town . . . full of festivity."[147]

The legislature also issued a resolve thanking Wright for his "great zeal for the interest and welfare of this province."[148]

Naturalist William Bartram was on hand as the Indian tribes began making their way into Augusta to finalize the deal in May 1773. In return for the discharge of their debts, Bartram noted, Georgia's merchants demanded "at least two millions of acres of land from the Indians." But among the Creeks, "being a powerful and proud spirited people, their young warriors were unwilling to submit to so large a demand, and their conduct evidently betrayed a disposition to dispute . . . and they could not be brought to listen to reason and amicable terms." It was only through the "cool and deliberate counsels of the antient venerable chiefs," coupled with plentiful gifts and rum, that their resistance began to crumble.[149] Although the Creeks begrudgingly acquiesced, they refused to surrender a single acre beyond the Ogeechee River, as Wright had sought. Even this proved too much for some of the young Creeks, who murdered the first family to move into those lands in the winter of 1773–74.[150]

Even though Wright had been applauded on both sides of the Atlantic for his efforts to expand Georgia's geography, economy, and imperial importance, a rather direct line can be traced from this achievement to the backcountry's participation in the upcoming revolution. There are two connecting dots on this line—two groups that were thoroughly dissatisfied with the cession and refused to quietly assent to its parameters. The Upper Creeks resented the Cherokees for surrendering land claimed by both nations, and many Crackers were livid that the government had priced the new lands beyond their reach. In fact, the opening act of this chain of events that led to frontier rebellion in 1775 and beyond was not 1773 but instead 1763, following the first great land cession at Augusta.[151] One cannot look at the cessions in isolation; they should instead be viewed as one large event with two parts. Moreover, they need to be viewed in conjunction with the nascent revolutionary movement unfolding across colonial America. The land cessions only provided short-term relief for the problems cited in Wright's memorial, in part because contradictory goals from the various participants—Wright, the merchants, the traders, and the Natives—and unrealistic expectations ensured future discord. Of course, these issues only came into focus after the event. In the moment, Wright displayed the acquired skills of a diplomat and imperial official in securing these significant cessions, much to the satisfaction of the home government, Georgians, and the Cherokees. As events would show, however, the seeds of discord were planted largely by Wright's own twin policies of seeking to protect the valuable Indian trade while also promoting the rapid settlement of the region by people vehemently opposed to both the Indians and their trade.[152] Additionally, the more his prominence and power had grown, the more vulnerable he became, because many Georgians began to view him with suspicion.

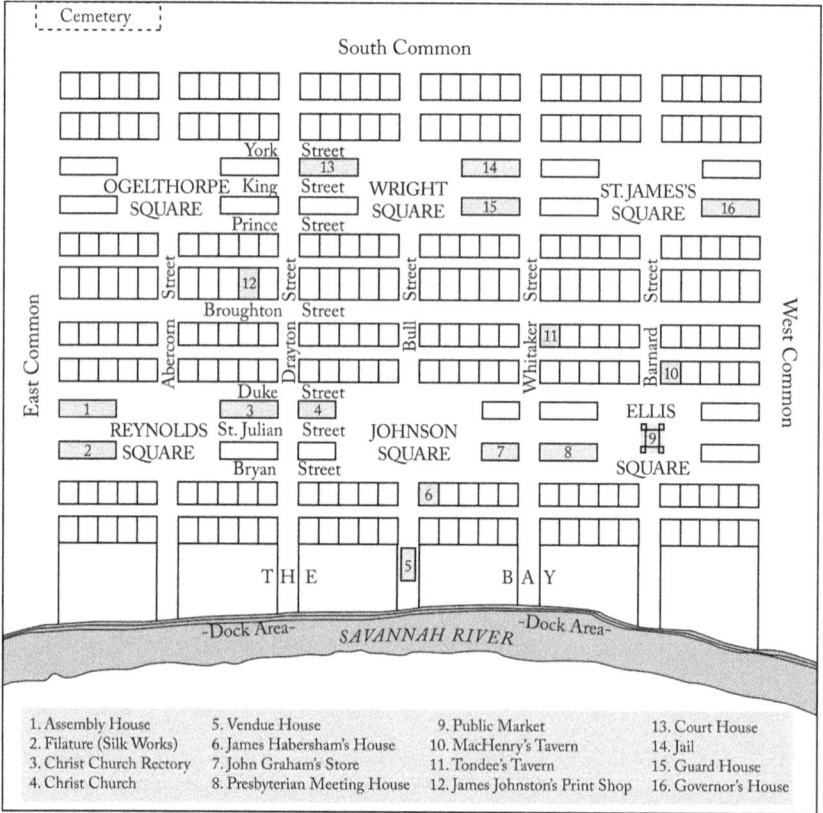

Cemetery

South Common

York Street
13 14
OGELTHORPE King Street WRIGHT ST. JAMES'S
SQUARE Prince Street 15 SQUARE 16
SQUARE

12
Broughton Street

11
10

Duke Street
1 3 4 ELLIS
REYNOLDS St. Julian Street JOHNSON
2 SQUARE SQUARE 7 8 9
Bryan Street SQUARE

6

THE 5 BAY

-Dock Area- SAVANNAH RIVER -Dock Area-

| 1. Assembly House | 5. Vendue House | 9. Public Market | 13. Court House |
| 2. Filature (Silk Works) | 6. James Habersham's House | 10. MacHenry's Tavern | 14. Jail |
| 3. Christ Church Rectory | 7. John Graham's Store | 11. Tondee's Tavern | 15. Guard House |
| 4. Christ Church | 8. Presbyterian Meeting House | 12. James Johnston's Print Shop | 16. Governor's House |

Savannah, 1770. Based on a plan by Thomas Shruder, deputy surveyor general, submitted 5 February 1770. Reprinted with permission from Paul Pressly.

CHAPTER 5

# A Governor's Authority
# Questioned

A true eighteenth-century conservative, Governor Wright believed government to be the purview of the independently wealthy and virtuous citizen.[1] Moreover, he consistently sought to align himself with the burgeoning
planter class in Georgia.[2] With his substantial salary, he bought, improved,
and cultivated immense tracts of land, becoming one of the largest slaveholders in Britain's North American colonies, owning a dozen plantations
and enslaving 526 humans.[3] His obituary portrayed him as a faithful and
obedient "servant of the king," a mostly accurate description that has been
adopted ever since by historians.[4] This claim, however, is only partially correct, for he devoted himself to serving the needs not only of his country but
also of his colony. When he ultimately sided with the Crown in its attempt
to quell an internal insurrection, he firmly believed that doing so was in the
best interest of Georgians.

By the mid-1770s James Wright possessed both a thorough familiarity
with the southern colonies and a keen understanding of the British imperial
system. Colonial Georgia experienced its greatest era of economic and territorial expansion during Wright's lengthy tenure, and he exemplified royal
government at its most effective in no small part because of his desire to
serve both the king and Georgians (see figure 5.1).[5] At the end of the 1760s,
Governor Wright saved Georgia from a backcountry movement similar to
the one in North Carolina.[6] To better regulate and maintain peace and order on the frontier, he advocated for the establishment of courts in Augusta
and hoped that expansion of the coastal areas would begin to fill the empty

FIGURE 5.1. Georgia's economic expansion, 1750–1780

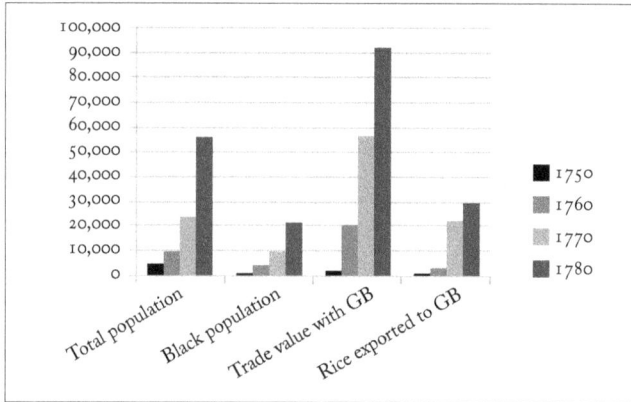

Data extracted from John McCusker, ed., "Colonial Statistics," in *Historical Statistics of the United States: Earliest Times to the Present*, ed. Susan B. Carter et al. (Cambridge, 2006), 5:627–772. The "trade value" is the value in pounds of both imports and exports with Great Britain. There are no data for 1760, so the value listed is a rough estimate utilizing the data from 1759 and 1761. Georgia's export value peaked in 1775 at £113,777. There are no data for the years 1776–1779. Rice exports are classified by number of barrels. There are no data for the years 1774–1780, so the value listed is for 1773.

space between that village and Savannah. To achieve these aims, he sought to augment Georgia's territory and fill it with the "better sort."[7] By the end of the decade, Wright had helped mold Georgia into something of an imperial jewel, at least economically. From the ministerial vantage point, Georgia remained true and loyal to the British Atlantic and Britain's mercantilist principles, and the executive and legislative branches worked in relative unity.[8]

## "Faithful Servant of the Crown"

Utterly pragmatic, James Wright understood the eighteenth-century world in which he lived and focused his boundless energies on making the most of the opportunities presented to him. In many ways his worldview resembled that of the realistic Massachusetts governor Thomas Hutchinson, who, according to historian Bernard Bailyn, "felt no elemental discontent, no romantic aspirations." Wright spent a lifetime relentlessly yet patiently accumulating land, wealth, and power, but, like Hutchinson, he "was never crudely avaricious . . . ruthless . . . [or] flamboyant." His lifelong quest for familial redemption, private wealth, and, perhaps most importantly, personal respect was grounded in a deep conservatism that required, according to

Bailyn, "a stable world within which to work, a hierarchy to ascend, and a formal, external calibration by which to measure where he was." Consequently, Wright's Weltanschauung left him ill-equipped to understand the moral passions driving the burgeoning rebellion, and his rigid, distant, and aloof personality handicapped his ability to navigate the crisis and chaos that soon enveloped and ultimately destroyed him. In these and later moments, Wright needed the same thing as many provincial officials, including Thomas Hutchinson. According to Bailyn, Hutchinson needed "an increasing sensitivity to the deepening difficulties of his position and a broadening responsiveness to the inner meanings of the opposition voices."[9] Yet he and Wright became more rigid and less imaginative. In the end, neither could fathom the rebels' state of mind and the fact that, even at his most persuasive, he could not effectively communicate with them.

Although Wright empathized with colonists who had become angry about parliamentary encroachments, he thoroughly believed in the British system of governance and insisted that the system could only be challenged through proper legal channels, not mob action. The very notion of aggressively defying British law was inconceivable to him, and such acts threatened to overturn the entire social, economic, and political foundation on which his world was based. Thus, when Wright would later write that the "powers of government are wrested out of my hands," his personal agony extended well beyond the political arena, for he fully comprehended that the rebels were, in the words of historian Gordon Wood, "indeed trying to destroy the ligaments of the older society and to reknit people together in new ways."[10] Amid the clamorous Tea Party days of 1773, Wright addressed the Georgia Assembly to explain the inherent contradiction of his position as both a royal official and a citizen of Georgia. "I ever [always] meant to discharge my duty as a Faithful Servant of the Crown," he insisted, "and can with the greatest truth declare I also meant at the same time to promote to the utmost of my power and abilities the true interest of the people."[11] The Assembly thanked Wright for his "affectionate speech" and extended their "greatest pleasure" at his success while in London.[12]

Two years later, as the imperial crisis reached a boiling point, the governor delivered an impassioned speech in which he reminisced about his nearly fifteen years in the colony and expressed his affection for the people of Georgia. "Believe me," he wrote, "I am at this time actuated by further motives than a show only of discharging my duty as the King's governor. I have lived amongst and presided over you upwards of fourteen years, and have other feelings. I have a real and affectionate regard for the people," he exclaimed, "and it grieves me that a province that I have been so long in . . . should, by imprudence and rashness of some inconsiderate people, be plunged into a state of distress and ruin."[13] These feelings and Wright's conflicted notions of duty were on full display as the imperial crisis unfolded. Until the end of his life in 1785, he steadfastly maintained his allegiance to king, country, and colony, persisting in his belief that many of the colonists, *his people*, had been led astray by a fractious minority. And here was the crux for a man like Wright. How does one serve two separate entities with occasionally divergent goals, wants, and needs? "No one can simultaneously serve two masters," Pennsylvania minister Henry Melchior Muhlenberg wrote in 1777, "who are opposed to each other. Anyone who adheres to one party will be hated and persecuted by the other."[14] Wright would learn this lesson all too well.

### "An Opulent and Considerable Province"

Although the struggle for hegemony occupied much of Wright's time throughout the next decade, Georgia's economy continued to boom.[15] The population—both European and African—continued to grow rapidly, and the enslaved planted and harvested more export crops than ever before. Governor Wright bragged that Georgia was "making a very rapid progress towards being an opulent and considerable province," if not the "most flourishing colony on the continent."[16] Even if we tone down Wright's hyperbole, Georgia was on the move. Future signer of the Declaration of Independence George Walton agreed, believing Georgia's recent rise was unparalleled anywhere on Earth.[17] Chief Justice Anthony Stokes remarked that "Georgia made but little progress in population and agriculture during the government of Mr. Reynolds, and his immediate successor Mr. Ellis; but under the long administration of Sir James Wright, the last governor, it made such a rapid progress in population, agriculture, and commerce, as no other country ever equalled in so short a time."[18] Even King George III "observe[d] with satisfaction [Wright's] unwearied endeavours to bring the negotiation with the Creek Indians to a happy issue."[19] Stokes, who was a friend of Wright, provided an admittedly favorable view that short-changed Governor Ellis. It was Ellis, after all, who had initiated Georgia's economic transformation, which Wright so capably built upon.[20]

Still, the growth under Wright was great. In 1761, Wright's first year in the colony, Georgia exported goods valued at £15,870. A dozen years later, it exported commodities valued at £121,677.[21] Its population exploded from two thousand in 1750 to more than forty thousand at the time of the revolution; rice exports increased from a few hundred barrels to twenty-three thousand; and only several dozen vessels sailed in and out of its ports in 1750, whereas over two hundred vessels docked in Savannah alone in 1775. By the 1770s, historian Paul Pressly observed, "Londoners had good reasons for confidence in the explosive growth" occurring in Georgia, and the financiers in Nicholas Lane and Lombard Street "saw Georgia as the next South Carolina and were willing to make the necessary investments" in the colony.[22] In examining this ascent, historian Jack Greene connected the colony's progress directly to Governor Wright. "The new hero of Georgia, its founding father," Greene noted, "became not Oglethorpe but James Wright." He had been instrumental, Greene argued, in making the province "a place of which inhabitants could be proud . . . [a place] with great opportunity" for small and large landowners alike.[23] It was during the latter part of the 1760s that Georgia became a bona fide slave society. Of course, this growth can almost wholly be attributed to the rise of the Caribbean slave plantation complex, with its hypercompetitive and "exploitative ethos" and in which Wright played such a pivotal role. Indeed, by the onset of the revolution, Georgia had become the second largest slave market in North America.[24] Governor Wright, in fact, invested in a slaving vessel, the *Governor Wright*, a 140-ton ship built in Bristol in 1768 and based in Charleston. Additionally, Wright worked with a Jamaican merchant to import slaves into Georgia.[25] In 1775 he contracted with Lachlan McGillivray and Joseph Clay, among others, to import about two hundred Gambian slaves, but the endeavor was disrupted by the onset of the revolution.[26]

In the early 1770s five of Wright's enslaved people fled for freedom, making their way to a "small paddling boat . . . to look for their own country." Their fate is unknown, as was that of four others who had escaped his Ogeechee plantation a few years prior. Wright believed that the Creeks, among other tribes, harbored runaways and even feared that they might arm them against the colonists.[27] Between 1763 and 1775, 13 percent of men and 18 percent of women who were enslaved "Georgians" who escaped did so with an intent to escape by sea. Another 25 percent of men and 22 percent of women headed for Savannah with the hopes of becoming anonymous in that town's larger population, which included free Blacks. It also seems logical that many of those headed for Savannah were likely heading to the sea as well. The timing of the recent escapes of Wright's enslaved may indicate that they had been motivated by the language of liberty then permeating the Lowcountry.[28] As the revolution began, the rebel government reported that many enslaved had flocked to the British.[29]

After being guided up the Savannah River to the city, a visitor to Savannah in the 1770s would likely have been shocked to see the number of ships and warehouses, most of which had been constructed with stone cellars. They sat atop a sandy bluff so high, one visitor noted, as to "put a man out of breath before he can reach the top."[30] Below the bluff, the Savannah River wound its way, snakelike, into the Atlantic Ocean eighteen miles to the southeast. Its harbor was often filled with ships. But the town of roughly four hundred houses symmetrically arranged along intersecting streets and around squares was still something of a frontier locale sitting in a smallish clearing amid a swath of pine forest. Savannah, according to historian Paul Pressly, "represented the classical ideals of proportion, harmony, and balance ... that probably had [their] derivation in the evolving pattern of London's West End."[31] One visitor described the houses of Savannah as being of such poor quality that Savannah "has a most wretched miserable appearance."[32] The buildings were so nondescript, soldier Peter Colomb recalled at the time, that "not one building can [he] describe."[33] In 1765, however, Lord Adam Gordon noted that the town was "extremely well laid out, and the buildings are increasing in number and size."[34] The wide streets consisted of "white sand so deep [that] it is just like walking through fresh fallen snow a foot deep."[35] The town was connected to the country by three roads. The Augusta or Ebenezer Road ambled westward through the pine barrens and across the vast piedmont. The Ogeechee Road made its way southward along a Native American trail past Midway and Darien. Lastly, the Sea Island Road crossed the swamps southeast of the town and meandered through the inland water settlements, such as Thunderbolt and Beaulieu.[36] In 1772 and 1773 customs officials cleared well over two hundred ships in Savannah compared to just a few dozen a decade earlier. The town proper was home to about thirty-five hundred people, about one-third that of Charleston but three times its own population in 1760. Those people now lived in over six hundred homes, including the three suburbs of Ewensburgh, Yamacraw, and Trustees' Garden. The city's merchants hawked everything from Jamaican rum to the finest cloth and manufactures from Britain, even if the variety failed to match that of Charleston. A visitor would have encountered many fine two-story homes with piazzas and fully staffed with servants and the enslaved. These six-to-ten-room homes were often painted and filled with mahogany, walnut, and cedar furniture. Whether thirsty, hungry, or eager for news of the day, a visitor had many taverns from which to choose, including Peter Tondee's, which was near the fresh market in Ellis Square.

Additionally, there were three libraries, three churches, a post office, and a theater.[37]

Wright's dual loyalty to Crown and colony had played a key role in the province's ascent during the previous two decades. The colony had grown by leaps and bounds between 1760 and 1774. Its boundaries had been significantly augmented by two land cessions, and its economy had become fully integrated into Britain's mercantilist system. Much of this progress can be attributed to Wright's steady political and aggressive economic leadership, which had nurtured the colony from infancy to maturity. But these were contingent times, and he had become quite worried.[38]

## "The Great Lenity and Generosity of the Crown and Parliament"

Georgia was at this time experiencing some of the growing pains colonies such as South Carolina had already experienced. These aches appeared simultaneously with the nascent revolutionary movement. For example, the Goose Creek Men of South Carolina had exerted a great deal of influence and run into opposition with provincial authorities earlier in the century.[39] In Georgia the Liberty Boys (a.k.a. the Liberty Party or the Sons of Liberty) appeared on the scene as the Stamp Act resistance emerged, just as the colony began to perceive itself as economically viable. As resistance to parliamentary legislation grew in subsequent years, the Liberty Party strengthened its grip on the Georgia House of Assembly. Their primary goal was to shift the balance of power from Wright to themselves. The battle over the Quartering Act (1764) was an early salvo. Led by Noble Wimberly Jones, a native Briton but a resident of Savannah since 1733, these early Liberty Boys initially failed to negate Wright's authority, largely because the Assembly was wary of offending the king or Parliament, who heavily subsidized the costs of colonial governance. This was a period of ever-shifting and tenuous alliances—one might be a Liberty Boy one week and loyal to the government the next. These issues, combined with Wright's executive abilities, best explain his success in stemming the revolutionary tide for so long.[40]

Parliament's repeal of the Stamp Act back in 1766 and its acquiescence in the face of mob violence endlessly frustrated Wright. He feared the consequences of that decision as the Assembly gathered for their first postrepeal session in November 1766 and was exasperated by what he perceived to be the Board of Trade's dismissive attitude about his objections.[41] Georgia's founder, James Oglethorpe, also expressed dissatisfaction with Parliament's dismission of colonial complaints.[42] Governor Wright's fears were temporarily allayed, however, as the House settled into their normal routines until Christmas, at which time they took their customary break.

But the tenor of the proceedings changed after the holiday recess, when Wright cautiously submitted Captain Ralph Phillips's request for provisions for the king's troops then stationed in Georgia. Although the Governor's Council responded positively, the Assembly submitted the matter to a subcommittee. Wright believed this to be a delaying tactic so the Assembly could consult with the radicals in South Carolina. Wright privately reached out to a few House members during the impasse, urging them to comply with the request. Failure to do so, he warned, might prompt a message from the governor that "would not be pleasing." But Wright now understood that "a very improper spirit was rising" in the Assembly, gaining more traction following the repeal of the Stamp Act.[43] Its members officially declined the request for provisions on 18 February 1767, stating that complying with such a request would be a betrayal of their constituents' trust and would set a dangerous precedent.

Carefully considering the situation unfolding before him, Wright decided not to "enter into an altercation" with the House. He knew that such a confrontation would require him to dissolve the Assembly with the hope that the colony would elect more amenable representatives. He had been told, however, that a subsequent election would be filled with "none but what they call Sons of Liberty," or those whom Wright still derided as "Sons of Licentiousness."[44] It was not uncommon in the eighteenth century for royal governors to dissolve the colonial assembly when its members acted in ways the governor believed to be inimical to the proper governance of the king's province. Colonial legislatures had never truly objected to this gubernatorial power prior to the Stamp Act, but it became an additional source of consternation afterward.[45]

During the next decade and more, the Liberty Boys symbolized for Wright a threat to the rule of law and to his position as royal governor.[46] The Assembly's response here seemed to indicate to Wright that the Stamp Act troubles were just an opening salvo, especially considering the nature of his prior positive interactions with the Assembly. Wright's keen insight here placed him outside of the traditional point of view emanating from London, where most believed the colonists had no real ability to "make effectual resistance."[47] By 1767 and likely responding to Wright's successful handling of the crisis the year before, a faction emerged within the House that seemed determined to challenge Wright's authority.[48] "The Assembly," he wrote to Lord Shelburne, "are now . . . follow[ing] the example and advice of some of their Republican spirited neighbours" in South Carolina. This is not to suggest that Georgia had no radical element prior to this but simply that Wright bemoaned the situation in Georgia as "rather hard and difficult," as he had barely a soldier to protect the province "against Indians, or negro insurrections, or even to be the least check on the licentiousness of the people." But, he added, "if check't at the beginning the matter will rest, and I am very hopefull everything will be set right."[49] Here Wright criticized the Board of Trade's handling of the stamp business and subtly encouraged them to respond more forcefully. "The great lenity and generosity of the Crown and Parliament," he lamented, "has only served to confirm [the Assembly] in their importance & the rectitude of their conduct on [the] occasion" of the Stamp Act. They now "cry out" about every single bit of legislation emanating from England, feeling that such behavior would result in repeal, as they believed it had in 1766.[50]

Wright believed that Parliament's repeal of the Stamp Act would have far-reaching and disastrous consequences. "The sovereignty of Great Britain in America," he wrote, "has rec[eiv]ed such a wound as I doubt it will scarce ever recover . . . [and the] acts of the British Parliament will I fear for the future, have very little weight in America," because the intention of Georgia's Liberty Boys was "to destroy or weaken the weight of the [Governor's] Council . . . [and] to assume to themselves unproper powers."[51] Wright's bluntness may have caused some officials in London to disregard his advice. This letter is remarkable for a couple of reasons. First, Wright accurately predicted the dire long-term consequences of Parliament's repeal. Second, this prediction was rooted in Wright's seemingly inherent paranoia about threats against parliamentary authority, which in turn threatened his own power. Sometimes paranoia can be perceptive prescience.

The House was astonished to learn that Wright had impugned their motives and character, especially "at a time when our conduct gave us no reason to entertain the least suspicion of our having merited" such a judgment.[52] They likely engaged the governor in a bit of self-righteous denial, as his interpretation of their motives would later prove correct. The governor responded indignantly several days later in a face-to-face confrontation with the Assembly. He unleashed a sanctimonious tirade reviewing their behavior over the past months. He complained of the lower house's refusal to comply with the Quartering Act (1764), which sanctioned the billeting and provisioning of British forces in the provinces. He also grumbled about their obstinance over the appointment of the colonial agent and their power struggle with the Council.[53] Lastly, Wright demanded the Assembly's subjugation to his and Parliament's prerogative. He had unequivocally drawn a line in the sand, as had, according to Wright, the "Pennsylvania Farmer," who possessed a "turbulent spirit."[54]

### "Enjoyment of Their Liberty & Property"

Despite the unprecedented growth of the colony, the Assembly continued to take aim at Wright's authority. They fully bypassed the Council in naming Charles Garth colonial agent to Great Britain. Garth's appointment followed the suspension of William Knox in the fall of 1765 after the latter published a pamphlet favorable to the Stamp Act. During that fall, the Council refused to assent to Knox's suspension, even though Governor Wright tacitly approved the measure. Moving forward, the House decided to avoid a disagreement with the Council altogether and joined Garth's official appointment with the 1766 tax bill, thus tying the Council's hands. The Council's primary complaint about Garth was that he was currently the colonial agent for South Carolina and could not truly represent the interests of both colonies. Council members' issue with the Assembly was that they believed they had the right to be joint participants in all provincial legislation, as well as the authority to cosupervise the distribution of all public monies and salaries. But ultimately the Council acquiesced, believing the passage of the tax bill to be of more importance than the appointment of Garth, in much the same way as Parliament viewed colonial commerce to be more important than collecting stamp duties.[55]

Two years later, as the upper and lower houses of the Assembly battled over the agent's remuneration, the Assembly wrote Governor Wright that while their "hearts overflow with gratitude and love" for the king, they expressed remorse that they could not "agree with your excellency either in the person or epithet of our agent, as we deem him the proper agent of the people."[56] Although the House installed Garth as agent, they ultimately lost their battle with the governor and Council when British officials in London ignored Garth, as Wright had encouraged them to do. The two sides eventually agreed on the appointment of Benjamin Franklin.[57]

Governor Wright emerged from this multiyear conflict with the Assembly and Liberty Boys with his power officially intact. He had, however, engendered some real animosity in certain circles. Moreover, this conflict illustrated to many Georgians their very limited political prospects within the imperial system. Historian Jack P. Greene referred to conflicts such as this one as the single most important development of the colonial era. Imperial officials, including Wright, endeavored to prevent Georgia's Assembly from following their Carolina neighbors' example. While their efforts were initially successful, the cost was high. It provoked significant animosity within the province. This power struggle festered, and neither side cared to compromise.[58]

Governor Wright called for new elections almost immediately after dissolving the Assembly in the spring of 1768. On the evening of 23 May, Georgia's Sons of Liberty met at the house of John Lyon, a local blacksmith, where they toasted the king, Whig member of Parliament Isaac Barre, and John Dickinson, the famed "Pennsylvania Farmer," and the "worthy fifteen who so nobly supported the liberties of their constituents in the late Assembly." They also expressed hope that the "ensuing Assembly correspond in sentiments with the generous fifteen of the last" and vowed to "maintain and support their rights and privileges."[59] In their pitch to the voters, the Sons, according to Wright, made a "distinction between the interest of the people & the interest of the Crown & Mother Country." Like Thomas Hutchinson in Massachusetts, Wright fretted that "this distinction, improper, ungenerous & groundless . . . had a vast effect upon the lower & more ignorant people." The Sons then created a narrative that Wright deemed baseless and false, arguing that Parliament intended to resuscitate the moribund Stamp Act, among other similarly nefarious pieces of legislation. The cure for such ominous plans, they maintained, was to elect Sons of Liberty to the Assembly, because only they could "protect & secure [the people] in the enjoyment of their liberty & property." Thus, only those who openly opposed the Stamp Act could be relied upon to support the people, while those who had aided in Wright's enforcement of the measure were enemies of the people. The *Georgia Gazette* reported that armed mobs had skulked around the polling place. Predictably, then, two-thirds of the assemblymen were reelected, and nearly three-quarters of those elected were devoted Sons of Liberty, including Noble Wimberly Jones, Archibald Bulloch, and Edward Telfair, all three of whom would become revolutionaries in the mid-1770s.[60] Henceforth, the Liberty Party controlled the House.

### "Seeds of Faction & Sedition"

The next legislative session began in November, and a hopeful Wright wrote about the existence of "the greatest harmony possible between the three branches." But things were not as sanguine or calm as he may have believed.

A former Speaker of the Assembly, Alexander Wylly, had received circular letters from both Massachusetts and Virginia concerning the Townshend Duties, and he promised that the Georgia Assembly would consider them.[61] The Townshend Acts, named after Charles Townshend, the chancellor of the exchequer, were a series of measures in 1767 and 1768 designed to better organize imperial administration and to raise revenue through taxes on commodities such as glass, paper, paint, and tea. Since Americans had exhibited such a visceral distaste for internal taxes, Townshend believed these external taxes would not likely cause a commotion, even though their proceeds would be used to pay the salaries of many provincial officials, including that of Wright.[62] He was wrong. Governor Wright, confident that the Assembly would heed his warning, immediately threatened its members with dissolution if they addressed the circular letters.[63] He, too, was wrong.

Members of the Assembly, however, had already laid the groundwork to voice their displeasure with the Townshend Duties. While they could effect little actual damage upon Wright's position, which was too deeply ingrained within the imperial system, they could lessen the prerogative of his right hand, the Governor's Council, which was, according to William W. Abbot, "the Achilles' heel of the governor [and] the mainstay of his power within the colony."[64] Inch by inch, the Assembly sought to bypass the Council on issues the Assembly deemed of real importance. Strong precedents for such behaviors had already been set in South Carolina, where the Assembly exercised great authority. Indeed, no colonial assembly had augmented its own power more than South Carolina's. A Wright family friend, Governor James Glen, once complained that "the people have got the whole administration into their hands, and the Crown is by various laws despoiled of its principal flowers and brightest jewels."[65] But Governor Wright would not idly stand by while "his" arm of the legislature was under attack. He used the full force of his authority, as well as his considerable influence, prestige, and patronage, to stunt any assault on the Council.

Assembly leaders had convinced the governor to officially sign off on bills before adjourning for the holiday break. To persuade Wright to break with the custom of waiting until after the New Year, the Speaker of the House assured him that the bills would be ready for his signature by 6:00 p.m. on Christmas Eve. But moments before Wright arrived, the Assembly drafted—and presumably sent—a properly supplicant address to the king that mimicked the Massachusetts and Virginia circular letters and sought redress from His Majesty. Their message acknowledged their proper "constitutional subordination to [Great Britain's] supreme legislature" but at the same time articulated "unexpressible concern . . . by their imposition of *internal* taxes."[66] The emphasis here is important. Americans insisted that they had no issue with external taxes because they offset the costs of transporting goods across the Atlantic. But Townshend's so-called external taxes were not intended to negate such costs, and the Assembly's actions showed their displeasure. An angry Wright decided to save what he could from the session and signed the bills. He then dissolved the Assembly. He had been duped.[67] In dissolving the Assembly, however, Wright reproached the legislators. "Be assured," he wrote, "that your true liberty, your property, and every thing that is valuable, must depend upon a free and uninterrupted course of law and government, under the protection of the mother country!" Wright earnestly believed this and wrote that no logical distinction could be made between internal and external taxes—such an argument was a "distinction without a difference." The colonists "are either bound by, and subject to, all the acts of the British Parliament . . . or are subject to none of any kind" and should be considered independent.[68]

This was the moment when the governor's relationship with the Assembly and his understanding of its worldview changed forever. He expressed his views in a letter to Lord Hillsborough that summer, promising his utmost efforts to "remove the prejudices which have been excited by the misrepresentations of the enemies to the peace and prosperity of Great Britain and her colonies . . . and to re-establish that mutual confidence and affection" that had for so long defined the relationship between the British government and the colonists. Although he believed that most Georgians remained steadfast in their loyalty to the Crown, he now feared that many had become convinced that Parliament did not represent them and thus could not tax them. Moreover, the late repeal of the Stamp Act "has so firmly fixt them in their opinion . . . that I am fully persuaded they never will be brought to change their sentiments." Seven full years before the Declaration of Independence, Governor Wright warned the Board of Trade that Americans would never accept parliamentary taxation. He then complained that Parliament's plan to also repeal many of the Townshend Duties would "not answer any effectual purpose," as it would not address the real issue: "the power or right of Parliament to tax America."[69]

Wright argued in a letter to Hillsborough that Parliament could have settled that issue had it simply remained steadfast during the Stamp Act crisis. Now, however, eight months after telling Georgians that Parliament possessed the absolute power of taxation, he suggested that nothing short of a constitutional change renouncing Parliament's right to levy internal taxes would settle the question. This was a monumental philosophical shift for a conservative like Wright and reveals his deep insight into the constitutional problem facing the Board of Trade. But the rebellious faction in America continued to grow, in no small measure because the board failed to read Wright's letter for *fifteen months*. An editor of various state papers at the British Public Records Office, W. Noel Sainsbury, left a truly remarkable note on top of this letter: "Had the British government taken Gov. Wright's advice instead of leaving it unread for fifteen months how different would have been the course of the events in America."[70] Instead, Wright was left to complain that the "Sons of Liberty . . . [may be] disposed to act improperly . . . as the Pensylvania [*sic*] Farmer . . . has most plentifully sown the seeds of faction & sedition to say no worse, & I'm sorry my Lords I have so much reason to say they are scattered in a very fertile soil, & that the well known author is adored in America."[71]

These were days of high tension, and the Assembly petitioned and remonstrated to the king, to no avail. In the fall of 1769, Councilman Jonathan Bryan presided over a public meeting in which the Governor's Council argued that Georgia had been "reduced to the greatest distress" by the Townshend Duties. The Assembly then approved eight resolutions. In these measures they promised to encourage local manufacturing and agreed to a nonimportation agreement, excepting "negro cloth" and firearms. They also agreed to import slaves only directly from Africa rather than from the West Indies.[72]

The new Assembly convened on 30 October with many new faces, including Button Gwinnett and Samuel Elbert, both of whom would become revolutionaries. The Assembly also boasted some older Liberty faction luminaries such as Noble Wimberly Jones, John Milledge, and Archibald Bulloch. Governor Wright described them as "men of turbulent spirits, great Liberty boys, and . . . men of bad hearts" who were only capable of "doing a great deal of mischief, especially amongst weak and rather ignorant people." These men, he argued, prevaricated, delayed, and obstructed the proceedings in such a way that conducting normal business became nearly impossible. Similar complaints would soon emanate from the pen of the Massachusetts governor, Thomas Hutchinson.[73] The revolutionary crisis was not merely a northern event; it stretched from Georgia to Massachusetts.

Governor Wright's struggles with the Assembly continued with increasing acrimony throughout the years. For instance, for nearly five years the colony had been working on a bill about the governance of the enslaved population that would meet with the approval of the Board of Trade. Essentially, the Assembly sought to pass the bill without the suspending clause, and the board would have none of it. All colonial legislation required a suspending clause, making the law provisional until Parliament reviewed the bill. This could be a transatlantic nightmare, because Parliament had to examine the provisions of the bill and send it back for changes. Back and forth it went, a process that often took years. This time, however, in a move designed to flex their muscles, the Assembly approved and sent the bill to the Council, but without the required suspending clause. The Council did not budge during this battle with the House, and the two sides eventually agreed that the suspending clause be added. The House, however, made it clear that their acquiescence arose "solely from the necessity of the case, and not from any conviction that such a clause ought to be inserted in any bill whatsoever." This "pernicious" suspending clause, they insisted, tended "to annihilate the rights of any Assembly."[74]

A second example of the Assembly's power struggle with Governor Wright during these years again concerned taxation without representation. Nearly five years after their Stamp Act resistance, in which they argued against just such a principle, the Assembly finally decided to care about the fact that they had been taxing four nonrepresented southern parishes. As the colony grew, it added parishes south of Savannah, but the Assembly failed to request from the Crown the right for residents of these provinces to vote and be represented in the Assembly. They now demanded elections for those parishes and would not listen to Wright's repeated assertions that he could not issue writs of election without explicit permission from London. The House held the annual tax bill hostage until elections were held in these parishes before finally relenting in March 1770.[75]

Although Wright seemed comparatively satisfied with the last legislative session, subsequent terms would be most notable for their increasing rancor. In the fall of 1770, the Assembly took umbrage with Parliament for not assenting to one component of their new election law. As usual, Wright bore the brunt of the lower house's frustration, and he dissolved the session when "some of the most violent [assemblymen] bellow'd on [about] their rights and privileges," which they believed to be equal to those of the House of Commons in London.[76] But Wright soon called for new elections, and the new House unanimously elected radical Noble Wimberly Jones as its Speaker. The governor rejected him outright, leading the House to object to Wright's "breach of the privilege of the House." He then dissolved the lower house once more. Wright wrote Hillsborough that the Assembly had become "intoxicated with ideas of their own importance and power" and that

it was past time for Parliament to remind the Assembly of its proper place-
ment within the empire, lest "they will become petty tyrants."[77] Thomas
Hutchinson echoed these exact sentiments within a month of Wright's
complaint. Mob rule, Hutchinson wrote, "has given the lower sort of people such a sense of their importance" that the rule of law would soon be useless unless firmly addressed by England.[78] Wright's friend James Habersham complained that the Assembly's behavior had become "most indecent
and insolent."[79] This was the situation in Georgia when Wright prepared to
leave for England to secure a Native land cession.[80] It may have seemed like
an inopportune time to leave the province, but much of that evaluation can
only be seen in hindsight. Issues with colonial assemblies were not uncommon in the eighteenth century, and Wright was desperate to obtain official
permission for the cession.

During Wright's absence, Habersham assumed the reins of government,
but the stalemate continued. The House pushed. Habersham refused to
yield. And round and round they went as if Wright had never left. Finally,
in the late winter of 1772, Georgians elected a less radical Assembly. This
may have been the result of Wright's successful negotiations concerning the
land cession. But the governor deliberated for a month before informing the
Board of Trade of the calm that seemed to have descended upon Georgia.
He wanted to gauge "how people and things in general appeared" and determined that "there is a rather pleasing prospect of harmony," even though
there remained "some discontented [and] factious persons" in Savannah.[81]
Wright busied himself during the summer negotiating and finalizing the
cession—a land deal that historian Kathryn Holland Braund decried as co-
ercion on a grand scale.[82] Wright, however, believed the cession played an
important role in the first return to "confidence and harmony" in Georgia
since 1765.[83]

### "All Commerce and Trade Almost
### Cease[d] in This Country"

But Georgia's political climate intensified, and provincial economic matters
receded into the background following Parliament's response to the Boston
Tea Party in 1773. The origins of this crisis date back to the Townshend Acts
of 1767, which taxed paper, paint, and tea, among other things. There was also
a provision that allowed these funds to be used to pay royal judges and governors such as Wright rather than paying them from local funds collected by
the provincial legislatures. Thus, the legislatures would lose any coercive au-

thority over these important officials. The Tea Party was the Sons of Liberty response to the Tea Act of 1773, which was designed in part to induce Americans to purchase East India Company tea. In doing so, however, the colonists would implicitly have agreed to Parliament's right to tax them, which they were unwilling to do.[84]

In response to the Tea Act, a group of Boston Sons of Liberty rather sloppily disguised themselves as Native Americans and dumped over three hundred chests of East India Company tea into the harbor on 16 December 1773. King George and Parliament had finally had enough and issued four laws that came to be known as the Coercive Acts. These laws closed the port of Boston and greatly limited the right of self-governance in Massachusetts. They sparked intense colonial reaction, but, for the most part, the furor over these measures remained largely muted in Georgia in 1774. Former Georgia governor Henry Ellis suggested that Bostonians "are likely to be a continual plague to us [but he had] no apprehensions from their power [or] courage [because] we know their weaknesses as well as their want of bravery." He expressed the common prejudice against colonists and was also certain that the Coercive Acts would surely "bring [the colonists] to reason."[85] Georgians that year were far more preoccupied with the Native unrest that followed the New Purchase. Christ Church rector Haddon Smith even reminded Georgians that Britain was their only source of protection against the Creeks.[86] During times of Native discord, which happened periodically in these years, Wright could always rely on Georgians to be "most dutiful and loyal subjects."[87]

According to a newly arrived immigrant from Glasgow, "it was not thought the [Tea Party] troubles would spread to the southward."[88] It was "thought" wrong. Georgia's Liberty faction had been emboldened by the Tea Party, and they soon lost their earlier inhibitions about offending Crown and Parliament. Savannah merchant Joseph Clay put it bluntly: "Mens minds at present are not bent on business," and "all commerce and trades almost cease[d] in this country."[89]

This is not to suggest that Georgians ignored the events in Boston. Following the Coercive Acts in the spring of 1774, Virginia sent out invitations for a national congress, and South Carolina rebels met in early July to discuss these latest events. Governor Wright reported that this action by South Carolina had ignited tempers in Georgia. Specifically, Wright referred to an announcement in the *Georgia Gazette* that the Liberty Boys had scheduled a meeting in late July at the liberty pole outside Tondee's Tavern.[90] Georgians erected their first liberty pole on 5 June 1775 during a Loyalist celebration of the king's birthday. The Liberty Boys raised this pole as a testament to their wish for reconciliation.[91] This produced a flurry of activity in the province, as supporters and opponents filled the colony with paper propaganda. Moreover, the opponents of this gathering feared that the Native situation in the backcountry was too serious to risk losing British assistance.[92]

## "Actually Begun a Civil War"

South Carolina's Liberty Boys spent the summer months of 1774 attempting to "stir up the people" of Georgia against the Coercive Acts. Wright described those South Carolinians as being "in great wrath" about the Boston Port Act and noted that they had passed "some very indecent resolutions."[93] On 20 July Noble Wimberly Jones, Archibald Bulloch, John Houstoun, and George Walton published an announcement in the *Georgia Gazette* requesting Georgians to make their way to the Vendue, or Auction, House the next week to discuss the constitutional crisis. They declared: "By the unrelenting fury of a despotick ministry, and with a view to enforce the most oppressive acts of a venal and corrupted Parliament, . . . an army of mercenaries under an unfeeling commander [Britain] have actually begun a civil war in America." Wright issued a proclamation limiting the freedom of speech by forbidding such sessions, and he denounced the "imaginary grievances" fostered by some "violent liberty people." Moreover, he announced that such meetings were "unconstitutional, illegal, and punishable by law."[94] The radicals paid little attention to his proclamation.

Two weeks later, Jones, Bulloch, Houstoun, and Walton resolved in the Assembly that they held the same rights as subjects in Great Britain and that recent parliamentary legislation was contrary to "our idea of the British Constitution," especially because it "blends . . . punishment [of] the innocent with the guilty." Georgia's rebels then appointed a committee to correspond "with our sister colonies."[95] Wright quickly condemned their efforts, again without effect. He then scribbled a missive to Dartmouth that echoed similar warnings he had sent since the Stamp Act crisis. "It is absolutely necessary that [the colonies] are brought to a point & clearly setled and established some how or other, and not suffered to remain as they are. Nothing but jealousies rancour and ill blood" now existed on this side of the Atlantic. "Everything [is] unhinged," he warned, "and running into confusion, so that . . . a man hardly knows what to do, or how to act and its a most disagreeable state to one who wishes to support law government & good order."[96] But no help would be forthcoming, because General Thomas Gage was otherwise occupied in Boston. Gage complained in a letter to Frederick Haldimand, a Swiss-born British general, that Wright believed the protection of the empire rested on a large cadre of troops in Georgia.[97]

By that fall, however, the pendulum seemed to swing in the opposite direction—toward Wright and the Loyalists, in no small part because of the peace treaty concluded with the Creeks.[98] Support had come from Augusta and elsewhere, and Wright's mood began to improve. The Reverend Haddon Smith, writing as Mercurius, urged Georgians to comply only with official government pronouncements: "We have nothing to do with resolves illegally entered into without doors."[99] The term "without doors" means extralegally, or resolves coming from an unsanctioned assembly. Governor Wright took an extraordinary step and essentially called for a meeting of Loyalists, which was heavily attended. Loyalists, according to historian Maya Jasanoff, "cut across the social, geographical, racial, and ethnic spectrum . . . making [them] every bit as 'American' as their patriot fellow subjects."[100] Wright now suggested that the radicals comprised a mere "junto" and rashly declared that "the sense of the people in this province is against these resolutions and . . . held in contempt."[101] Wright's proactive and perhaps aggressive decision to call for a countermeeting was not matched by any other colonial governor and likely helped stall the revolutionary fervor in Georgia. Of course, it is also possible that his antagonism fed the rebellious spirit in Georgia.[102]

## A Continental Congress

With John Glen at their head, a committee of thirty was appointed at the 27 July meeting of the Assembly and tasked with writing resolutions against the Coercive Acts. Before doing this, however, they decided to adjourn until parishes beyond Savannah's environs could be represented.[103] Much of the rancor and opposition to Wright and parliamentary policies sprang from Christ (modern Chatham County) and St. John's (modern Liberty County) Parishes. Early in the crisis, perhaps dating back to the Stamp Act days, a cadre of small businessmen and artisans had joined with younger sons from some elite Savannah families to oppose Wright. St. John's Parish, on the other hand, was unified in its opposition to government policy. As Wright said, residents of that parish strongly adhered to "Oliverian principles," that is, strongly antimonarchical.[104] Wright shared this experience with Thomas Hutchinson, who echoed similar concerns in Massachusetts.[105] Meanwhile, Wright issued a public proclamation warning of the illegality of such meetings.[106]

Discouraged and exasperated, yet lucid and insightful, Governor Wright scrawled a lengthy epistle to Lord Dartmouth that vividly illustrated the rebellious inclination of

> a junto of a very few only.... Every thing my Lord was done that could be thought of, to frustrate their attempt, but this did not totally prevent it.... I am to be reflected upon & abused for opposing the licentiousness of the people.... I apprehend there will be nothing but cabals & combinations and the peace of the province & minds of the people continually heated, disturbed & distracted and the proclamation I issued against [treasonous gatherings] is termed arbitrary & oppressive.... I conceive that the licentious spirit in America has received such countenance & encouragement from many persons, speeches, and declarations ... that neither coercive or lenient measures will settle matters.... America is now become, or indisputably ere long will be, such a vast, powerful & opulent dominion, that I humbly conceive [that] in order to restore & establish real & substantial harmony affection & confidence ... it may be found advisable to settle the line with respect to taxation.... [In short], nothing [exists] but jealousies rancour and ill blood.[107]

This is an extraordinary letter. In 1774 Wright predicted that America was on the path to independence if Parliament did not concede that it did not possess the right to directly tax the colonists. Thomas Hutchinson also believed that transferring the power to tax was "advisable." In 1773 he wrote to John Pownall in the House of Commons that such a measure "would greatly tend ... to conciliate the affections of the colonies to the parent state."[108] Wright later advised Lord George Germain, the secretary of state for America and the engineer of Britain's war effort, that Parliament should grant representation to the Americans. Wright understood America's promise. It was growing at an incredible rate, and governing such a land would soon prove problematic under any circumstances.[109]

Committee chairman Glen sent out invitations to the 10 August committee meeting with great celerity, and each parish responded to his call, despite Wright's warning that such meetings were indeed illegal.[110] These representatives claimed to possess the same rights as Britons, including the right to only be taxed by their elected assemblies. They also declared their unanimity with their sister colonies. Rather than being truly revolutionary, however, these resolutions mimicked previous declarations dating back to the Stamp Act crisis a decade prior. Statements such as these emanated from loyal subjects, not revolutionaries. Perhaps to emphasize this, they declined to send delegates to the Continental Congress in Philadelphia.[111]

While decrying this meeting as a "junto of a very few" men, Governor Wright meanwhile chose to not publicly further oppose this meeting or its resolutions for fear of antagonizing the radicals.[112] His intuition seemed to have real merit, because progovernment flyers soon began circulating across the province. These messages suggested that the 10 August meeting had not in fact been a true reflection of Georgia's sentiments and warned Georgians that such illegal gatherings might discourage the Board of Trade from sending troops to protect the frontier. Signatories of these petitions included future revolutionaries, including James Habersham Jr., Alexander Wylly, William Few, and Elijah Clarke. And round and round they went.[113]

Following the refusal of the 10 August meeting to send delegates to the Continental Congress, Assembly members from St. John's Parish reconvened several times to reignite the flame of liberty and finally succeeded in getting a few other parishes to nominate Dr. Lyman Hall as a delegate to the national convention. He refused to go, likely because he felt that he lacked sufficient colony-wide support.[114] It is safe to say that by the end of August 1774 a majority of Georgians either belonged to or sided with Governor Wright's faction, and the word "independence" remained anathema to most, if not all, of them.[115] Things remained relatively quiet until South Carolina's delegates returned from the Continental Congress, "as they call it," which had convened on 5 September.[116] Georgia's Assembly had been scheduled to resume its normal business in mid-November, but Wright thought it wise to prorogue the meeting for January, because Georgia's neighbors had used every means available to "raise a flame again in the province . . . and we have been in hot water ever since." Wright added in his letter to Dartmouth that he hoped Parliament would soon show some resoluteness, because "things cannot continue long in this state."[117]

St. John's Parish led the movement to join the Continental Association, which had been adopted by the First Continental Congress on 20 October 1774, and which called for the nonimportation of British goods as well as the nonexportation of goods to Britain. The Scottish-dominated parish St. Andrews also early joined the revolutionary movement. The constitutional crisis was especially personal for many of these recent immigrants. They insisted that "neither we nor our fathers were able to bear" such oppressions. In a statement that must have raised Wright's eyebrows, the Scots complained of "monopolizing our lands into a few hands" who live in "extravagance [and] luxury."[118]

Wright still believed in late December 1774 that he needed additional succor from the Board of Trade. "I think I should be able to keep every thing quiet & orderly," he wrote, but as it was, the Liberty Boys had been "very active in fomenting a flame" throughout the province.[119] After proroguing the Assembly in November, Wright allowed the Assembly to convene on 17 January in the hopes that permitting their meeting would prevent the provincial congress, that extralegal radical body, from also meeting. Wright's liberal use of his power to dissolve the Assembly back in November ultimately resulted in a desire among certain members to simply create their own legislature. Wright's gambit failed, and they met the next day. In that case, he hoped that simultaneous meetings might at least dilute the radicals' hold on the provincial congress by adding some conservative voices from the Assembly.[120] Wright soon revealed to Dartmouth that it now appeared likely that the radicals would join with the Continental Congress. Their passions had stirred Georgians to a "height of phrenzy," he wrote that December.[121]

Shortly thereafter, radicals elected members to attend the Continental Congress, and the Sons of Liberty had the Continental Congress's nonimportation agreement published in the *Georgia Gazette*. Furthermore, they implored all parishes to send representatives to Savannah on 15 January 1775 to determine if Georgia should adopt the accord. Wright had been correct in gauging the influence of Georgia's neighbor. South Carolina's radicals provided much of the impetus for such actions, and their influence on the province would only continue to grow.[122]

Since Wright's days as South Carolina's attorney general, that province's Assembly had been an incessant thorn in his side. They withheld salary due to his father, the chief justice, and for years they constantly haggled with Wright over his fees as attorney general and again as the colonial agent to Great Britain. Their Liberty Boys hounded him during the Stamp Act crisis, and now they were quickly losing patience with what they perceived as Georgia's less than ardent revolutionary ardor. "In short my Lord," Wright complained to Dartmouth, "every engine was set to work, and every method used by our neighbors the Carolinians to draw the people of this province in."[123] Wright in fact had complained about their mischief for years. He warned Lord Hillsborough in 1769 that "there will be no real or proper harmony till there is a thorough settlement of the matters in dispute."[124] Two years earlier he directed his frustrations to Lord Shelburne, complaining that South Carolinians had infected Georgians with their republican ideas. "If check[ed] at the beginning the matter will rest," but if not, those people "will endeavour to trample further upon the Council and King's authority."[125] In another letter, he added that they had spread "many false-hoods ... pretences, and threats ... and it was given out they could come and burn the barns" of all those who stood in their way.[126]

The South Carolina rebels were not alone in burning Wright's barns at his various plantations. Georgia rebel James Jackson was a willing participant in such destruction. In fact, he later purchased one of Wright's sequestrated plantations.[127] Generally, according to Georgia lieutenant governor John Graham, a plantation's barns, rice machines, overseer's house, and Negro houses cost about £450, so these were substantial pressures indeed.[128] The intimidation from South Carolina continued: if Georgians failed to approve the Continental Congress's measures, "blood and devastation should stalk through every corner" of the colony. Perhaps what most infuriated Wright was that South Carolina's acting governor, William Bull, seemed to turn a blind eye to these actions, leaving Wright to suffer alone for his defense of the Crown. Wright even told officials in London about the threatening of government officials who "dare do their duty [but] Bull will be very safe." He had echoed these same concerns during the Stamp Act crisis.[129] Georgia's Liberty Boys soon acquiesced to their South Carolina brethren and chose representatives to send to the proposed Second Continental Congress.[130]

Although he lacked adequate military support, Governor Wright tried to complicate the rebels' designs. In an attempt to pull several important radical leaders from the Liberty Boys' meeting, he called the legislature into session on the very day the rebels planned to meet. The governor opened the legislative meeting with an impassioned and convincing plea. He called on Georgia's leaders to not "be led away by the voices and opinions of men of over-heated ideas" but rather to "consider coolly and sensibly ... the terrible consequences" of adopting the Continental Congress's resolutions. He forcefully conceded to the Liberty Boys that "you may be advocates for liberty, so am I, but in a constitutional and legal way." A conservative to his core, Wright assured them that "where there is no law there can be no liberty. It is the due course of law, and support of government, which only can insure to you the enjoyment of your lives, liberties, and your estates." His intensity and passion had now reached a crescendo. "I exhort you," he exclaimed, "not to suffer yourselves to be drawn in, to involve this province in the distresses of those who may have been offended; we are in a very different situation, and on a very different footing from the other colonies."[131]

Here, Wright referred to Georgia's thriving economic condition and the annual stipend it received from Parliament. Thus, Wright warned Georgians in much the same way as Thomas Hutchinson had warned Massachusettsians, suggesting that independence "must prove their ruin."[132]

Wright had indeed capably led Georgia, both economically and otherwise. Thomas Wooldridge of His Majesty's Forty-Eighth Regiment, then stationed in Pensacola, commented that while West Florida governor James Grant was an excellent military officer, he was a tyrannical governor. On the other hand, he praised Governor Wright's methods and credited his leadership for the "flourishing state of the province."[133] As late as January 1775, Wright boasted that most Georgians believed his policies "proceeded from an honest principle and resolution to discharge his duty to His Majesty." He was right, and this would ultimately make him an outsider to many of them.[134]

Regardless of Wright's exhortations, the provincial congress chose Archibald Bulloch, Noble Wimberly Jones, and John Houstoun as delegates to what would become the Second Continental Congress. They also adopted a toned-down version of the Continental Association. Their version delayed its initiation and disregarded the nonconsumption component, among other reductions.[135] Part of the reason for this abridged version of the Continental Association was because the provincial congress only represented five of the twelve Georgia parishes. Georgia was still divided on the association, and the congress believed it pushed the envelope as much as possible without "immediately commencing a civil war among ourselves." They adjourned on 25 January 1775 and left final approval of their resolutions to the full Assembly.[136]

In February Wright gratefully acknowledged receipt of the king's speech of 10 December 1774, which affirmed Parliament's full legislative authority "over all His Majesty's dominions." He hoped that such a declaration would be "sufficient to remove the false impressions" of colonists, "rouse them from their delusion ... and put an end to their wild expectations and unwarrantable pretensions." But he realized that it might now be too late, because "a great many people have work't themselves up to such a pitch of political enthusiasm with respect to their ideas of liberty ... and of their right to resist ... that it is very difficult" to convince them otherwise.[137] In a letter to Dartmouth, he complained again of the deleterious effect of South Carolina's rebels, who had again "raise[d] a flame" in this province. Only "God knows what the consequences may be," he cried.[138] A significant portion of Georgians, he complained, "have work't themselves up to such a pitch of po-

litical enthusiasm with respect to their ideas of liberty [and] their right to resist what they call unconstitutional laws, that I do not expect" they will ever
give up. In short, he wrote, "they have not forgot certain speeches in the beginning of the year 1766."[139] In other words, in Wright's mind, the Stamp
Act was the powder keg that ignited the revolutionary troubles.

On 24 April the pendulum had swung again. Prior to learning of the
clashes at Lexington and Concord, Governor Wright informed the Board
of Trade that he had the "great satisfaction to acquaint your Lordship
that I think I may venture to say I have succeeded in my endeavours to
Counter Act and Prevent" many of the machinations of the colony's radical element.[140] Wright's success in stemming the tide must have been common knowledge in rebel circles. In late May 1775 Henry Laurens wrote that
"Georgia is, notwithstanding all the flattering accounts of Governor Wright,
in commotion."[141] Wright actually would have agreed, although he complained that Georgia was still "threatened by our Carolina neighbors that
if any blood is spilt in the Massachusetts Bay they will come here and cut
our throats."[142] Blood had been spilled, and Wright was certain that the
bloodletting would rapidly spread throughout British North America. In
fact, Wright predicted that the rebels were ready, if not eager, "to oppose and
engage the Kings Troops."[143] The king, his ministers, and his troops were
also eager to engage if necessary. It seemed that very few people held compromise in their heart.[144] A few weeks later, one Virginian screamed, "Give
me liberty, or give me death!" In Georgia the ailing James Habersham cried
that the people here "are generally almost in a state of madness and des-
peration."[145] Such were the convictions of many during these tumultuous
times, and on 16 April General Gage decided to send one hundred troops to
Georgia.[146]

But Governor Wright continued in what must have seemed a futile exercise in bridging the gap. His experiences as a transatlantic Briton made him
especially attuned to the arguments emanating from London as well as the
colonies. But the hyperpolemical 1770s and the ever-widening ideological
gap between the colony and the metropole proved to be much more than he
could successfully negotiate. He was simply too inflexible. But his pleas that
spring seemed to have the desired impact. Shortly after his speech, the leaders of the Liberty faction despaired of ever regaining the upper hand.

Unfortunately for Wright, the news that fighting had erupted on Lexington Green in Massachusetts soon reached Savannah and rejuvenated the Liberty Boys. They seized the opportunity to unleash their anger abruptly and
violently upon Wright, and they raided the royal arsenal. Georgians "hur-

ried fast into rebellion," Governor Wright said, as soon as they received word about the opening salvo in Massachusetts. The situation worsened and rapidly devolved from one of hopeful optimism to utter despair, leaving the governor fearful for his life and requesting permission to return to England.[147] A young Loyalist named Elizabeth Lichtenstein wrote, likely echoing the governor's sentiments, "Everywhere the scum rose to the top."[148]

Meanwhile, the Liberty Boys met across town. The meeting was thinly attended, with fewer than half the parishes sending representatives. Those few in attendance were left to feel "a good deal embarrassed."[149] They managed to agree to form a committee to oversee the nonimportation of goods from Britain but accomplished little else. This half-hearted measure was derided as "mock" and "lukewarm," and, moreover, many of the city's merchants opposed nonimportation. "I truly blush," Andrew Elton Wells wrote to his brother-in-law Samuel Adams of Boston, "for the want of spirit of the greatest part of this province."[150] The radicals in the Assembly planned to secretly unleash their own resolves by having their members rush those schemes through the Assembly before Wright could act. The governor, however, had been notified of their plot and quickly dissolved the Assembly, certain that there was "no doubt" that their measures would have been adopted. The Assembly blamed Wright for their conduct. Instead of dismissing the comments, his defense against the charge helped to legitimate the provincial congress.[151] Here is a nice example of what can happen in contingent moments like this. Both sides felt frustrated that the other side had the advantage.

Sentiments in Georgia continued to "fluctuate between liberty and convenience" in the months following the dissolution of the Assembly that February, and the Liberty Boys feared they might not gain the upper hand. In fact, they refused to send delegates to the Continental Congress. "Alas!" they wrote to John Hancock, "with what face could we have appeared for a province whose inhabitants had refused to sacrifice the most trifling advantages to the public cause, and in whose behalf we did not think we could safely pledge ourselves."[152] Historian Mary Beth Norton has opined that "Sir James Wright could claim greater success in obstructing the efforts of resistance leaders than all but one other governor—Cadwallader Colden of New York."[153] Thus, there was a veritable draw in Georgia. On the one hand, Governor Wright complained of the lack of military support from Britain to buttress his administration. He always believed Georgia needed more forces than it currently had. On the other, the radicals realized that they still had failed to garner the support of even half of Georgia's inhabitants.[154]

In fact, back in the fall of 1774, hundreds of Georgians signed petitions in support of the governor and Crown.[155] Governor Wright's spirits remained relatively high into the spring, especially after receiving an incredibly complimentary letter from the Board of Trade.[156] First, Lord Dartmouth conveyed his earnest approval of Wright's actions during the past year. "I have already so repeatedly expressed to you," he wrote, "of your meritorious conduct, in the prudent and proper measures you have pursued for preventing, as far as you are able, the contagion from spreading itself through the province of Georgia." Second, Wright learned that troops and a sloop of war were to be sent to Savannah. Additionally, the governor received word from London that Parliament was unanimous in its determination to reduce the radicals "to a state of due obedience." Finally, even though Wright expressed skepticism about "what turn things may take, . . . I doubt it will not be that favourable . . . [because] a very contrary spirit still prevails in general."[157] He feared that Britain's newly found determination to exert its authority might have been discovered too late. But Wright maintained hope that the Liberty Boys in Georgia had failed to win the hearts and minds of enough Georgians to effect any significant changes to his regime. While the Liberty Boys tended to agree, the situation was fluid and often dependent upon outside forces—even distant ones.

### "A General Rebellion throughout America"

The shedding of blood on Lexington Green in Massachusetts proved to be the fulcrum on which colonial Georgia's future would pivot. Wright lamented that "the unhappy affair of the 19th of April . . . have at length drawn and forced the people of this province into the same predicament with others. . . . I see no probability of any tolerable quietude, unless the prudence and moderation of the Continental Congress should lay a foundation for it."[158] Wright laid it bare: only the Americans themselves could prevent a civil war, and the recent "unhappy turn" at Lexington and a recent Lowcountry rumor that the British planned to "liberate the slaves and encourage them to attack their masters, [throwing] the people . . . into a ferment," made it unlikely that the Americans would prevent that war.[159] No measures from London could stem the tide. The Reverend John Joachim Zubly later said that "a civil war in America is begun!"[160] Barnard Elliott, a South Carolinian recruited by Georgia's rebels, wrote that "he had formerly been averse to the American Measures . . . but that he had now altered his mind. . . . [S]ince the Battle of Lexington he was convinced that America was to be hard

rode, & drove like slaves."[161] He now had to choose sides, and he would be
no Cain.[162] Certainly the bloody Battle of Bunker Hill in June 1775 hardened others to join the rebel standard and left Prime Minister Frederick,
Lord North nearly speechless.[163] Nearly. He finally realized that the rebels
would not simply wilt in the face of British might. "The war is now grown to
such a height," he cried, "that it must be treated as a foreign war."[164]

Georgia's radicals wasted no time in concocting a propaganda war, one
that Wright would never successfully counter.[165] News of the events outside Boston made its way to Savannah via Charleston on 10 May, interestingly, on the same day the Second Continental Congress convened. Radical
leader Noble Wimberly Jones shared with Benjamin Franklin the feelings
of many in Georgia: "The present situation is truely alarming. . . . God only
know where such matters may end." In something of a tip of the cap to Governor Wright, he added, "Our province has not appeared outwardly forward
in the mat[ter] thro' [the] influence of some tools of administration, yet am
of oppinion a large majority do heartily join in sentiment with the other colonies."[166] It took the Liberty Boys no time to break into the public powder
magazine and steal six hundred pounds of gunpowder. The governor issued
a proclamation offering a reward for information about the theft but did not
"expect or suppose it will have any effect."[167] A few months later, the rebels had taken full control of the "Publick Magazine," prompting Wright to
complain of the "unparalleled insolence" now present in the province.[168]

Wright now realized that the momentum had shifted yet again. "In short,"
he wrote, "things are in a most disagreeable state, and I see no prospect of a
change for the better."[169] Two weeks later, at the end of May, he reported a
rumor that the South Carolinians planned to "raise an army . . . [and] seize
on all the Kings officers in So. Carolina, & in this province." Georgians,
moreover, Wright complained, "are much changd & many seemed disposd to
follow" South Carolina's example, and he predicted "nothing but a prospect
of a general rebellion throughout America."[170] This seemed especially likely
following either a rumor or a clever example of rebel propaganda. According to reports from Charleston, the British planned to "liberate the slaves &
encourage them to attack their masters." This report threw the Lowcountry
"into a ferment . . . [and] will involve us all in the utmost distress."[171] It did.

While utilizing freed bondsmen against the rebels appealed to Virginia's
governor, John Murray, the Earl of Dunmore, James Wright found it nox-
ious, even if he likely appreciated part of Dunmore's rationale. Like Wright,
Dunmore strongly believed in the rule of law and took his role as Britain's

representative quite seriously. He believed his proclamation, which was issued on 7 November 1775 and which threatened to free Virginia's enslaved,
to be "disagreeable" but necessary because Virginians had committed treason
and could not be punished through "the ordinary course of the civil law."[172]
While most white Americans reacted with contempt to Dunmore's proclamation, the Continental Congress would use a similar tactic in 1779 when it
urged Georgia and South Carolina to "take measures immediately for raising [and arming] three thousand able-bodied Negroes."[173] At that time, one
Georgian fearfully predicted that the British would be able to quickly re-
conquer Georgia and South Carolina once the enslaved flew to the British
standard.[174]

Georgians' fears were not merely rhetorical. In early December 1774, half
a dozen "new Negro fellows and four wenches" belonging to a Captain Morris "killed the overseer . . . murdered his wife, and dangerously wounded a
carpenter named Wright." A young boy had also been mortally wounded.
The runaways then made their way to the home of Angus McIntosh, whom
they "dangerously wounded." From there, they made haste to Roderick Mc-
Leod's home and "wounded him very much, and killed his son." The killing
spree soon ended. Some of the men were "taken and burnt, and five of the
wenches returned to the plantation."[175] The growth of this original group
of enslaved and their violent actions raised the anxieties of white Georgians
and played no small role in Georgia's revolutionary movement.[176]

From London in the late fall of 1775, a brother-in-law of Wright's son,
South Carolinian Ralph Izard, wrote that former governor William Henry
Lyttelton "was particularly rancorous against America" and approved of the
idea of "encouraging the Negroes in the Southern Colonies to drench themselves in the blood of their masters."[177] Some historians have rather persuasively argued that these apprehensions actually pushed many whites to the
rebel cause.[178] In fact, the South Carolina Council of Safety made a horrific
suggestion to its Georgia counterpart in March 1776 when its members advocated the "destr[uction of] all those rebellious Negroes upon Tybee Island
or wherever they may be found" and even thought that Native Americans
might be the "most proper hands" employed in this business.[179] In reality,
though, the British themselves were quite reluctant to fully engage Blacks as
weapons in their war against the rebels.[180]

The events in Massachusetts and rumors of the mother country's plan
to arm slaves compelled the Liberty Boys to further action, and Wright's
friends told him that those in South Carolina intended "to seize on my per-

son in all events." Georgia's Liberty Boys informed Wright that although they disapproved of this plan, they could not guarantee his safety. Fearful for his safety, Wright complained to officials in London that Georgia's Loyalists believed the Crown had left them "to fall a sacrifice to the resentment of the people." Furthermore, he protested that if his advice had been heeded earlier, "all the southern provinces" would have been kept out of the "rebellion."[181] Perhaps—perhaps not.

Wright was exhausted. With his liberty and life threatened, he believed he could give no more to Georgia. He no longer wished to "continue in this very uncomfortable situation, without the means of protection & support, and therefore must [again] humbly request . . . leave to return home . . . next spring, or sooner as things may be circumstanced."[182] News of Wright's concern spread beyond Savannah. A Charleston correspondent confirmed that he was "much alarmed for his safety," as he should have been, because South Carolina's Committee of Intelligence urged Whig leaders in Savannah to maintain a watchful eye on him.[183] The Council of Safety had been created in the summer of 1775 in response to the Battles of Lexington and Concord and the rumors of Native and enslaved insurrections. The Committee of Intelligence was just one of many committees created by South Carolina's provincial congress.[184] Publication of some of Wright's letters encouraged a situation in which, according to Wright, an element of the population was "ready to tear to pieces any man who writes something contrary to their own opinion." He was ready to retire to the land of his birth. After all, why should he stay, he wrote, when Loyalists "expose their lives" without either protection or support from the government?[185] Ten years of fighting the Assembly, ten years of sporadic insecurity, ten years of threats to his conservative temperament. He had now given up hope.

### "Treasonous Gatherings"

By the summer of 1775, the revolutionary fervor in Georgia had placed royal governance of the colony in deep peril, especially because many of Savannah's leaders had come to believe that their business prospects were closely connected to the power struggle with Governor Wright. Dejected and hopeless, Wright repeated his request to return to England. His desire to leave soon increased upon learning that "all the King's officers in Charles Town are prisoners." Knowledge of Wright's request may have aided the king's cause if not Wright's own. The rebels "did not attempt to commit any open riot or abuse" in the ensuing days after learning the governor planned to leave the colony. The liberty flag, however, remained defiantly flying.[186] Wright encouraged Lieutenant William Grant of the Royal Navy to remain in Savannah for as long as possible and asked militia leaders to "stand by him in case Carolina should make him prisoner."[187] In the meantime, Wright made incessant appeals for military assistance, but without success. "I begin to think," he wrote in July, that "a King's governor has little or no business here."[188] But the Board of Trade had grown weary of Wright's pleas for help.[189] On 4 July 1775 the Governor's Council was "unanimously of opinion that as the powers of government are at present totally unhinged, . . . prosecutions [for any offenses] would be useless."[190] The royal government now had no ability to enforce the law—in the summer of 1775, a full year prior to the Declaration of Independence.[191]

South Carolina's royal governor, Lord William Campbell, concurred. In a letter to Thomas Gage, he declared: "All legal government is now at an end."[192] He queried which southern governor had suffered the greatest indignations—Governor Wright, Governor Josiah Martin of North Carolina, or himself—adding that many backcountry inhabitants were inclined to support the Crown and wanted only a little military support and encouragement. South Carolinian Henry Laurens, who had taken in Wright's son, Alexander, as an apprentice in his mercantile firm, noted that Georgia's Assembly had "made [Wright's] pillow rough."[193] Interestingly, Laurens remained cordial with the younger Wright, who left South Carolina at the onset of the crisis. Wright's wife and children remained in Charleston.[194] Worse yet for Governor Wright was that he had to endure these difficult times without his best friend. James Habersham had just "gone to Philadelphia for the recovery of his health."[195] He would die several months later. Wright named John Hume, "a relation of mine," to replace Habersham on the Governor's Council.[196]

Wright's pillow was especially rough in no small part because the South Carolina Council of Safety intercepted several of his letters. The rebels' ability to disrupt government communications proved quite fruitful and delayed the British military response in the South.[197] At the end of June 1775, Wright mailed several letters to British officials in which he advised them of the deplorable situation in Georgia. On 27 June he warned Lord William Campbell, South Carolina's newly appointed royal governor, of the "disorder'd state of pub[lic] aff[ai]rs." Moreover, Wright insisted, that "without any protection or support I am much afraid. . . . I see no probability of any sober quietude."[198] South Carolina's rebels intercepted this letter as well as two letters from Wright to Gage. While it is unclear if the rebels replaced the Campbell letter, they did replace Wright's letters to Gage and Admiral Samuel Graves. In the first letter, Wright lamented that the "unhappy affair of 19th of April . . . have at length drawn and forced the people of this province" into such disaffection that "I see no probability of any tolerable quietude." He also advised Gage to either send no troops or "five times" the number he previously requested, because too few would "only inflame the whole province." Additionally, Wright suggested that England would be a better locale for governors than America, lest they "have the mortification to see their powers executed by Committees and mobs." He concluded that he was "amazed that these southern provinces should be left in the situation they are, and the governours and king's officers [left] naked and exposed to the resentment of an enraged people."[199] The Rebel Council of Safety replaced this letter to Gage with one that portrayed the province to be in relative peace. Concomitantly, the governor of East Florida asked a naval officer to hand deliver a private message to Governor Wright and advised the officer to observe and be "circumspect as he proceeded," because the governor was unsure who could be trusted.[200] But Wright had not used such caution, and the rebel seizure of his correspondence worked like a charm, leaving Admiral Graves and General Gage to suspect that "Georgia [has] not suffered."[201] Patriot lore has it that Wright asked Gage after the war why he had been negligent in sending help. Gage responded that he had letters from Wright stating that all was calm in Georgia. It was then that Wright inspected the letters and declared them forgeries.[202] Henceforth, the governor did his best to communicate via "a trusted friend," although to what effect no one can know.[203] What is known is that no military leader paid much attention to the crisis in the southern provinces.

The forged letter mimicked Wright's talking points. Regarding Lexington, the forged letter stated that "I am happy that . . . there is nothing really formidable . . . in the designs of our neighbours of South Carolina" and that all was well. Furthermore, the letter stated that the new governor, Campbell, was "inexperienced in affairs of government" and might "express apprehensions," but there was nothing to worry about. "I assure you," the phony letter read, "no danger is to be apprehended" and no troops whatsoever were needed in South Carolina and Georgia.[204] How did General Gage interpret this letter to be legitimate? He had corresponded with Wright for years, and Wright had constantly harped about the need for additional men. Of course, Gage was preoccupied in Boston and may not have been able to send relief in any event.

On the same day, Governor Wright also penned a letter to Admiral

Graves. He inquired about the whereabouts of the vessel Graves was supposed to have sent to Georgia and stated that there were then "four or five boats from [South Carolina], full of armed men" on the Savannah coast. These men, according to Wright, had blocked the port and had "it in their power to plunder any thing that arrives here, and do just what they please." Therefore, he maintained, we need "immediate assistance." Unfortunately for the governor, this letter was also intercepted and forged. The false letter stated that Wright had no "occasion for any vessel of war."[205] So as far as the British military command in America knew, Georgia and South Carolina remained tolerably peaceful.

Georgia's second provincial congress convened at Tondee's Tavern on 4 July 1775. With Christ and St. John's Parishes at the fore, this congress chose Archibald Bulloch as its president. The Reverend John Joachim Zubly then delivered something of a moderate sermon. A monarchist at heart, Zubly told Georgians that the king had fallen victim to nefarious ministers. Moreover, he reminded Americans of their common ancestry with Britons. Quoting from 2 Chronicles, he preached that while the "Gospel of Jesus is the law of liberty," one should never "go up, nor fight against your brethren."[206]

The congress requested Governor Wright to announce a day of fasting and prayer, which he did for 19 July, though without acknowledging the congress's request. At the same time, the Continental Congress proclaimed 20 July as a national day of fasting and prayer. Christ Church rector Haddon Smith refused to observe the national holiday and soon found himself forbidden by the Committee of Safety from again preaching in Savannah.[207]

The provincial congress adopted sixteen resolutions that month that fully brought it in line with the other colonies. The congress promised to adhere to all Continental Congress recommendations.[208] The next day, 7 July, members of the congress chose five delegates to the Continental Congress: Archibald Bulloch, John Houstoun, John Zubly, Noble Jones, and Lyman Hall. They then sanctioned an audacious petition to the king written by Zubly, who suggested the king listen to Americans rather than his ill-intentioned ministers. He also urged George III, as the "sovereign of the most important empire in the universe," to repeal Parliament's recent unconstitutional measures.[209]

A few days later, the congress published its first indication that separation from the mother country might lie ahead. The nineteen resolutions passed by the members of the congress on 10 July included a statement of their natural rights, their equality of rights with all Britons, an acknowledgment that the British Empire and constitution were the best in the world, and a re-

statement of their belief in no taxation without representation and that the
Coercive Acts were unconstitutional. The pinnacle of their resolves, however, was a warning that nothing but the deprivation of their natural rights
"could ever make the thought of a separation otherwise than intolerable."[210]
So one can see in this bold message a compromise between the moderate
and radical elements in Georgia. While there is a recognition of Georgians'
membership in the British Empire, there is also an acceptance that that affiliation is tenuous and dependent upon the Americans' understanding of the
British Constitution. The next day, the extralegal provincial congress oddly
stated that "in these very critical and alarming times, [they] shall always pay
due respect to" Governor Wright, who dubiously wrote, "Pray God grant a
happy and speedy reconciliation."[211]

Supposedly with all due respect to Wright, the congress created the
Council of Safety and gave its members full executive authority to act in the
congress's stead during its recess until mid-August. The congress further instructed its delegates to the Continental Congress to apply for full membership. This provincial congress, Georgia's second, would become its first revolutionary government.[212] To illustrate the point, members used a variety of
methods to coerce all Georgians to join with them. In addition to the seemingly benign methods of economic and social pressures, the congress used
more violent measures. Wright angrily wrote that the rebels "threaten[ed]
to proscribe," or banish, recalcitrant Georgians. Failing that, they threatened
to take or destroy their property, banish them from the province, or even tar
and feather them.[213]

## "Where There Is No Law There
## Can Be No Liberty"

The next six months proved to be increasingly miserable for Wright and his
fellow Loyalists. The governor of South Carolina, Lord William Campbell,
wrote that "it is a matter of doubt to me, whither [*sic*] Sir Jas Wright, Governor [Josiah] Martin [of North Carolina], or myself, is in the worst situation, as . . . we seem equally abandon'd by the whole world."[214] Campbell
would soon learn that he was in the worst situation: he would be forced to
leave the province in two short months.[215] Writing from London, Ralph Izard, the brother-in-law of Wright's son, Alexander, wrote that he soon expected South Carolina's rebels to "have marched to Georgia and taken possession of Savannah."[216] He was onto something. Georgia's radicals began
to take control of the provincial militia in July and, by winter, possessed the

courts as well. By September Wright lamented that "the King's governor remains little else than nominally so," especially as "the poison [of liberty] has infected the whole country," from Lowcountry to backcountry.[217] On 8 August the Council of Safety complained to Wright that many militia officers were detrimental to the service of Georgia. Governor Wright opined that this was because these men had refused to sign the Continental Association. Alas, he wrote, "the Liberty People" have taken over the militia. "My Lord," he complained to Dartmouth, "are these things to be suffered in a British government?"[218] By November the Council of Safety had taken full control of the commissioning of officers.[219]

Loyalists daily faced insults from the Sons of Liberty. Failure to sign the rebel oath could result in banishment or worse. "Advertisements are put up throughout Georgia," Wright wrote, "requiring . . . all persons to take the new state oaths." Refusal meant confiscation and banishment.[220] For example, Wright was startled on the evening of 24 July by a "very great huzzaing in the streets." He sent someone to investigate and learned that river pilot John Hopkins had been kidnapped and tarred and feathered, which Wright described as the "most horrid spectacle I ever saw." Hopkins's offense was to have made derogatory remarks about the Sons of Liberty, who paraded him past the governor's home, surely in an attempt at intimidation.[221] Even Wright's minister at Christ Church, the Reverend Haddon Smith, had been forced to "flee from the violence of the people . . . [after having] been continually persecuted," even though Wright came to his aid.[222]

In early August members of the rebel congress penned a fascinating letter to the governor in which they suggested unity "in times like [the] present." Moreover, they suggested that such unity would require a reorganization of militia leadership. They assured Wright that they "exclude even the most distant idea of an attack upon the prerogatives of our most gracious sovereign" or his provincial officers. Wright and his Council wisely understood this letter as an attempt to "wrest the command of the militia out of the hands of the [Royal] government."[223] Later in the fall, Wright grieved over the "wretched state" of affairs and cried that his "government [has been] totally annihilated," leaving him to face daily "the greatest acts of tyranny, oppression, [and] gross insults."[224] His situation was so dreadful that rumors circulated throughout the British Atlantic world that he had been "made prisoner by the people."[225] Not yet.

In the face of such affronts, Governor Wright and the Loyalists believed that they, and not the rebels, were beacons of liberty because they defended constitutional government against a violent mobocracy.[226] In a message to the Assembly, Wright wrote, "You, gentlemen, are Legislators, and let me entreat you to take care how you give a sanction to trample on Law and Government; and be assured it is an indisputable truth, that where there is no law there can be no liberty." He wrote that only the proper application of government "can insure to you the enjoyment of your lives, your liberty, and your estates."[227] This would be the central tenet of his political ideology. After all, the governor reasoned, how could lovers of liberty excuse the rebel treatment of Augusta's Thomas Brown? Wright reported in August that the Liberty Boys had "most cruelly treated" and tortured the Augustan.[228] Three months later, Brown had recuperated enough to describe the horrific episode to his father: "People here are under immense pressure to subscribe to a Rebel oath, including me.... [I explained to them] that my situation was particularly delicate [and] that I did not wish to take up arms against that country which gave me being. On the other hand, it would be equally disagreeable to me to fight against those amongst whom, it was probable, I should spend the remainder of my days. Additionally, I told them I desired to live in peace and tranquility without meddling with politics." The rebels had no patience for neutrality, and after a short scuffle, they fractured Brown's skull with the butt of a rifle. The "cowardly miscreant[s]" then carried him off and tortured him "with unparalleled barbarity" by tying him to a tree and lighting a fire under his feet.[229] Brown's treatment pushed him into a corner, and he became an aggressive Loyalist militia leader.[230] He later responded to claims that he behaved barbarically by insisting that he did not use his mistreatment as an excuse to betray his moral compass. "I can say with truth," he wrote, that "I never deviated from the line of conduct the laws of war and humanity prescribed."[231]

Rebel treatment of nonrebels intensified in 1775. A recent Georgia immigrant advised his father to discourage others from his hometown (Firth, Orkney) from immigrating to Georgia because the "Americans will kill them like deer in the woods.... I seed the Liberty Boys take between two and three hundred Torrys" and drive them like sheep and put them "in gaile."[232] Rebel authorities arrested Councilman John Hume in October, presumably to be "torn to pieces," according to Wright. "However ... as a matter of great humanity and tenderness, they condescended to order him out of the province," Wright continued. Loyalists were in great need of assistance, and if none was soon offered, he complained, "every officer and friend of government will either be forced out of the province, or must submit to a worse fate."[233]

The second half of 1775 proved painfully confused and contingent. Oftentimes both Loyalists and rebels believed themselves to be losing ground in the battle for hearts and minds. Part of this was a result of ever-shifting alliances. As Wright mourned the loss of his authority, certain rebels bemoaned the lack of revolutionary zeal within their own ranks. A full month after Wright lamented the virtual dissolution of his government, Peter Taarling confided to John Houstoun, one of Georgia's delegates to the Continental Congress in Philadelphia, "I wish it was in my power to give you a reciprocal acc't of the warlike spirit of Georgia. . . . [Instead] I'll therefore leave it and begin to hope, perhaps a few months more, may rouse us and we will be more used to drums & politicks, than what we are at present."[234] Time would indeed rouse them.

That November the king declared the Americans to be in "open rebellion" and sent seven regiments of infantry to the American South.[235] The next month, just two months after Taarling penned his frustrated letter to Houstoun, Wright learned that the king had indeed approved his request for leave. The governor informed Lord Dartmouth that "all the King's officers and friends to government write for my continuance amongst them. . . . I am well informed and have [even] been told by several of the Liberty people that they [also] express great concern and uneasiness at my intention of leaving the province at present."[236]

It appeared Wright's nearly two-decade tenure in Georgia had come to an end. In that time, he had worked tirelessly to promote its growth. He had been unimaginably successful, and most Georgians personally liked him. But with that growth came an increasing desire for independence among the colonists. They had started to feel constricted by "parental" guidance, and that feeling often expressed itself in fits of animosity. Although Wright had spent all but fifteen of his fifty-nine years in the southeastern Lowcountry, he was always a "faithful servant of the Crown," and that loyalty would prove costly.[237]

Beginning with the Stamp Act crisis, some Georgians began to lose faith that their governor fully represented their interests and theirs alone. They realized that, first and foremost, Wright's duty rested with the Crown. As time passed and as events in the other colonies unfolded, radical Georgians determined that they needed neither James Wright nor Great Britain. But as Wright maintained throughout the remainder of his life, "If we could have got any support or assistance [we] should have kept [Georgia] out of the rebellion." Right or wrong, this was his position until he died.[238]

*Portrait of Joseph Habersham*, by Richard West. Savannah, 1884.
From Georgia Historical Society: GHS 1361-AF047,
Georgia Historical Society collection of portraits.

Andrea Soldi (Italian, 1703-1771), Sir James Wright, c. 1736-1771,
oil on canvas, 35⅞ x 27⅝ inches (91.1 x 70.2 cm),
Telfair Museum of Art, Savannah, Georgia.

*Engraving of James Habersham.* Foltz Photography Studio (Savannah, Ga.). Savannah, undated. From Georgia Historical Society: GHS 1360-PH-25-10-03, Georgia Historical Society collection of photographs.

# CHAPTER 6

# A Governor Arrested

## "Sir James, You Are My Prisoner"

With any semblance of normality crashing down around him, Wright desperately tried to maintain some appearance of authority. He dispatched letter after letter, imploring the Board of Trade to provide succor, though history had surely taught him that little relief would be forthcoming. During the first week of January 1776, Wright complained to Dartmouth that "if we had proper support and assistance, I think [substantial] numbers would join the King's standard." But, he continued, "no troops, no money, no orders, or instructions [coupled with] a wild magnitude [of Liberty people] gathering fast, what can any man do in such a situation?" Moreover, he complained, the rebels "are a parcel of the lowest people chiefly carpenters, shoemakers, blacksmiths &c with a few at their head . . . [of the] better sort of men." He suggested that this lower sort were merely tools of the elite, something Thomas Hutchinson also stated.[1] Wright added that it was doubly shameful that "His Majesty's officers and dutiful & loyal subjects [should] be suffered to remain under such cruel tyranny and oppression."[2] Even more disheartening was the death in Edinburgh of Wright's eldest sister, Isabella.[3]

In December 1775 Dr. Thomas Taylor of Savannah wrote that two-thirds of Georgians supported the Crown, but without protection, "they know it is vain to oppose the current."[4] One Loyalist had even been forced to live "in the swamp; having lost" most of his property and possessions.[5] On a personal level, Wright had the foresight to have all of his lands and properties appraised, because he anticipated "the storm." Since he "had not the small-

TABLE 6.1. An inventory of the enslaved, rice crops, and animals on eight of Wright's plantations

| Plantation | Men | Women | Boys | Girls | Total | Rice | Animals |
|---|---|---|---|---|---|---|---|
| Orange Green | 30 | 24 | 12 | 6 | 72 | 468 | 224 |
| Knob | 16 | 16 | 5 | 1 | 38 | 255 | 0 |
| Canoochee | 18 | 17 | 7 | 2 | 44 | 231 | 20 |
| Mound Laurell | 19 | 18 | 9 | 1 | 47 | 229 | 0 |
| River | 20 | 15 | 4 | 1 | 40 | 408 | 0 |
| Point | 22 | 16 | 5 | 0 | 43 | 397 | 0 |
| Mulberry Hill | 22 | 14 | 5 | 6 | 47 | 523 | 0 |
| Sedge Field* | 22 | 15 | 6 | 1 | 44 | 112 | 0 |
| TOTALS | 169 | 135 | 53 | 18 | 375 | 2,623 | 244 |

* Sedgefield had plantation tools as sufficient quantity for the use of [all] eight plantations. A study of Lowcountry Georgia plantations for estates from 1755–1760, reveals that the average number of enslaved per plantation was 14.9. The average in areas where Wright's plantations predominated was closer to 27. From 1766 to 1777, the average Georgia plantation consisted of 25.1 enslaved.

SOURCES: *GGCJ*, 1778–1779, 4–5; and Paul Pressly, *On the Rim of the Caribbean: Colonial Georgia and the British Atlantic World* (Athens, 2013), 44, 137.

TABLE 6.2. An inventory of Governor Wright's furniture at his Canooche plantation, which appears to have been his primary "country residence" (original spelling retained)

**FRONT ROOM BELOW STAIRS**
1 mahogany bureau, 3 mahogany tables, 10 walnut chairs
3 dozen stone plates, 13 dishes, 5 knives & forks, 9 wine glasses
2 tumblers, 2 decanters, 4 teapots, 1 coffee pot, 1 sugar dish
2 milk pots, 14 coffee & tea cups & saucers, 2 China bowls
5 wash hand basons, 2 salts, 1 candle stick

**BED CHAMBER BELOW STAIRS**
1 bedstead, bed bolster & pavillion, 2 blankets, 2 coverlids, 9 table cloths, 4 napkins, 5 pair sheets, 1 pine table

**LARGE CHAMBER ABOVE STAIRS**
1 bedstead & pavillion, 2 walnut chairs, 2 rush bottom chairs, and 1 old table

**SMALL CHAMBER ABOVE STAIRS**
1 bedstead, 1 mattrass & 2 bolsters, 2 pillows, 3 blankets, 2 coverlids, 2 chairs, 3 chamber potts.

SOURCE: *GGCJ*, 1778–1779, 5.

est" doubt that Britain would prevail, he wanted to be able to "prove the value when the rebellion should be quelled."[6] Just a few days later, the rebels erected a new liberty pole in the middle of Johnson Square in Savannah.[7]

A much more tangible and overt oppression awaited Wright when he learned the lengths to which the rebels would go to exercise their tyranny. Having received a promise of support and aid from the Continental Congress, Georgia's radicals determined to press forward and take full control of the province. The rebel Council of Safety appointed Samuel Elbert, Edward Telfair, and Joseph "Joe" Habersham to secure war matériel. The men had been authorized to purchase four hundred stands of arms, twenty thousand pounds of gunpowder, and sixty thousand pounds of lead and shot.[8] A few days later, on 7 January, the Council of Safety discussed a report that two British warships were en route to Georgia. The rebels suspected that the British intended to either purchase or plunder for provisions. Thus, "fearing for the public safety," the council issued orders to raise its own militia. In the meantime, ships in the harbor were forbidden from sailing for fear they would be captured and looted by the British. Moreover, royal officials were forbidden from "going without the limits of Savannah." Lastly, "all houses of all overseers and negroes" would be immediately searched, and weapons and ammunition should be confiscated except "one gun and thirteen cartridges for each overseer."[9]

With British ships seemingly hovering on the horizon, the Council of Safety augmented its security preparations by ordering the arrest of certain suspected Loyalists and submitting a request for reinforcements from South Carolina.[10] On 13 January the council received word from its South Carolina compatriots that H.M.S. *Tamar* had been sighted off Tybee Island, which was located at the mouth of the Savannah River, twelve miles downstream from the city.[11] Three more warships, along with auxiliary vessels, arrived five days later. The news gave Wright hope that Georgia would soon be restored. Rebel leaders had other plans.

Joseph Clay and Noble Wimberly Jones, and Joseph Habersham, the son of a close friend of Governor Wright, made haste for Tondee's Tavern, a rebel haven just a few blocks from the governor's home at the northwest corner of Broughton and Whitaker Streets.[12] After a fiery discussion, the Council of Safety resolved to irreversibly plunge Britain's youngest colony deep into the maelstrom of rebellion by ordering the arrest of Governor Wright and Governor's Council members John Mulryne, Josiah Tattnall, and Anthony Stokes. These men had now been deemed a dangerous threat to the liberty of the people.[13] That night, rebel major Joe Habersham, whose recently deceased father had been Wright's closest friend, happily volunteered to apprehend the royal officials. The younger Habersham had been an officer in the provincial militia but resigned as the imperial crisis began. When Wright asked him why he would resign this important commission, Habersham said, according to Henry Laurens, that he "would not hold a commission under an enemy to his country."[14] With ominous orders in hand, he and a small, hand-picked party made their way through the chilly darkness to Governor Wright's home.

At that moment, Wright and the Governor's Council had sat down to dinner at the governor's home, also known as the Government House. This was no ordinary dinner party, however. It was a meeting of Georgia's highest-ranking ministerial officials, and the discussion focused on the town's ever-growing mobocracy.[15] As governor and Council labored through a difficult meal at Wright's mahogany dining table under the comforting gaze of a portrait of King George II, a sudden noise at the front door halted the conversation. Seemingly out of nowhere, Habersham's posse descended upon the home and rushed past the guard stationed at its entrance. Major Habersham entered the dining room amid a cacophony of loud voices, boots on wood, and confusion. With apparent grace and dignity, he bowed to the assembled guests and marched to the head of the table. In this moment, Wright learned what Thomas Hutchinson later opined: "Everything in American affairs happens contrary to probability."[16] Placing his arm on Governor Wright's shoulder, Habersham declared, "Sir James, you are my prisoner."[17] Without waiting for Habersham to complete his sentence, most of the dinner guests scattered for an exit. John Martindale, Wright's butler, was unable to escape and soon found himself on a ship headed for England. The capture of the governor proved to be the final motivation for many non-rebels, who made haste for St. Augustine and other safer environs. One such emigrant, Martin Jollie, confided to East Florida's royal governor, Patrick Tonyn: "These deluded people has made every prudent thinking man withdraw from the party."[18]

The Council of Safety reconvened a few hours later and resolved that each of those arrested be permitted to return "to their respective homes upon their parole assuring that they will attend his Excellency the Governor's house, at nine o'clock to-morrow morning." The council then granted Wright's parole upon the conditions that he remain in his home and not correspond "with any of the officers or others on board the ships of war now at Tybee [Island], without the permission of this Board." Governor's Council member James Edward Powell later complained of the "repeated instances of outrage, insult, and imprisonment" during this time of parole and added that Wright experienced "as much ill treatment as [any officer] of the Crown."[19] The denial of Wright's personal liberty in the name of liberty prompted at least one member of Georgia's rebel government to renounce his own oath to the rebels. Years later, Basil Cowper wrote that he "continued with [the rebels] till the Governor and Council were made prisoners when he quitted them," indicative of the limits of Cowper's passion for reform.[20] From Massachusetts, Lieutenant General Thomas Gage succinctly commented about what Wright already believed: "America is a mere bully."[21]

### "Daily Deliberate Murders"

The deeply personal nature of this rapidly unfolding civil war made Wright's parole a precarious and dubious condition, and the revolution in Georgia and South Carolina was a civil war. The Reverend Oliver Hart wrote of "the greatest appearance of civil war" then brewing in the backcountry. Loyalist South Carolinian Sir Egerton Leigh wrote that the revolution honored "no law, no friendship, no alliance, [and] no ties of blood."[22] Continental Army officer Otho Holland Williams, who fought in the southern campaigns, wrote to his brother Elie in Baltimore: "The daily deliberate murders committed by pretended whiggs and reputed tories . . . are too numerous & too shocking to relate."[23] Georgia's chief justice, Anthony Stokes, identified the beginning of that civil war a few years later but agreed that that was indeed the nature of the conflict in Georgia. After the war, he wrote that a "Civil War broke out in Georgia . . . after the King's Government was re-established there."[24] Even the rebels thought of this conflict as a civil war. In the summer of 1775 Georgia's provincial congress wrote to the inhabitants of the backcountry: "It is with great sorrow we are to acquaint you that what our fears suggested . . . is actually come to pass. A Civil war in America is begun," twelve months before independence had been declared.[25] Back in Boston, General William Howe informed Lord Germain, who had replaced Lord Dartmouth, that Lieutenant Colonel James Grant had recently returned from Georgia and found the entire "country in open rebellion [and Governor Wright] & many of the Kings Friends prisoners at large."[26] Georgians now had to prepare for the worst of the worst—what Thomas Hobbes described the previous century. "Now all such calamities as may be avoided by human industry," Hobbes had written, "arise from war, but chiefly from civil war, for from this proceed slaughter, solitude, and the want of all things."[27] Loyalist Thomas Brown, who had been attacked by the rebels in the early stages of the conflict, concurred, calling civil wars "one of the greatest evils incident to human society," because "men whose passions are inflamed by mutual injuries, exasperated with personal animosity against each other, and eager to gratify revenge, often violate the laws of war and principles of humanity."[28] And the civil war in the South was thoroughly "woven into the fabric of life." Georgians "lived in constant fear," and every individual was personally affected by the war's violence.[29]

Following his arrest, Wright summoned two radical leaders to his home. He expressed confidence that the British had orders to treat Georgia as in a state of rebellion, but if the rebels promised to allow the British vessels to purchase provisions, Wright would personally persuade the commander to leave the town unscathed. Otherwise, the British "would certainly take it by force."[30] This was indeed no choice whatsoever. If the rebels complied, their movement would become a mere fiction; if they refused, their town would be destroyed. The two rebel leaders, Noble Wimberly Jones and Joseph Clay, reported Wright's message to the Council of Safety. The message only served to embolden the members of the council. They voted to put Wright and the Governor's Council on parole, forbidding them to leave town or interact with the British ships.[31] Two days later, as militia filtered into town, the Governor's Council surrendered authority to the rebel government. Divisions then became apparent, as the congress now had the authority it had long sought. The time had come to defend Savannah.

The previous November, the Continental Congress had authorized a Continental battalion from Georgia, with its officers chosen by the rebel government. The debate over this issue proved contentious and ultimately deadly. The most radical element, commonly known as the "popular or country party," chose Button Gwinnett as Georgia's military commander. Gwinnett was a radical firebrand. Georgia doctor Lyman Hall mused that Gwinnett was, "if possible, a Whig to excess." The "conservative" wing within the rebel ranks, mostly from the merchant class, selected Samuel Elbert. Tempers boiled as the factions hunkered down, but cooler heads prevailed. They agreed on Lachlan McIntosh as a compromise candidate, even though it was written that "the flame of war is now burst forth . . . the cry of young and old is liberty or death."[32] The factionalism, however, persisted.[33]

Exacerbating Governor Wright's situation, the Council of Safety issued a resolution requiring all prisoners to be relocated to the backcountry upon entry of British vessels into the Savannah River.[34] Worse yet, at least according to Chief Justice Stokes, the rebels planned to forcibly draft Loyalists into the militia and use them as cannon fodder should the British invade.[35] Just days after Wright and his cohorts received their paroles, royal lieutenant governor John Graham privately learned that the rebels were "determined to confine [him], upon which Graham was obliged to conceal himself night and day in Swamps for a considerable time." Worse yet, he wrote, he had been "exposed to all the inclemencies of the weather, until he fortunately made his escape on board the King's ships."[36] The council's promised safety of parole seemed more uncertain with each passing day.

Wright now believed that the rebels had broken, or planned to break, the terms of his parole. These combined factors compelled him to seek the security of H.M.S. *Scarborough*, then in the harbor.[37] Moreover, rabble-rousers continually harassed the governor and his family and on more than one occasion subjected his home to scattered musket shots. Such behavior would have been a violation of a resolution passed by the rebel Council of Safety on 16 January, which forbade Georgians from "idly fir[ing] a gun in the town." Though it can be supposed that these were not idle shots. In the face of these insults and threats, Wright bemoaned that he could avail himself of "not the least means of protection, support, or even personal safety," which proved far "too much" to endure.[38] Additionally, Josiah Tattnall further defended Wright's actions, stating that the governor's parole stipulated that he could "quit the country if he should be insulted. [Thus when] he & his family being afterwards insulted, [I] assisted him with a boat & men to carry [them] off."[39] Georgia's provincial congress, which had first convened the previous July, accepted no such justification, tersely noting that "Governor Wright observed his parole of honor for a time, but after nearly four weeks of confinement broke it, and, escaping through a back door of his house, fled in the night time and made his way, under cover of darkness, to an armed British ship anchored in the harbor."[40]

During the late-night hours of 11 February, Wright, his youngest son, Charles, and his two daughters escaped through his back door and "down the river about five miles by land to Bonaventure, where [John] Mullryne [sometimes spelled Mulryne] lived, and where a boat and crew were waiting for him."[41] Josiah Tattnall was later arrested for "having assisted the Gov. Sir James Wright in withdrawing himself from Savannah." He was imprisoned for nearly two months, had his property confiscated, and was forced into exile in the Bahamas.[42] Additionally, to help feed the men aboard His Majesty's ships, Wright also "ordered a boat load of rice to be brought" with him, but the boat was "stopt and seized" by the rebels.[43] Wright justified his actions by declaring that "in order to avoid the rage and violence of the

Rebels, [I] was reduced to the necessity of leaving the town of Savannah in the night."[44] According to General Howe, the Wrights "narrowly escap[ed] the search of a detachment of 150 men sent to seize him."[45] The *Scarborough* saluted Wright's safe arrival.[46] Wright's flight changed the calculus for everyone.

## "Total Ruin And Destruction"

Wright's escape meant that the rebels could no longer use him as a bargaining chip, and McIntosh, the new rebel military commander, ramped up his defensive preparations. Wright's getaway also brought about the official end of royal government, a situation that seemed to require a military response from Captain Andrew Barkley (sometimes spelled Barclay), the British naval commander. Two days later, Wright again assured the rebels that Barkley would not harm the town if his ships were allowed to purchase supplies. In fact, Wright implored them to accept these terms, adding that he was "(probably) the best friend the people of Georgia have." If they failed to accede to his conditions, "it may not be in my power to insure them the continuance of the peace and quietude they now have."[47] He then informed his former Council that the king had granted his return to England, but Wright's "regard for the province and people is such that I cannot avoid exhorting the people to save themselves and their posterity from that total ruin and destruction."[48] The provincial congress paid no heed to Wright's letters, and the Governor's Council was paroled and powerless. The two sides continued to prepare for the ensuing encounter.

In considering Wright's message, McIntosh lamented his scarce martial resources: roughly 350 Georgia militia and Continentals and approximately 100 South Carolinians with which to protect the "open, straggling, defenseless and deserted town" against the British ships in the harbor.[49] As Captain Barkley of the Royal Navy considered his limited options, he now reached out and reminded the Council of Safety that he simply wanted to purchase provisions at market value, "which I had great reason to expect in any part of his Majesty's dominions."[50] Of course, Barkley operated from an outdated calculus. Georgians had just arrested their royal governor and no longer considered the colony part of anyone's dominion, and they refused the request.

The British commander now understood that his only chance of procuring provisions rested on his ability to access the two dozen or so merchant vessels (or rice boats) then in the harbor, which the rebels had quarantined and moored against Hutchinson Island, a little tract of land located across the river from Savannah proper and separated from South Carolina by numerous swamps and streams with varying and changing navigability. The rice boats sought by Captain Barkley were located at the northern tip of Hutchinson Island, which meant that the British would have to pass Savannah's defenses, mediocre as they were, to reach them.[51] "Our distress here," Wright now wrote to Major General Henry Clinton, "is beyond description [and] I must in the strongest manner possible request your immediate assistance."[52] With such assistance, Wright assured the Board of Trade, "I shall think it my duty to continue here for some time." Without troops, he wrote, "I don't see how I can possibly be of any material service."[53]

Several weeks prior to this plea, Governor Wright had arrived aboard the twenty-gun H.M.S. *Scarborough* at Cockspur Island at 9:00 in the morning of 12 February. A newspaper soon reported that Wright, "with his two daughters, has retired on board the *Scarborough*, thereby abdicating his government, and leaving behind him an estate valued to at least £80,000 sterling."[54] Some of the items lost included "two English horses, three other horses, a phaeton, and a chair with harness for horses."[55] Some of his missing furniture included mahogany bureaus, writing desks, dining tables, a cistern, miscellaneous tables, a fire screen, card tables, tea tables, beds, and a breakfast table. He also lost a guitar, a pianoforte, china, a portrait of King George II, carpets, and much more.[56]

Captain Andrew Barkley's deafening salute honoring Wright's safe arrival to his ship startled Savannahians and angered the rebel Council of Safety.[57] Moreover, Wright believed that his journey to the protection of the British vessel would be short-lived. As it turned out, he either lied to or attempted to deceive the rebel Council of Safety when he said that Barkley only wanted provisions. In a letter to the American secretary of state, Lord George Germain, who had just replaced Dartmouth, Wright wrote: "When I left Savannah from many accounts I had received my full expectation was that the King's ships & troops . . . were come to our relief and assistance, and that I should have returned to Savannah [within] 48 hours."[58]

Although the British would have to pass the town to reach the rice boats, there was good news for Captain Barkley: Savannah's defenses were woefully inadequate, and its defenders were thoroughly discombobulated. Many of the "numberless avenues" leading into the city were left unguarded, and many of the men in town were "under no control or command whatsoever," McIntosh carped, adding that the Council of Safety had not even "met for some time," leaving Savannah in a state of "anarchy and confusion."[59] Moreover, the Continental Association, which had restricted the disembarkation

of vessels, was set to expire on 1 March. At that point, they would all be free
to leave and conduct their business as usual.

## "Growing Worse Every Hour"

McIntosh decided that the time had come for him to take control of Georgia's ambiguous power structure "least [*sic*] the colony should be tamely
given up."[60] Believing that Barkley's intent was not simply to provision but
to restore royal authority under Governor Wright, McIntosh reconnoitered
the area, about which he knew very little. He placed men where he believed Barkley's men would land and set up ambushes along several roads
leading into the town. Of course, these measures "reduced our number in
town greatly," making a full-throated defense of the waterfront quite difficult. Many of the elite remained neutral or supported the British and made
their way to the interior. Others made their way from the interior, including many Congregationalists from Midway. The Midway Congregational
Church, founded in the mid-1750s, reported in early March that their attendance had been greatly affected by the crisis. "Few met," they reported, because "this province [is] in a state of alarm, and the major part of the men of
this district [are] at Savannah," about thirty-five miles northeast.[61] As these
preparations were under way, the British made their move. H.M.S. *Cherokee*
led a flotilla of armed vessels and transports up the river, stopping about two
and a half miles from the town, where, according to McIntosh, the rebels
"sank a hulk in the channel of the river" opposite to the Brewton plantation.
Here McIntosh stationed Colonel Archibald Bulloch and 150 men with orders to prevent a British landing.[62]

The Council of Safety reconvened in the first days of March. It acted
quickly, allowing only certain vessels to depart the harbor, ordering the rigging and rudders removed from all others, and requesting an appraisal of
the property of "friends of America" so that remuneration could be made
from the Continental Congress. Lastly, the council made a dire decision. If
defeat seemed imminent, council members would burn the town and destroy all shipping in the harbor "so that the minions of the King would find
themselves in possession, not of a town, but a heap of smoldering ruins." A
meeting of rebel property holders unanimously approved this ominous measure.[63] Likely aware of these circumstances, Captain Barkley acted.

The British commander accompanied H.M.S. *Hinchinbrook* and H.M.S.
*St. John* up the Savannah. To protect the town, McIntosh sent three hundred
men and three cannons to Yamacraw Bluff, a small village about a thousand

feet upriver. Barkley, however, was not gunning for Savannah: he wanted the rice boats at the northern tip of Hutchinson Island. He landed a few men on the South Carolina side of the island, out of sight of Savannah. His troops crossed the swampy marshes and boarded the boats. Fortunately for the British, the orders to remove the rigging and rudders had not yet been carried out. The next morning, however, rebel captain Joseph Rice made his way to the ships and was "without any noise, or the smallest knowledge of us, kidnapped," said William Ewan (sometimes McEwan), president of the rebel provincial congress. With no sense of irony, the rebels complained that the taking of their rice boats could "not be justified upon any principle whatsoever."[64] In retaliation, Wright wrote, the rebels "seized upon" several Loyalists, including Anthony Stokes and Josiah Tattnall. Additionally, the rebels "scalp't" a British marine. With each passing day, cried Wright, "things . . . are growing worse," and there was no assistance in sight.[65] Savannahians of all persuasions felt the gravity of the situation. "All the women, children, and valuable effects are removed from Savannah," a correspondent wrote, "which is filled with armed men, who live there in the true livery stile, breaking into stores and knocking in the heades of the rum punches."[66]

A few hours later, two additional British ships sought to make their way to the northern tip of Hutchinson Island, where they could protect the recently commandeered rice boats as they made their way back down the river. Unfortunately, problematic river currents delayed the British ships several hours. About this time, McIntosh heard that the British had taken the rice boats and captured Captain Rice and his men. To confirm the report, McIntosh sent two unarmed men to confer with the British. Ewan later wrote that "contrary to all principles which cement society and govern mankind," these men were also taken prisoner. The rebels responded, according to Ewan, by firing two four-pounders "directly into them."[67] A smattering of fire continued from both sides for several hours. McIntosh later wrote that the news of the capture of Captain Rice "inflamed" the rebel militia, and they directed their ire at those "who had treacherously joined the enemy"—the Loyalists.[68] Lacking the resources to fully assault the British as they desired, the rebels made another attempt to negotiate the prisoners' release. Failing on this front, they decided to scorch as many British vessels as possible.[69]

The rebels' first attempt on this front failed, as their fireship proved too large and ran aground. The rebels then dispatched a torched sloop, with some success. The sloop ignited two of the rice boats, but the British ships and remaining American boats made it out of harm's way.[70] Although the ships made their escape, several soldiers were left behind and, according to one contemporary, fled across the marshes "in a laughable manner."[71] The British then used a "channel never known before" to pick up their remaining troops and make off with sixteen hundred barrels of rice.[72] Of those, over one-quarter were owned by Governor Wright, who made sure to bill the Board of Trade for the provisions.[73] Before long, however, the two sides agreed to a ceasefire. McIntosh acknowledged that the rebels had lost "two white men killed and one Indian wounded slightly," while the British acknowledged six wounded. McIntosh, however, dubiously claimed, "They must have many [more] both killed and wounded."[74]

Following the cessation of martial hostilities, the rebel Council of Safety ordered several members of the Governor's Council to be imprisoned. The Council of Safety hoped these men could be used in a prisoner exchange for those held by the British. But the governor himself sailed away aboard H.M.S. *Scarborough* a few days later. The military postmortem of the so-called Battle of the Rice Boats was mixed for both sides. The British obtained the needed provisions but were unable to restore royal authority, if indeed that was ever their intention. The rebels, however, maintained control of the province and forced the governor to flee.[75]

During the month of March, both before and after the battle, Governor Wright attempted to conduct professional and private business from aboard the *Scarborough*, but the rebels quickly seized these messages.[76] An exasperated Wright informed Germain that the situation was "growing worse every hour," as the Loyalists are "in the greatest distress possible."[77] The governor knew personally whereof he spoke. On 26 March the rebels attempted to recapture him. Wright wrote that "an attempt was made on Tybee Island, where the Rebels expected to find me on shore, with several officers & gentlemen, but happily none were on shore. . . . [T]heir chief intention was to surprise me, and that they are much disappointed."[78] He also complained to Clinton that although approximately three-quarters of the Georgia militia had been loyal, "many have [changed their opinion] lately, some persuaded by others, some [persuaded by a supposed British plan] to raise an insurrection amongst the blacks, and some, say many, intimidated by threats of personal injuries, loss of property."[79] Thus, according to Wright, revolutionary decisions in Georgia rested upon three issues: personal pressure applied from friends and loved ones, the fear of a slave uprising, and/or local intimidation. Some of his own property, in fact, had been destroyed. Although the *Scarborough* secured the personal safety of the governor and his family, it proved unable to protect many of his personal effects and professional communications. The rebels destroyed a British vessel containing Wright's baggage in the Savannah River, which explains the dearth of his personal correspondence.[80]

## "The Prospect of Death"

The situation was indeed dire, necessitating the *Scarborough*'s embarkation for Massachusetts and other northern colonies, where the crew planned to deliver the seized rice. There is no extant correspondence that reveals Wright's personal thoughts as he and his family fled Georgia, but he likely felt much the same way as Governor Thomas Hutchinson did when he made a similar departure from Massachusetts in 1774. Exhausted and forlorn, Hutchinson admitted that "five years constant scene of anxiety would weary a firmer mind than mine."[81] Generally speaking, oceanic travel was a cause of intense anxiety, especially for someone like Wright, who had lost a wife and three daughters at sea. "The prospect of death," wrote Presbyterian minister Samuel Davies, "strikes me with a shuddering horror." Such prospects intensified during the revolution. Bostonian William Cheever bemoaned that his "mind [was] filled with the thoughts of leaving my home . . . at this most dangerous warlike season, when not only death and the sea perched on one hand, but the cruill enemy stands ready on the other."[82] Wright, like his Bostonian counterpart, faced, in Thomas Hutchinson's words, an unbearable "mixture of improper, unnatural sentiments and reasoning, rude and indecent language, sophistical and fallacious reasonings and evasions, oblique allusions . . . below [even] the dignity of Robin Hood or even a schoolboy."[83]

More than indecent language awaited Wright. Three weeks later, while en route to Nova Scotia in April, the rebels engaged the *Scarborough* in battle at Goat Island, near Newport, Rhode Island.[84] Though Wright was physically unscathed, the howl of gunfire hissing overhead must have made him fear for his life and that of his family. The *Scarborough* finally concluded its hazardous voyage when it docked at Halifax on 21 April.[85] (Life for the ship got much worse four years later, when it was lost at sea during the Savanna-la-Mar hurricane in Jamaica.)[86] But in May 1776 Wright sailed for London via H.M.S. *Glasgow*, arriving on 7 June, according to Thomas Hutchinson.[87] Two weeks later, the men attended a king's levée, or formal reception, and then dined at William Knox's.[88] The Knox family home at Soho Square became a hub for American Loyalists, especially for his old friend Governor Wright.[89]

Georgia was the last of the thirteen mainland colonies to officially rebel, in no small part because of the "utmost endeavors" of Wright to "induce the inhabitants ... to continue in and adhere to their duty and allegiance to his Majesty."[90] He added that his colony failed to send delegates to the First Continental Congress, and, in a common refrain of his, "if we could have had or got any support or assistance we should [have] kept [Georgia] out of the rebellion."[91] Wright later wrote that Georgia "resisted the Rebellion for a long while, and for many months there were only twelve united states."[92] This is mostly true. Savannah in fact was the last of the major cities in the original thirteen colonies to receive news of the Declaration of Independence. Those Georgians that remained in the Lowcountry soon "interred" George III, solemnly declaring, "We therefore commit his political existence to the ground, corruption to corruption, tyranny to the grave, and oppression to eternal infamy."[93]

Back in London, Wright and Hutchinson, the two exiled governors, met numerous times during the next few years to discuss the situation in America.[94] From the outset, Wright, along with the other provincial officials, assailed the Board of Trade with incessant calls to shift the focus of the war southward. No official expressed himself perhaps more zealously than Wright, who, Hutchinson remarked, "speaks freely of past measures, and as freely" of his ideas for prosecuting the war. James Wright was no sycophant, and the ease with which he proffered suggestions triggered an agitated Germain to complain: "Sir James Wright can be of little use at present, his ideas of military operations are most extraordinary." To the point, Germain scoffed, Wright suggested an invasion of Georgia and the Carolinas employing the "assistance of all the Indians and only eleven thousand regular troops."[95] Wright had been Georgia's commander in chief for nearly fifteen years and quite successfully directed the colony's complex Native relations. He may have lacked a thorough understanding of military strategy, but he understood the situation in Georgia and the southern colonies better than any British minister. He also rightly gauged the pulse of many Georgians who were dissatisfied with the rebel government. These Loyalists, or would-be Loyalists, were significant in number and of great potential usefulness if properly supported, a case cogently argued by historian Jim Piecuch.[96] Germain thoroughly underappreciated Wright, often keeping him in the dark and rarely, if ever, seeking his advice.[97] But Wright persisted and proved, according to historian Ira Gruber, "particularly skillful in emphasizing the advantages of campaigning in the South."[98]

Wright penned a dramatic letter to Germain in February 1777, insisting that his ideas "flow[ed] from an honest zeal." Although there is little reason to doubt the genuine nature of Wright's agenda, his motives must have also been connected to his personal finances. The rebels had confiscated "523 Negro slaves" valued at £27,787 and nearly £11,000 of rice from his Lowcountry plantations.[99] Later, upon his return to power in 1779, he claimed to have retrieved only 323 of the enslaved. He purchased an additional thirty-seven and witnessed the birth of forty-eight more between 1779 and the end of the war. Additionally, the governor said that 3 percent of his enslaved died annually.[100] During the war, many of Wright's enslaved were "employed" by both the rebels and the Loyalists. Thomas Brown noted that the rebel "galleys are laying manned entirely with Governor Wright's Negroes."[101] The theft of human property was widespread in the revolutionary South, perpetrated by rebel and Loyalist alike.[102] Lord Germain would later instruct Wright that "too much care therefore cannot be taken to prevent the carrying out of the province, or the secreting, or otherwise purloining, any of those Negroes." Moreover, he wrote, "Good usage is not only what is due to them from humanity, but will be the most likely means to encourage others to seek the same asylum."[103]

Regardless of his mixed motives, the exiled governor argued that the issue of taxation and taxation alone was the casus belli, and he proffered many suggestions in the hopes of ending the crisis. To provide for a mutually beneficial and practical relationship between Great Britain and America, Wright suggested, the Crown must grant "a generous plan or constitution for America. . . . [Additionally], all past treasons and offense &c. shall be forgiven and buried in oblivion, and pardon granted to all persons whatsoever as to their lives, except certain persons. . . . In the future all taxes in America," he recommended, "shall be granted and levied in the respective colonies."[104] These were essentially restatements of his earlier suggestions and might have prevented war if they had been granted prior to the fighting at Lexington and Concord. These suggestions also predated the famous Carlisle Commission of 1778, a too-late British attempt to negotiate an end to the war by acceding to American demands long since passed.[105]

## Colonists Would Flock to the King's Standard

In the summer of 1777, Wright joined fellow exiles John Graham, Georgia's lieutenant governor, South Carolina governor Lord William Campbell, and William Bull, South Carolina's lieutenant governor, in sending a lengthy petition to Germain. They warned of the danger of delaying the shift of military operations southward, because the Loyalists there maintained their patriotism at their own peril. The men proffered two reasons for this strategic

shift in their thinking: the strength of southern loyalism and the importance of southern trade to the empire.[106] They argued that "from our long
residence" in the Lowcountry, "we are enabled to form a pretty clear opinion how ... to reduce [the rebels] to His Majesty's obedience." They insisted
that they had "every reason to believe" that colonists would flock to the king's
standard in "great numbers [if] a sufficient body of His Majesty's troops" appeared. They assured Germain that "we are well informed and persuaded,
that there are great divisions in those provinces, and that many still retain
their loyalty to their king." These people would "exert themselves" for His
Majesty "if protection could be afforded them, or [if] they *saw a certainty*
of relief and support at *hand*" [emphasis in the original]. Former Georgian
William Knox, now Germain's deputy, played an important role in the development of a southern strategy based on the exiles' suggestions. Knox was
their most direct link to the Board of Trade, so his support was significant. A
close friend of Knox, Wright also served as his attorney and plantation manager while Knox resided in London.[107] This important relationship no doubt
gave Wright's suggestions added weight. In fact, much of Wright's correspondence with Knox was unfiltered and not meant for the eyes of Germain
or the king. But southern exiles were not the only ones pushing this message.
Pennsylvania's Joseph Galloway testified before Parliament that "more than
four-fifths of Americans would prefer a union with Great Britain to independence." Thomas Hutchinson and Benjamin Thompson of Massachusetts
offered similar statements.[108]

But Germain, who was circumspect and wanted to avoid "being deceived
in our expectations," sought intelligence that might corroborate these sentiments. He sent South Carolina's former attorney general, James Simpson,
to investigate. Simpson discovered that "there are still too many amongst
[the Americans] who will use all their influence to prevent a restoration of
the public tranquility," but many were fatigued by the exigencies of war. Although he assured Germain that many held out hope for relief from the
British, their loyalty was connected to the protection the army could provide.
Thus, if the British could protect them from their neighbors, they preferred
British governance over independence. He also opined that "whenever the
King's Troops move to Carolina, they will be assisted, by very considerable
numbers."[109] Although there is much debate about the veracity of these
"considerable numbers," two important facts may corroborate them. First, in
1782 Georgia's rebel legislature disqualified 279 Loyalists. Second, in 1780 the
British government had only found 161 rebels to disqualify. Perhaps Simpson
and Wright were onto something.[110] Simpson's report was confusing and

perhaps contradictory, which should have been a warning to Germain, but the real flaw of Simpson's account was that he only interviewed those "people of the first fortune" and not a sampling from all classes. The preponderance of information garnered by Simpson, however, convinced Germain to proceed. In fact, according to historian Paul Smith, the anticipated strength of southern Loyalists was the "most important factor in the reorientation of British strategy."[111]

But Wright and the others warned the Board of Trade that reconquering Georgia and South Carolina would be no easy task. Those currently in power in the southern provinces who believed "their past behaviour has precluded any expectation of pardon, will strenuously endeavour to keep up the spirit of rebellion, and oppose any forces." Also, they emphasized both the importance of controlling the backcountry and the need to fully commit to the plan, as "no partial sufferings or temporary distresses, will induce the southern colonies to submit, and that nothing will do there but force." This was important. Wright fully believed that half measures would be of little service and that the British must wholly commit sufficient troops and monies to regain Loyalist support. Moreover, the exiles added that "we must observe that the Rebels in these provinces are becoming more powerfull every day," as they have offered "large tracts of land" to Virginians willing to come to Georgia and provide military assistance.[112] The displaced leaders were correct in their assessment of Loyalist numbers. If properly protected and deployed, the Loyalists could shift the course of the war.[113] The following July, Wright and Graham petitioned Germain. They insisted that at the very least Georgia should be subdued, even if it were not yet possible to also subjugate South Carolina.[114]

Governor Wright continued to badger Lord Germain. Writing from his home on Somerset Street, a few blocks from the Thames, Wright conveyed to Germain some interesting news from Georgia. Rebel brigadier general Lachlan McIntosh, "a great Rebel," had been confined in Georgia for killing Button Gwinnett, a Whig politician and signer of the Declaration of Independence, in a duel in one of Wright's meadows.[115] More importantly, Wright observed, the divisive nature of political affairs in the colony "seems to present a most favourable opportunity," as many people "may be disposed to return to their allegiance, especially if they had any assistance." Furthermore, Wright offered "to go out myself and join in the [reconquest of Georgia]."[116] Two months later, in December 1777, he expressed to Thomas Hutchinson the need for "more vigorous exertion" of British military power in the southern colonies.[117]

## "Prosecution of the War"

Wright met privately with the king a few months later, presumably to discuss his ideas concerning the conquest of Georgia. If this meeting was anything like Thomas Hutchinson's encounter four years prior, then Wright met with a sovereign who possessed great knowledge of Georgia and seemed desirous of learning as much as he could about every circumstance and rebel in the strife-ridden colony.[118] Concomitantly, and certainly in part because of the repeated entreaties of Loyalists like Governor Wright, Germain fully revived the southern strategy.[119] Aside from his lobbying efforts, Governor Wright penned a personal letter to Lord North in which he sought relief for his children. With the loss of most of his property upon his expulsion from Georgia, his family needed government assistance. Wright stated that his oldest son, twenty-seven-year-old James Wright Jr., possessed a "very liberal education, and [had] been brought up equal to his expectation." Describing an entitled young man, Wright wrote that his son was "totally unprovided for, and . . . thinks himself too old to have some introductory employment." His second son, Alexander, was married and had been quite well settled in South Carolina until the revolution. Now he lived in London and was "only in part provided for." For his third son, Charles, the governor had "purchased an ensign's commission in the 64th Regiment at Halifax" in May 1776. Such a commission would have cost Governor Wright around £900 sterling.[120] The now twenty-two-year-old Charles had been present "in all the attacks on Long Island and Peachs Hill, and Danbury, also in those in Pennsylvania, and is now with Gen. Howe at Philadelphia." As for his "two daughters," they had been "educated here, and have always lived suitable to my rank and character in life, and to their expectations from my Estate." In closing, Wright tugged on North's sentiments as both a father and a government man, trusting that His Lordship "will judge of the feelings of a man turned of 60, who has laboured hard in an intemperate climate for 40 years and after receiving with honor a fortune sufficient to provide handsomely for the support of his family, is totally deprived of it in this manner."[121] A few months later, the governor again wrote Lord North, seeking "any opening . . . for an employment" for his eldest son.[122]

In addition to being pressured by colonial officials, Germain was forced to recalculate his strategy after the rebel victory at Saratoga, New York, which led to the Franco-American Alliance of early 1778. The entry of France into the war required the British to rethink their priorities southward, toward

the more profitable southern and Caribbean colonies. This, in turn, necessitated a reallocation of forces. Germain dispatched a "Most Secret" letter
to Howe's successor, Lieutenant General Sir Henry Clinton, on 8 March
1778. In this important missive, he informed Clinton that he had been appointed commander in chief in America and outlined the plan for subduing
the southern colonies, which was partly based on the information and plans
provided by Wright and his Lowcountry compatriots. Germain told Clinton that the "power, reputation, and future welfare of this nation" depended
upon the results of the contest. He said that "so speedy & happy a termination of the war could not fail to give the greatest pleasure to the King."
While the king expected and sought a negotiated peace, he did "not think fit
to slacken any preparation." Germain assured Clinton that the king, Parliament, and the nation fully supported the "prosecution of the war" and suggested that although his forces would be presently reduced, Germain hoped
that reinforcements would soon be on their way. But the king insisted that
"the war must be prosecuted upon a different plan," and troops must be stationed to protect an array of American possessions from Nova Scotia to the
Caribbean, from the coast to the frontier.[123]

Eleven pages into this secret letter, Germain informed Clinton that "it is
the King's intention that an attack shall be made upon the southern colonies with a view to the conquest and possession of Georgia & South Carolina" because the Board of Trade had received "various reports" that represented the "distress of the inhabitants, and their general disposition to return
to their allegiance." Therefore, Germain continued, "it is the King's wish that
every means were employed to raise and embody the well affected inhabitants." Furthermore, Germain told Clinton that if the move south proved
successful, "the intention was to leave those to the northward to their own
feelings and make them suffer every distress which cutting off their supplies and blocking up their ports might occasion."[124] Thus, the reconquest
of Georgia was central to the board's plan. The military subjugation of the
province would afford Loyalists time to return to the British standard, after
which civil governance would be established. If successful, this plan would
form a blueprint and be used from South Carolina northward.[125] General
Clinton was skeptical of these plans, feeling that his forces were already
spread far too thin, but Germain was adamant.[126] Clinton also had others
warning him to place "no confidence in any of those loyal Americans near
you. Many are spies upon you, sending home what they know will please."[127]

Accordingly, an unenthusiastic Clinton assembled a force of British, German, and Loyalist troops under the leadership of Lieutenant Colonel Archibald Campbell of the Seventy-First Regiment of Foot (Fraser's Highlanders), whose primary directive was to possess Savannah. Clinton also gave Campbell, a twenty-one-year veteran in the army, a commission as civil governor of the province, though he was eager for Wright to return.[128] Commodore Hyde Parker would oversee their journey and command the naval forces. From East Florida, Brigadier General Augustine Prévost was ordered to march to Georgia and rendezvous with Campbell. Although as "brave as Caesar," Prévost came across as "very diffident" and without an "opinion of his own."[129] Campbell viewed him as a "worthy man" but "too old & inactive for this service."[130] Prévost himself may well have understood that his days of active campaigning had passed, because he had for many months sought to be relieved of his post. His replacement was on his way.[131]

Upon forming a junction with Campbell, Prévost was to then assume command of their combined forces. The rebels in Georgia had been warned of a possible invasion, but neither Major General Robert Howe of the Continental Army nor the rebel government seemed particularly concerned, even after a British deserter confirmed the previous intelligence.[132]

Rebel defenses had been bungled from start to finish. Neither Howe nor Georgia's local authorities—Governor John Houstoun and militia colonel George Walton—could (or would) coordinate their efforts. Campbell arrived at the entrance of the Savannah River on 23 December 1778 after an arduous six-week voyage from New York. A French volunteer for the rebels, Lieutenant Pierre Colomb, stated that "the sudden appearance of this fleet flew everyone into consternation." He added that a defense of the town seemed implausible "either through lack of courage or because more than half of them favored England [and] only 600 men could be found" to defend Savannah.[133] Here, a rebel confirmed Wright's argument: large numbers of Georgians favored Britain.

As for the British voyage itself, a Hessian officer in the convoy wrote that "trunks and portmanteaus were hurled helter-skelter, and every minute you had fear you would be thrown. . . . [T]he sea was composed of terrific mountains and valleys."[134] The city that was their objective rested on the sandy bluffs of the Savannah River. It was well-planned, laid out in a large rectangle, with straight streets intersecting in a grid. Many fine homes and busy shops lined the organized streets, which contrasted nicely with the verdant squares. The design of Savannah has been described as "the most original and brilliant plan of any American city before [Pierre] L'Enfant planned Washington, D.C." But the city's fortifications had become so dilapidated in the past few years that the rebel general Howe contemplated giving up Savannah entirely and retreating into the interior.[135]

## "By the Back Doors and Windows"

After surveying the ground as best he could, Campbell decided to disembark at Girardeau's plantation, a few miles from the city proper. The British landing began two days later, on the morning of 29 December. General Howe believed that the landing at Girardeau's was a simple feint, and he left only a single company of South Carolina Continentals of fewer than fifty men, who failed to adequately harass the British from nearby Brewton Hill. Campbell's men marched in battle formation from the plantation toward the South Carolinians, about six hundred yards and a forty-foot rise from their landing. To securely disembark their remaining troops and provisions, the British had to take the thinly guarded hill, just south of the town.

As the British approached, Campbell could not understand why the rebels had not more robustly defended the bluff. "Had the Rebels stationed four pieces of cannon on this bluff with 500 men," he wrote, "it is more than probable, they would have destroyed the greatest part of this division of our little army."[136] The rebels unleashed an ineffective volley as the British approached the buildings on Brewton Hill. Rather than return fire, the British advanced with great celerity, bayonets at the ready. This allowed them to maintain their momentum rather than getting bogged down in a firefight, and they took the field in less than five minutes as the "Rebels retreated with precipitation by the back doors and windows" of the buildings sitting atop the hill. General Howe held a quick council of war, where it was decided that a full retreat should be a last resort. The rebels would stand and fight.[137]

Meanwhile, with the British safely ensconced atop the bluff, their remaining troops landed. The disembarkation, however, took nearly six hours, leaving the rebels with a second opportunity to harass the British. But again, the rebels lacked any initiative and made no attempt to counterattack or pester the landing troops in any way whatsoever. The British began their march toward the city around noon, arriving at one of Governor Wright's former plantations two hours later and discovering that Howe had established a very strong defensive position near the plantation. A slave found on the Wright plantation, later identified as Quamino—sometimes referred to as Quash—Dolly, led "the troops without artillery through the swamp" upon the rebels down a path that rebel colonel George Walton had often frequented "with young ladies, picking jessamines."[138] Campbell ordered Captain Sir James Baird's Light Infantry Corps to follow his new guide around the British rear and through a narrow swampy path to the American flank, while the rest of the British troops kept the rebels' attention focused on a possible frontal attack.

Again, Howe proved negligent. He failed to post pickets on his right rear flank at the exact spot where Quamino Dolly led the British. Without forewarning, Baird's corps descended upon Howe's unsuspecting troops, signaling to Campbell to advance his own units. Now realizing his predicament, Howe immediately ordered a retreat. It was too late. British forces advanced with an unbridled intensity, and many of the rebels simply dropped their firearms and fled. According to Campbell, "Their retreat was rapid beyond conception."[139] George Walton, a signer of the Declaration of Independence and a constant thorn in Wright's side, was shot from his horse, taking a bullet in the thigh. Fortunately for Walton, his British captors never discerned that he had signed that traitorous document.[140] Mordecai Sheftall and his son tried to make their escape across Musgrove Creek, but the water was too high, and the son could not swim, and they were forced to surrender. One of the officers they encountered called them "poor, deluded wretches" and could not fathom how they could follow their so-called leaders. Sheftall's unrecorded reply so angered the officer that he placed Sheftall "to be confined amongst the drunken soldiers and Negroes, where [he] suffered a great deal of abuse."[141] Governor Wright would have likely agreed with this decision. The Sheftalls were members of Savannah's Jewish community, and Wright referred to Jews as "violent rebels and pursecutors of the King's Loyal subjects."[142]

After the fighting ended, Campbell's bounty included the capture of 38 officers, 415 noncommissioned officers and privates, 48 cannons, and significant quantities of provisions and war matériel, along with the city of Savannah. "In short," Campbell wrote, "the capital of Georgia [and] the shipping in the harbour [are] in our possession." In addition, he wrote, eighty-three rebels were "found dead" and eleven were wounded. British losses totaled twelve.[143] Campbell then issued a proclamation that promised protection to all loyal subjects. His arrival prompted Jacob Bühler to emerge from the woods, where he had been hiding from the rebels for two years, and join Campbell's forces.[144] Importantly, and discouraging to the Loyalists, he added that loyalty would be solely based on future, not past, actions. In a move designed to animate Loyalists, Campbell encouraged them to report "ringleaders of sedition" to British headquarters.[145] Such mixed signals would cost the British in the future. This British tendency toward lenity, excepting certain commanders, such as Lieutenant Colonel Banastre "Bloody Ban" Tarleton, resulted in the alienation of Loyalists.

The British commander then adopted a rebel policy from 1775 by promising to "expose to the rigors of war" all who would not sign the loyalty oath. What about the promise to look only at future actions? Campbell believed Georgians received his proclamation "with every demonstration of joy." It actually received mixed results, and it forced Georgians into one camp or another. Of course, hindsight provides much more clarity. In the moment, Campbell saw much of what he wanted to see, and his vision was aided by the arrival of "many Loyalists" from Augusta. So he moved forward with his plan. He informed Prévost of his plan to complete the subjugation of Georgia by moving to Augusta, the province's backcountry seat. In a few short days, Campbell boasted, he planned to become the "first officer . . . to take a stripe and star from the rebel flag of Congress."[146] Doing so would have been a personal coup of sorts. Campbell had earlier endured hellish conditions in a rebel prison, and he had described the "shameful and unprecedented barbarity" of his captors.[147]

Campbell's success in Savannah was welcome news to the British. New York Loyalist Peter Van Schaack wrote that the "affair in Georgia have given new life and spirits to the friends of administration."[148] In a letter to General Clinton, Captain John Jervis wrote, "Your coup in Georgia . . . [has] preserved the nation from despair and the ministry from perdition. There never was a thing more well timed as the Georgia business."[149] Consequently, the fall of Savannah worried some rebels. From Paris, Edmund Jennings informed John Adams that Campbell sought reinforcements from Clinton. "They do not mean to stay in Georgia," he opined, "but will plunder and leave it."[150] Rebel leader Lachlan McIntosh confirmed Jennings's fears: "The whole state of Georgia, & every farthin of property I have in the world are in the possession of the enemy."[151] Prévost approved Campbell's plan to march on Augusta, and off he went.[152]

It took Campbell leading one thousand of his troops about a week to traverse the frontier roads from Savannah to Augusta.[153] An energetic crowd of supporters greeted their arrival, and Campbell soon received the loyalty oaths of about fourteen hundred men, who were soon formed into twenty militia companies. But these men, according to a British engineer, could provide "no real substantial services . . . [because they were primarily] Crackers, whose promises are often like their boasts."[154] Campbell agreed: the Crackers were a "race of men whose motions were too voluntary to be under restraint, and whose scouting disposition is a quest of pillage."[155] Both statements reflected Wright's own sentiments. Following his defeat at Savannah, General Howe had fled across the river into the camp of Continental major general Benjamin Lincoln, who had assumed command in September 1778. Thus, Campbell failed in one of his top priorities, which had been to prevent the rebels' communication with South Carolina.

On the other hand, Lincoln primarily sought to prevent Campbell from winning the hearts and minds of Georgians as well as from reconnecting with Native leaders. Lincoln had much to fear on this second front. A union between the British and the Indians could prove catastrophic to the rebel cause. Indian superintendent John Stuart promised imperial authorities that they could rely upon the cooperation of the Creeks and Cherokees. Fearful of just such an alliance, South Carolinians forced Stuart to flee into East Florida and held his property as security, confined his wife and daughter to their home, and arrested his son-in-law for aiding his escape.[156] His family later wrote that the "fury of a merciless and ungovernable mob" had forced his flight.[157] The next month, while in Savannah, Wright encouraged Stuart to "take steps for the security of [his] person."[158] Stuart took his advice and, according to Florida governor Patrick Tonyn, "narrowly escaped [the rebels'] fury."[159]

While Germain seemed to have no reservations about using the Indians (not the enslaved) against the rebels, Clinton was again unenthusiastic. Ultimately, this lack of unified strategy would minimize the utility of Natives in the Southeast, but that did not seem to matter in the moment.[160] Campbell wrote that within the "space of ten days, [I] settled the frontier of Georgia in a state of tranquility" and closed "all the avenues leading from South Carolina."[161] He had not.

## "Rented Allegiance"

Within a few weeks, Georgia's rebels had rebounded from the loss of Savannah and begun to organize themselves, which included promising relief and protection for any who swore allegiance to their cause. These must have been terribly complicated and contingent times for Georgians. They felt tugged by the British on one side and by the rebels on the other, and the intensity of these factors constantly varied, especially once the two sides began offering land or seemed more capable of protecting settlers' property.[162] Many loyalties also veered according to which army commanded the neighborhood in question. Survival was paramount. A South Carolina rebel, Brigadier General William Moultrie, noted that people on the frontier were "waiting to see the event between the two armies."[163] Wright correctly estimated the extent of Loyalist support (or American disaffection) with the rebel government, but he misjudged the Loyalists' willingness to commit.

By and large, American Loyalists remained loyal only insofar as the British could protect them. General Charles Cornwallis complained that they were "dastardly and pusillanimous" and grumbled that giving them weapons is simply "throwing away good arms."[164] He especially held Lieutenant Colonel Thomas Brown and Governor Wright's son James in contempt. Cornwallis particularly disagreed with their methods of raising troops and of dealing with prisoners, even though their procedures were like those used by the rebel militia.[165] Cornwallis himself suffered from a widespread problem in the British civil and military command. As a rule, the British failed to understand the numbers of soldiers required to fully prosecute the war, they failed to properly establish rule in regained territories, and they failed to comprehend the intensity of the civil war in America, especially in the southern provinces.[166] James Wright leveled these same criticisms both during and after the war. Historian Andrew Jackson O'Shaughnessy referred to the supposed temperamental loyalty in the South as "rented allegiance."[167] There is good reason for this. Unlike General Cornwallis, who bemoaned the efforts of the Loyalist militia, General Francis, Lord Rawdon, understood that the primary reason for the failure of Loyalists to flock to the British standard "was the atrocious cruelties exercised upon them whenever they fell into the hands of the Rebel militia, cruelties so great that they exceed all belief."[168] "The poor proscribed Tories," former royal governor of New York Cadwallader Colden wrote in 1775, "are hunted and worried like beasts of prey."[169] Such temporary allegiances, however, existed on both sides. For example, a man Wright had known for twenty years signed the rebel oath, but according to Wright, the rebels "never considered him as one of their party" and declared him a "loyal subject."[170] And during a vicious civil war, it is easy to understand the necessity of riding the fence. One historian characterized the civil war in Georgia as a "fratricidal conflict characterized by ruthlessness and undisguised brutality."[171] Another stated that he "was not prepared [to encounter the depth of] the violence and savagery of the partisan warfare" in the Lowcountry. Additionally, he wrote, "The patriotic gore written by contemporaries depicting the brutish villainy of the Tories I had more or less dismissed as gross exaggerations. It was not. What was exaggerated was the purity and nobility of our patriotic ancestors . . . [who] were every bit as vengeful as their enemies."[172] For this reason, rebel officer William Moultrie opined that "what was called a 'Georgia parole' and to be shot down were synonymous."[173]

In the backcountry, rebel militia colonels Elijah Clarke, John Twiggs, and John Dooly began assembling considerable forces. Their presence and growing numbers convinced many people to reconsider the British loyalty oaths they had just taken.[174] Additionally, Brigadier General John Ashe of the Continental Army crossed the Savannah River with more than a thousand North Carolina troops. Campbell overestimated Ashe's strength and withdrew from Augusta on 14 February. The Loyalists felt wholly betrayed by this decision, and their fear of abandonment by the British would shape the nature of this conflict, especially because "many of the Prisoners taken ... are treated with a severity by no means justifyable."[175] One cried that the British evacuation "left the poor Loyalists exposed to the Fury of the Rebel army."[176] Historian Martha Condray Searcy succinctly summed up the situation. Even though "British expectations [of widespread Loyalist support] seemed perfectly plausible ... they left their sympathizers ... with no defense but themselves.... [Actions like this] gave some Loyalists ... clear evidence that they could not depend on the British government for protection."[177]

But Campbell, hoping to return to Britain, did not simply leave the backcountry without any British presence. He left the younger brother of General Prévost, Lieutenant Colonel Mark James Prévost, in command and suggested that he should attempt to strike at Ashe's flank if the opportunity arose. At the same time, about 112 miles away, Georgians Dooly and Clarke joined forces with South Carolina militia colonel Andrew Pickens. These militiamen chased several hundred Loyalists from North and South Carolina. The Loyalists were led by Colonel John Boyd and were attempting to reach the British army, which they thought still held Augusta. Many of Boyd's men had joined this march reluctantly or under threats, and they deserted in droves.

The rebels led their men to victory over Boyd's remaining Loyalists at Kettle Creek, northwest of Augusta. Boyd fell, mortally wounded.[178] In less than a month after Campbell wrote about the subjugation of the province, the rebels had forced him from Augusta and defeated a nearby Loyalist force. Worse yet for the British was the treatment of Loyalist prisoners by the rebels. Colonel Andrew Pickens carried them to South Carolina and put them on trial for treason. He made an example of their leaders and hanged five men. The backcountry inhabitants learned a painful lesson about the

cost of Loyalism.[179] General Clinton later complained that Campbell's journey to Augusta had needlessly angered the rebels, and at what cost?[180]

Over the next few weeks, Lieutenant Colonel Prévost ascertained Ashe's
true numbers and decided to take Campbell's suggestion to surprise the
North Carolinian. Prévost quietly led a small expeditionary force toward the
confluence of the Savannah River and Briar Creek, but they were discovered
by John Ross's South Carolina light horsemen. Prévost learned from a few
prisoners that the rebels were "trusting much to their superiority in numbers, [and] were in the utmost perfect security." Perhaps this overconfidence
was the reason Ross never informed Ashe that a body of British troops lay
nearby, or perhaps it was a reflection of the widespread discontent between
Ross and Ashe and in fact within all of Ashe's command. His men were
low on rations and exhausted from long marches. Several had mutinied, and
many simply longed to return home.[181]

On the afternoon of 3 March 1779, after a long trek to outflank the American opposition, Lieutenant Colonel Prévost's combined British and Loyalist forces approached Ashe's contingent of North Carolina and Georgia
Continentals and sundry militiamen at Briar Creek.[182] Ashe had been thoroughly surprised by their arrival. In fact, his first warning of an attack was
the appearance of his panicked pickets fleeing pell-mell toward his camp.
In addition to being ill-prepared, the rebels were also ill-equipped. Their
cartridges were distributed too late and often did not match the caliber of
their weapon. Recognizing the disorder in the rebel ranks, Prévost ordered
an immediate assault. Within minutes, British forces overwhelmed the rebels. Many of the rebels panicked and fled through the nearby swamps or attempted to cross the healthy-sized Briar Creek. One British soldier related
that "many were swallowed up by the one and drowned in the other."[183] Colonel Samuel Elbert, who had long been a thorn in Wright's side, and his
Georgia Continentals were the last to fall. All eighty of them were either
killed or captured. In a letter to North Carolina's governor, General Ashe
simply stated: "Things here wear a melancholy appearance."[184] This bloody
battle, in which the rebels suffered 30 percent casualties while inflicting just
1 percent on the British forces, guaranteed British hegemony of Georgia's
coast and left the frontier in an uncomfortable and contested state of flux.[185]
And James Wright sought a return to this?

Unaware of the preparations at Whitehall, Wright spent the second half
of 1778 fraternizing with London's most important players, undoubtedly discussing the issue most dear to him—Georgia. His "calling card list" included,

among others, William Pitt, 1st Earl of Chatham, John Stuart, 3rd Earl of
Bute, George Germain, Jeffery Amherst, Thomas Gage, Thomas Hutchinson, Sir William Howe, and John James Percival, 3rd Earl of Egmont. Additionally, he maintained consistent contact with John Murray, 4th Earl of
Dunmore and royal governor of Virginia, William Campbell, royal governor of South Carolina, and Josiah Martin, royal governor of North Carolina, all exiled in London.[186] Campbell's victory in Savannah and Prévost's
triumph in the Georgia backcountry in the early spring of 1779 would prove
to be of monumental importance for Wright.[187] "The feeble resistance" of
those in the Lowcountry, Lord Germain wrote to Clinton, provided "in-
dubitable proof of the disposition of the inhabitants to support the Rebel
government."[188]

In January 1779 and prior to learning of Campbell's successful campaign
in Savannah, Wright presented a petition to Germain from Georgia's Loyalists, "praying that their property, especially their Negroes, [will] not be damaged by British forces in Georgia."[189] This issue would have likely been the
most important personal issue Wright faced during his exile, since his human property comprised such a substantial part of his estate. According to
historian Benjamin Quarles, Georgia "was the scene of the most widespread
seizure of British-held blacks."[190] Meanwhile, Campbell urged Germain to
send a governor to Georgia with all speed.[191] It is unclear exactly when
Wright learned that the province had been restored to the Crown, but on 27
February he outlined the triumph to Hutchinson. Wright did not, however,
mention a possible return to America.[192]

The extant evidence indicates that while Germain prepared to exploit
Campbell's triumph, he had not bothered to consult the man who best understood Georgia's colonists. Wright clearly was in the dark and received
information from the secretary on a purely need-to-know basis, which occurred abruptly on 8 March when Germain ordered him to "prepare to return to Georgia" aboard H.M.S. *Experiment*, commanded by Commodore
James Wallace, who would soon marry into Wright's family.[193] Earlier in
the war, Wallace had an opportunity to destroy Newport, Rhode Island, but
"spare[d] the town from attack" in exchange for provisions.[194] Rather quickly,
however, Germain began to question his decision. In a letter to his secretary, William Knox, he expressed his "doubt whether [Wright] is equal to
the undertaking of governing a province under the circumstances of Georgia."[195] On that point, Germain may have been correct, but only in the sense
that no one might be equal to that challenge. With France in the war, Britain's resources were now stretched beyond its capabilities. It is difficult to as-

certain exactly why, but Germain clearly had little respect for Wright's abilities, despite his many letters that commended Wright's management of the province. Additionally, the rebels understood Wright's skill. In her impressive multivolume history of the war, Mercy Otis Warren wrote that "the influence of Sir James Wright . . . prevented that state" from early joining the revolutionary movement.[196]

## "Possession of the Provinces Themselves"

Despite Germain's nagging concerns, preparations were made for the governor's return, both personally and professionally.[197] Personally, Wright worried about his finances upon returning to Georgia. As a Crown official, he would be expected to be a man of sufficient means. He had lost nearly £80,000 sterling in 1776. Although some of his losses had been recovered following Campbell's victory, Wright believed himself to be destitute. "Therefore," he cried in a letter to member of Parliament John Robinson, "let me entreat you, for Godsake, . . . to do something for me" as a representative of the king.[198] Before the war, Wright estimated that his total net income had approached £8,000 per year.[199]

Professionally, Germain painted for Wright a glowing portrait of the situation in Georgia, promising that nothing would be "wanting to complete the public tranquility but the declaration of His Majesty's commissioners putting it at the peace of the King."[200] Was Germain overconfident, wishful, deceitful, or just naive? Benjamin Franklin and James Madison provided a much more accurate assessment of the situation. Writing from his compound in a posh Parisian neighborhood, Franklin scoffed at Britain's "possession of the capitals of five provinces" because Americans still maintained "possession of the provinces themselves." Madison surmised that Georgians "have been sorely infested with [the British army] for the greatest part of a year, and will no doubt cooperate [with the rebels], by the most decisive exertions."[201] Prior to his departure, Wright was given a lengthy list of instructions and suggestions. Despite his reservations and critical assessment of Wright's ability, Germain told the governor that his "knowledge of the temper and disposition" of Georgians would be indispensable in determining the exact course of action. Most important, perhaps, was that Germain's instructions heeded many of the suggestions Wright had repeatedly given during his exile.[202]

James Wright now prepared to return to Georgia, his home for most of his adult life. Emotions and memories must have overwhelmed him as he contemplated this next journey. He had experienced tremendous growth during his time in Georgia; he had reached the pinnacle of power in colonial America; he had become wealthy beyond his imagination; he had made many friends and connections; and he had experienced great pain and sorrow during these years. His wife and three daughters died during his time as governor; he had negotiated, with varying success, several imperial crises; he had been shot at and arrested; and he had fled in the middle of the night to the safety of a British man-of-war. He now would make another transatlantic voyage with the daunting task of restoring a rebellious colony to the king's standard.[203]

# CHAPTER 7

# A Governor Redeemed?

## "Sir James, You Are Hurt, You Bleed Profusely!"

In the late spring of 1779, James Wright embarked on a figurative and literal sea of difficulties. Shortly after departing the British coast, Commodore James Wallace encountered several French vessels in the choppy English Channel waters and impetuously chased these ships into Cancale Bay in the northwest corner of France. He urged Wright below deck to look after his daughters, but the governor refused. He insisted that he be allowed to remain on deck and aid in the vessel's defense. In so doing, he found himself in the thick of a firefight, with the hiss of balls overhead and the popping of cracking beams all around. At one point Wallace stated, "That ball must have come very near, for I felt it on my face." Moments later, Wallace noticed blood running down Wright's face and onto his clothes and said, "Sir James, you are hurt, you bleed profusely!" Wright reluctantly retired below, where his daughters tended to his wounds.[1]

The Wrights finally reached Savannah on 14 July. Historian Leslie Hall convincingly argued that Wright "firmly established British rule," being the only man to reestablish civil government in America. She proffered seven compelling reasons British rule "very nearly succeeded." Parliament provided an annual stipend to the province. Under British rule, the local economy would be based on the pound sterling, and local troops would be paid with official specie and, thus, spend it in Georgia. Wright's government was unified, whereas the rebel government was rife with faction. While Georgia's rebels failed to consistently cooperate with Continental forces, Wright always worked in cohesion with the British military, even when their efforts frustrated him. Wright aided backcountry and Lowcountry refugees. Lastly and concomitantly, he helped Georgians rebuild their lives.[2]

After arriving, Wright quickly discovered that Germain's rosy appraisal of the situation had been grossly inaccurate. In fact, Major General Augustine Prévost informed General Clinton that the rebels had taken a position to "make us jealous for Georgia," and Wright soon described Georgia's situation as "wretched."[3] Georgia's Loyalists tried to help Wright by copying the Massachusetts Sons of Liberty and formed their own version of the Minutemen.[4] Governor Wright reinstated civilian control of the government but worried that "things are not as pleasing here as I hoped. I expect Rebel movement against us in October." He also concurred with Prévost. Britain's foothold in Georgia was tenuous, and the "Rebels are very busy in keeping up the expiring flame of Rebellion." In what had been an incessant cry before the war and intensified during it, Wright argued that more troops were necessary for the defense and maintenance of the colony. To that effect, he encouraged General Clinton to "make an early movement this way."[5]

Clinton understood the importance of Wright's request, informing Germain that he would sail southward in October, but with Charleston on his mind rather than Savannah. He believed that if "we do not conquer South Carolina everything is to be apprehended for Georgia." Wright's assessment of Georgia's political climate grew gloomier by the day. His reports sounded much like those of 1775 and 1776, and he became convinced that the colony would soon be "totally lost" because the army had abandoned Georgia by carrying operations into South Carolina, leaving the backcountry Loyalists "skulking about to avoid the Rebel parties."[6] Prévost's raid into South Carolina in the spring of 1779, however, was only temporary, and by summer most of the British troops had returned to their positions in and around Savannah. The governor was not opposed to hyperbole as a means of emphasizing his needs.

But Wright would soon have more pressing concerns than the Georgia backcountry. On 16 August, just one week after he sought Clinton's prompt assistance, French vice admiral Charles Hector, comte d'Estaing, embarked from Cape François in the West Indies and set sail for America for what he thought would be a relatively minor engagement on the Georgia coast. D'Estaing was a devoted officer, a fearless warrior, and incredibly ambitious. South Carolinian Thomas Pinckney declared him to be "as brave as Julius Caesar."[7] But he believed this expedition to be a "cruel task" that had been "irrevocably imposed [on him] by national honor and by an irresistible train of events."[8] Two weeks later he opened discussions with Continental army general Benjamin Lincoln concerning a joint venture in the southern theater.

Wright himself learned on 3 September that what was believed to be some "Cork Victuallers" (provision ships from Cork, Ireland) was actually part of d'Estaing's fleet. Captain John Henry of H.M.S. *Fowey* confirmed the identity of the vessels the next day. These were moments of intense anxiety in Savannah. On the fifth, Prévost rushed two messages to Lieutenant Colonel John Maitland, who had been left to garrison Beaufort, South Carolina, ordering him to remain there but to prepare to quickly move toward Savannah upon a moment's notice.[9] Maitland, a "gallant" officer, was "so beloved" by his Highland troops that they would have gone anywhere for him with the "greatest alacrity."[10]

Word of the French arrival off the coast of Georgia spread through the Lowcountry with incredible celerity and served as a catalyst for both Loyalist and rebel alike, initiating a new terrible, atrocity-filled, internecine civil war in the Lowcountry. Rebel general William Moultrie of South Carolina regretted his inability to participate and to have "shared the glory" but soon anticipated hearing the "joyful news of the surrender of Savannah."[11] "His Majesty's well-affected subjects," wrote royal chief justice Anthony Stokes, "rushed to Savannah's defense. Likewise scores of Rebels" who had recently taken the royal loyalty oath "descended upon Savannah like a swarm of locusts, wreaking havoc all the way" in anticipation of a swift rebel victory.[12] "Accept my most hearty and sincere congratulations upon the new and glorious face of our affairs," wrote rebel George Walton just days before allied forces stormed Savannah. He bemoaned his absence from the field "while the liberty & independence of my country are about to be restored."[13]

News of d'Estaing's arrival also reverberated throughout the Atlantic. Common wisdom indicated that the Franco-American Alliance would soon triumph in Georgia and quickly convert that victory into something much greater. A correspondent of Benjamin Franklin expressed optimism in d'Estaing's ability to render the "most essential services to the common cause." The prospects of victory in Georgia, he said, were "almost certain." James Madison wrote that the impending victory at Savannah "will thoroughly cure [the British] of their rapacious zeal for the rich & flourishing metropolis of S. Carolina." He added that "it will be a great disappointment to me I confess if any of them escape."[14]

The Continental Congress prematurely set aside a "day of public and solemn thanksgiving to Almighty God" for returning Georgia to her rightful owners. Former president of the congress, Henry Laurens, confidently informed George Washington that "every body [was] in full prospect of repossessing Savanna & having the British general[,] his troops & the *wrong governor Sir James Wright* [his former close friend] prisoners of war within a week." But this was not simply bluster or overconfidence. Hessian chaplain Johann Waldeck (the Hessians were German allies of the British) reported that d'Estaing's arrival spelled doom for the combined British forces in Georgia. "Everything is going amiss," he cried, "and this affair will end as it did for Burgoyne's army."[15] These were bleak days indeed for James Wright.

General Prévost correctly speculated that d'Estaing "cannot, I should think, venture to continue long in their present exposed situation, on this coast, at this season of the year." Upon his arrival, d'Estaing informed the Americans that it would be "criminal" if he remained on land more than eight days.[16] As it turned out, the count's six-week stay proved deadly for his seamen, who lacked provisions. One nearly mutinous sailor maintained a deep-seated anger toward d'Estaing. "The ambitious vice-admiral," he wrote, "is advised of the condition of the men and the ships but he seems to have absolutely no regard for them. Of all the scourges which plague the poor human race an ambitious master of its fate is the worse."[17]

## "A War about Slavery, If Not a War over Slavery"

On 6 September, with d'Estaing hovering over Savannah like a vulture, Wright ordered all capable citizens to send thirty "negroes" apiece to aid Captain James Moncrief and his engineers in fortifying the town. In all, about a thousand Blacks were "employed" during the siege. It was not the first time the British employed Blacks in His Majesty's service in Georgia, and they would continue to exploit Blacks as guides, couriers, and laborers throughout the conflict. In addition to the menial chores involved in constructing fortifications, the British employed "some armed negroes" as soldiers, including about two hundred garrisoned on Hutchinson Island. One such combatant, Scipio Handley, escaped from Charleston in 1775, volunteered to serve with the British while in Barbados, and participated in the defense of Savannah, receiving a musket ball in the leg for his service. He later received twenty pounds in compensation.[18]

Governor Wright later expressed his great pride that his enslaved left their new rebel owners to return to him. If so, they returned to a life of enslavement, both during and after the revolution, as did many others who flocked to the British standard.[19] In the spring of 1780, Georgia and South Carolina militia under Colonels John Twiggs and Andrew Pickens raided British-controlled areas of Georgia and fought a company of armed slaves on one of Wright's plantations. Five dozen enslaved, with two white overseers, fought for the right to remain on Wright's plantation and against white "Liberty men" determined to sell them as plunder. Their motivations could be many, and it is impossible to tell what compelled each to fight. Most plausible is the desire to maintain the life they currently knew and to avoid being separated from home and family.[20] Historian Alan Gilbert has written that "visions of victory motivated black fighters" on both sides of the contest as they fought for self-determination.[21]

Unsurprisingly, not all Savannahians were comfortable with arming the enslaved. During those tense fall weeks of 1779, nearly two dozen residents petitioned the Governor's Council, complaining that a "number of slaves appear in arms and behave [wi]th great insolence . . . [and] commit great outrages and plunder in and about the town." Two months later, the "grand jurors" of Savannah presented an additional grievance, upset by the "great numbers of Negroes, that are suffered to stroll about, both in town and country, many with fire-arms and other offensive weapons, committing robberies and other enormities, to the great terror and annoyance of the inhabitants."[22] In fact, this issue had been raised by the Governor's Council shortly after he returned from England. Their records indicated that "Negroes have run away from their masters . . . in South Carolina [and] taken shelter in this province." Others, they claimed, had "run away from their owners in this province" and are causing great "evil [and] it becomes absolutely necessary that some vigorous exertions be made" to control them.[23] While white Savannahians had problems with Blacks, Blacks held Savannah in contempt, at least according to the famous enslaved man Olaudah Equiano, who would later write one of the most important slave narratives. Free Blacks, he wrote, "live in constant alarm for their liberty, which is but nominal, for they are universally insulted and plundered without the possibility of redress." Thus, when Equiano "took [his] final leave of Georgia . . . [he] determined never more to revisit it."[24]

Back on 30 June, General Clinton had issued the Philipsburg Proclamation, granting refuge to any enslaved persons who reached British lines. Slave labor would build (and later defend) the fortifications around Savannah.[25] Hessian captain Johann Ewald observed that "three hundred Negroes [whose labor Wright had secured] had to work head-over-heels" in a frantic effort to bolster the town's defenses. The Reverend John Joachim Zubly, a zealous defender of American liberties and former Continental Congress member, observed that "few men have suffered more from the Rebels" than the enslaved. In a letter to Wright, he added: "During the siege eight or more of my slaves were constantly in arms, for which I would not expect any pay[,] but wish that something by way of encouragement as they have risk'd their lives might be allowed to themselves." He apparently did not consider their freedom an appropriate "encouragement."[26]

The rhetoric of the American Revolution compelled many Lowcountry slaves to seek their independence either by pursuing safety within British lines or by escaping outright. Rather than passively praying that freedom would be bestowed upon them by their grateful enslavers, they often seized liberty, at great risk. Historian Douglas Egerton correctly noted that rebel militias "regarded black guerillas as runaways and slave rebels, rather than as legitimate enemy combatants [and] often resorted to summary execution of those captured." In *Three Peoples, One King,* Jim Piecuch persuasively argued that African Americans, "driven by their desire for freedom . . . refused to remain idle during the struggle."[27] William Prince claimed to have been born a free man but "was cheated out of his freedom and sold to an American in Georgia." As the British arrived in 1778, his enslaver "ordered [him] to fight against the English," but he ran away and joined them. In doing so, "he gained his liberty."[28] In fact, according to Sylvia Frey, "actual or potential resistance [by the enslaved] was a main factor in the development of Britain's southern strategy." This, however, created something of a "rallying cry" for the rebels and made the American Revolution in the South "a war about slavery, if not a war over slavery."[29] Gary Nash declared the American Revolution to be the "largest slave uprising" in American history as Blacks discovered the "power of the revolutionary ideology of protest." In fact, as many as one-third of Georgia's enslaved flocked to the British lines during the siege, and according to historian Maya Jasanoff, "almost all of the five thousand enslaved blacks in Savannah would [ultimately] leave." So many enslaved fled their plantations that the price for a "seasoned Negro" in the region rose from forty pounds to eighty-five pounds during the war. Although neither the rebels nor the British officially offered outright emancipation to slaves for their service, Lowcountry Blacks had become quite adept at negotiating the "terms" of their servitude. Also, there was an implicit understanding within the British military command that the enslaved who assisted them might be considered free from bondage. Accordingly, many of the enslaved sought to take advantage of the Revolutionary War to further their own plans for independence.[30]

The actions of the enslaved and formerly enslaved in Georgia's Lowcountry doubtless served as a critical episode in the ongoing negotiation between owner and owned—what Ira Berlin termed the master/slave "minuet." He characterized this "revolutionary generation" of slavery as remarkably fluid and diverse, in large measure a response to the republican rhetoric of the age. Although the behaviors of "insolent" slaves unquestionably expanded Black liberty, they also curtailed it by provoking the reactionary reinforcement of the plantation system.[31]

The mass exodus of the enslaved required deft handling on the part of both British military officials and James Wright. He observed "several thousand" Blacks in Savannah, many of whom had fled their enslavers or "had been captured by the King's army and brought in." The presence of so many restless Blacks caused great anxiety to Savannah's white population. Aware that the situation "was of the utmost importance and consequence," especially since the "mischief has greatly increased and seems to be a growing evil," Wright believed in the need for "vigorous exertions" to find equitable solutions. Although he and the Council promptly responded to such concerns, the situation was infinitely complex and required creative and flexible solutions. "Captured Negroes belonging to loyal subjects," the Council determined, should be restored to their masters "at a future and proper time." Chattel belonging to the rebels could "in due time . . . be legally confiscated and forfeited to His Majesty to be applied to such uses as he may be graciously pleased to direct." In the interim, however, a commission would be established "to take under their care and management" all such slaves, but they agreed to leave the management of those "captured by the army" to General Prévost. Lastly, a decision was made that a "strong and convenient house or prison be provided" as a detention center for "all such Negroes as may prove unruly."[32]

There were also about two hundred enslaved in possession of the Indians at Savannah, a situation that caused the civil government great consternation. Wright believed that Native enslavers in town could have "very serious and dangerous consequences," so he attempted to purchase them, even bringing "several head men to his own house." The Natives were uninterested. The headmen insisted that Prévost had assured them that "whatever plunder they got should be their own." Alas, Wright resolved, "It is not in [my] power to do anything with respect to those Negroes."[33]

## "To Make Reprisals and to Retaliate"

Wright had other concerns besides the influx of Black people into the city. As the French fleet filtered into the harbor, d'Estaing ordered Count Albert de Rions to trap Lieutenant Colonel Maitland's force at Beaufort, South Carolina. Such a trap would greatly weaken British chances of holding Savannah. "I fain hope we are not in much danger," Prévost wrote to General Clinton, "if we are fortunate enough to get our detachment from Beaufort."[34] Meanwhile, the true danger that confronted Wright and Georgia's Loyalists shifted from the theoretical to the actual when a Lieutenant Whitworth was dispatched to New York on 7 September 1779 to inform Clinton of the situation. The French quickly intercepted his vessel and forced him back up the Savannah River. The next morning, a Wednesday, brought more bad news when Wright was awakened from a restless slumber with news that the French fleet had increased to forty-two ships. "It is astonishing to me," he wrote East Florida governor Patrick Tonyn, "that such a formidable fleet should come on this coast, likely with plans to reduce our provinces."[35] More astonishing was the news that his friend Robert Baillie had been captured by the French during their landing and disembarkation near the Orphan House. He was later exchanged after the siege had been lifted.[36]

Defending Savannah proved to be no easy task for at least two reasons. First, as one soldier reported, the heat and humidity were "so severe" that "malignant fevers" were all too common. One participant cried that "during the day we were exposed to the most intense heat."[37] A Hessian officer asserted that this was the reason why only the poor stayed in Savannah during the summer.[38] Another officer complained about the "great heat and the amount of sand flies . . . snakes and crocodiles."[39] Second, the British, like their rebel counterparts the previous year, failed to adequately prepare for an invasion. Prévost "did nothing more for his defense against the Rebels," Hessian officer Johann Ewald wrote, "than have the four old redoubts repaired and construct several new ones for support." He added: "On every occasion during this war one can observe the thoughtlessness, negligence, and contempt of the English toward their foe." According to Wright, thirteen redoubts and fifteen artillery batteries were soon raised throughout the town.[40] That said, Savannah also possessed significant natural defensive barriers. The rice fields, marshes, drainage ditches, and streams could impede movement and amplify the strength of the defensive positions that tied into them. The sandy soil absorbed artillery shot and was easily repaired. Also, the Savannah River itself was an effective defense if one controlled it.[41]

As the British awaited Maitland's hopeful arrival, there was deep concern about whether the town could be saved. The *Gazette* summed up the general feeling: "To all thoughtful persons," his safe arrival from Beaufort seems "more and more doubtful." General Prévost and Governor Wright echoed those doleful sentiments. Prévost expressed dubious "hope that Colonel Maitland will be here this day," 8 September.[42] Wright feared that "if we do not hear something of [Maitland] today I shall be in great pain."[43]

"Great pain," indeed! Chief Justice Stokes complained of allied threats of "bloody menaces" awaiting the Loyalists.[44] British lieutenant colonel John Harris Cruger insisted that the rebels "talk'd of nothing but putting all to the sword."[45] This idea that no quarter would be offered put fear in every Loyalist heart and may help explain the nature of the ensuing conflict.[46] Georgia's rebel chief justice, John Glen, echoed these sentiments when a Loyalist expressed hope that the rebels would be lenient with them. Glen replied that "it was not now a time to use gentle & moderate measures, but to make reprisals and to retaliate."[47]

The pulse around the city accelerated as the French made a descent on 9 September and discovered that the British fort on Tybee Island at the entrance of the Savannah River had been evacuated. Prévost hurriedly sent out dispatches ordering every British post to retire to Savannah posthaste, even though he was not yet convinced Savannah was in true danger.[48] He needed all the British regulars he could procure because he had lost some faith in the Loyalists. While acknowledging the importance of the southern provinces, he articulated a deep concern about the utility of provincials in this campaign. "North American troops are unequal to the task of defending the southern colonies . . . [because of] their despondency whenever attacked."[49] Concomitantly, d'Estaing began assembling his troops for debarkation.[50] Within short order, Cruger's command from the port of Sunbury arrived in Savannah, and the nature of the conflict changed dramatically for Wright when a flag of truce from John Wereat, president of the rebel executive council of Georgia, arrived, seeking "to treat an exchange of prisoners and to claim" Wright as their prisoner. Although nothing came of this request, Wright certainly understood that less than a successful defense of Savannah stood between him and either a rebel prison or the gallows.[51]

Meanwhile, General Lincoln began the Continental army's descent upon Savannah at the same time as Polish volunteer Brigadier General Casimir Pulaski led an advanced scouting party across the Savannah River near Ebenezer, about twenty-four miles northwest of the capital. A disgruntled Pulaski complained that "nothing less than my honour . . . retains me in a service, which ill treatment makes me begin to abhor."[52] The remaining rebel force crossed the river the next day, 12 September. Later that day, Maitland hastily set out for Savannah via an inland waterway "with an intent to push through Skull Creek, and join General Prévost in Savannah."[53] Had Lincoln posted a man-of-war at that creek's mouth, he likely would have captured Maitland. In fact, the rebels had previously intercepted a Prévost communication at this exact spot. But Lincoln blamed the French for the failure, arguing that they had agreed to "block up the enemy in Port Royal."[54] Independent of any promises, d'Estaing said he ordered Albert de Rions to complete this task, but de Rions said the Charleston River pilot refused to help. Moreover, d'Estaing insisted it was the Americans who were supposed to prevent the junction with Maitland from reaching Savannah.[55] In any event, a failure to block Maitland could prove costly to the allies, because if they had been able to prevent Maitland's troops "from getting into [Savannah]," a rebel claimed, the Loyalists "would have capitulated without firing a gun."[56]

Regardless, General Lincoln was certain that the British would ultimately surrender. "My tranquil colleague," d'Estaing wrote, "happy in his imperturbable tranquility, entertained no doubts" that Prévost would surrender after the "first bomb [was] thrown into the city." Moreover, d'Estaing complained, Lincoln had already begun haggling over the expected distribution of British and Loyalist prisoners.[57] Young Joe Habersham shared Lincoln's boundless confidence. "Most people are of opinion," he wrote to his wife, "that the enemy will capitulate after 24 hours bombarding as their honour will oblige them to hold out til that takes place."[58] In late September, Joseph Clay expressed a similar sentiment: "We . . . expect we shall be able to carry the place in a very few days."[59] James Wright began to feel his world shrink.

As Maitland departed Beaufort, d'Estaing led his troops in a night landing at the hauntingly beautiful Beaulieu plantation on the Vernon River, about fourteen miles south of Savannah. D'Estaing chose Beaulieu upon the recommendation of former Savannahian Philip Minis, who said it was the "best place for landing, on account of its facilities both for disembarking and for forming any number of troops."[60] In d'Estaing's estimation, however, Minis had "very badly chosen" this spot, because "a post of a hundred men would probably have repulsed us."[61] Fortunately for the French, no such post existed.

The lack of resistance at the landing filled d'Estaing with great confidence. "I am at the moment of persuading myself," he journaled, "that the resistance of Savannah will be very feeble." Lieutenant Meyronnet de Saint-Marc of the French navy quoted d'Estaing as telling an aide: "I am convinced that if we march right on the city sword in hand, we will take it in spite of our small number." General Lincoln concurred. "There can hardly be a doubt," he wrote, "but if the British were closed in by the French and American troops they would be forced to surrender immediately."[62] Even Dr. Alexander Garden, a Loyalist, agreed that "the only deliberation was how to render submission as little disgraceful as possible."[63] Prévost himself expressed great concern about the strength of the allied forces. "We are not afraid of any of them," he said, "but both together may be too many for us."[64]

As it were, "Foul weather" delayed d'Estaing's landing, according to an anonymous French journal, and it was not until 18 September that the allies reached the outskirts of Savannah. Although some would later criticize d'Estaing for his cautious approach, the diarist dismissed criticisms of d'Estaing's delayed approach as having only been raised "after the event." Rebel general Lachlan McIntosh joined Lincoln's force the next day, bringing the aggregate American force to fifteen hundred. After learning on 15 September that French forces were on land and moving toward the city, General Lincoln hastened his own march and reached Cherokee Hill, about ten miles distant from the town.[65]

Once at Savannah and "convinced that . . . resistance would be very weak," d'Estaing wasted no time in making his intentions known. He initiated what would become a six-letter exchange with Prévost, beginning with a summons for surrender. The rebels were incensed that the count had assumed such a dominant position within the alliance. Wright wrote that in the summons, the Frenchman "boasted of his formidable armament by sea and land . . . and that it was totally in vain to think of opposing or resisting his force." Prévost politely replied that he "delayed to answer till [he] had shown" the summons to Governor Wright and because he could not in good conscience surrender his post without receiving official terms. Although "sensible" of the need for the British to discuss terms, d'Estaing complained that the British had used the twenty-four-hour truce he granted them to continue "intrenching yourself. It is a matter of very little importance," he continued, "however, for form's sake, I must desire that you desist during our conferences." D'Estaing then ordered his since-halted column to resume its march, but "without [actually] approaching [the British] posts." In a postscript, he notified Prévost that General Benjamin Lincoln would soon form a junction with his forces.[66] Two Black deserters soon reported to the British that General Benjamin Lincoln had formed that junction. Georgia's Black population quickly realized that their best opportunities for freedom generally rested in British hands.[67]

## "The Gallant Maitland Flew"

D'Estaing would soon regret his lack of urgency. At noon on 16 September, Maitland's battalion of the Seventy-First Highlanders, with the assistance of a Loyalist and some Gullah fishermen, hazarded "swamps, bogs, and creeks, which had never before been attempted but by bears, wolves, and runaway Negroes" to reach the safety of Prévost's defenses, augmenting his force by nearly seven hundred men. Although hyperbolic, the account given by Georgia Loyalist Samuel Douglass accurately recorded the difficulty of Maitland's journey. Douglass claimed to have aided in Maitland's safe arrival by loading some three hundred troops on his various boats.[68] A poem was later written about Maitland's exploits: "With rapid wings, but not before untried, from Beaufort's banks the gallant Maitland flew."[69] Their accomplishment was magnified by the fact that their leader suffered with "bilious fever," a malarial malady. More important than the obstacles Maitland faced was the fact that the French and the rebels failed to obstruct his advance, which d'Estaing lamented was "an unpardonable [and incalculably important] mistake," because Maitland's troops "were the ones the enemy always put in the fore, and they evinced the most audacity during the siege."[70]

Maitland's arrival caused the allies much consternation. D'Estaing and Lincoln observed from Brewton Hill as the last of Maitland's men streamed into town. "I have had the mortification," D'Estaing cried, "of seeing troops of the Beaufort garrison pass under my eyes."[71] A French participant, defending against criticism aimed primarily at d'Estaing for allowing Maitland to reach Savannah, sensibly noted that Prévost had been inclined to surrender after making a face-saving "apparent defense." This was quite common in eighteenth-century warfare, although granting the British twenty-four hours to deliberate had been quite generous of d'Estaing. Unfortunately for him, Maitland's arrival "changed all at once these pacific dispositions." Of this fact there is no doubt.[72]

Wright accurately expressed the sentiments of many within the town. Maitland's triumphant arrival, he said, brought "inexpressible joy to the whole army." Loyalist Elizabeth Lichtenstein Johnston stated that the arrival of Maitland's troops "raised the spirits of the people very much." One British officer stated that Maitland's arrival strengthened their forces and "made us . . . so very saucy."[73] At noon on 17 September, as Maitland's forces streamed into Savannah, Prévost held a council of war to determine their course of action. Maitland himself promised that anyone who "utters a syllable recommending surrender, makes me his decided enemy." He had worked to hard to come to the town's defenses to see it so meekly given away.[74] Wright and Lieutenant Governor John Graham were in attendance when, as the governor wrote, "it was unanimously decided to defend the town." Nineteenth-century historian Lorenzo Sabine made the claim that Wright's friends insisted it was the governor's determination that swayed the discussion. Moreover, they asserted, Wright had cast the deciding vote when the others were equally divided. There is no contemporary evidence to support this, and such councils were held to determine a sense of those involved rather than to be directly counted. That said, Wright clearly exerted himself to the fullest in arguing for a stand and, according to Graham, "behaved with more zeal for [the] King's service" than any "man could."[75] In his account, Captain Moncrief stated that a "member of the Council [suggested that Wright] was prejudiced in favor of the defense of the place as he had great property in the province. Sir James declared . . . that he had rather see his whole property torn to pieces than so shameful a thing should be done as to surrender the town without fighting." There was likely truth in both statements. Wright certainly wanted to do everything to save his property, but he would have cared much more about defending the king's realm. He later told Germain that he had been "happy in being here at the time of the siege" and that his "King and Country . . . have every right to my best services & shall have them to the utmost of my power and abilities."[76] Thus, on 17 September, Prévost notified the count that after "having laid the whole correspondence before [Governor Wright] and the military officers of rank . . . , [it was] the unanimous determination . . . that though we cannot look upon our post as absolutely inexpungible, yet that it may and ought to be defended."[77] The decision to defend Savannah, Wright told Germain, "made me very happy as I had some strong reasons to apprehend & fear the contrary."[78] All of this, of course, had been made possible by Maitland's arrival.

In a letter to his family written shortly after the siege, Cruger boastfully admitted that the British had "nothing else in view but to steal time till we could be reinforced" by Maitland's men. Rebel General Henry Lee, the father of Robert E. Lee, argued that "any four hours before" Maitland's junction "was sufficient to have taken Savannah."[79] A French officer argued that there was little inclination to mount a serious defense of the town prior to Maitland's arrival but that a "brave officer had engaged them in a vigorous defense."[80] D'Estaing later regretted his generosity in granting a twenty-four-hour truce, realizing he had fallen victim to a painful "trick." In fact, he now worried about his chances of taking the town, but he believed he must stay and lay siege to Savannah lest he jeopardize France's alliance with the rebels, especially after Generals John Sullivan and Nathanael Greene had accused him of betrayal.[81] "London, America and even Paris," he wrote, "would have dishonored me," and the alliance was already strained.[82] But even so, one Hessian feared that "there was no hope that [our] troops could be saved in any way."[83] During the next few days and nights, the two sides busied themselves preparing for an assault. There was scattered and minimally offensive firing from both land and sea, and on 20 September Prévost ordered the sinking of several vessels in the channel in the vain hope of preventing French access to the town.

By 22 September the allies had completed the investment of Savannah, as the French had moved their camp just east of the Ogeechee Road and the rebels had moved to their left. Chief Justice Stokes feared that the allies "had entrenched themselves up to the chin." The first face-to-face encounter occurred that evening between an advanced British post and a French reconnaissance party, but an assault was not yet forthcoming. D'Estaing continued with his preparations, inching ever closer to Prévost's forces. In the morning hours of 24 September, Prévost dispatched Major Colin Graham on a sortie to both reconnoiter the enemy and "draw them exposed to our cannon." This scheme exceeded the general's expectations. Although forced to pull back, Graham inflicted significant casualties on the French. Wright wrote in his journal that the French "were much galled by our cannon and the fire of musquetry & lost we were informed 84 killed & about 100 wounded."[84] Many of those French soldiers were the Haitian and Caribbean volunteers in d'Estaing's army, whose rearguard action made an allied escape possible.[85]

That same day, Wright again experienced the personal nature of the rebellion. At 8:30 that evening, near Hilton Head Island, the French vessel *Le Sagitaire* captured the *Experiment*, captained by Wright's son-in-law, James Wallace. The ship carried two of Wright's daughters, Anne ("a young lady of great beauty and merit") and Isabella. Demasted during a hurricane and wobbling to the South Carolina coast, Wallace's ship proved easy prey for the French. His state of mind may also have aided the French, at least according to Henry Remsen, an American merchant and member of the Continental Congress who mocked the captain for being "so drunk that he did not destroy the dispatches, orders, and code of signals." Wallace was later court-martialed for his actions but "honourably acquitted." In fact, he was later "highly complimented [by the king] on his late meritorious behaviour."[86]

That said, the French did obtain the payroll for the British forces in Georgia as well as a bevy of supplies. This loss was a severe check to the British cause, as one Hessian bemoaned: "The naval hero, who has captured ships

and thereby created such an impressive fortune, Sir James Wallace, is reportedly captured with the ship [but] surely sold his capture at a high price."
Fortunately, Wallace and his new bride, Anne, were released on parole on 6
February 1780. It is unclear when exactly Wright learned of his daughter's
capture, but a Charleston paper announced the capture on 1 October. This
must have been an immeasurably trying time for the governor. Two of his
daughters had endured a naval battle and had been captured by the French,
and his son Major James Wright was stationed inside the town's defenses,
while another son, Charles, was with Clinton's army.[87]

The allies' initial bombardment of the besieged city began on 25 September 1779. Prévost and Moncrief responded two days later by demolishing and
then converting the British barracks located in the middle of their line into a
sturdy breastwork. That very day, the French blundered into a British patrol
they mistakenly assumed to be merely an engineering party. The rising ca-
sualty toll endured by the French up to this point, as well as the various de-
lays in both the landing of their force and subsequent forward actions, began causing a stir within the French camp.[88]

## "Savannah Was at One Time Deplorable"

The allies increased the frequency and ferocity of their bombardment of Savannah as September rolled into October. On 29 September, rebel general
McIntosh requested that his family, along with the other women and children within the city, be allowed safe conduct from Savannah, and for good
reason: "There was not a single spot where the women and children could
be put in safety," according to the royal chief justice. Elizabeth Lichtenstein
Johnston later mentioned that she darted about the town seeking safety and
ducked her head with each explosion, "as if that could save me."[89] Regardless
of their safety, General Prévost denied the request, likely feeling that would
afford the allies fewer inhibitions when attacking.

A few days later, on 2 October, the allies "kept up a continual firing upon
the town for a whole day," according to Cruger, "doing no other mischief
than breaking some windows and frightening the women and children."
Wright reported that from 11:30 p.m. to 1:30 a.m., a total of 123 shells "were
thrown into every part of the town, but without doing any material damage." Justice Stokes provided a much fuller and more vivid description of this
attack in a letter to his wife. He said that "while the women and children
were asleep, the French opened a battery of nine mortars, and kept up a very
heavy bombardment for an hour and a half," forcing "a number of gentle-

men" to the relative safety of Yamacraw Bluff, where, in fact, the royal government had erected a holding pen for the enslaved. "In short," he confided, "Savannah was at one time deplorable."[90]

At daylight on 4 October, the French began a daylong salvo, resulting again in little damage. According to Prévost, other than "killing a few helpless women and children and some few Negroes and horses in the town and on the common," there was no real damage to report.[91] Many Georgia Loyalists filed compensation claims for the loss of their human property during the siege.[92] Even though the damage may have been minimal according to military authorities, Wright described the assault as "most furious and incessa[nt]," resulting "only in the deaths of the daughter of Mrs. Thompson and a Mr. Pollard."[93] George Washington had described the psychoemotional impact of his New York campaign, and Wright's description implies that the impact must have been similar in Georgia. "When the men-of-war passed up river," Washington wrote, "the shrieks and cries" of the children and women were "truly distressing."[94]

Lieutenant Colonel Cruger stated that during this attack the French began throwing carcasses, or incendiary shells, into the town, which "only burnt 2 houses. Their shells, tho perpetually flying, did little or no damage, but their shott greatly injured the town; scarcely a house has escaped, [and] several are irreparable." Another Loyalist defiantly wrote in her memoir nearly sixty years later that though the French "hope was by incessant fire to burn the town and force a surrender, a merciful God protected us." Not everyone, however, had been spared, and the damage was by no means minimal. No fewer than eleven Blacks were killed this day, four of whom were huddled in Lieutenant Governor John Graham's wine cellar. Seven more burned to death in a fire near the church.[95]

Major T. W. Moore said the cannonade was "one of the most tremendous firings I have ever heard."[96] Stokes found his home directly in the line of and eventually burned by French fire, and he took flight for the safety of Yamacraw. "When I got to the common and heard the whistling of a shot or shell," he wrote, "I fell on my face." He picked himself up in the middle of the night and finally reached "an encampment made by Governor Wright's negroes . . . and it being dark I fell down into a trench which they had dug."[97] The firing only stopped, according to Meyronney de Saint-Marc, when d'Estaing feared he would run out of ammunition. Colonel Luis-Marie de Noailles, however, proffered a different reason. He said that the French naval cannoneers had mistakenly been plied with rum rather than beer that evening, and they tended to fire with "more vivacity than precision."[98] Savannah was subject to an excess of a thousand shells over the course of the next five days that "shook the ground."[99]

The allies, according to rebel major John Jones, expected to begin the cannonade in the predawn hours of 3 October, but there was a delay. But Jones held out hope that the British "will think it prudent to surrender" soon. If not, he feared, then "many valuable lives must be lost in taking the town by storm."[100] The next day he informed his wife that the bombardment had begun at midnight, "a sight that I would not miss seeing." He expected the shelling to last for two days, after which "I hope Savannah will have surrendered. I feel most sincerely for the poor women and children; God only knows what will become of them." Although he prayed for a British capitulation following the bombardment, he was "now of the opinion the enemy will make a very vigorous and desperate defence, and it is more than probable that we shall be driven to the disagreeable necessity of storming."[101] A few days later, on 7 October, Major Jones complained that the "enemy still continue very obstinate, and a more cruel war could never exist than this. The poor women and children have suffered beyond description." Many were "put to death" by the bombardment, and others were "killed in their beds," including one "poor woman, with her infant in her arms." Although the allies' incessant firing had burned "only one house," he expected that "this night the whole [town] will be in flames."[102] Mary Jones sent at least two replies to her husband during these tense days. "I would to God the great affair was over," she cried. She added that although she knew he would act bravely, she implored him to "not run rashly into danger, if you can avoid it. Consider you have two dear children and a wife whose whole happiness depends on yours."[103] With two sons for soldiers and two daughters in an allied prison, James Wright could empathize.

The civilian impact had not been confined simply to houses damaged by cannon shot. Savannah Loyalist Catherine Eirick petitioned General Prévost a few months after the battle. She said that the British army used her home as a hospital and promised to return the home in three weeks, "yet she has been kept out of it ever since, and never received any rent for it nor had she another place given to her to go to." Moreover, much of her extensive property had been torn down and utilized as firewood, while her animals and garden had been "taken or destroy'd," leaving her in "great distress."[104] In time, according to Elizabeth Lichtenstein Johnston, the cannon fire "gave us far less fear" than did the "appalling sound of the small arms." Moreover, she wrote, "the colored children got so used to the shells that they would run and cover them with sand, and as we were rather scarce of ammunition they would often pick up the spent balls and get for them seven-pence apiece."[105]

Seeking to escape the allied bombardment, Wright moved to Prévost's camp, pitching a tent next to Maitland's near the Spring Hill redoubt.[106] Interestingly, d'Estaing believed the area around the Spring Hill redoubt to be "the least fortified, the one where we ... [must] attack in force."[107] Wright retreated just in time, or so historians have believed. However, an early nineteenth-century newspaper article tells a different tale.

> In the siege of Savanna, by Count D'Estaing, in the year 1779, Sir James Wright was walking along what is called the Bluff, a high sandy bank of the river, during a violent cannonade, when he was struck down insensible by a double-headed shot which passed near him. He soon recovered his senses, nor was the smallest hurt, bruise, or impression of any kind to be perceived on any part of his body. On his becoming sensible, the first object that struck him was a woman standing over the body of her daughter, which the same shot had divided quite in two, about fifty yards before it passed Sir James. The mother and daughter had been standing in the door on the opposite side of their house from the French lines, the mother leaning on the daughter's shoulder, when the daughter dropped from under her arm, divided in two by the fatal shot. This was on the side of the town the most remote from the French lines; the shot must have passed through many objects, and was probably near exhausted when it passed Sir James Wright. Sir James was soon able to get under the Bluff, where he was safe till he could be conveyed home and felt no lasting consequences from the accident.[108]

## "Did Him High Honor and Credit"

On 5 October the allies continued their relentless shelling of the town. A Mrs. Lloyd's home, near the church, was burned. "Mrs. Laurie's house, on Broughton Street [one block north of Wright's residence]," was substantially damaged, resulting in the deaths of "two women and two children."[109] All told, according to Jean Rémy, the chevalier de Tarragon, "forty women or children of various colors" were killed during the siege.[110] The firing became so hot that on the sixth, Prévost sought permission from d'Estaing "to send women and children [including his own wife and children] out of town on board of ships, and down the river ... until the business should be decided."[111] Perhaps remembering the British general's refusal of McIntosh's earlier request, d'Estaing and Lincoln refused, reminding Prévost of his personal and sole responsibility "for the consequences of your obstinacy."[112]

The incessant cannonade destroyed the dwelling in which Chief Justice Stokes had stored his belongings. It also killed four of his enslaved, and four others were "so much scorched that they died in a few days."[113] Wright wrote that by 7 October, "most of the houses in town were much damaged by the shot" and the "cannonade & bombardment continued" throughout that day, burning another home, though "no body [had been] kill'd."[114] The conflict became even more personal for the governor when his son escaped a close call after French grape shot bombarded Major Wright's redoubt in the Trustees' Garden. According to Lieutenant Colonel Alured Clarke, Wright performed "with a degree of zeal that gave me great satisfaction, and that did him high honor and credit."[115] Unfortunately, though typically, the governor's account of this episode was of a purely professional nature. D'Estaing began another shelling around midnight.[116] D'Estaing himself had already had enough of this affair. He called "this strange siege" something of a "Penelope's web," meaning it never progressed. As the second week of October emerged, he realized his forces must finally "take sword in hand."[117]

After a heated council of war on 8 October, the allies resolved to attack the British lines the next day, focusing their energies primarily on the Spring Hill redoubt, where Wright had repositioned himself days before. David Hopkins, a rebel from South Carolina, hoped the end was near. The allies were "all in high spirits and determined for victory," he wrote, adding that "in a few days we shall have [the] town and every villain in it."[118]

The allies also planned to make a feint along the center of the British line. The previous week, on 2 October, General Prévost recorded his prescient expectation that the allies' strongest exertions would be made on the British right, and his preparations reflected that intuition. The combined forces against him took arms at midnight and began, in Governor Wright's words, "a bombardment which continued till the firing of the morning gun at daybreak." As the sun rose on that unseasonably chilly morning of 9 October, the allies began their march into "the valley of the shadow of death" at daybreak.[119]

As the allies began their descent upon Savannah, d'Estaing expressed deep concern over their prospect for success, saying "he had a very poor opinion of this attack." Many of his officers and men seemed to have a similar gut feeling. There were last-minute changes that morning as many regulars were quickly drafted into service to fill out depleted militia units. Many companies were to be led by new officers under whom the men had never before served. Many Americans also deserted on the evening of 8 October. Complicating the issues even more, some American guides leading the French troops out of their camp seemed to have no real geographical understanding of the ground. One such guide admitted that he "did not know the road and at the first shot disappeared."[120]

The ensuing battle on that "dark and foggy" morning was one of the bloodiest during the revolution, exceeded only by Bunker Hill in sustained casualties by one side. The invasion began with an allied predawn feint against the British right in the Trustees' Garden, where Governor Wright's son was stationed. According to the governor, this assault was repulsed by "Major Wright." D'Estaing's main assault, however, targeted the Ebenezer and Spring Hill redoubts, near the governor's tent, where the compact space of the battlefield rattled with the sound of muskets and the screams of the wounded. The French admiral personally led the assault on the Spring Hill redoubt and was in the thick of the melee from beginning to end. Wright wrote that this "attack was made with great spirit on the part of the French . . . [and] lasted 1½ hour."[121]

During the assault, Hessian lieutenant colonel Friedrich von Porbeck urged Prévost to order a sortie that helped thwart the allied advance at a critical juncture. The defenders met them with a merciless hail of musket and artillery fire that repulsed them, but only with great difficulty. Writing a couple of years later, Frenchman Pierre Charles L'Enfant admitted he had the "satisfaction to have been among troops who among the distresses of that unfortunate day, acquired as much glory as if they had been crowned with success." He told General Washington, "I say that never were greater proofs of true valour exhibited than at the assault at Savannah."[122]

After ninety severe minutes, Wright wrote, "the enemy were beat back & retreated with great precipitation." Ever the salesman, he stated that the day had been won in large part thanks to the "persevering resolution & bravery of the Loyalists." He also praised the work of the engineer, Captain Moncrief, "whose eminent services contributed vastly to our defence and safety." Before long, deserters, prisoners, and the wounded informed the besieged that the French had suffered terrible casualties. Among those, according to Wright, were d'Estaing, who "received a musket shot in his arm & another in his thigh, Count [Casimir Pulaski] a wound in the hip by a grape shot & since dead." D'Estaing wrote that "General Pulaski was mortally wounded because he got too close in order to exploit more promptly the pathway we were supposed to open for him. His death is an incalculable loss for the

American cause."[123] The *Royal Georgia Gazette* disagreed, suggesting that "no European power . . . would have employed him."[124] Another loss that was certainly felt across the Lowcountry was that of Major Jones. On the eve of the battle, he "staggered" his friends with his foreboding certainty that he would perish in the ensuing struggle. His fear proved warranted, as a "four pound ball" struck him dead.[125] His corpse was then tossed into a shallow burial pit until, reportedly, a friend recognized his hand protruding through the grave and provided him a more decent burial.[126]

Wright reported French losses at nearly one thousand "of the flower of their army." The rebels, he believed, suffered half that number. "It is astonishing to think," he wrote, "that in this attack we had only lost Capt. Tawes [actually, Lieutenant Thomas Tawse] & 7 privates kill'd and 14 wounded."[127] Tawse had been killed defending a parapet on the Spring Hill redoubt.[128] Historian Alexander Lawrence determined that the French actually suffered 11 officers killed and 34 wounded, with an additional 140 soldiers killed and 335 wounded. He estimated that the total rebel loss amounted to 21 officers killed and 16 more wounded and a count of 210 soldier casualties (with no differentiation between killed and wounded). The British losses, he suggested, were paltry by comparison: eighteen killed, of whom three were officers, and thirty-nine total wounded.[129] Major Moore, Prévost's aide, wrote that the postbattle scene was horrific. "The ditch was filled with dead," he wrote, and "many hung dead and wounded on the Abbatis," a makeshift impediment leading to a fort. D'Estaing had been stretchered to the Thunderbolt settlement, where he lamented to a surgeon, "I have a deep wound which is not in your power to cure."[130] While recovering from this wound, d'Estaing dined in Paris with John Adams, who served only a Bordeaux of the "very best quality."[131]

The battle also may have been the most ethnically and racially diverse of the Revolutionary War. Redcoats, Scottish Highlanders, Hessians, African slaves, Cherokee and Creek Natives, and Loyalists from Georgia, the Carolinas, New York, and New Jersey were led by a Swiss-born commander, and all fought under the British banner. Matching up against this foe were French grenadiers, American rebels, Irishmen, Polish hussars, Afro-Caribbean mulattos, and Black troops.[132]

The days following the battle witnessed sporadic artillery exchanges interrupted by the occasional flag of truce to collect the wounded and bury the dead, although, as Prévost wrote, many of the dead "were self-buried in the mud of the swamp." A French war council determined on 11 October that a retreat via Charleston should be their next move. Even so, Governor Wright and the British forces remained on high alert. "[F]rom ye 9th," Colonel Cruger wrote, "we continually expected a second attack from Monsieur, in hopes of recovering their lost reputation." But by the twelfth, it appeared that the French and the rebels were pulling back. Reports indicated that rebel militia "were daily going off in numbers," Wright noted, and that the French "seem'd now to fire from two pieces of cannon only."[133]

Many white Savannahians again expressed discomfort about the number of armed Blacks in the city. William Hanscomb of South Carolina led a group of two hundred armed slaves in protecting the city's perimeter. All told, more than six hundred Blacks temporarily served in the British lines during the siege. Many of them were wounded or died during the siege. All the while, white citizens complained that the armed Black men roamed the countryside, wreaking havoc.[134] Moreover, as the British garrisons within the city shrunk from disease and desertion, Blacks became increasingly important to the town's defense. The British army in Georgia even created the African American King of England's Soldiers unit. They served valiantly. As the British evacuated at the conclusion of the war, some four thousand Blacks, many in bondage, left with them.[135] Some of those troops engaged in a skirmish on 16 October when they engaged a rebel party on Lachlan McGillivray's plantation. On that same day, Wright recorded that the Haitian volunteers, a "French black & mullatoe brigade," prepared to embark for the West Indies.[136] The British counted about 200 "armed" Blacks in their lines, while the allies could count 156 soldiers from Port-au-Prince and an additional 545 "mulatto and blacks" from San Domingo.[137]

## "To Check the Spirit of Rebellion"

On 16 October 1779, the manager of Wright's Ogeechee plantation brought intelligence that the allies "were preparing for a retreat." Wright confirmed this two days later and confidently reported that the French had embarked from Causton's Bluff and headed down the river toward Tybee Island.[138] To celebrate this news, the governor proclaimed a day of public thanksgiving on 29 October. A few days later, the remnants of d'Estaing's fleet departed, and the count reached Brest on the northwest coast of France five weeks later. General Clinton explained the importance of Georgia to overall British strategy. "Should Georgia be lost," he wrote to Lord Germain in November, "I shall have little hope of recovering that province and also of reducing and arming South Carolina."[139] Moreover, a defeat at Savannah may have toppled Lord North's ministry.[140] The British repulse of the allies was indeed no small action.

Regarding this significant victory, Governor Wright wrote to Germain: "The southern parts of No. America I conceive are now in your Lordships power whereas had the French got footing here, I fear they wou'd have been lost."[141] Although Wright could revel in the fact that Savannah had been saved and, perhaps more important, that his son had escaped injury and even earned military laurels, his personal thanksgiving must have been tempered by the knowledge that James and Anne Wright Wallace were taken to France as prisoners of war. In a very sincere gesture, though, d'Estaing allowed Wright's other daughter, Isabella, to return to Savannah to be with her father. It seems plausible that the count also afforded Anne the same opportunity, but she preferred to stay with her new husband. In Wright's words: "Sir James Wallace being taken was an unfortunate affair. My daughter Bella was allowed by Count d'Estaing to come to me."[142]

These personal concerns would not, however, interfere with Wright's duty. Before the French had even departed, he began badgering Germain about the situation in Georgia and the need for additional support. On 6 November he wrote a lengthy missive to the American secretary, complaining of the tenuous nature of royal authority in Georgia and adding that Loyalists were in "very great distress." Furthermore, he wrote, "I am now, my lord, taking every step . . . to check the spirit of Rebellion by compelling all those" who should have but did not come to Savannah's defense to "give a very circumstantial account" of their behavior. Such a move likely drew the ire of those inclined toward neutrality as well as those who simply feared the violence of the moment. Three days later, his mood had changed, and he cheerily informed Germain that the rebels were in great disarray and that Charleston could be easily conquered—no wonder Wright endlessly frustrated Germain. Nonetheless, British success in Georgia and Wright's occasionally rosy portrait during the aftermath of the siege led to the Board of Trade's full support of the southern strategy. The British hoped the events of 1779 in Savannah would be the linchpin to victory.[143] "By the blessing of God," Wright would write, the French and rebels had been "totally defeated & routed by the united & spirited efforts of His Majesty's Troops & his loyal & faithful subjects."[144]

It would not be long before official word from Savannah would dominate correspondence on both sides of the Atlantic, initially reporting a rebel victory. The *Boston Gazette* reported on 1 November that allied forces had been successful in recapturing Georgia. Such conjecture was rampant. James Madison wrote from Williamsburg that "reports already begin to prevail that the British Army is in part if not wholly captivated." John Bondfield, a Quebec merchant then settled in Bordeaux, informed Benjamin Franklin of "very pleasing" intelligence that confirmed that d'Estaing had "destroyed the British armd [*sic*] vessels on the coast and made prisoners at Beaufort eight hundred soldiers." John Adams also mentioned in a letter to Franklin that he had received word from America confirming d'Estaing's success in Georgia.[145]

Facts slowly emerged from Savannah, and rebel responses to the events of 9 October vacillated between forlorn and cautiously optimistic. In early December Horace Walpole read about the ending of the siege in the *Extraordinary Gazette* but remained skeptical because "there seems to be a great hiatus in the authority."[146] Abigail Adams wrote to her husband about the "unfortunate" affair in Georgia. Two weeks later, their son wrote in his diary that d'Estaing had been "repulsed at Savannah" with considerable loss. John Adams himself proclaimed his "mortification" at the recent events in the southern states. But one correspondent of the American diplomats in France was more sanguine. Though he was "greatly disappointed" by the affair at Savannah, he did "not apprehend the effects so dreadful as painted. The English are weakened by their loss of stores[,] ships & men . . . and will thereby be prevented from attempting any thing material this winter." Even the typically dour John Adams suggested that "these small triumphs . . . [are] a poor compensation for the blood and the millions [the British] are annually wasting." Lieutenant Colonel John Laurens, the son of Wright's former friend Henry, responded in much the same manner. In a letter to his father, he confided that d'Estaing's "efforts though not entirely successful had been of some service, and his capture of [James Wallace's] *Experiment* [as well as] *Ariel* had lessened the number of infesters of the coast."[147]

In early November 1779 a thoroughly exhausted James Wright took a moment to reflect upon the past few months. "We have met with a very unexpected alarming scene," he wrote to Germain, as "no man could have thought or believed that a French Fleet . . . would have come to the coast of Georgia." The month-long siege proved an arduous trial indeed for the sixty-three-year-old governor. He was involved in the daily military discussions, found himself constantly exposed to enemy fire, endured the capture of his daughter by the French, experienced the uncertainty of having a son serving within the British lines, and had to deal with the prospects of losing his city, his freedom, and his life. Validation of Wright's important services during this ordeal may be found in a letter written by the chief engineer. Captain James Moncrief wrote that Governor Wright's "conduct and behavior . . . was of material importance, and that in the first instance he was very instrumental in saving the place, and that his behavior tended materially to confirm the minds of the wavering."[148]

## "Greatest Event Since the Beginning of the War"

The British and Loyalists responded to the successful lifting of the siege with unalloyed joy. Lieutenant Colonel Lewis V. Fuser held a celebratory ball in St. Augustine in honor of the victory. Royal chief justice Anthony Stokes praised the bravery of the militia and volunteers, insisting that their efforts during the siege "proves how well men will behave when they are fighting in a good cause."[149] On 6 November James Rivington's *Royal Gazette* in New York became the first pro-British paper outside of Savannah to report the news. In that issue the renowned poet Jonathan Odell began each of the twelve stanzas in his poem "The Congratulation" by poking fun at the rebels: "Joy to great Congress, joy an hundred fold / The grand cajolers are themselves cajol'd." Clinton effusively praised the events in Georgia and penned a letter to the duke of Newcastle, declaring the lifting of the siege to be the "greatest event since the beginning of the war." Word from Savannah reached British East Florida on 15 November, which, according to a Hessian chaplain, "suddenly raised the spirits of all the English" and "instilled in the people of Georgia a great confidence in our troops."[150]

News would not reach Britain until 20 December, and the response was euphoric. Playwrights galore appended their works to include laudatory lines of the recent triumph. The king ordered the firing of artillery at the Tower of London for the first time since the 1763 Treaty of Paris. He also opened the November 1780 session of Parliament by lauding the "signal successes which have attended the progress of my arms in the provinces of Georgia and Carolina, [which have been] gained with so much honour to the conduct and courage of my officers, and to the valour and intrepidity of my troops." Moreover, George III expressed his hope that these victories would bring the rebellion to a precipitous and "happy conclusion."[151]

A Scottish paper reported a "general illumination throughout the city and suburbs of Edinburg to celebrate the victory."[152] *Lloyd's Evening Post* printed a celebratory poem titled "British Arms Triumphant, on D'Estaing's Defeat at Savannah":

> Proud the Gallic Cock was grown
> But that pride is now come down
> British valour cuts his comb
> And drives the traitor bleeding home.[153]

A Paternoster Row newspaper also printed a congratulatory poem, "Punchinello to the King," which reveled in the British triumph:

> D'Estaing is again put to sea, Sir, Bibbity bobbety, bo
> Though like a French Dog, not content with his own
> He has carried off two of your Ships—and hid one
> But the Siege, G[od] be praised, Of Savannah is raised.[154]

Despite these loud proclamations and assertions of British might, historian Richard Cole points out that not all periodicals shared in the joy. London's *St. James's Chronicle* proffered a quite sobering ode:

> It is a mortifying reflection
> Amidst the sound of the tower and park guns
> And the peels [*sic*] from our steeples
> That our gain is only that we have not lost.[155]

However, the cheers were far louder than the jeers, and in mid-January Germain notified Wright that "His Majesty commands me to express to you his particular satisfaction in your firm and spirited conduct, and to assure you that he imputes much of the successful resistance made to the enemy to that ardor and resolution of which you have been the example." William Murray, 1st Earl of Mansfield, and General Prévost echoed these sentiments. Mansfield described Wright's "signal service . . . which every hour shews more & more the importance of the defense of Savannah. I hope you will live long to enjoy the fruits of public applause & gratitude." Prévost added that "Wright most cheerfully determined to fare as we might in every respect."[156] Whether one cheered or cried, perhaps the most important result of the British victory at Savannah was the continuation of the war and its human cost. Historian and biographer William Johnson opined a few decades later that an allied victory "would have saved oceans of blood."[157]

Historian George Clark put forth three explanations for the British victory at Savannah: the failure of the allies to prevent Maitland's Scottish Highlanders from reaching Prévost, d'Estaing's "unpardonable" delay in actually assaulting the city, and his "courteous, but ill-advised" truce. Hessian captain Johan Ewald echoed such sentiments, wondering what might have happened had d'Estaing only granted a two-hour truce rather than a full twenty-four. He concluded, however, that the British "had luck alone to thank [that] they repelled the enemy." A French participant, however, defended d'Estaing's decisions as having to be made without the benefit of hindsight. The foremost authority of the siege, Alexander Lawrence, agreed. In his 1951 *Storm over Savannah*, he opined that "America indeed owed Vice Admiral d'Estaing a great deal," and "if Mr. d'Estaing had been luckier his name would be as familiar in America as Lafayette's."[158] Perhaps.

Lafayette himself feared that the worst possible consequences would result from the allied defeat: "The miscarriage of our great preparations in Europe, the defeat at Savannah, . . . the total ruin of commerce, the devastation of the coastal cities [and] the very dangerous extension of British power in the southern states" could render the American cause a death blow: "Our aid [to them is now] almost indispensable."[159] The predictable finger-pointing began immediately. Although the irascible John Adams refrained from directly blaming the French for the defeat, he opined that "it has always been the deliberate intention and object of France, for purposes of their own, to encourage the continuation of the war in America, in hopes of exhausting the strength and resources" of both Britain and the United States. Adams may have had a point, but it would be odd for d'Estaing to sacrifice so many of his men and nearly himself to achieve that aim. Across the Atlantic, "a Loyal American" suggested that the French performance at the siege "was evidence of their plan to encircle the American colonies." In a sense, they may have been correct. A lengthy civil war would certainly bolster France's position both in Europe and globally. However, once the French were committed to a particular contest, anything less than a fully concerted effort would only serve to weaken the French Empire. That said, the severe loss in the Lowcountry gave both France and the rebels pause concerning future joint operations.[160]

A clear anti-American bias appeared in many postmortem analyses. Most British and French accounts of the battle held the rebels in contempt, and most rebel accounts failed to credit the Loyalists for their role in the victory. Wright also failed to acknowledge the valor of his local foes, even though he acknowledged that of the French. Stokes wrote that the "French behaved with great bravery . . . but they all accuse the Rebels of backwardness." Not all Frenchmen, however. Agathon Guynement, the chevalier de Kéralio, declared, "There had been [no] betrayal from the U.S.," adding, "they served us

and served well ... [and] all held with equal firmness [as] that of the troops
of the King." Meyronnet de Saint-Marc agreed. The Continental troops,
he said, "showed the greatest courage ... without wavering until they received" d'Estaing's order to retreat.[161] Years later, President George Washington toured the United States and spent several days in the Georgia Lowcountry. In the early evening hours of 14 May 1791, he visited the Spring
Hill redoubt and offered a diplomatic assessment of that fateful day. His diary entry that night indicated that many had solicited his opinion of the allied assault, but "to form an opinion of the attack at this distance of time,"
he wrote, "and the change which has taken place, in the appearance of the
ground by the cutting away of the woods, &c. is hardly to be done with justice to the subject."[162]

## "I Thought Myself Happy in Being Here"

So what did the siege of Savannah mean to Governor Wright? D'Estaing's
fleet was spotted in southern waters just a few months after Germain promised Wright that Georgia was securely settled. It was not, and soon after his
arrival late in the summer of 1779, he had to deal with the possible, maybe
expected, capitulation of his government and British arms in Georgia. He
witnessed the marriage of a daughter, the active military engagement of a
second son, bullets and mortar fire that whizzed above his head and at his
feet, and the capture of his son-in-law and two daughters by the French. It is
not surprising, therefore, that in early December Wright requested His Majesty's permission "to return to Great Britain."[163] He had given all he could.

What, then, did the repulsion of the joint Franco-American Alliance
mean to the British war effort? The long-term consequences are much more
complicated because the geopolitical implications of a long-drawn-out
world war altered the importance of the events of September and October
1779 and because those effects would only emerge in time. Most immediately, however, it meant that the British retained possession of their youngest
North American colony, which allowed them to, in quite short order, reduce
Charleston, their most valuable continental city. Sir James Wright himself
may have offered the best analysis of the importance of the siege of Savannah. In a letter to Lord Germain, he wrote: "I thought myself happy in being here at the time of the siege" because "if this province then fell, America
was lost and this I declared on every occasion & urged the necessity of every
exertion possible to defend this place."[164]

There is validity in Wright's assessment. General Clinton's long-delayed campaign to take Charleston might never have happened had the siege of Savannah succeeded or even lasted longer. Clinton wrote that he likely would have given up on his expedition to South Carolina if Savannah had fallen to the American and French armies. As it was, his fleet risked destruction in storms along the coast of North Carolina to rush southward. The journey, as had South Carolina governor Lord William Campbell's earlier voyage, took five full weeks. A typical journey should have taken closer to ten days. But because of the successful repulse of the Franco-American assault, the British army would go on to thoroughly defeat two Continental armies at Charleston and Camden, South Carolina.[165]

# CHAPTER 8

# A Governor Evacuated

## "Harassed and Ruined by Rebels"

From his residence at Craven Street, roughly equidistant between Covent Garden and the government offices at Whitehall in central London, James Wright composed a lengthy letter to British home secretary Thomas Townshend in September 1782 describing his experiences during the Revolutionary War. Following the 1779 siege, Wright stated, "we flattered ourselves with hopes that we should have been able to remain in peace & quietness . . . [and safe] from the tyranny & oppression of the rebellion." Tranquility, however, would not be in store for the governor and the king's loyal subjects or, for that matter, his rebellious subjects. "But alas!" exclaimed Wright, "before the minds of the people were settled and wholly reconciled to a return to their allegiance & authority of the King's government, the troops were withdrawn." According to Wright, Britain's utter disregard for the province soon resulted in a "very rapid revolt" in the backcountry during which the rebels "assassinated and otherwise cruelly murdered as many Loyalists as they could come at & upwards of an hundred good men in the space of one month *fell victims to their loyalty.*"[1] No wonder he desired to leave. The final two and a half years of the American Revolution in Georgia witnessed a ruthless cycle of civil strife unmatched during the rebellion. Moreover, it was a period of an equally unmatched cycle of frustration and anger for Governor Wright because of British disregard for his province. Wright's myopic and provincial view of British strategy blinded him to the global situation, which shrank Georgia's overall importance in imperial planning.

The governor's irritation with the home government's indifference, perceived or otherwise, can be traced to the very beginning of his governorship.[2] More recently, in fact, although Wright departed London for Georgia in the spring of 1779, he still had "not had the honor to receive a line" from Lord George Germain, the American secretary, in nine months.[3] Perhaps it was this very deep-seated and long-lasting frustration, this sense of truly feeling isolated in a dangerous and distant peripheral land, that led to his request to again return home. At the end of November, the Reverend John Joachim Zubly, the passionate rebel turned Loyalist, wrote a lengthy letter to Wright outlining his own sufferings related to the siege. In that letter, he noted that the governor was widely expected to leave Georgia, "it being reported that your excellency is now to take your departure from this place."[4]

To make matters worse, Savannah was soon besieged again, but this time by an outbreak of smallpox. This deadly disease occupied much of Wright's time in January 1780 and spared few neighborhoods and plantations, "particularly [the] Negroes," he wrote.[5] Moreover, additional problems plagued the governor. "I wish it were in my power," he remarked to Germain, "to give your Lordship an agreeable or satisfactory account" of the province's situation. Wright chided the ministry for not adequately fortifying the backcountry, leaving Georgia's loyal inhabitants to be constantly "harassed and ruined by Rebels from Carolina and villains in the back country here, who joined them for the sake of plunder." In short, he said, the "province had been suffered to relapse into rebellion again." An example of such depredations happened at a plantation owned by Wright's friend Lieutenant Governor John Graham. A "most daring robbery had been committed," the Governor's Council reported, in which "upwards of 100 slaves were carried off."[6] According to historian Benjamin Quarles, Georgia was home to the "most widespread seizure of British-held blacks" in America. Wright believed rebel commanders were most concerned about seizing the enslaved, even more so than destroying British provisions and materiel.[7] Moreover, he insisted that if his repeated entreaties to station British regulars in Augusta had been heeded, Georgia would now be at peace and a haven for Loyalists from other colonies.[8]

But it was not simply the rebels that confiscated the enslaved. One historian concluded that "a group of kidnappers were now quietly making a profit by selling black children to the West Indies." On 5 January 1781 Wright touched on this issue in a letter to Nisbet Balfour, commandant at Charleston: "I gave directions, & made all the inquiry I cou'd about the negroes &c. you mentioned you were apprehensive were brought into this province with an aim to sell or ship off, but could not discover that any were." Concerns, however, persisted. The commissioner of sequestered estates in Charleston published a proclamation to that effect and later discovered the truth about this illicit trade as surviving victims came forth with disturbing details in 1782.[9]

But tranquility was not possible for James Wright because, at least in part, British officials had always considered his pleas excessive.[10] In fact, cantankerous British admiral Marriot Arbuthnot shockingly exclaimed that Wright "ought to be hanged" for his conduct and temper.[11] Lieutenant Colonel Nisbet Balfour also expressed real frustration with Wright and the Governor's Council, calling them "the most absurd of all people."[12] But the disconnect was largely a matter of perspective: British officials viewed Georgia as a peripheral concern, whereas Wright considered it as part of the core. "The Generals," Wright whined, "have always set their faces against this province . . . and they will do nothing for us."[13]

Perhaps illustrating that point, the previous year General Henry Clinton had begun making final preparations for the launch of Britain's "southern strategy."[14] As previously mentioned, this plan had been outlined in Germain's "most secret" letter to Clinton of 8 March 1778 and had called for Clinton's shifting his focus to the southern colonies "with a view to the conquest and possession of Georgia and South Carolina."[15] In short, this stratagem sought to "Americanize" the war based upon four principles: (1) the intense and incessant assurances from southern colonials, especially officials like Governor Wright, that the South was filled with Loyalists who only needed the arrival of some British troops to make their presence felt; (2) the British desire to cut off rebel trade, in the words of historian John Shy, "through which foreign aid for the rebellion was being purchased"; (3) the belief that the southern colonies were sparsely populated and thus more likely to be subdued; and (4) the fact that the southern colonies offered a base from which to deal with the impending French threat in the Caribbean. Moreover, the southern frontier offered the support of many pro-British Indian tribes, as well as that of thousands of potential allies then laboring on large plantations in the Lowcountry.[16]

Historians have generally condemned the British for foolishly listening to exiled southern officials who, so the story went, grossly exaggerated Loyalist numbers. Historian Jim Piecuch has disproven this theory as being both far too simplistic and incorrect. He has asserted that Britain's error was not in relying on southern Loyalists, Indians, and Blacks but in neither developing a coherent plan nor convincing its field commanders that such a plan would produce the desired results.[17] For example, General Clinton complained to Wright that he was "greatly disappointed" in the number of Loyalists he found in North Carolina in 1776. That colony's governor, however, noted in a letter to Clinton that he (the governor) had "not so much been deceived in my expectations from the good disposition of People . . . as I have been disappointed with regard to the arrival" of British troops.[18] Additionally, the British either failed to or could not commit the necessary resources to the southern colonies to achieve their aims.

Once word reached New York that the siege of Savannah had been lifted, Clinton resumed the plan to retake the southern colonies. Although Wright viewed Clinton's plans as an abandonment, Wright accurately predicted that without conquering South Carolina, "everything is to be apprehended for Georgia."[19] In late December, about the same time as Clinton set sail from New York, Wright wrote him a panicky letter: "We are now anxiously looking out for your arrival here and I must request in the most earnest manner you will not lose a single day."[20] A few weeks later, the governor acknowledged his fear that South Carolina rebels, whom he always believed to be the instigators of the rebellion in Georgia, would soon attack the province. "I am no soldier," he noted, "but I don't like many things I hear and see. . . . [L]et me entreat you, Sir, to make a movement this way."[21] In this letter, Wright validated Clinton's interest in South Carolina. He also only expressed what the generals had long thought about him: he was not a soldier.

### "Exposed to the Utmost Danger"

On 24 January 1780 rebel general Benjamin Lincoln notified Thomas Jefferson that he had learned that a fleet of about ninety ships had sailed for Georgia from New York with South Carolina as "their object."[22] The next week he informed Jefferson with absolute certainty that the British fleet was "now in very great force at Savannah."[23] Although the convoy had been scattered by inclement weather, most of the ships had reached Georgia by early February. By the eighth, Clinton had already advanced in force toward Charleston, leaving none of his troops behind in Savannah. In fact, to Wright's dismay, Clinton ordered most of the troops in Georgia to join the operations against Charleston. The governor stated that the removal of most British regulars from Georgia would leave "this province . . . exposed to the utmost danger . . . [as] almost any trifling force may come up the River, and

destroy everything in it."[24] Later, he declared that their removal had actually precipitated a "general and very rapid revolt" in Georgia.[25] Even worse
for Georgia's Loyalists was the fact that none of these British troops ever returned to the province.

Wright soon acknowledged that although Savannah was in no "immediate" danger, he generally "face[d] incredible obstacles operating under such
dire conditions in Georgia."[26] But the situation was not as rosy throughout
the Lowcountry, because "not 20 miles from Town," Wright wrote," the rebels "plundered and carried off both white men and Negroes."[27] Rebel mili-
tiaman McKeen Greene later wrote that "under Colonels [Andrew] Pickens
and [John] Twiggs ... we dispersed some Negroes of Governor Wright."[28]
Although Wright continued to beg for assistance, and Lieutenant Colonel
Alured Clarke wanted to help, none was forthcoming. Simply put, the entry
of France and Spain into the contest thinned British resources beyond their
capacity.[29]

General Augustine Prévost's tune had changed by early March, when
he complained to Clinton that both Savannah and St. Augustine had been
rendered defenseless and were presently in the "greatest danger."[30] Clinton
promised relief when practicable but insisted that Savannah was in no immediate danger.[31] Although Clinton was stretched too thin, he certainly
understood that Georgia was in trouble.[32] He did, however, assure Wright
that if he took Charleston, "we shall probably carry on operations upon the
Upper Savannah [Augusta]."[33] Wright viewed such an operation as critical to maintaining peace in Georgia, because "it is the key."[34] In fact, he
advised Germain: "Hold Carolina and Georgia, and America may yet be
recovered."[35]

The governor soon responded to Clinton that while he fully understood
the importance of Charleston, "tak[ing] care of what you have got" was also
essential. Moreover, Wright pressed, "this province is or will be broke up totally ruined if something is not speedily done."[36] Neither Clinton nor Cornwallis proffered a useful response. Meanwhile, as he prepared to lay siege
to Charleston, Clinton continued South Carolina governor Lord William
Campbell's practice from January 1779 and issued a general amnesty to all
rebels for actions taken prior to 3 March.[37] Wright and the Council viewed
the proclamation as potentially dangerous for Georgia, fearful that

> many persons formerly inhabitants of this province may come in under
> Your Excellency's proclamation and claim of you their pardon even [those
> who] were most active in leading men then in rebellion here and who

were not seduced by the acts of faction or hurried away by their loyalty and by the tumults and disorder of the times but men who seduced others and practiced and encouraged the acts of faction themselves, men who seriously and deliberately promote[d] treason and rebellion, men who have had great time and frequent opportunities of returning their allegiance and duty but have not, men who were in arms when this province was reduced in January 1779, men who were then invited by Colonel Campbell to submit themselves but *who then and ever since have obstinately persisted in their treason and rebellion, men who have sat in judgment and men who have exercised and enforced under the rebel powers every act of cruelty, tyranny, and oppression against His Majesty's truly loyal subjects* who have wantonly proscribed and passed laws or bills of attainder against innocent and loyal subjects. Men who were many of them in the lines during the siege of this place and who joined in the attack here on the 9th of October last and men *who are hard and dangerous and obstinate rebels.*[38]

Wright also suggested that instead of rewarding the rebels with blanket pardons, the British should "encourage and reward Loyalists."[39] Loyalist spirits indeed needed lifting. In early April the governor grumbled to Germain that Georgia is "truly in a grievous situation, [as the Loyalists are] continually harassed and plundered by parties of Rebels." This lawlessness in the backcountry could have been prevented, Wright believed, if only Clinton had sent a small force to Augusta.[40] In fact, Wright was so fixated on subduing the backcountry that Clarke, who had taken command of the nominal troops at Savannah when Prévost returned to Britain in May, bemoaned that "Wright seems rather tenacious of the post at Augusta."[41]

Instead, that important frontier post belonged to the rebels under the leadership of South Carolina militia general Andrew Williamson. As Clinton carefully made his way to the outskirts of Charleston by land, General Lincoln withdrew all Continental troops from Georgia and rushed to Charleston. Just as Wright and the Loyalists were angered by Clinton's decision, Georgia's rebels protested Lincoln's reaction. The rebels sought South Carolina's assistance in guarding their shared border near Augusta, and now those troops would be moving to defend their own capital. Without their aid, Williamson marched his rebel militia into Augusta in early March.[42]

Shortly thereafter, the war reached Wright's backyard when three hundred rebels raided Wright's "plantations at Ogechee [about fifteen miles from Savannah] and burned and destroyed seven of my barns . . . and did me other damage to the amount of at least £8,000. . . . [Moreover], they shot four of my Negroes dead and wounded three more, one of which it's thought will dye, and how many they have carried off with them, it's not yet in my power to say with certainty."[43]

Concomitantly, the British began constructing siege works around Charleston. Approximately six weeks later and with great difficulty, Clinton completed his investiture of the city and immediately made plans to extend the British sphere of influence in that colony.[44] What Clinton did not do was make a movement in force toward Augusta, leaving the region defenseless against rebel "plundering parties."[45] The rebels clearly believed Georgia to be ripe for the picking. Wright even suggested that the reconquest of Charleston worsened the situation for Georgians because roaming "parties of Rebels [had come] from Carolina and plunder[ed] kill[ed] and carr[ied] off the inhabitants within 5 or 6 miles" of Savannah. Additionally, another "party of Rebel plunderers . . . carried off some prisoners and about 20 Negroes" within a few miles of Savannah.[46] Wright feared that these rebel incursions, emboldened by the dearth of British soldiers in the province, might force Loyalists to make decisions of loyalty based on personal safety.[47]

Back in Augusta, rebel general Williamson occupied the town from early March until he evacuated on 29 May, after which Loyalists under Colonels Thomas Brown and James Grierson moved in and occupied the town. Both Wright and Brown fervently believed throughout the summer that loyalism might prevail.[48] They were buoyed in this opinion by the surrender of whole units of rebel militia in the backcountry, and they doubted the fidelity of many who signed the rebel oath, believing that they played a waiting game in the hopes that Loyalists or the British would regain the advantage. Only Wilkes County and part of Richmond County, in northeast Georgia, were under rebel control.[49]

### "Peace Will Soon Be Re-established"

But these were contingent times. In mid-August rebel Elijah Clarke and about four hundred of his followers marched toward Augusta. Their attack on the Loyalist post there nearly forced the immediate capitulation by Colonel Brown, who held out for several days, thanks to the assistance of some Native Americans. British reinforcements under Lieutenant Colonel John Harris Cruger arrived from Ninety-Six, South Carolina, in the nick of time and forced Clarke's speedy exodus. This was an important victory for the British, "for had [the rebels] succeeded," Wright wrote, "I am . . . certain they would soon have become formidable."[50]

After Cruger's arrival, according to an early historian who claimed to write from British accounts in his possession, Brown picked a dozen wounded rebels and hanged them from the staircase of a house outside of town.[51] Governor Wright reported that "thirteen of the prisoners who broke their paroles & came against Augusta have been hang'd," adding that "I hope [it] will have a very good effect."[52] Brown himself denied ever having acted outside the bounds of "the laws of war and humanity," and it is likely that the men had been hanged for breaking their paroles of honor, not uncommon during this era.[53] It is worth mentioning that by the end of 1780, Wright's attitude toward the rebels had become much more harsh, as he eschewed the more paternalistic pretensions he had exhibited throughout his career. According to historian Edward Cashin, the execution was simply a matter of policy that "no one on the British side questioned."[54] In any event, Clarke's survivors would continue to pester the British, notably at the pivotal Battle of Kings Mountain the following month, likely the battle that initiated the collapse of royal authority in the South.[55]

The behaviors of Brown and his men were emblematic of the tactics used by both sides, who sought to intimidate would-be foes and punish opponents. Both sides were culpable. General Williamson's evacuation of Augusta back in May left many backcountry rebels to ponder, according to a Wright correspondent, "in what manner [they should] apply to [Wright], to solicit peace, or obtain some kind of pardon." The governor had also heard that many South Carolinians were "preparing petitions to Sir Henry Clinton with the same views." If this were true, Wright wrote to Germain, "I am very hopeful my Lord peace will soon be re-established in these provinces and doubt not but (as I have always said) the reduction of them will give a mortal stab to the rebellion."[56] But, again, these were contingent times. Clinton left the task of securing peace in the Lowcountry to General Charles Cornwallis and sailed for New York on 8 June, fully confident that Georgia and South Carolina were firmly under British control.[57] Before departing Charleston, however, the British commander issued a proclamation that would have long-lasting negative consequences for Wright and the Loyalists. In this proclamation, Clinton revoked the paroles he had given to rebels in May, stating: "It is fit and proper that all persons should take an active part in settling and securing his Majesty's Government, and delivering the Country from the Anarchy, which for some time past hath prevailed." Moreover, this proclamation "restored to all [such prisoners and parolees] the Rights and Duties belonging to Citizens and Inhabitants" but obligated them to bear arms against the rebels, if called upon.[58] Ironically, both Clinton and Cornwallis insisted they did not want anyone of dubious loyalty serving in the royal militia. A commissary under General William Howe, Charles Stedman, argued that Clinton's decree compelled the neutrals to join the rebels. Moreover, he insisted that Loyalists were extremely embittered by Clinton's offer of full benefits of citizenship to those who had taken up arms against the Crown. Ultimately, Stedman maintained that the proclamation laid the "foundation of mutual jealousy and distrust ... amongst the inhabitants themselves."[59] While this last statement was erroneous because the region was already embroiled in a civil war, Stedman correctly observed the proclamation's effect on both the neutrality of the rebel parolees and the morale of the Loyalists.

The extant evidence concerning Wright's sentiments about Clinton's 3 June proclamation is ambiguous. On the one hand, Georgia's chief justice, Anthony Stokes, arrested prominent Georgia rebels upon their return to Savannah under charges of treason.[60] Such behavior by Loyalist officials drew Cornwallis's ire, and he ordered Lieutenant Colonel Clarke to notify Wright that "detaining a prisoner of war on parole to bring him to tryal for treason at Savannah is highly improper and unwarrantable."[61] On the other hand, in response to a number of backcountry petitioners "praying to be received and restored to His Majesty's peace and protection," Wright urged the Governor's Council to extend leniency to them and to, in the Council's words, "bury in oblivion all past offences."[62] Here we see a rare instance in a changing Wright philosophy—whereas he had always rigidly sought the persecution of defiant Americans, he now saw the need for clemency.

In the meantime, that summer Wright complained that "our most violent Rebels ... are preparing to return here" because they had not been punished and there were insufficient means to stop them. Contingent times, indeed, and Wright's complaints failed to align with the advice he had proffered his Council. He then asked for and suggested that 800 troops and 150 horsemen would likely ensure that the "rebellion cannot rear its head again in Georgia."[63] But, again, support would not be forthcoming, even though Cornwallis assured Wright that he would "pay the greatest attention to the security and protection of Georgia." Cornwallis reasoned, though, that so long as he possessed South Carolina, a post at either Savannah or Augusta would provide Georgia "the most ample and satisfactory protection."[64] Wright responded dubiously, reminding Cornwallis that the great distance of 140 miles between the two "gives great opportunities to ill disposed people."[65] The situation was so dire that Wright summoned a special session of the Assembly to discuss defending Savannah. They passed an astonishing bill that would draft slaves to build fortifications and even arm them during an emergency.[66]

## "Wanton Cruelty and Barbarity"

In August 1781 Benjamin Franklin informed diplomat Charles William Frédéric Dumas that "the enemy now have nothing left in Georgia but Savannah."[67] Governor Wright again reminded the military commanders that most Georgians were loyal and "have given the strongest proofs of their loyalty [but see themselves and] relatives put to death solely on that account. To give them up is the height of cruelty and the worst policy."[68] Lieutenant Colonel Nisbet Balfour wished he could do more for Georgia's Loyalists and empathized with their suffering, "which I am the better enabled to judge of, from the similar situation of many deserving persons" then in Charleston.[69] Wright did not concede the point and implored Balfour to act. "I am well persuaded," he said, "if you saw and knew the consequences of not [coming to Georgia's aid] . . . you would strain a point to do it" because the conflict there was simply brutal.[70]

The British never truly possessed the Georgia backcountry because the British military deemed Georgia to be somewhat insignificant and because the nature of the conflict on the frontier was incredibly personal and dominated by atrocity and reprisal. As Thomas Brown later wrote, "A civil war being one of the greatest evils incident to human society, the history of every contest presents us with instances of wanton cruelty and barbarity [because] men whose passions are inflamed by mutual injuries, exasperated with personal animosity against each other, and eager to gratify revenge, often violate the laws of war and principles of humanity."[71] Additionally, as historian Kenneth Coleman opined, Georgia's rebels "must have had a remarkable intelligence system," because they seemed to always be a step ahead of their Loyalist counterparts.[72] The rebel cause also received the continued assistance of South Carolina's rebels.

But the Lowcountry militia alone would not win this war. Later that summer, on 16 August, Cornwallis scored a complete victory against General Horatio Gates at Camden, South Carolina, seemingly cementing British control of South Carolina.[73] While the "reduction of South Carolina . . . certainly afforded us great security," Wright wrote, "we had danger again at our doors." Wright admitted that both Cornwallis's victory over Gates and Lieutenant Colonel Banastre Tarleton's victory over rebel general Thomas Sumter eased their difficult situation, but "we are not even now in a state of security."[74] Governor Wright's son Alexander, in fact, occasionally accompanied Tarleton (and Major Patrick Ferguson, the British officer best known for his fighting in the backcountry) on their backcountry excursions and served as a superintendent of police during the British occupation of Charleston.[75] If a silver lining was to be found for the rebels following their catastrophic defeats on the Carolina frontier, it was the appointment of General George Washington's hand-chosen successor to the disgraced Gates, General Nathanael Greene.[76] Greene's instincts were like Washington's, and he planned to take the offensive.

Rebel efforts so frustrated Wright that he angrily advised Balfour, the commandant of Charleston, that "the most effectual and best method of crushing the rebellion in the back parts of the province is for an army to march without loss of time into the ceded lands and to lay waste and destroy the whole territory . . . for these people . . . have by their late conduct forfeited every claim to any favour or protection." This is quite the turnaround from his earlier appeal for moderation. He somewhat humanely added that "if in the execution of this measure any women or children shou'd be left destitute, we shall be ready to subscribe towards their support."[77] Wright also advised the Georgia Assembly that "vigorous measures are still necessary to crush the rebellion in the back parts of the province."[78]

General Cornwallis finally agreed. In a letter to Cruger, he insisted that the rebels "must be dealt with in the most severe manner . . . [and] I give you my sanction to any act of rigour you may think necessary."[79] "In a civil war," he wrote, "there is no admitting of neutral characters . . . [and] every measure taken to prevent" those in opposition from being armed must be taken.[80] He ordered his subordinates to send "Loyalists into the countryside to burn the houses of villains, drive off their cattle and burn and plunder their property." Such measures were indeed adopted by Colonel Cruger, who sent "out patrols of horse to pick up the traitourous Rebels in the neighborhood."[81] One of Cruger's officers confided to a friend, "We have now got a method that will put an end to the rebellion in a short time—by hanging every man that has taken protection and is found acting against us."[82] He was wrong. Wright penned an angry letter to Clinton a year later that highlighted the uselessness of such an atrocious policy. "The Rebels are in possession of the whole country above Ebenezer," he wrote, and "they have sent [Loyalist] wives and children [to Savannah and] threaten to reduce [the city] by famine." In short, he wrote, they were about "to lay waste the country so that the province is ruined and lost for want of a little assistance."[83] Wright bears some culpability for rebel behavior. South Carolina judge Aedanus Burke noted that the governor of Georgia's rebels were "the [fittest] people ... for dealing [with] the Tories in their own way [because of the] disfranchisements, confiscation & high hand of Govr Wright & his crew in the hour of success."[84]

Wright busied himself in these months attempting, with little support from the British military, to provide for Georgia's defense.[85] His inability to convince British commanders to provide even nominal aid had convinced him yet again to seek a return to London.[86] "I am humbly to request that his Majesty will be graciously pleased to grant me his Royal leave of absence," he wrote Germain in December 1780, "and that I may be at liberty to return to Great Britain as circumstances may happen or appear in the course of next summer & to remain there for such time as his Majesty in his great wisdom may think proper. Possibly my Lord, I might be useful for a while."[87]

This situation would soon worsen. General Greene arrived from West Point and took command of the Continentals in the South.[88] On 17 January 1781 General Daniel Morgan and the rebels earned a dramatic victory over the vilified British lieutenant colonel Banastre Tarleton at the Battle of Cowpens, along the border of the Carolinas.[89] General Clinton later described the Battle of Cowpens "as the first link of a chain of events that ... ended in the total loss of America."[90] General Washington declared that this "decisive and glorious" victory would "have an important influence on the affairs of the South."[91] Both men were correct, though Clinton's "chain of events" should probably have started with the Battle of Kings Mountain. Governor Wright's son Major James Wright married Sarah Smith, the daughter of a Charleston gentleman, the very next day.[92] The British loss at Cowpens threw "us into the utmost confusion & danger, for this province is still left in a defenseless state," Wright wrote. As it stood, he moaned, Savannah still had "many thorough rebels and villainous incendiaries."[93]

In mid-February close to one hundred South Carolinians crossed the Savannah River and, according to Wright, "assassinated eleven persons in their houses." The governor continued: "This base conduct of the Rebels, I consider my Lord, as the strongest proof of the rebellious spirit which still continues amongst many of the people and that as they are not strong enough to retake the province they will endeavor to murder & harass & distress his Majesty's good and loyal subjects."[94] Two months later, Colonel Isaac Shelby darted into Wilkes County and killed several dozen settlers, and the Loyalists lacked the manpower and resources to mount a campaign against him.[95] These incursions greatly reduced Loyalist forces in the backcountry and prompted Wright to complain of the "very great distance Lord Cornwallis and his army are at," because it "give[s] every opportunity to the disaffected to collect, & murder, plunder &c in a most cruel & shocking manner."[96] The governor proved prophetic. The situation was especially troublesome because the Loyalist militia were under constant alarm and "without either pay or subsistence."[97]

General Greene finally engaged the British a few months after taking over the Continental army's Southern Department. On 15 March his army met General Cornwallis at Guilford Courthouse—named after a patron of James Wright's grandfather—outside modern-day Greensboro, North Carolina. Although Greene relinquished the field, the British triumph, which Wright hoped would be a "signal victory," was clearly of a Pyrrhic nature: Cornwallis endured substantial casualties, and the rebels lived to fight another day.[98] MP Charles James Fox soon declared that "another such victory would ruin the British Army."[99] Even though some Loyalists believed that Cornwallis's "victory" had "settled the peace of the back country," the rebels had been emboldened by Greene's efforts in North Carolina.[100]

Wright complained to Germain that Cornwallis's great distance from Georgia encouraged rebel intransigence. He continued, seemingly incredulous with the way in which the ministry and the army had disregarded the Loyalists: "It's a cruel hard case that loyal subjects struggling to support His Majesty's government . . . should be suffered to be thus murdered for want of a few troops." Throughout the spring and summer, Wright continued to tell his superiors that Georgia "has many good & faithful subjects . . . who will do everything in their power to support his Majesty's government."[101] There are many Loyalists in Georgia, he wrote, "but [they are] doomed to death & destruction."[102] Military historian Ian Saberton has argued that "it is no exaggeration to say that [Cornwallis's] decision was critical in a series of events that lost Britain the southern colonies and cost it the entire war."[103]

The governor soon received disturbing news from the backcountry. He learned that rebel colonel Isaac Shelby and a few hundred overmountain men had gone into the ceded lands and viciously "assassinated upwards of 40 people . . . and the unheard of cruelty of the Rebels was so shocking that the generality of the people took to the swamps for shelter against these worse than savages, who say they will murder every loyal subject in the province." Rumors were now running rampant that rebels were collecting in force at numerous places in the South Carolina backcountry with the intent "to come over into this province & lay waste the whole lower part of the country." Wright surmised then that Georgia had now been "reduced to a precarious & dangerous situation."[104] He could not escape soon enough.

Back in Savannah, the fears of a Spanish assault on St. Augustine prompted British Lieutenant Colonel Clarke to remove a contingent of his troops in Savannah and march to East Florida. His departure left only a nominal force in Georgia commanded by Hessian lieutenant colonel Friedrich von Porbeck, who despised his duty in Georgia and who was equally detested by Governor Wright.[105] Clarke's departure also meant that loyal Georgians would suffer greatly in the coming months because the rebels realized their raids would now involve fewer risks.

In addition to trying to oversee Georgia's defense, Wright spent a great deal of time feeding and clothing Loyalist refugees and paying Loyalist militia out of his own rapidly depleting pockets.[106] "Partys of Rebels," the Governor's Council lamented, continue to "skulk about in the woods & swamps & avail themselves of the opportunity of attacking men separately & at their own homes."[107] In fact, the inhabitants of Wrightsborough feared that "a dangerous insurrection" would break out and force them to "quit their settlements."[108] The following month, according to the *Royal Georgia Gazette*, "a set of the most barbarous wretches that ever infested any country, amounting some say to 200 . . . surprised and murdered several Loyalists at Wrightsborough."[109]

There simply were not enough soldiers to defend the province. If only it had been provided 150 cavalry, "Georgia would by this time have been intirely at peace," Wright complained.[110] But without that military deterrent, Elijah Clarke began to again lay siege to Augusta in early May 1781.[111] His force was soon augmented with men under militia general Andrew Pickens and Continental lieutenant colonel Henry Lee. The Loyalist defenders of Augusta repeatedly begged for assistance, but without success.[112] Wright even suggested that without this succor, "the province will be broke up & ruined." In this letter to Germain, Wright mentioned that he and his Council had entreated von Porbeck to consider and reconsider sending immediate aid to Augusta. He refused.[113]

## "Laid Waste & Totally Destroyed"

As spring turned into summer, the rebels tightened their grip on Augusta while also, according to Wright, "murdering, plundering, laying waste & doing all the mischief they possibly can." In fact, he argued that Whig atrocities and intimidation had led many Loyalists to flock to the rebel standard. Loyalist Thomas Taylor noted that the rebels "were spreading devastation all around."[114] Wright once again argued that a few well-placed troops could have prevented such "assassinating partys [who] still continue going about the country."[115] No aid would be forthcoming, however, as Lieutenant Colonel Balfour informed Wright that the British posts at Wright's Bluff, Buck Head, and the Congaree had all been taken by the rebels. Balfour added that Britain's overall position in the region had reached a critical level and that he lacked the "power to succour the garrisons of Ninety Six [South Carolina] and Augusta."[116]

Writing that same day from General Greene's headquarters, Captain Nathaniel Pendleton presciently opined that Augusta would collapse within the week.[117] The first of Augusta's two forts fell on 25 May. Growing increasingly frustrated, angry, and isolated, Wright dispatched a diatribe to Balfour, arguing that it might now "be too late to prevent the whole [of Georgia] from being laid waste & totally destroyed & the people ruined, we are now in a most wretched situation."[118] The Governor's Council also suggested that a "sufficient force should march immediately . . . to Augusta, to retake that place and establish a strong post."[119] They held on to hope in the face of overwhelming odds. Within weeks, the rebels had captured the second post guarding Augusta, killing Colonel Grierson in the process, "after the capitulation & laying down his arms."[120] Wright later wrote to Grierson's widow that the rebels had "murdered him in cool blood after the capitulation."[121] Wright surely felt that the end must be near.

Although Savannah remained in British hands, the fall of Augusta meant that rebels fully controlled the Georgia frontier. Wright's world was shrinking at an alarming rate. In June the governor bemoaned the lack of soldiers to "keep the Rebels from destroying & laying waste" to Savannah itself. In short, he wrote Germain, "our prospect is wretched."[122] His pleas finally produced some action, as Lieutenant Colonel Francis, Lord Rawdon, wrote during the siege of Augusta: "Sir James Wright represented so strongly the want of troops at Savannah that I thought it necessary to send the King's American Regiment thither with all dispatch; tho at that time we could ill spare them."[123] In spite of the celerity with which royal authority in Georgia seemed to crumble, Lord Germain expressed great pride in Wright's accomplishments, in spite of his earlier reservations. "I trust the example of Georgia," Germain wrote, "will be followed by all the other provinces when they are restored to the King's peace." Moreover, he gushed, "it must be highly pleasing to you to reflect that you have led the way in measures, which have the fairest tendency to heal the unhappy breach."[124] Although Wright's efforts to fully restore Georgia were, in most cases, sensible, Germain still had very little understanding of the nature of this civil war in the southern colonies.

Georgia's prospects grew much bleaker weeks later following Cornwallis's defeat at Yorktown, Virginia, in October 1781.[125] General Greene reported to Robert R. Livingston, U.S. secretary of foreign affairs, that all the southern states were now under rebel control, "Charleston and Savannah excepted."[126] The catastrophic event nearly propelled Parliament to terminate the prosecution of the war and prompted Wright's anger. He wrote Germain in mid-December: "I always dreaded it, from the moment Lord Cornwallis went into Virginia. . . . I fear [it] has ruined the King's Cause in America."[127] Although Governor Wright failed to fully realize the siege's consequences, Lord North did. He wailed, "O God, it is all over!"[128] But, Wright wrote, "we are at this moment in the utmost danger & distress & expect every day" the arrival of a "formidable force" commanded by General Greene. Moreover, Wright wrote, "we have also intelligence that the Marquess de la Fayette is on his way."[129] One Savannahian lamented that the "Loyalists have been brought to utter ruin."[130] In preparation for the seemingly inevitable assault, Governor Wright stated that "we have now 500 Negroes at work on our fortifications, and this place will be very secure and tenable if we get men sufficient to man the works."[131]

By early 1782, Hessians were deserting in droves, and Continental forces were inching ever closer to Savannah as General "Mad" Anthony Wayne led about five hundred men into the Lowcountry, prompting Wright to order the destruction of the "rice and provisions" in the Ogeechee district.[132] Wayne, who exhorted his men forward with the battle cry that "sanguine God is rather thirsty for human gore," had Wright on his mind.[133] General Alexander Leslie sent two hundred British troops from Charleston to augment Georgia's meager forces, and Wright ramped up colonial defenses by bringing in three hundred Choctaws.[134] In January a still seething Wright informed Germain that the British "ought to have supportd [sic] these southern provinces," because without them, New York would "be of little consequence." Although this may seem ridiculous or even self-serving, Wright was likely correct. Savannah and Charleston were the primary connection with British possessions in the West Indies, which were the financial key to empire.

James Wright again requested permission to leave Georgia.[135] Historian Kenneth Coleman correctly observed that Wright's correspondence by now "took on the note of pessimism of a man who knew that he was doomed."[136] There was much reason for such an attitude, because according to Wright, "we are now confined almost to our lines around the town & are expecting a powerful attack every day & probably [another] siege."[137] A few days later,

Wright sent another letter to Germain by way of the governor's brother, Jermyn, "who has been buffeted about by the Rebels for these past five or six years past."[138]

In early February General Wayne forced the British and Loyalist forces to withdraw closer and closer to Savannah proper.[139] Wayne suggested that he could take Savannah if Greene would send reinforcements.[140] Dejected and hopeless but ever the dutiful Loyalist, Wright found himself "continually hurried" by the rapidly unfolding events of the time, and a sense of doom permeated his every letter. He closed one letter by simply stating, "I will stop, for I can tell you nothing pleasant, I shall say no more."[141] He truly resigned himself to his deplorable lot, lamenting to his old friend William Knox, "I am convinced nothing will be attempted any where.... [E]very insult & every depredation the Rebels choose to offer or commit will be suffered with impunity."[142]

Additionally, Wright's correspondence since the summer of 1781, if not earlier, revealed a man who wanted to make sure that the blame for the fall of Georgia would be placed elsewhere.[143] He especially attacked the British decisions to show "lenity" to the rebels and to abandon Georgia and South Carolina prior to the subjugation of the rebels: "I have not either seen or heard anything like peace or tranquility here or in South Carolina since last February [1780]—We might have had both if the troops had not gone into Virginia."[144] Governor Wright believed so desperately in the need for additional troops or horsemen that he paid for patrols of horse out of his own pocket.[145]

But without the Loyalists being given relief of any note, the rebels comfortably crossed the Altamaha River and "murdered 12 or 13 Loyal Subjects" in St. Andrew's Parish, just south of Savannah.[146] At the end of the month, Wright sent a personal protest to his superiors. He complained that he "ought to have been in England long ago" but had remained in Georgia, where he had "been informed beyond a doubt that my life is threatened & that offers have been made to General Wayne to assassinate me."[147] Yet he stayed, performing his duty to Crown and Parliament until the bitter end.

## "God Knows What Our Fate Will Be"

In late April, as many of his own men deserted in droves, German baron Ludwig von Closen, an aide-de-camp to French general Jean-Baptiste Donatien de Vimeur, comte de Rochambeau, confided to his journal that British headquarters had received intelligence that Savannah would soon be evacuated.[148] A week later General Sir Guy Carleton arrived in New York to replace Clinton. His first orders called for a quick evacuation of the colonies, and he determined to begin by evacuating the southern provinces.[149] All of this, however, was unknown to Governor Wright, who continued with his doomed efforts to procure British troops with which to dislodge General Wayne.[150] Wayne's arrival, Wright wrote, "reduced [many Loyalists] to the dire necessity of quitting their very comfortable settlements in the country" and to flee "almost naked & destitute of every thing" to the relative safety of Savannah.[151] But even Wright began to understand that the writing was on the wall. Earlier in the year he had written that he had been "persuaded there was a time" when he could have saved Georgia, but because "I can get nothing from" the ministry, there was no hope. "God knows what our fate will be," he continued, but the "fault . . . does not lye with me."[152] Regardless of culpability, Wright knew full well that his freedom, if not his life, was on the line.

His efforts, of course, were destined to fall on deaf ears. Shortly after Wright made this last request, General Alexander Leslie, who had assumed command in the South, received notification that peace negotiations had begun.[153] As Leslie received this communication, Carleton dispatched a letter to Charleston ordering him to evacuate Savannah.[154] Leslie then forwarded the information to Wright.[155] Wright responded with utter contempt and amazement:

> We his Majesty's most dutiful & loyal subjects, feel ourselves at a loss for language to express the astonishment we experience, at the intelligence received, of an intention to withdraw his Majesty's troops. . . . We can with the greatest confidence assert that a greater proportion of the inhabitants of Georgia have attached themselves to the royal cause, than in any other British colony in America, and that numbers of them have been inhumanly murdered, and others stript of their property. . . . We little expected that the town of Savannah would have been evacuated, to the utter ruin of many Loyalists who have suffer'd the greatest hardships in defending it.[156]

The stripping of Loyalist property was near, as the evacuation fleet reached Charleston by 20 June and proceeded to Savannah without delay, arriving on 1 July.[157] Just days prior to the evacuation of Georgia, Wright again lamented "the distress & misery brought on his Majesty's loyal subjects . . . for the want of 4 to 500 men [who] would have effectually held the country."[158] Wright fought beyond the bitter end. George Washington observed similar distress upon the evacuation of New York, writing that the Loyalists were "little better than a medley of confused, enraged, and dejected people. Some are swearing, and some crying, while the greater part of them are almost speechless."[159] This assuredly was the case in Savannah.

The evacuation itself was hectic, according to Wright. "Alas!" he exclaimed. "We were hurried away with our Negroes, without the least notice & had not provisions for six weeks in hand for their future subsistence."[160] The governor had successfully requested that the British transport some two thousand enslaved to Jamaica on the H.M.S. *Zebra*.[161] The town that Wright had called home since 1761 was evacuated ten days later. With about eight hundred "Loyal refugees," Wright departed from Tybee Island, still bitterly complaining about the "cruel order for the evacuation."[162] From London that September, Wright penned a scathing letter to Thomas Townshend recounting the innumerable sufferings of the Loyalists. Although they had been encouraged by the Crown and given "assurances of protection & support," they were deserted by their country, to their "very great mortification, grief & astonishment."[163] Historian Michael Hattem argued that the revolution was not so much against king and Parliament as it was against "the exercise of arbitrary power over the colonies without recourse or redress. Just as their British ancestors had resisted arbitrary rule of Charles I and James II" a century before, "so did the colonists in the eighteenth century."[164] Thus, James Wright is historically linked to his grandfather. Both men chose arbitrary power. Both lost.

# A Governor's Final Act

## "The King's Most Loyal & Faithful Subjects"

At the end of May 1782, prior to the evacuation of America, Governor Wright composed an emotional letter to General Sir Guy Carleton, Britain's final commander in chief in America. Wright informed the general that Georgia's Loyalists "have been firm in their allegiance throughout . . . [and] have suffered every kind of distress for their loyalty," including the confiscation of their property. "Justice and equity," he added, gave them just "claim to the interference and protection of government," especially as it pertained to their possessions. He also suggested at this very late date that Georgia could still be held and then be used as a bargaining chip in the subsequent "treaty for peace." From a purely financial standpoint, no one had suffered as much as Wright. He recorded his losses that spring at more than £40,000 sterling and expected that number to more than double soon.[1] A London newspaper correspondent from New York opined that Wright "is the only capital sufferer for his loyalty in America, but that he has taken care not to be very poor."[2]

The next day, 31 May, Georgia's royal Assembly dispatched their own memorial to Carleton. "From a very early period," they stated, "we have taken arms in defense of our happy Constitution, and shewn an unshaken loyalty to the best of kings." In return, they insisted, "we have been persecuted by our enemies, deprived of our possessions, and some hundreds have been most cruelly murdered." Moreover, they now advised Carleton that they had been forced inside the confines of the city and "are now doing duty within

[British] lines," while their "estates are [left alone] and confiscated by the Rebels, and are now advertized for sale" by their very enemies.[3]

The rebel government passed two confiscation acts during the Revolutionary War. In March 1778 Governor Wright headlined a list of 117 Georgians (including his brothers Charles and Jermyn) declared guilty of high treason by the Whig government. Four years later, he topped another list of 279 Loyalists charged with disloyalty, "murder, rapine, and devastation." These offenses justified the confiscation of their estates and their permanent banishment from the state under penalty of death. Wright's sons, James Jr., Alexander, and Charles, joined him and his brother Jermyn (Charles had died in the interim) on this second list.[4]

After receiving orders to evacuate on 14 June, Wright grumbled bitterly to Carleton that "the situation of affairs here was not properly & sufficiently known to your excellency or I trust such steps would not have been taken" to evacuate this province "when a reinforcement of 4 or 500 men would have effectually held the country."[5] Wright worked tirelessly and without success to maintain royal control of the province. In fact, he had fought beyond the bitter end and had become thoroughly disenchanted, disillusioned, and perhaps a tad delusional in the waning days of the American Revolution, bemoaning that "the King's most loyal & faithful subjects" had been abandoned by king and country.[6] The failure to subdue the rebellious colonists signaled for Wright the end of his long tenure at the pinnacle of provincial power, the end of familial redemption, and the end of his American dream.

In the last extant and likely final issue of the *Royal Georgia Gazette*, publisher James Johnston announced the forty-fifth birthday celebration of King George III with a firing of the cannons at noon. Soon thereafter Governor Wright "gave an elegant entertainment to a more numerous company than was ever assembled on the like occasion in this place."[7] On 2 July the governor bade a final farewell to Georgia, his home for more than two decades. The British fleet made a brief stop in Charleston to procure supplies and additional passengers. Charleston had been Wright's home for more than three decades prior to his appointment as governor of Georgia. He had been raised, learned the law, met and married his wife, and witnessed the birth of most of his children in the city. One week later, he left America for the final time, arriving in Great Britain five weeks later.[8]

"Poor Sir James Wright I hear, is come home," wrote former South Carolina royal governor William Henry Lyttelton to William Knox, "and I hope he has done travelling for the rest of his life, and will have a competent allowance from [the] government to make him live comfortably."[9] Back in

1777 Wright had written a letter to the Earl of Shelburne about the plight of the Loyalists: "[I] have reason to believe independence is to be granted to America & that a negotiation is now actually carrying on." He begged that "restitution should be made . . . as in right & justice ought to be."[10] But Wright would go to the grave seeking both this peace and a "competent allowance," spending his final years at the head of the American Loyalist Claims Commission laboring to secure compensation for himself and Britain's loyal Americans.

On 29 August King George III held a levee at St. James's Palace where the "great officers of state [and] the foreign ministers, &c. were present. . . . Sir James Wright, Baronet, Governor of the province of Georgia, was at the levee, it being the first time since his return from America, when he was most graciously received, and had the honor to kiss His Majesty's hand." Wright utilized this special meeting to deliver a memorial to his sovereign, "stating the distressed condition and sufferings of His Majesty's loyal and faithful subjects of Georgia."[11] His task would prove difficult; indeed, one exiled and well-to-do Loyalist from Massachusetts lamented that "the state is not to reward the loyalty of every subject. . . . I cannot foresee what I may hereafter do, but easily that I must suffer hunger and nakedness in the comfortless mansions of the wretched."[12]

In the fall of 1782, newly elected prime minister William Petty, Lord Shelburne, appointed MPs John Eardley-Wilmot and Daniel Parker Coke "to enquire into the cases of all American sufferers," a duty that they began in October. Each Loyalist desirous of receiving compensation was required to submit a petition attesting to their fidelity and outlining their property losses. In addition, the petitioners were required to attend a hearing and produce affidavits "to confirm or to explain the merits, the losses, and other circumstances of [their] case."[13] Back in 1775 Wright had spent a great deal of time advocating for the safety, rights, and pecuniary compensation of Loyalists. He would now occupy the few remaining years of his life in that same quest. His efforts were not merely selfless; they also served the greater Loyalist communities, as his hundreds of affidavits attest.[14] Many of these Loyalists (mostly men) desperately needed Wright's assistance, for, as Abigail Adams observed, they were "very desperate bitter and venomous."[15]

In mid-February 1783 the *London Chronicle* announced the list of "agents chosen by the loyal American sufferers" to represent each former colony.[16] In his account of the commission, Eardley-Wilmot wrote that Wright's "activity and zeal, as well as abilities and large property, placed [him] at the head of the Board of Agents." He added that "being much respected, both in his public and private character, he kept his province, as long as possible, free from the general contagion." Later, Eardley-Wilmot wrote, the "government being determined to support him with energy, encouraged him to return in the spring of 1779. . . . [During] the siege [of Savannah], the [French and rebels] were repulsed in a most gallant manner . . . aided by the determined zeal and spirit of Sir James Wright himself, which made the successful defence of Savannah one of the most brilliant events of the War."[17]

Writing from Paris to Ralph Izard, an in-law of Wright's son Alexander, during the postwar peace talks, Wright's former friend Henry Laurens inserted a significant block quote in his letter from an unnamed acquaintance concerning the peace talks. In addition to denigrating Lord Shelburne as "rotten, deceitful, treacherous, & the very essence of Toryism," the acquaintance commented that "it is egregious in [the Loyalists] to appoint L[o]r[d] Dunmore, Govr Franklin, S[i]r James Wright, and even Arnold to be their agents."[18] Loyalist compensation proved the most acrimonious issue of those peace talks in Paris. Benjamin Franklin and John Jay were absolutely opposed to such compensation, and their intransigence, accompanied by Prime Minister Shelburne's acquiescence on the point, nearly ruined the peace talks.

## "They Have Lost and Sacrificed All"

At approximately the same time, the agents, with Wright at their head, published a pamphlet titled *The Case and Claim of the American Loyalists: Impartially Stated and Considered*. The thirty-eight-page pamphlet mimicked Wright's persistent complaint throughout the war: "Though destitute of that protection and support which they had a right to expect from the state, they were called upon 'to withstand and suppress the rebellion.'" The Loyalists even quoted Thomas Paine's work *The Crisis*: "The British have lost their interest in America with the disaffected."[19] Certainly the Loyalists had long believed this to be true.

The second part of the pamphlet set out to justify the agents' claim for remuneration. Their central argument, just like Thomas Jefferson's Declaration of Independence, drew heavily on Lockean theory. The "great aim and end of civil society," they insisted, "is protection of the persons and properties of individuals, by an *equal contribution* to whatever is necessary to attain and secure it." They offered commonsense examples of this contract as well as historical references to justify their right to compensation. In short, they maintained that "they have lost and sacrificed all that men can possibly lose or suffer, *life itself excepted*."[20]

Loyal Georgians also submitted their own petition to King George III because they deemed their situation, as the only southern colony in which Britain reestablished civil government, to be unique. They submitted an extract of a letter from Lord Germain to Governor Wright in which the king "assure[d] them that his loyal and faithful subjects of Georgia may always rely upon his Majesty's protection, and constant attention to their prosperity and happiness." It was just such a promise, which was oft repeated, that instilled in them an even deeper resilience than they had already exhibited.[21] The most resilient of these loyal Georgians, James Wright, occupied the final three years of his life advocating for their cause.

This unrelenting task involved attending daily hearings and incessant meetings with officials and other Loyalists, as well as providing hundreds of affidavits for his fellow Georgians, including many from the lower rungs of society.[22] For example, Wright wrote a letter in support of Henry Ferguson, a militia officer of nominal means. Ferguson, Wright wrote, was "in very distressed circumstances at present & deserves assistance."[23] In another letter to the American Loyalist Claims Commission, Wright noted that George Johnston, "a poor man" from the backcountry, had evacuated in 1782 and "knows no body here & has applied to me for assistance." Three other men joined Johnston on the last day of September 1784. "I know the men to be honest & loyal," Wright observed, "tho poor & ruined . . . , and I have been obliged to assist them, or they might lye in the streets, starve, and perish."[24] Lastly, for example, Samuel Montgomery praised Wright's generosity in helping feed Montgomery and his three children.[25]

Wright also spent a great deal of energy pressing for his own compensation package. He procured an impressive list of supporters, including, among others, King George III; William Pitt the Younger; William Murray, 1st Earl of Mansfield; George Germain, 1st Viscount Sackville; Thomas Townshend, 1st Viscount Sydney; William Legge, 2nd Earl of Dartmouth; Wills Hill, 1st Marquess of Downshire; and Sir Henry Clinton. The rebels had confiscated Wright's estates three times during the revolution. He had lost nearly £5,000 worth of furniture in 1776 and all his furniture upon the evacuation from Savannah. In 1783 he submitted the largest claim of any Georgian, claiming to have lost 231 slaves and more than twenty-six thousand acres of land dispersed over eleven plantations and additional tracts.[26] The commission accepted a claim valued at £100,260.11 and awarded him

£35,347.00 sterling, in addition to his £500.00 annual pension. A subsequent parliamentary act provided a reduction of all claims exceeding £10,000 and ultimately awarded Wright £32,977 plus £1,000 per annum as a pension for his service as governor.

According to Robert Mitchell's examination of Georgia Loyalist claims, Wright's individual claim represented 11 percent of all Georgia claims, and his award comprised about 15 percent of all compensation.[27] Wallace Brown's groundbreaking study of Loyalist claims indicated that Wright's claim was one of thirty in Georgia to exceed £5,000 sterling; another forty claimed less than £2,000; twenty-five less than £1,000; and thirteen less than £500. Furthermore, Brown found that Georgia's Loyalists came from all socioeconomic backgrounds, and 60 percent of them had lived in Savannah. Nearly 6 percent of all the town's white inhabitants filed claims, easily the highest of all colonial cities. Most Georgia claimants arrived after 1763.[28]

### "A Stable World within Which to Work"

Wright, however, would not live to learn of the commission's final decision. He was quite ill during his final year. In February 1785 he mentioned that he was "still confined & unable to go out" and that he must communicate by writing.[29] He died later that year at his home on Fludyer Street in southeast London on Sunday, 20 November 1785, and was interred in the north transept at Westminster Abbey one week later.[30] His death was reported on both sides of the Atlantic. The most thorough of these reports was the *Morning Chronicle and London Advertiser*:

On Sunday last died Sir James Wright, Baronet, late Governor of Georgia, in the 71st year of his age. As he presided in that province for two and twenty years with distinguished ability and integrity, it seems to be a tribute justly due to his merit as a faithful servant of his king and Country. Before the commotions in America, his example of industry and skill in the cultivation and improvement of Georgia was of eminent advantage; and the faithful discharge of his executive and judicial commission was universally acknowledged, by the people over whom he presided, none of his decrees as Chancellor having ever been reversed. Under all the difficulties which attended the latter period of his government, his spirited conduct in defence of that province was singularly manifested. *His loss is deeply felt and sincerely lamented by his family and friends, as well, [sic] as by his unfortunate fellow-sufferers from America, whose cause he most assiduously*

*laboured to support and solicit; and the success which attended his active exer-*
*tions in their behalf afforded him real comfort under his languishing state of*
*health for some time before his death.*[31]

The *Gazette of the State of Georgia* was much less laudatory, simply stating: "Died. Yesterday at his house in Westminster, Sir James Wright, Bart., many years Governor of Georgia."[32] Thus, after having dedicated more than two decades of his life to the province of Georgia, overseeing its rapid economic growth and geographic expansion, James Wright's life was reduced to a hollow afterthought.

Historian Bernard Bailyn concluded that Massachusetts governor Thomas Hutchinson, Wright's fellow exiled governor, "felt no elemental discontent, no romantic aspirations." The same certainly held true for the pragmatic James Wright, who spent a lifetime relentlessly accumulating land, wealth, status, and power. He thoroughly understood the eighteenth-century world into which he was born and focused his boundless energies on making the most of the opportunities presented to him. Like Hutchinson, however, Wright "was never crudely avaricious . . . ruthless . . . [or] flamboyant." His lifelong quest for familial redemption, private wealth, and, perhaps most importantly, personal respect was grounded in a deep conservatism that required, according to Bailyn, "a stable world within which to work, a hierarchy to ascend, and a formal, external calibration by which to measure where he was."[33]

Wright's upbringing left him ill-equipped to understand the moral passions of a revolutionary world. He was simply too rigid, distant, and aloof, and by the mid-1770s he found himself trapped by the chaos, which soon enveloped and ultimately destroyed him. Insecurity was Governor Wright's most evident character defect and can be seen in his correspondence. Unbending and industrious, he had an almost obsessive need to be appreciated, especially by his superiors. This, however, is not to say that he was a sycophant, because he was not. He rarely hesitated to critique the performance of his superiors, although he was careful to couch such criticisms in the proper deferential tone of the era.

Wright earnestly believed that British and Georgian interests were entirely compatible, and he worked assiduously to achieve both. Furthermore, he sincerely believed that he was possessed with a unique insight into the psyche of both Briton and Georgian alike and thus capable of successfully mediating the imperial crisis. He was born in England and spent roughly twenty years in London, usually near the centers of power, yet he spent most of his life on the periphery, building long-lasting relationships with colonists from Charleston to Savannah.

A consummate conservative, Wright nevertheless empathized with colonists who had become angry with parliamentary encroachments, and he understood the vital importance of the colonies to the British Empire and to the mercantilist system. Importantly, though, he believed in the British system of governance and insisted that the system could only be challenged through proper legal channels and not mob action. The very notion of aggressively defying British law was inconceivable to him. Such acts threatened to overturn the entire social, economic, and political foundation on which his world was based. Thus, during the sweltering summer of 1775, when Wright wrote that the "powers of government are wrested out of my hands," his personal agony extended well beyond the political arena, for he fully comprehended that the rebels were trying to tear down the foundation his life rested upon and replace it with an entirely new one.[34]

# LIST OF SOURCE ABBREVIATIONS

*AA*      Peter Force, ed. *American Archives: Fourth Series, Containing a Documentary History of the English Colonies in North America from the King's Message to Parliament of March 7, 1774, to the Declaration of Independence by the United States.* 6 vols. Washington, D.C., 1837–1846.

AO      Audit Office Papers, TNA.

*BGLC*    Mary Bondurant Warren, comp. *British Georgia Loyalists' Claims.* Athens, 2014.

BHO      British History Online. https://www.british-history.ac.uk/.

CL      William L. Clements Library, University of Michigan, Ann Arbor.

CO      Colonial Office Papers, TNA.

*ColRG*   Allen D. Candler, ed. *Colonial Records of the State of Georgia.* 39 vols. Atlanta, 1904–1986. Unpublished volumes are in the collection of the Georgia Historical Society, Savannah.

CP      Henry Clinton Papers, CL.

CRNC     Documenting the American South. Colonial and State Records of North Carolina. https://docsouth.unc.edu/csr/index.php/volumes.

*DAR*     K. G. Davies, ed. *Documents of the American Revolution, 1770–1783.* 21 vols. Shannon, Ireland, 1972–1981.

DLAR     David Library of the American Revolution, Washington Crossing, Pa.

*EAID*    Alden T. Vaughn, gen. ed. *Early American Indian Documents: Treaties and Laws, 1607–1789.* 20 vols. Bethesda, Md., 1979–2004.

*FM*      Benjamin Franklin Stevens. *B. F. Stevens's Facsimiles of Manuscripts in European Archives Relating to America, 1773–1783.* 25 vols. London, 1889–1898.

FO      Founders Online. https://founders.archives.gov/.

GA      Georgia Archives, Morrow.

*GG*      *Georgia Gazette.*

*GGCJ*    Mary B. Warren et al. *Georgia Governor and Council Journals.* 9 vols. Athens, 1991–2011.

*GHQ*     *Georgia Historical Quarterly.*

GHS　　　　Georgia Historical Society, Savannah.
*GHS Coll*　　*Collections of the Georgia Historical Society.* 21 vols. Savannah, 1840–1989.
　　　　　　https://dlg.usg.edu/collection/g-hi_g-hiia?per_page=20&sort=year+desc.
GP　　　　Thomas Gage Papers, American Series, CL.
*HCG*　　　George White. *Historical Collections of Georgia.* New York, 1855.
*JCC*　　　*Journals of the Continental Congress, 1774–1789.* https://memory.loc.gov
　　　　　　/ammem/amlaw/lwjclink.html.
*JCHA*　　　J. H. Easterby et al., eds. *The Journal of the Commons House of Assembly.* 14
　　　　　　vols. Columbia, 1951–1996.
*JSH*　　　*Journal of Southern History.*
KP　　　　William Knox Papers, CL.
LP　　　　William Henry Lyttelton Papers, CL.
*ODNB*　　*Oxford Dictionary of National Biography.* https://www.oxforddnb.com/.
*PHL*　　　David Chesnutt et al., eds. *The Papers of Henry Laurens.* 16 vols. Columbia,
　　　　　　1968–2002.
*PNG*　　　Richard K. Showman et al., eds. *The Papers of Nathanael Greene.* 13 vols.
　　　　　　Chapel Hill, 1976–2005.
*RAM*　　　*Report on American Manuscripts in the Royal Institution of Great Britain.* 4
　　　　　　vols. London, 1904–1909.
*RG*　　　William W. Abbot. *The Royal Governors of Georgia, 1754–1775.* Chapel Hill,
　　　　　　1959.
*RGG*　　　*Royal Georgia Gazette.*
*RRSG*　　Allen Candler, ed. *Revolutionary Records of the State of Georgia.* 3 vols.
　　　　　　Atlanta, 1908.
SCDAH　　South Carolina Department of Archives and History. https://www
　　　　　　.archivesindex.sc.gov/.
*SCG*　　　*South Carolina Gazette.*
*SCHGM*　　*South Carolina Historical and Genealogical Magazine.*
*SCHM*　　*South Carolina Historical Magazine.*
SP　　　　William Petty, Lord Shelburne Papers, CL.
TNA　　　The National Archives at Kew, United Kingdom.
*WMQ*　　*William and Mary Quarterly.*
WO　　　　War Office Papers, TNA.

# NOTES

## Introduction

1. "Proceedings," 18 January 1776, p.m., in *GHS Coll*, 5.1:38. Also see Frank Lambert, *James Habersham* (Athens, 2005); and Lambert, "'Father against Son, and Son against Father': The Habershams of Georgia and the American Revolution," *GHQ* 84, no. 1 (Spring 2000): 1–28.

2. For more information about the publicly funded governor's house, see *ColRG*, 1:388–392.

3. For Wright's property, see James Wright, Loyalist claim, in *BGLC*. (In order to provide clarity and a single, more accessible source for Georgians' Loyalist claims, I will only cite Mary Bondurant Warren's *BGLC* when referencing a Loyalist claim, even though her volume was first released after the completion of my dissertation, on which this book is based.) Wright does not mention his arrest, only that "in Feb. 1776 I was under the necessity of retiring & went on board His Majesty's ship *Scarborough*" (Wright to Jon Forster, 3 November 1783, in *BGLC*).

4. "Discourse delivered before the Georgia Historical Society, at the celebration of their second anniversary, by William Bacon Stevens, M.D.," in *GHS Coll*, 2:28–30; William Bacon Stevens, *A History of Georgia* (Philadelphia, 1859), 2:127–129; Charles Colcock Jones Jr., *History of Savannah* (Syracuse, 1890), 219–221; Jones, *The History of Georgia* (Boston, 1883), 2:211–212; and Hugh McCall, *History of Georgia* (Atlanta, 1909), 300–301. Later in the war, Wright exacted a measure of revenge by confiscating Habersham's estate. See *London Courant, and Westminster Chronicle*, 30 December 1780.

5. "Proceedings," 18 January 1776, 11:00 p.m., in *GHS Coll*, 5.1:39.

6. Jones, *History of Georgia*, 2:212; Jones, *History of Savannah*, 220; Stevens, *History of Georgia*, 2:128.

7. The veracity of the account concerning shots fired into Wright's home cannot be conclusively affirmed. He did not mention such an episode in either his Loyalist claim or any extant correspondence. However, Josiah Tattnall, who was arrested at the same time as Wright, mentioned in his claim that Wright had been continually harassed and "insulted." See Josiah Tattnall, Loyalist claim, in *BGLC*. Stevens and Jones have produced well-researched and generally trustworthy histories of Georgia.

8. Wright to Lord George Germain, 12 February 1776, folder no. 5, document no. 657, CO.

9. I have chosen to utilize the contemporary spelling even though colonial Charles Town did not adopt its current name until after the Revolutionary War.

10. For a fuller review of Wright's ancestry, see Greg Brooking, "'My Zeal for the Real Happiness of Both Great Britain and the Colonies': The Conflicting Imperial Career of Sir James Wright" (PhD diss., Georgia State University, 2013), https://scholarworks.gsu.edu/cgi/viewcontent.cgi?article=1038&context=history_diss.

11. Stuart Handley, "Wright, Sir Robert (c.-1689)," in *ODNB*, http://www.oxforddnb .com/view/article/30056; John Venn, *Biographical History of Gonville and Caius College* (Cambridge, 1897), 1:265. Also see S. H. A. Hervey, *Biographical List of Boys Educated at King Edward VI Free Grammar School, Bury St. Edmunds, from 1550–1900* (Bury St. Edmunds, 1908), 434; and R. W. Elliott, *The Story of King Edward VI School, Bury St. Edmunds* (Bury St. Edmunds, 1963), 19–20.

12. He gained admission to Lincoln's Inn on 14 June 1654 and was called to the bar on 25 June 1661. See Handley, "Wright." His father, Jermyn, entered Lincoln's Inn on 27 November 1626. See Venn, *Biographical History*, 1:265. Also see Augustus Jessopp, ed., *The Lives of the Right Hon. Francis North, Baron Guilford; the Hon. Sir Dudley North; and the Hon. and Rev. Dr. John North by the Hon. Roger North* (London, 1890), 1:324.

13. Handley, "Wright"; Sir James Wright, pedigree chart, College of Arms, London, www.college-of-arms.gov.uk; and "Collection of Pedigree and Genealogical Memoranda of the Family of Wright," in Davy's Suffolk Collections, vol. 80, British Library.

14. For example, he became embroiled in the Popish Plot (1678–1681). See John Kenyon, *The Popish Plot* (Ann Arbor, 1972); John Pollock, *The Popish Plot: A Study in the History of the Reign of Charles II* (London, 1903), 317–332; and Roger North, *The Lives of the Right Hon. Francis North [. . .]* (London, 1826), 312–326.

15. John Miller, *James II* (New Haven, 2000), 184–185; Scott Soberby, *Making Toleration: The Repealers and the Glorious Revolution* (Cambridge, 2013); Peter Ackroyd, *Rebellion: The History of England from James I to the Glorious Revolution* (New York, 2014), chap. 45; and William Gibson, *James II and the Trial of the Seven Bishops* (New York, 2009), esp. 116–139.

16. For "profligate," see John Campbell, *The Lives of the Chief Justices of England* (London, 1874), 2:356. For "odious," see Richard Hildreth, *Atrocious Judges: Lives of Judges Infamous as Tools of Tyrants [. . .]* (New York, 1856), 387.

17. "Norfolk, England, Church of England Baptism, Marriages, and Burials, 1535–1812," database with images, Ancestry, https://www.ancestry.com/discoveryui-content /view/2867615:61045?tid=&pid=&queryId=4bdee5c3cb78ebdeecd6ca21e265873e& _phsrc=YqT443&_phstart=successSource; John Burke, *A Genealogical and Heraldic History of the Commoners of Great Britain and Ireland* (London, 1835), 2:615.

18. Venn, *Biographical History*, 1:473–474; Henry Macgeagh, *Register of Admissions to the Honourable Society of the Middle Temple, from the Fifteenth Century to the Year 1944* (London, 1949), 1:159.

19. The two were wed on 7 October 1689. See "Marriages from the Sedgefield Registers (1581–1729)," database with images, Ancestry, https://www.ancestry.com/ discoveryui-content/view/608290:2056?tid=&pid=&queryId=ee1b59abe376bd835c6d

25a49c9ede12&_phsrc=YqT439&_phstart=successSource. Parish records indicate that she died on 27 November 1723.

20. "London and Surrey, England, Marriage Bonds and Allegations, 1597–1921," Ancestry, https://www.ancestry.com/discoveryui-content/view/608290:2056?tid=&pid=&queryId=ee1b59abe376bd835c6d25a49c9ede12&_phsrc=YqT439&_phstart=successSource.

21. For an alternative or secondary possibility concerning the family's relocation, see Charles Sanderson to William Cotesworth, 23 January 1726, folder no. 1, document no. 68, Cotesworth MSS CK, Gateshead Public Library, Gateshead, U.K. This letter was transcribed by Joyce Ellis, author of *A Study of the Business Fortunes of William Cotesworth* (New York, 1981).

22. Arch. Hutcheson to Mr. Delafaye, 16 June 1730, in Hoyt Canady, "Gentlemen of the Bar: Lawyers in Colonial South Carolina" (PhD diss., University of Tennessee, 1984), 152.

23. Elizabeth Hyrne to Burrell Massingberd, 21 January 1725, in Pauline Loven, "Mr. Robert Wright," in *Hyrne Family Letters, 1699–1757*, http://hyrneletters.wordpress.com/genealogy/mr-robert-wright/.

24. Edward McCrady, *The History of South Carolina under the Royal Government, 1719–1776* (New York, 1899), chaps. 5, 6; Robert Weir, *Colonial South Carolina: A History* (Columbia, 1997), chap. 6; and Walter Edgar, *South Carolina: A History* (Columbia, 1999), chaps. 6, 7. For his appointment, see item 633, 28 May 1725, in *Calendar of State Papers Colonial, America and West Indies*, ed. Cecil Headlam (London, 1936), 34:367–381. For his royal appointment, see *London Evening Post*, 15–17 December 1730; Charles Hart to Governor Robert Johnson, 23 February 1730, in ST 463, 62 B, p. 654, SCDAH; and Robert Johnson to Robert Wright, 24 March 1731, in ST 464, 64, pp. 187–188, SCDAH.

25. Thomas Lowndes to Alfred Popple, 23 December 1729, in Headlam, *Calendar*, 36:565–578; and McCrady, *History of South Carolina*, 107–109.

26. W. Roy Smith, *South Carolina as a Royal Province, 1719–1776* (New York, 1903), 44–45; Jack Greene, *The Quest for Power: The Lower Houses of Assembly in the Southern Royal Colonies, 1689–1776* (Chapel Hill, 1963). For the issues most relevant to Wright, see 129–147, 330–343.

27. For example, *SCG*, 5 and 12 May 1733; and *Daily Courant*, 13 April 1733. See also Carl Vipperman, *The Rise of Rawlins Lowndes, 1721–1800* (Columbia, 1978), 32–37; McCrady, *History of South Carolina*, 150–163 and, generally, chap. 9; Leonard Labaree, ed., *Royal Instructions to British Colonial Governors, 1670–1776* (New York, 1967), 1:370–371; Smith, *South Carolina*, 42–48, 129–131, 294–303; James Haw, *John & Edward Rutledge of South Carolina* (Athens, 1997), 4; Ella Lonn, *Colonial Agents of the Southern Colonies* (Chapel Hill, 1945), 279; and Eugene Sirmans, *Colonial South Carolina: A Political History* (Chapel Hill, 1936), 181–182.

28. "Proceedings," 4 February 1738, in *JCHA, 10 November 1736 to 7 June 1739*, 470. For Bull the enslaver, see Kinloch Bull, *The Oligarchs in Colonial and Revolutionary Charleston: Lieutenant Governor William Bull II and His Family* (Columbia, 1991), esp. 232.

29. McCrady, *History of South Carolina*, 182, 460–464; and, for example, *SCG*, 15 May 1736.

30. *SCG*, 27 October, 24 November 1739. See also Peter McCandless, *Slavery, Disease, and Suffering in the Southern Lowcountry* (Leiden, 2011), 70.

31. James Oglethorpe to the Duke of Newcastle, from Savannah, 12 October 1739, in *DAR*; Oglethorpe to Trustees of Georgia, 5 October 1739, in *DAR*; Jim Murphy, *An American Plague: The True and Terrifying Story of the Yellow Fever Epidemic of 1793* (New York, 2003); William Bull to Board of Trade, 20 November 1739, in Headlam, *Calendar*, 45:215–234; George Dunbar to Herman Verelst, 7 October 1739, in Headlam, *Calendar*, 45:198; *Daily Post* (London), 5 December 1739; *London Evening Post*, 6 December 1739; *Universal Spectator and Weekly Journal*, 8 December 1739; and *SCG*, 1 December 1739.

32. For example, series S372001, vol. 00R0, pp. 100, 421, in "Explore," SCDAH. These two documents indicate his lease and/or sale of 10,400 acres plus land in Amelia Township in 1737 and 1739. Also see his numerous land grants and plats, also in SCDAH. See, for example, series 213019, vol. 0002, p. 390, for a land grant of 302 acres in Craven County on 25 June 1736 and series S213184, vol. 0003, p. 210, for a plat for 2,000 acres in Queensboro Township on 1 October 1736.

33. George Rogers, *Charleston in the Age of the Pinckneys* (Columbia, 2002), 68.

34. For example, series 213003, vol. 0002, p. 46, in SCDAH lists the sale of six thousand acres to George Anson. There are also numerous advertisements for the sale of land in *SCG*, 30 August 1735, 6 April 1738.

35. The Wright family placed an advertisement for a 25 June 1741 estate sale "at the plantation late of Robert Wright, Esq.; deceased, near Dorchester, a parcel of very good slaves, and sundry other things" (*SCG*, 11 June 1741). Additionally, there are at least two instances in which slaves fled the chief justice's Dorchester plantation listed in *SCG*, 4 October 1735, 23 July 1737.

36. McCrady, *History of South Carolina*, 63.

37. I owe a great debt to two professional genealogists, the late Mary Bondurant Warren (Athens, Ga.) and Kenneth H. Thomas Jr. (Decatur, Ga.), for their inexhaustible assistance and endless support in tracking down the Wright family pedigree, a project that they began prior to my own project. The key sources for Wright's genealogy are "Collection of Pedigree and Genealogical Memoranda"; Wright, pedigree chart; James Wright, Loyalist claim, in *BGLC*; and Burke, *Genealogical and Heraldic History*.

38. For a full examination of relevant historiography, see Brooking, "'My Zeal.'"

39. Sydney Mintz, "Enduring Substances, Trying Theories: The Caribbean Regime as Oikoumene," *Journal of the Royal Anthropological Institute* 2, no. 2 (June 1996): 292. See also John McCusker and Kenneth Morgan, eds., *The Early Modern Atlantic Economy* (New York, 2000).

40. Trevor Reese to Kenneth Coleman, 29 November 1954, MS3478, box 8, Kenneth Coleman Papers (unprocessed), Hargrett Library, University of Georgia, Athens. Also see Kenneth Coleman, "James Wright," in *Georgians in Profile: Essays in Honor of Ellis Merton Coulter* (Athens, 1958), 40–60; Coleman, "James Wright and the Origins of the Revolution in Georgia," in *The Human Dimensions of Nation Making: Essays on Colonial and Revolutionary America*, ed. James Kirby Martin (Madison, 1976), 105–120; Coleman, "Oglethorpe and James Wright: A Georgia Comparison," in *Oglethorpe in Perspective: Georgia's Founder after Two Hundred Years*, ed. Phinizy Spalding and Har-

vey Jackson (Tuscaloosa, 1989), 122–130; Coleman, "James Wright and the Growth of Georgia, 1760–1776," paper presented at the annual meeting of the Southern Historians Association, 1960; Coleman, "Sir James Wright: Georgia's Last Colonial Governor," paper presented at Valdosta State College, 1967; Edward J. Cashin, "Sowing the Wind: Governor Wright and the Georgia Backcountry on the Eve of the Revolution," in *Forty Years of Diversity: Essays on Colonial Georgia*, ed. Harvey H. Jackson and Phinizy Spalding (Athens, 1984); Cashin, "'But Brothers, It Is Our Land We Are Talking About': Winners and Losers in the Georgia Backcountry," in *An Uncivil War: The Southern Backcountry during the American Revolution*, ed. Ronald Hoffman, Thad Tate, and Peter Albert (Charlottesville, 1985); *RG*; Robert Calhoon, *The Loyalists of Revolutionary America, 1760–1781* (New York, 1973); and Calhoon, Timothy Barnes, and Robert Davis, eds., *Tory Insurgents: The Loyalist Perception and Other Essays* (Columbia, 2010).

41. James Wright to Lord George Germain, 19 February 1776, in *ColRG*, 39:226–231.

42. See Calhoon, *Loyalists*; Calhoon, Barnes, and Davis, *Tory Insurgents*; William Nelson, *The American Tory* (Boston, 1961); Moses Coit Tyler, *The Literary History of the American Revolution, 1763–1783* (New York, 1957); Claude H. Van Tyne, *The Loyalists in the American Revolution* (New York, 1929); Esmond Wright, ed., *Red, White, and True Blue: The Loyalists in the Revolution* (New York, 1976); Wright, *A Tug of Loyalties: Anglo-American Relations, 1765–85* (London, 1975); Wallace Brown, *The Good Americans: The Loyalists in the American Revolution* (New York, 1969); Leslie F. S. Upton, *Revolutionary versus Loyalist* (Waltham, 1968); North Callahan, *Royal Raiders: The Tories of the American Revolution* (Indianapolis, 1963); Callahan, *Flight from the Republic: The Tories of the American Revolution* (Indianapolis, 1967); Janice Potter-MacKinnon, *The Liberty We Seek: Loyalist Ideology in Colonial New York and Massachusetts* (Cambridge, 1983). See also William Pencak, *America's Burke: The Mind of Thomas Hutchinson* (Washington, D.C., 1982); Joseph Tiedeman, Eugene Fingerhut, and Robert Venables, eds., *The Other Loyalists: Ordinary People, Royalism, and the Revolution in the Middle Colonies* (Albany, 2009); John Ferling, "The American Revolution and American Security: Whig and Loyalist Views," *Historian* 40, no. 3 (May 1978): 492–507; Paul Smith, *Loyalists and Redcoats: A Study in British Revolutionary Policy* (Chapel Hill, 1964); Wallace Brown, *The King's Friends: The Composition and Motives of the American Loyalist Claimants* (Providence, 1965); and Mary Beth Norton, *The British-Americans: The Loyalist Exiles in England, 1774–1789* (Boston, 1972).

43. Jim Piecuch, *Three Peoples, One King: Loyalists, Indians, and Slaves in the Revolutionary South, 1775–1782* (Columbia, 2008); Maya Jasanoff, *Liberty's Exiles: American Loyalists in the Revolutionary South* (New York, 2011); Cassandra Pybus, *Epic Journeys of Freedom: Runaway Slaves of the American Revolution and Their Global Quest for Liberty* (Boston, 2006); Ellen Wilson, *The Loyal Blacks* (New York, 1976); Gary Nash, *Red, White, and Black: The Peoples of Early North America* (Upper Saddle River, 2000); Nash, *The Unknown American Revolution: The Unruly Birth of Democracy and the Struggle to Create America* (New York, 2006); John Pulis, ed., *Moving On: Black Loyalists in the Afro-American World* (New York, 1999).

44. For a multiethnic emphasis, see Piecuch, *Three Peoples*; Pybus, *Epic Journeys*; Jasanoff, *Liberty's Exiles*; Wilson, *Loyal Blacks*; and Pulis, *Moving On*.

45. Potter-MacKinnon, *Liberty We Seek*. This is specifically noted by Wright's best

friend, James Habersham, who wrote: "It is easy for people in England to speculate," but in Georgia "we must act as necessity requires. [The Board of Trade] do not truly understand our local circumstances" (see Habersham to James Wright, 4 December 1772, in *GHS Coll*, 6:217).

46. See, for example, Brown, *King's Friends*.

47. Bernard Bailyn, *The Ordeal of Thomas Hutchinson* (Cambridge, Mass., 1974), vii.

48. Andrew Walmsley, *Thomas Hutchinson and the Origins of the American Revolution* (New York, 1999); Ed Cashin, *Governor Henry Ellis and the Transformation of British North America* (Athens, 1994); Cashin, *The King's Ranger: Thomas Brown and the American Revolution on the Southern Frontier* (New York, 1999); Carol Berkin, *Jonathan Sewall: Odyssey of an American Loyalist* (New York, 1974); John Ferling, *The Loyalist Mind: Joseph Galloway and the American Revolution* (University Park, 1977); Sheila Skemp, *William Franklin: Son of a Patriot, Servant of a King* (New York, 1990); Frank Lambert, *James Habersham: Loyalty, Politics, and Commerce in Colonial Georgia* (Athens, 2005); and James Corbett David, *Dunmore's New World: The Extraordinary Life of a Royal Governor in Revolutionary America—with Jacobites, Counterfeiters, Land Schemes, Shipwrecks, Scalping, Indian Politics, Runaway Slaves, and Two Illegal Royal Weddings* (Charlottesville, 2013).

49. John Ferling, *Setting the World Ablaze: Washington, Adams, Jefferson, and the American Revolution* (New York, 2000), x–xi.

50. Thucydides, *History of the Peloponnesian War*, trans. Richard Crawley (London, 1910), 133.

51. Frederick Jackson Turner, *The Frontier in American History* (New York, 1920), 1. See also James Merrell, *The Indians' New World: Catawbas and Their Neighbors from European Contact through the Era of Removal* (New York, 1989).

52. N. Scott Momaday in *Ken Burns Presents: The West, a Film by Stephen Ives*, DVD, directed by Stephen Ives (Florentine Films, 2004).

53. Leonard Thompson and Howard Lamar, "Comparative Frontier History," in *The Frontier in History: North America and Southern Africa*, ed. Leonard Thompson and Howard Lamar (New Haven, 1982), 3–14.

54. Richard R. Beeman, *The Evolution of the Southern Backcountry: A Case Study of Lunenberg County, Virginia, 1746–1832* (Philadelphia, 1984); Gregory Nobles, "Breaking into the Backcountry: New Approaches to the Early American Frontier, 1750–1800," *WMQ* 46, no. 4 (October 1989): 643–644; Bernard Bailyn and Philip D. Morgan, eds., *Strangers within the Realm: Cultural Margins of the First British Empire* (Chapel Hill, 1991); George William Franz, *Paxton: A Study of Community Structure and Mobility in the Colonial Pennsylvania Backcountry* (New York, 1989); Michael A. Bellesiles, *Revolutionary Outlaws: Ethan Allen and the Struggle for Independence on the Early American Frontier* (Charlottesville, 1993); Alan Taylor, *Liberty Men and Great Proprietors: The Revolutionary Settlement on the Maine Frontier, 1760–1820* (Chapel Hill, 1990); Eric Hinderaker, *Elusive Empires: Constructing Colonialism in the Ohio Valley, 1763–1800* (New York, 1997), 195–199; Carville Earle, "Place Your Bets: Rates of Frontier Expansion in American History, 1650–1890," in *Enduring and Evolving Geographic Themes*, ed. Alexander B. Murphy and Douglas L. Johnson (Lanham, 2000); Joshua Piker, "Colonists and Creeks: Rethinking the Pre-revolutionary Southern Backcountry," *JSH* 70, no. 3 (August 2004); Wilma Dunaway, *The First American Frontier: Transition to Capi-*

*talism in Southern Appalachia, 1700–1860* (Chapel Hill, 1996); Bernard Bailyn, *The Peopling of British North America: An Introduction* (New York, 1988); Carl Bridenbaugh, *Myths and Realities: Societies of the Colonial South* (Baton Rouge, 1952); David Hackett Fischer, *Albion's Seed: Four British Folkways in America* (New York, 1989); Rachel Klein, *Unification of a Slave State: The Rise of the Planter Class in the South Carolina Backcountry, 1760–1808* (Chapel Hill, 1990); Klein, "Frontier Planters and the American Revolution: The South Carolina Backcountry, 1775–1782," in Hoffman, Tate, and Albert, *An Uncivil War*; Klein, "Ordering the Backcountry: The South Carolina Regulation," *WMQ* 38, no. 4 (October 1981): 661–680; Klein, "Who Should Rule at Home? The Revolution in the Carolina Backcountry," in *Major Problems in the History of the American South*, ed. Paul Escott, David Goldfield, Sally McMillen, and Elizabeth Turner (Boston, 1999); Alan Gallay, *Formation of a Planter Elite: Jonathan Bryan and the Southern Colonial Frontier* (Athens, 2007); and Joan E. Cashin, *A Family Venture: Men and Women on the Southern Frontier* (New York, 1991).

55. James Wright to the Earl of Shelburne, 15 August 1767, in *ColRG*, 37:240–242.

56. Piker, "Colonists and Creeks," 510. Inhabiting this region, he stated, "meant liminality for all concerned."

57. Richard White, *The Middle Ground: Indians, Empires, and Republics in the Great Lakes Region, 1650–1815* (New York, 1991); Alan Taylor, *Divided Ground: Indians, Settlers, and the Northern Borderland of the American Revolution* (New York, 1996); Merrell, *Indians' New World*; Colin Calloway, *New Worlds for All: Indians, Europeans, and the Remaking of Early America* (Baltimore, 1997); Claudio Saunt, "'Our Indians': European Empires and the Native American South," in *The Atlantic in Global History, 1500–2000*, ed. Jorge Cañizares-Esguerra and Erik Seeman (Upper Saddle River, 2007); Evan Haefeli and Kevin Sweeney, *Captors and Captives: The 1704 French and Indian Raid on Deerfield* (Amherst, 2003); Gregory Evans Dowd, *A Spirited Resistance: The North American Indian Struggle for Unity, 1745–1815* (Baltimore, 1992); Ned Blackhawk, *Violence over the Land: Indians and Empires in the Early American West* (Cambridge, Mass., 2006); Claudio Saunt, *A New Order of Things: Property, Power, and the Transformation of the Creek Indians, 1733–1816* (Cambridge, 1999); James Axtell, *The Invasion Within: The Contest of Cultures in Colonial North America* (New York, 1986); Edward J. Cashin, *Guardians of the Valley: Chickasaws in Colonial South Carolina and Georgia* (Columbia, 2009); Daniel K. Richter, *Facing East from Indian Country: A Native History of Early America* (Cambridge, Mass., 2003); Fred Anderson, *The Crucible of War: The Seven Years' War and the Fate of Empire in British North America, 1754–1766* (New York, 2000); Gary Nash, "The Forgotten Experience: Indians, Blacks, and the American Revolution," in *The American Revolution: Changing Perspectives*, ed. William Fowler and Wallace Coyle (Boston, 1979); and Piecuch, *Three Peoples*.

58. Eugene Genovese, *The Political Economy of Slavery: Studies in the Economy and Society of the Slave South* (New York, 1965); Bertram Wyatt-Brown, *Honor and Violence in the Old South* (New York, 1986); James Oakes, *The Ruling Race: A History of American Slaveholders* (New York, 1998); Eugene Genovese, *Roll, Jordan, Roll: The World the Slaves Made* (New York, 1974); Daniel Kilbride, "Cultivation, Conservatism, and the Early National Gentry: The Manigault Family and Their Circle," *Journal of the Early Republic* 19, no. 2 (Summer 1999): 221–256; S. Max Edelson, *Plantation Enterprise in Colonial South Carolina* (Cambridge, Mass., 2006); Mart A. Stewart, *"What*

*Nature Suffers to Groe": Life, Labor and Landscape on the Georgia Coast, 1680–1920* (Athens, 2002); Jeffrey R. Young, *Domesticating Slavery: The Master Class in Georgia and South Carolina, 1670–1837* (Chapel Hill, 1999); Erskine Clarke, *Dwelling Place: A Plantation Epic* (New Haven, 2005); Michael O'Brien, *Conjectures of Order: Intellectual Life and the American South, 1810–1860* (Chapel Hill, 2004); Stephanie McCurry, *Masters of Small Worlds: Yeoman Households, Gender Relations, and the Political Culture of the Antebellum South Carolina Lowcountry* (New York, 1997); Ulrich B. Phillips, *American Negro Slavery: A Survey of the Supply, Employment and Control of Negro Labor as Determined by the Plantation Regime* (New York, 1918); Kenneth Stampp, *The Peculiar Institution: Slavery in the Ante-Bellum South* (New York, 1956); Frank Tannenbaum, *Slave and Citizen: The Negro in the Americas* (New York, 1947); Stanley Elkins, *Slavery: A Problem in American Institutional and Intellectual Life* (Chicago, 1968); Peter Kolchin, *Unfree Labor: American Slavery and Russian Serfdom* (Cambridge, 1987); Philip Morgan, ed., *African American Life in the Georgia Lowcountry: The Atlantic World and the Gullah Geechee* (Athens, 2010); Carl Degler, *Neither Black nor White: Slavery and Race Relations in Brazil and the United States* (New York, 1971); Peter Wood, *Black Majority: Negroes in Colonial South Carolina from 1670 through the Stono Rebellion* (New York, 1975); Ira Berlin, *Many Thousands Gone: The First Two Centuries of Slavery in North America* (Cambridge, 1998); Berlin, *Generations of Captivity: A History of African-American Slaves* (Cambridge, 2003); John Hope Franklin, *From Slavery to Freedom: A History of American Negroes* (New York, 1947); John Blasingame, *The Slave Community: Plantation Life in the Antebellum South* (New York, 1972); Timothy Lockley, *Lines in the Sand: Race and Class in Lowcountry Georgia, 1750–1860* (Athens, 2001); Barbara J. Fields, "Ideology and Race in American History," in *Race and Reconstruction: Essays in Honor of C. Vann Woodward*, ed. J. Morgan Kousser and James M. McPherson (New York, 1982); Benjamin Quarles, *The Negro in the American Revolution* (Chapel Hill, 1961); Sylvia Frey, *Water from the Rock: Black Resistance in a Revolutionary Age* (Princeton, 1992); Winthrop Jordan, *White over Black: American Attitudes toward the Negro, 1550–1812* (Chapel Hill, 1968); Gary Nash, *The Forgotten Fifth: African Americans in the Age of Revolution* (Cambridge, Mass., 2006); Philip D. Morgan, *Slave Counterpoint: Black Culture in the Eighteenth-Century Chesapeake and Lowcountry* (Chapel Hill, 1998); Eric Williams, *Capitalism and Slavery* (Chapel Hill, 1944); Phillip Curtain, *The Atlantic Slave Trade: A Census* (New York, 1969); Joseph Inikori and Stanley Engerman, eds., *The Atlantic Slave Trade: Effects on Economics, Societies, and Peoples in Africa, the Americas, and Europe* (Durham, 1992); Herbert Klein, *The Middle Passage: Comparative Studies in the Atlantic Slave Trade* (Princeton, 1978); Hugh Thomas, *The Slave Trade: The Story of the Atlantic Slave Trade* (New York, 1997); David Eltis, *The Rise of African Slavery in the Americas* (New York, 2000); Paul Lovejoy, *Identity in the Shadow of Slavery* (New York, 2009); Manisha Sinha, "To 'Cast Just Obliquy' on Oppressors: Black Radicalism in the Age of Revolution," *WMQ*, 3rd ser., 64, no. 1 (January 2007): 149–160; Simon Schama, *Rough Crossings: Britain, the Slaves, and the American Revolution* (New York, 2006); and Peter Wood, "'The Facts Speak Loudly Enough': Exploring Early Southern Black History," in *The Devil's Lane: Sex and the Race in the Early South*, ed. Catherine Clinton and Michele Gillespie (New York, 1997).

59. James Wright to the Duke of Hillsborough, 31 May 1768, in *ColRG*, 37:311–313;

Wright to Upper House, 15 February 1773, in *ColRG*, 17:688–690. For the best study of the limited power wielded by Britain's southern colonial governors, see Ruth Carol Cunningham, "The Southern Royal Governors and the Coming of the American Revolution, 1763–1776" (PhD diss., University of New York at Buffalo, 1984).

60. The appointment did not become official until 25 February 1731. See Walter Edgar, ed., *Biographical Directory of the South Carolina House of Representatives* (Columbia, 1977), 2:30. James Wright's grandfather, also named Robert, served as lord chief justice of England from 1685 to 1688. See William Cobbett, *Parliamentary History of England* (London, 1809), 5:279–340, for example.

61. *SCG*, 20 February 1742.

62. *Pennsylvania Gazette*, 29 November 1764.

63. "Proceedings," 4 March 1737, in *JCHA, 10 November 1736 to 7 June 1739*, 282–283; "Proceedings," 28 June 1737, in Brent Holcomb, *Petitions for Land from South Carolina Council Journals* (Columbia, 1996), 1:89; and *SCG*, 5 November 1737.

64. On the eve of the revolution, Wright's estate was valued at £80,000, making him the wealthiest man in Georgia. See *RG*, 84.

65. James F. Cook, *Governors of Georgia* (Huntsville, 1979), 19.

66. *RG*, 83; Calhoon, *Loyalists*, 21; and Ronald G. Killion and Charles T. Waller, *Georgia and the Revolution* (Atlanta, 1975), 6.

67. Cook, *Governors of Georgia*, 20. For the determined resistance concerning Wright's land policies, see Gallay, *Formation*.

## Chapter 1. The Making of an Aristocrat

1. *Middlesex Journal and Evening Advertiser*, 1 May 1776, which stated that Sir James Wright's "baggage" had been "burnt" by the rebels. It is also possible that he had his papers (or remaining papers) burned following his death.

2. *SCG*, 23 July 1737.

3. *SCG*, 21 August 1737, 29 December 1737, 28 December 1738.

4. Ric Berman, *Loyalists and Malcontents: Freemasonry & Revolution in South Carolina and Georgia* (Goring Heath, 2017), 22.

5. "Original Rules and Members of the Charlestown Library Society," *SCHGM* 23, no. 4 (October 1922): 163–170.

6. Berman, *Loyalists and Malcontents*, 2.

7. Jessica Harland-Jacobs, "'Hands across the Sea': The Masonic Network, British Imperialism, and the North Atlantic World," *Geographical Review* 89, no. 2 (April 1999): 239.

8. Immanuel Wallerstein, *World-Systems Analysis: An Introduction* (Durham, 2004); Jack P. Greene, *Peripheries and Center: Constitutional Development in the Extended Polities of the British Empire and the United States, 1607–1788* (New York, 1986); and Amy Turner-Bushnell, "Center-Periphery Analysis," in *Atlantic History*, ed. Joseph C. Miller (Princeton, 2015), 86–87.

9. *SCG*, 28 May 1737.

10. George Farquhar, *The Recruiting Officer, a Comedy* (London, 1819).

11. *SCG*, 28 May 1737.

12. *SCG*, 28 December 1738.

13. *SCG*, 3 January 1743. Also see Clay Ouzts, *Samuel Elbert and the Age of Revolution in Georgia, 1740–1788* (Macon, 2022), 49–53.

14. David Ramsay, *History of South Carolina* (Newberry, 1858), 69; Walter Edgar, *South Carolina: A History* (Columbia, 1998), chap. 8; George C. Rogers, *Charleston in the Age of the Pinckneys* (Columbia, 1980), 9–11, 68–74; Emma Hart, *Building Charleston: Town and Society in the Eighteenth-Century Atlantic World* (Columbia, 2010), 65–66; and Russell Menard, "Financing the Lowcountry Export Boom: Capital and Growth in Early South Carolina," *WMQ* 51, no. 4 (October 1994): esp. 659–661, 675.

15. Kenneth Morgan, "The Organization of the Colonial American Rice Trade," *WMQ* 52, no. 3 (July 1995): 433–434; and Alan Gallay, *The Formation of the Planter Elite* (Athens, 2007), 11.

16. George Washington to John Park Custis, 26 May 1778, FO.

17. George Frakes, *Laboratory for Liberty: The South Carolina Legislative Committee System* (Lexington, 1970), 57–58; James Glen to Board of Trade, March 1751, in *The Colonial South Carolina Scene: Contemporary Scenes, 1697–1774*, ed. Roy Merrens (Columbia, 1977), 182; Rogers, *Charleston*, 40–43; Edgar, *South Carolina*, chap. 5; and Marion Eugene Sirmans, *Colonial South Carolina: A Political History, 1663–1763* (Chapel Hill, 2012), 226–227.

18. Henry Laurens to James Laurens, 15 April 1774, in S. Max Edelson, *Plantation Enterprise in Colonial South Carolina* (Cambridge, Mass., 2011), 1; and Henry Laurens to James Wright, 14 September 1764, in *PHL*, 4:423.

19. The others included a baker and a ship captain.

20. Edelson, *Plantation Enterprise*, 1.

21. Gallay, *Formation*, 62, 5, 18. During this period, land in South Carolina was fairly cheap and plentiful, but the necessary labor to create an actual plantation was truly scarce. Also see Paul Pressly, *On the Rim of the Caribbean: Colonial Georgia and the British Atlantic World* (Athens, 2013), 7.

22. Frederick George Mulcaster to unknown, 6 November 1768, in Joyce Chaplin, *An Anxious Pursuit: Agricultural Innovation and Modernity in the Lower South, 1730–1815* (Chapel Hill, 1993), 1–2; and Edelson, *Plantation Enterprise*, 191–192.

23. Henry Laurens to Duncan Rose, 5 June 1785, in *PHL*, 16:565–566.

24. Henry Laurens to Edward Bridgen, 23 September 1784, in Chaplin, *An Anxious Pursuit*, 2.

25. Chaplin, *An Anxious Pursuit*, 8–10; and Edelson, *Plantation Enterprise*, 286.

26. William G. Bentley, "Wealth Distribution in Colonial South Carolina" (PhD diss., Georgia State University, 1977), 109.

27. Gallay, *Formation*, chaps. 3 and 4; and Klein, *Unification*, chap. 1.

28. Klein, *Unification*, chap. 1; Gallay, *Formation*, chap. 1; Betty Wood, *Slavery in Colonial Georgia, 1730–1775* (Athens, 1984), chap. 6; Julia Floyd Smith, *Slavery and Rice Culture in Low Country Georgia, 1750–1860* (Knoxville, 1985), chap. 2; Pressly, *On the Rim*, chap. 8; Morgan, "Rice Trade," 433; Matthew Mulcahy, *Hubs of Empire: The Southeastern Lowcountry and British Caribbean* (Baltimore, 2014), 4, chaps. 4–5; Darold Wax, "Georgia and the Negro before the American Revolution," *GHQ* 51, no. 1 (March 1967): 63–77; and Karen Bell, "Rice, Resistance, and Forced Transatlantic Communi-

ties: (Re)envisioning the African Diaspora in Low Country Georgia, 1750–1800," *Journal of African American History* 95, no. 2 (Spring 2010): 157–182.

29. Joseph Clay to James Jackson, 16 February 1784, in *GHS Coll*, 8:194–195.

30. Hart, *Building Charleston*, 127.

31. Timothy Lockley, *Lines in the Sand: Race and Class in Lowcountry Georgia* (Athens, 2004), 7.

32. For Jack, see series S213003, vol. 2H, p. 150, SCDAH; for Cesar, see series S213003, vol. 2H, p. 133, SCDAH. For the phrasing, see Jourden H. Banks, *A Narrative of the Events of the Life of J. H. Banks* (Chapel Hill, 2000), 82; and Daina Ramey Berry, *The Price for Their Pound of Flesh: The Value of the Enslaved, from Womb to Grave, in the Building of a Nation* (Boston, 2017).

33. See series S213003, vol. 2I, p. 647, SCDAH. Their names were Simon, Hopes Prince, Bullock Prince, Essex, Sarah, Betty, Carolina, Bella, and Hagar. For Cato, see series S213003, vol. 2I, p. 642, SCDAH.

34. *SCG*, 26 December 1754, 9 January 1755.

35. Wright owned land in a variety of locations, including in Berkeley County on the Cooper River, in Craven County on Turkey Creek, and in Queensboro County on the Pee Dee River and on Lynche's Lake. See Katie-Prince Ward Esker, comp., *South Carolina Memorials, 1731–1776* (Cottonport, 1973), 1:41; Brent Holcomb, *South Carolina's Royal Grants* (Columbia, 2009), 4:77, 5:137, 6:232.

36. Eugene D. Genovese, *The Political Economy of Slavery: Studies in the Economy and Society of the Slave South* (Middletown, 1989), 28; Bertram Wyatt-Brown, *Honor and Violence in the Old South* (New York, 1986); and Eugene D. Genovese, *Roll, Jordan, Roll: The World the Slaves Made* (New York, 1974), 602. For the genesis of paternalism in the colonial Lowcountry, see Alan Gallay, "The Origins of Slaveholders' Paternalism: George Whitefield, the Bryan Family, and the Great Awakening in the South," *JSH* 53, no. 3 (August 1987): 369–394.

37. Henry Laurens to Lachlan McIntosh, 3 March 1773, in Gregory Massey, *John Laurens and the American Revolution* (Columbia, 2000), 14. Also see Gallay, "Origins."

38. Henry Laurens to Elias Ball, 1 April 1765, in *PHL*, 4:595–597.

39. James Habersham to William Knox, 9 March 1764, in *GHS Coll*, 3:15–17.

40. Wood, *Slavery*, 148–149.

41. Frank Lambert, *James Habersham: Loyalty, Politics, and Commerce in Colonial Georgia* (Athens, 2005), 116–117.

42. Bentley, "Wealth Distribution," abstract and chap. 3. Bentley provides a thorough study of "estates of deceased individuals" in the Charleston Probate Office. Also see George Rogers Taylor, "Wholesale Commodity Prices at Charleston, South Carolina, 1732–1791," *Journal of Economic and Business History* 4 (February 1932): 356–377; Rogers, *Charleston*, 7–11; Hart, *Building Charleston*, 122, 127–128, 145–146, 187–188; Sirmans, *Colonial South Carolina*, 207–210; Robert Weir, *Colonial South Carolina: A History* (Columbia, 1997), 145–147, 174–176, 177, 214, 231; and Peter Wood, *Black Majority: Negroes in Colonial South Carolina from 1670 through the Stono Rebellion* (New York, 1975), 48–49, 55–63, 150–152, 280–285.

43. Bentley, "Wealth Distribution," abstract and 12.

44. Lambert, *James Habersham*, 116.

45. James Wright, Final Will and Testament, 22 April 1786, in Prerogative Court of Canterbury and Related Probate Jurisdictions: Will Registers, PROB 11/1141/229, TNA. The will was transcribed by genealogist Sandra J. Boling of Atlanta. Also see Brooking, "Sir James Wright and Jenny, His Free 'Black Servant,'" *The Junto: A Group Blog on Early American History*, 28 January 2014, https://earlyamericanists.com/2014/01/28/sir-james-wright-and-jenny-his-free-black-servant/.

46. James Wright, Loyalist claim, in *BGLC*.

47. For related studies, see Marissa Fuentes and Brian Connolly, "Introduction: From Archives of Slavery to Liberated Futures," *History of the Present* 6, no. 2 (Fall 2016): 105–116; Saidiya Hartman, "Venus in Two Acts," *Small Axe* 12, no. 2 (June 2008): 1–14; Jennifer Morgan, *Reckoning with Slavery: Gender, Kinship, and Capitalism in the Early Black Atlantic* (Durham, 2021); and Jenny Shaw, "In the Name of the Mother: The Story of Susannah Mingo, a Woman of Color in the Early English Atlantic," *WMQ* 77, no. 2 (April 2020): 177–210.

48. James Wright to John Forster, 8 April 1784, in AO, 13/37.

49. The historical record, however, provides much more fodder concerning James Wright the slave-owning governor, a topic that will be discussed in subsequent chapters.

50. During the revolution the cost had increased to £2,476. See *ColRG*, 39:464–465.

51. Phillip D. Morgan, *Slave Counterpoint: Black Culture in the Eighteenth-Century Chesapeake and Low Country* (Chapel Hill, 1998), 35–42.

52. The quote is from James Graham, in James Wright, Loyalist claim, in *BGLC*.

53. Hoyt Canady, "Gentlemen of the Bar: Lawyers in Colonial South Carolina" (PhD diss., University of Tennessee, 1984), 269.

54. *SCG*, 29 November and 6 December 1735; and Peter Charles Hoffer, *Law and People in Colonial America* (Baltimore, 1998), 6.

55. Samuel Johnson, *Dictionary of the English Language* (Dublin, 1768), www.books.google.com.

56. For example, see *SCG*, 3 April and 22 November 1742, 31 January and 11 April 1743, 8 October 1744, 18 February and 28 October 1745; Gallay, *Formation*, chap. 4; and Hart, *Building Charleston*, 1–2.

57. Without mentioning a source, Canady wrote that Wright attended Eton, Cambridge, and Gray's Inn ("Gentlemen," 227). I can find no primary source for Wright's attendance at Eton, Cambridge, or Gray's Inn.

58. Robert Blackham, *Story of the Temple, Gray's and Lincoln's Inn* (London, 1932), 84–86.

59. Francis Bacon, "Of Gardens," in *The Essays* (New York, 1985), chap. 46; William R. Douthwaite, *Gray's Inn: Its History & Associations* (London, 1886), chap. 8; and Andrée Hope, *Chronicle of an Old Inn: Or, A Few Words about Gray's Inn* (London, 1887), 70–92.

60. R. Campbell, in David Lemmings, *Professors of the Law: Barristers and English Legal Culture in the Eighteenth Century*, (Oxford, 2000), 64.

61. Joseph Foster, *The Register of Admissions to Gray's Inn, 1521–1889* (London, 1889), 375–376; George Edward Cokayne, ed., *Complete Baronetage* (Exeter, 1906), 5:163;

Canady, "Gentlemen," 438; and Alfred Jones, *American Members of the Inns of Court* (London, 1924), 221–223.

62. *SCG*, 17 October 1741.

63. *SCG*, 9 January 1742.

64. See *SCG*, 13 February, 3 April, and 22 November 1742, 31 January and 11 April 1743 (which announced Wright's election to the vestry of St. Philip's Church), 2 April (the paper indicates that Wright was in Charleston in December 1743 and April 1744) and 8 October 1744, and 18 February 1745. These are just a few of many such evidences that Wright lived in Charleston through much of 1746. Wright continued his active leadership at St. Philip's until he left Charleston for good in 1757. See, for example, *SCG*, 10 April 1749.

65. *SCG*, 20 February 1742.

66. C. E. E. Hollis Hallett, comp., *Early Bermuda Wills, 1629–1835, Summarized and Indexed, a Genealogical Reference Book* (Bermuda, 1993), 373, 385; and David Dobson, *Directory of Scottish Settlers in North America, 1625–1825* (Baltimore, 1986), 61.

67. Hallett, *Early Bermuda Wills*, 373, 272. She had remarried by 16 December 1731, the date of the will of Walter Mitchell, stepfather of Martha Dolphin Heron, indicating her remarriage by then.

68. David Dobson, *Scots in Georgia and the Deep South, 1735–1845* (Baltimore, 2000), 80; *ColRG*, 28.1:260. He was granted land in Georgia in 1738. See Alexander Heron to Benjamin Martin, 18 May 1750, *ColRG*, 25:488–491. There was a significant number of Bermuda settlers in Georgia. See Henry C. Wilkinson, *Bermuda in the Old Empire* (London, 1950), 83, 315, in which Heron and others are mentioned. See also Samuel Charles Hill, *Yusuf Khan: The Rebel Commandant* (New York, 1914), 21–32.

69. Reginald Fletcher, *The Pension Book of Gray's Inn, 1699–1800* (London, 1910). Wright does not appear in the manuscript pension records either.

70. Wright did not appear in the *SCG* between 24 November 1746 (legal announcement) and 18 April 1748 (elected vestryman).

71. Series S213003, vol. 2H, p. 1, SCDAH. Wright replaced James Abercromby. Additionally, there is no mention of Wright in the London newspapers from 1741 to 1750.

72. Lemmings, *Professors*, 62–64, 119, 230–231, 302. Alfred Jones stated that Wright entered Gray's Inn in 1741 and was later called to the bar. See Jones, *American Members*, 221–223.

73. Julie Flavell, *When London Was Capital of America* (New Haven, 2010), chap. 4; and Lemmings, *Professors*, 144.

74. Andrew Mussell, archivist at Gray's Inn, personal correspondence, spring 2018.

75. For the notion of gaining a fine polish in London, see Eric Stockdale and Randy J. Holland, *Middle Temple Lawyers and the American Revolution* (Eagan, 2007), 42–43; and Sheila Skemp, *William Franklin: Son of a Patriot, Servant of a King* (New York, 1990), 28. For the importance placed on the legal profession, see Wilfrid Prest, *The Professions in Early Modern England* (Kent, 1987), 64–89; and Lemmings, *Professors*, chaps. 3 and 4.

76. Jones, *American Members*, xxviii. Six Americans attended multiple inns. Seventy-four South Carolinians attended an inn. For a slightly lower but still hefty percentage,

see Stockdale and Holland, *Middle Temple Lawyers*, T11–T17. Also see Lemmings, *Professors*, chap. 6; and William Sasche, *The Colonial American in Britain* (Madison, 1956), chap. 5.

77. Stockdale and Holland, *Middle Temple Lawyers*, 42–43. See also Flavell, *When London*, chap. 4.

78. *London Magazine*, July 1746; and for the quote, see Lemmings, *Professors*, 203.

79. Skemp, *William Franklin*, 39–42.

80. Stockdale, *Middle Temple Lawyers*, 39–41, quote on 39. See also Flavell, *When London*, 91–95.

81. Lemmings, *Professors*, 134 and, more generally, chap. 4; for the quote, see Canady, "Gentlemen," 3.

82. Flavell, *When London*, 67.

83. 4 March 1737, in *JCHA, 10 November 1736 to 7 June 1739*, 282–283; 28 June 1737, in Brent Holcomb, *Petitions for Land from the South Carolina Council* (Columbia, 1996), 89; and *SCG*, 5 November 1737.

84. Several years later, the *SCG* simply referred to Wright as "attorney at law," indicating that the position had indeed been temporary. *SCG*, 9 January 1742. Wright would later serve as the official full-time attorney general throughout much of the 1740s and 1750s.

85. 4 March 1737, in *JCHA, 10 November 1736 to 7 June 1739*, 282–283.

86. See, for example, 2 February 1738, in *JCHA, November 1736 to 7 June 1739*, 450, 456, and various dates, 636, 661; see also *JCHA, 12 September 1739 to 26 March 1741*, 59, 109; *JCHA, 14 September 1742 to 7 May 1743*, 109, 375, 377, 401, and 521; *JCHA, 20 February 1744 to 25 May 1745*, 87, 93, 113, 325, 396, 410, 416–417, 428; and *JCHA, 10 September 1745 to 17 June 1746*, 61, 74, 144, 147, 159. Similar such disputes can be found in the *JCHA* throughout Wright's entire tenure as attorney general, which ended in 1757. Regarding the House's miserly ways concerning other officials, see *JCHA, 20 February 1744 to 25 May 1745*, 396, in which the House disallowed certain charges submitted by attorney general James Abercromby. Also see Canady, "Gentlemen," 70, 336; and Jack P. Greene, *The Quest for Power: The Lower Houses of Assembly* (Chapel Hill, 2012), chaps. 3–6.

87. Canady, "Gentlemen," 213.

88. Canady, "Gentlemen," 323.

89. John McCusker and Russell Menard, *The Economy of British America, 1607–1789* (Chapel Hill, 1991), 61; John McCusker, W. Robert Higgins, Richard Bean, Alice H. Jones, James Shephard, Carville Earle, and Russell Menard, "Colonial and Pre-federal Statistics," in *Historical Statistics of the United States, Colonial Times to 1970*, ed. William Lerner (Washington, D.C., 1975), 2:1175; and Peter Lindert and Jeffrey Williamson, "American Incomes 1774–1860," 5 January 2023, http://emlab.berkeley.edu/users/webfac/cromer/e211_f12/LindertWilliamson.pdf. See also "American Incomes 1650–1870," http://gpih.ucdavis.edu/tables.htm.

90. John Ferling, *Jefferson and Hamilton: The Rivalry That Forged a Nation* (New York, 2014), 21.

91. James Glen to South Carolina Council, 21 February 1756, in *JCHA, 20 November 1755 to 6 July 1757*, 120.

92. Holcomb, *Petitions for Land*, 3:114.

93. Edward McCrady, *The History of South Carolina in the Revolution 1775–1780* (New York, 1969), 108. Also see Anne King Gregorie, ed., *Records of the Court of Chancery of South Carolina, 1671–1779* (Washington, D.C., 1950), 401–402, who determined that Wright, "like his father was a man of character and ability."

94. Series S213003, vol. 2G, p. 265, SCDAH; and Holcomb, *Petitions for Land*, 3:199. This case was resolved in Wright's favor on 3 September 1753 (3:262).

95. Huw David, "James Crokatt's 'Exceeding Good Counting House': Ascendancy and Influence in the Transatlantic Carolina Trade," *SCHM* 111, no. 3/4 (July–October 2020): 157.

96. 4–5 May 1743, in *JCHA, 14 September 1737 to 7 May 1743*, 431, 434.

97. Edward S. Farrow, *Farrow's Military Encyclopedia: A Dictionary of Military Knowledge* (New York, 1885), 1:386–387.

98. Series S213003, vol. 2F, p. 90, SCDAH; 21–22 February 1745, in *JCHA, 20 February 1745 to 25 May 1745*, 355, 357.

99. Charles McLean Andrews, *The Colonial Period of American History: England's Commercial and Colonial Policy* (New Haven, 1938), 245.

100. Various dates, in *JCHA, 28 March 1749 to 21 November 1749*, 68–269, 272, 277–278.

101. Canady, "Gentlemen," 271–273. This number only considers cases prior to 1750. Wright was one of the few attorneys to thrive before and after 1750. Additionally, only 14 percent of South Carolina lawyers during this period tried more than one hundred cases.

102. Canady, "Gentlemen," 276–277, 443–444, 439–440.

103. Canady, "Gentlemen," 282–283. Canady ascribes this high percentage of merchant clients to Wright's "favorable reputation."

104. Rogers, *Charleston*, 15; and Canady, "Gentlemen," 3, 18, 282–283.

105. Michael G. Kammen, *A Rope of Sand: The Colonial Agents, British Politics, and the American Revolution* (Ithaca, 1968), 48–52; Ella Lonn, *Colonial Agents of the Southern Colonies* (Chapel Hill, 1945), chap. 4; and Greene, *Quest for Power*, chaps. 9–10. In fact, as governor, Wright became involved in controversies over three different such appointments.

106. For the debate and appointment of Wright, see 5, 9, 11, 16, 17, 18, 19 November 1756, in *JCHA, 20 November 1755 to 6 July 1757*, 288–299. For the controversy, see South Carolina Agent Act, 19 November 1756, in CO, 324/60; and Thomas Cooper and David McCord, eds., *The Statutes at Large of South Carolina* (Columbia, 1841), 4:34–35. For Wright's appointment, see South Carolina Committee of Correspondence to James Wright, 8 July 1757, in LP.

107. Board of Trade to William H. Lyttelton, 10 February 1757, and James Wright to Lyttelton, 9 November 1757, both in LP.

108. *SCG*, 3, 10, 17, 24 February 1757.

109. *SCG*, 3, 10 March 1757; Charleston Deed Book, vol. VV, pp. 476–484, accessed via C-Film #008139577 (familysearch.org), SCDAH. For Brailsford's occupation, see Flavell, *When London*, 20. Brailsford also had a place in London's West End, where Carolinians like Wright often stayed or lived.

110. 21 May 1757, in *JCHA, 20 November 1755 to 6 July 1757*, 466; and *SCG*, 23 June, 21 July 1757.

111. *SCG*, 18 August 1757.

112. *SCG*, 4 August 1758. The advertisement suggests that Cato may have been "harboured" in Amelia Township, the locale of his former master.

113. *SCG*, 3, 10 March 1757.

114. Quoted in "Q&A: Settle in Georgia or Carolina?," National Humanities Center, 5 January 2023, http://nationalhumanitiescenter.org/pds/becomingamer/growth/text9/carolinasgeorgia.pdf. Data from Georgia confirmed this bias. From 1755 to 1767, 35 percent of all slaves imported to Savannah came from Gambia. The next highest percentage was 13 (from St. Kitts). Bell, "Rice, Resistance," 162.

115. *SCG*, 11, 18 August and 1, 15 September 1758.

116. James Wright Loyalist claim, in *BGLC*.

117. James Wright to W. H. Lyttelton, 9 November 1757, in LP. The previous agent, Charles Pinckney, noted that Wright arrived in October. Francis Leigh William, *A Founding Family: The Pinckneys of South Carolina* (New York, 1978), 380. Interestingly, prior to receiving Wright's letter, Lyttelton wished Wright's "voyage proved in all respects a prosperous one [with] little unpleasantness" (Lyttelton to James Wright, 29 December 1759, in LP).

118. Greene, *Quest for Power*, 266.

119. Flavell, *When London*, 22–25, 84–85, and, generally, chap. 4; Maurice D. McInnis, *In Pursuit of Refinement: Charlestonians Abroad, 1740–1860* (Columbia, 2015), 104; Carl Vipperman, *The Rise of Rawlins Lowndes, 1721–1800* (Columbia, 1978), 79–85; Kammen, *A Rope of Sand*, 16–17; and Henry Laurens to Richard Oswald, 18 September 1766, in *PHL*, 5:202–203.

120. Anna Brinkman-Schwartz, "The Heart of the Maritime World: London's 'Mercantile' Coffee Houses in the Seven Years' War and the American War of Independence, 1756–1783," *Historical Research* 94, no. 265 (August 2021): 508–531.

121. For example, the House directed Wright to occasionally send it "three setts of the votes of the House of Commons, and four setts of such acts of Parliament as they related to America" (*JCHA, 6 October 1757 to 24 January 1761*, 345–346). For context, see Greene, *Quest for Power*, 266; Kammen, *A Rope of Sand*, 4–5, 16–17; and for the best examination of the colonial agency in the South, see Lonn, *Colonial Agents*, esp. chap. 5.

122. Kammen, *A Rope of Sand*, 62.

123. Franklin to Pennsylvania Assembly, 10 June 1766, in FO.

124. William Bollan to James Bowdoin, 29 September 1773, in Kammen, *A Rope of Sand*, 125.

125. William Bollan to Josiah Willard, 19 April 1754, in Kammen, *A Rope of Sand*, 59.

126. Peter Manigault to Andrew Rutledge, 26 February 1754, in Greene, *Quest for Power*, 266.

127. Lonn, *Colonial Agents*, 309; and L. B. Namier, "Charles Garth, Agent for South Carolina: Part II (Continued)," *English Historical Review* 54, no. 216 (October 1939): 634.

128. Kammen, *A Rope of Sand*, 43, 47–48, 60; and Lonn, *Colonial Agents*, 319.

129. James Wright to Lyttelton, 18 May 1758, in LP. See also Lonn, *Colonial Agents*, 319, 337–338; and James Abercromby to the Council of Virginia, 15 February 1760 and 20 April 1760, in *The Letter Book of James Abercromby, Colonial Agent, 1751–1773*, ed. John C. Van Horne and George Reese (Richmond, 1991), 338–339, 348–350.

130. Kammen, *A Rope of Sand*, 39–42; and Lyttelton to James Wright, 15 April 1759, in LP.

131. James Wright to South Carolina Assembly, 15 May, 5 August, 4 September, and 26 November 1759 and 13 February 1760, in Letterbook of Charles Garth and James Wright, SCDAH.

132. Lyttelton to James Wright, 15 April 1759, in LP.

133. For example, James Wright to Lyttelton, 9 November 1757, 15 February, 1 March, 15 May, 5 August, and 25 November 1758, and 31 March and 4 September 1759, in LP.

134. James Wright to Lyttelton, 15 February, 1 March, 25 November 1758, in LP; James Wright to South Carolina Assembly, 26 November 1758, in Letterbook of Charles Garth and James Wright, SCDAH. For context, see Lonn, *Colonial Agents*, 186; Daniel Tortora, *Carolina in Crisis: Cherokees, Colonists, and Slaves in the American Southeast, 1756–1763* (Chapel Hill, 2016); and Jeffrey Dennis, *Patriots & Indians: Shaping Identity in Eighteenth-Century South Carolina* (Columbia, 2017).

135. James Wright to South Carolina Assembly, 5 August 1758, in Letterbook of Charles Garth and James Wright, SCDAH; and R. C. Simmons, ed., *Proceedings and Debates of Parliament Respecting North America* (White Plains, 1987), 290. For context, see Lonn, *Colonial Agents*, 205.

136. Board of Trade to Lyttelton, 9 November 1757, in LP; James Munro and Almeric Fitzroy, eds., *Acts of the Privy Council of England, Colonial Series* (London, 1966), 4:363; and 7 April 1760, in *Journals of the Board of Trade and Plantations* (London, 1935), 11:123.

137. Board of Trade to Lyttelton, 21 April 1758, in LP; James Wright to South Carolina Assembly, 25 March 1759, in Letterbook of James Wright and Charles Garth, SCDAH; Munro and Fitzroy, *Acts of the Privy Council*, 4:363, 5:363–367; and Lonn, *Colonial Agents*, 187–188.

138. Shelburne to Gage, 14 August 1767, in GP.

139. Lonn, *Colonial Agents*, 192.

140. James Wright to South Carolina Assembly, 13 June 1758, in Letterbook of James Wright and Charles Garth, SCDAH.

141. William Brownrigg quoted in Mark Kurlansky, *Salt: A World History* (New York, 2003), 10.

142. James Wright to South Carolina Assembly, 13 June 1758, in Letterbook of James Wright and Charles Garth, SCDAH; James Abercromby to Francis Fauquier, 16 March 1758, in *Official Papers of Francis Fauquier*, ed. George Reese (Charlottesville, 1980–1983), 1:3–6; Benjamin Franklin to James Wright, 9 July 1759, in FO; Lonn, *Colonial Agents*, 327–328, 355; Kammen, *A Rope of Sand*, 35; Abercromby to Richard Corbin, 6 March 1758, Abercromby to Arthur Dobbs, 13 March 1758, and Abercromby to Dobbs, 20 April 1758, in Van Horne and Reese, *Letter Book*, 233–234, 242–243, 256–257.

143. Quoted in Lonn, *Colonial Agents*, 167.

144. Lonn, *Colonial Agents*, 239; and Abercromby to John Blair, 25 June 1759, and Abercromby to the Committee of Correspondence of North Carolina, 20 July 1759, in Van Horne and Reese, *Letter Book*, 299–300, 312–314.

145. *SCG*, 1 December 1758.

146. *SCG*, 3 March 1759. Their names were, in the likely order of birth, Sarah (fif-

teen), Robert (thirteen), James Jr. (twelve), Ann (ten), Alexander (eight), Isabella (seven), Martha (six), and Charles (four). Their firstborn, Martha Isabell, died at the age of two.

147. James Wright to Lyttelton, 29 December 1759, in LP; James Wright to South Carolina Assembly, 5 January 1760, 25 March 1759, in Letterbook of Charles Garth and James Wright, SCDAH. Wright's departure in the summer is confirmed in Abercromby to Francis Fauquier, 1 November 1761, in Reese, *Official Papers*, 1:417–419.

148. Lyttelton to James Wright, 7 August 1758, in LP. For similar such sentiments, see Lyttelton to James Wright, 19 February, 1 September 1759, in LP.

149. R. C. Simmons, "Colonial Patronage: Two Letters from William Franklin to the Earl of Bute, 1762," *WMQ* 59, no. 4 (January 2002): 122.

150. Gordon S. Wood, *The Radicalism of the American Revolution* (New York, 1992), 57.

151. Simona Piattoni, "Clientelism in Historical and Comparative Perspective," in *Clientelism, Interests, and Democratic Representation: The European Experience in Historical and Comparative Perspective*, ed. Simona Piattoni (Cambridge, 2001), 2.

152. Kristen Block, "Patron-Client Networks," in *Atlantic History*, ed. Joseph C. Miller (Princeton, 2015), 371–373.

153. Lord Hillsborough to James Wright, 29 May 1764, in *ColRG*, 34:352; and Bamber Gascoyne to James Wright, 29 May 1764, in *ColRG*, 34:538–542. Also see Hillsborough to James Wright, 1 February 1772, in *ColRG*, 34:619–621, in which Hillsborough and his cosignees address Wright to be their "trusty and wellbeloved" friend.

154. The first sentiment is in Lyttelton to James Wright, 7 August 1758, in LP; the quote in Lyttelton to James Wright, 18 September 1759, in LP.

155. Abercromby to Robert Dinwiddie, 3 November 1757, in Van Horne and Reese, *Letter Book*, 211–212.

156. John Monson to Newcastle, 25 October 1742, in James Henretta, *Salutary Neglect: Colonial Administration under the Duke of Newcastle* (Princeton, 1972), 132, 225.

157. *SCG*, 23 February, 1 March 1760; and *New-York Gazette*, 31 March 1760. Also see Henry Ellis to Lyttelton, 7 March 1760, in Ed Cashin Papers, Augusta State University, Augusta, Ga.; 13 May 1760, in Munro and Fitzroy, *Acts of the Privy Council*, 4:397–398; Abercromby to Fauquier, in Reese, *Official Papers*, 1:417–419; and 13 May 1760, in *Board of Trade Journal*, 11:107.

158. 13 May 1760, in *Board of Trade Journal*, 11:107; Earl of Halifax to King George III, 13 May 1760, in *ColRG*, 34:363–364. The king received Wright's commission three days later. See 19 May 1760, in *ColRG*, 34:365–366.

159. Knox to ———, 20 May 1760, in William Knox and Howard Vicenté Knox, *Manuscripts of Captain H. V. Knox* (Boston, 1972), 83–85. Knox received the appointment in 1762. Knox to Lyttelton, 10 February 1762, in KP.

160. Journal entry, Reverend Samuel Urlsperger, 17 March 1760, in *Detailed Report on the Salzburger Emigrants Who Settled in America*, ed. George F. Jones (Athens, 1993), 17:140–141.

161. *SCG*, 6 September 1760; and *London Chronicle*, 14 June 1760.

162. Abercromby to Fauquier, 1 October 1761, in Reese, *Official Papers*, 1:417–419.

## Chapter 2. A New Governor

1. Paul Demere to Lyttelton, 24 June 1758, in LP; Lachlan McIntosh to Lyttelton, 5 June 1758, in *Documents Relating to Indian Affairs, 1754–1765*, ed. William McDowell (Columbia, 1970), 462; and for Byrd, see Daniel J. Tortora, *Carolina in Crisis: Cherokees, Colonists, and Slaves in the American Southeast, 1756–1763* (Chapel Hill, 2015), 53.

2. Fred Anderson, *Crucible of War: The Seven Years' War and the Fate of Empire in British North America* (New York, 2000), 219–236; and Tortora, *Carolina in Crisis*, 44–53.

3. Ellis to Board of Trade, 25 October 1758, in *ColRG*, 28.1:165–167. Ellis's complaints about the colony's defenses were staunch indeed. He notified the board that he had repeatedly requested aid from the secretary of state as well as the commanders in chief in America but without success. He specifically called out General James Abercromby, who did not bother to reply to any of four letters. As for other such complaints during his tenure, see, for example, Ellis to Pitt, 10 July 1760, in *ColRG*, 28.1:280–283. It is important to note that the term "Creeks" can be misleading, as the region, town, and family could often be of more importance than the "nation." See Joshua Piker, *Okfuskee: A Creek Indian Town in Colonial America* (Cambridge, 2004); and David Corkran, *The Creek Frontier, 1540–1783* (Norman, 1967).

4. Ellis to Pitt, 10 July 1760, in *RG*, 81.

5. Louis DeVorsey Jr., "Indian Boundaries in Colonial Georgia," *GHQ* 54, no. 1 (Spring 1970): 63.

6. Kenneth Coleman, *Colonial Georgia: A History* (Millwood, 1989), 217–220; and Helen Shaw, "British Administration of the Southern Indians, 1756–1783" (PhD diss., Bryn Mawr, 1931).

7. William Richardson, 5 February 1759; and William Richardson, "An Account of my Proceedings since I accepted the Indian Mission on October 2d, 1758, to go and exercise my office as a Minister among the Cherokees or any other Indian Nation that would allow me to preach to them," 12, both in William Richardson Davie Papers (1758–1819), Wilson Library, University of North Carolina, Chapel Hill.

8. Tortora, *Carolina in Crisis*, 62, 68.

9. *RG*, 78–79.

10. *SCG*, 12 May 1759. For the Anglo-Native conflict in the Southeast from 1758 to 1763, see Tortora, *Carolina in Crisis*; Jeff W. Dennis, *Patriots & Indians: Shaping Identity in Eighteenth-Century South Carolina* (Columbia, 2017); Anderson, *Crucible of War*, 457–471; Corkran, *Creek Frontier*, 193–228; Louis DeVorsey, *The Indian Boundary in the Southern Colonies, 1763–1775* (Chapel Hill, 1966), 112–180; Gary Nash, *Red, White & Black: The Peoples of Early North America* (Upper Saddle River, 2000), 233–239, 252–262; and Claudio Saunt, *A New Order of Things: Property, Power, and the Transformation of the Creek Indians, 1733–1816* (Cambridge, 1999), 38–63. For this conflict's impact on Georgia, see Ed Cashin, *Governor Henry Ellis and the Transformation of British North America* (Athens, 1994), 73–94; and *ColRG*, 28.1.

11. James Wright to Lyttelton, 29 December 1759, in LP.

12. "Journal of Lord Adam Gordon," in *Narratives of Colonial America, 1704–1765*, ed.

Howard H. Peckham (Chicago, 1971), 237–240; and Nathan Alexander to Lyttelton, 4 May 1759, in McDowell, *Documents*, 485.

13. John Juricek, *Endgame for Empire: British-Creek Relations in Georgia and Vicinity, 1763–1776* (Gainesville, 2015), 6; Anderson, *Crucible of War*, 456–461; Tortora, *Carolina in Crisis*, chap. 7; Steven C. Hahn, *The Invention of the Creek Nation, 1670–1763* (Lincoln, 2004), chap. 7; and Corkran, *Creek Frontier*, chap. 14.

14. Ellis to Board of Trade, 16 April 1760, in *ColRG*, 28.1:246–247; Ellis's War Appeal to the Creeks, 15 February 1760, and Ellis to the Upper and Lower Creeks, 26 May 1760, in *EAID*, 11:310, 319–320. Also see *SCG*, 24 May 1760.

15. It should be noted that South Carolina waged war against the Cherokees in the late 1750s and early 1760s. See Edward J. Cashin, *Lachlan McGillivray, Indian Trader: The Shaping of the Southern Colonial Frontier* (Athens, 1992), chap. 10.

16. Ellis to Board of Trade, 7 June 1760, in *ColRG*, 28.1:250–252. This is not to suggest that Cherokee violence ceased entirely. See, for example, 7 November 1760, in *ColRG*, 8:415–416.

17. 2 June 1760, in *ColRG*, 16:498–499. For Ellis's sympathy, see *RG*, 77–80. For his overall diplomatic skills, which were considerable, see Cashin, *Governor Henry Ellis*, chaps. 6, 9.

18. Ellis to William Pitt, 10 July 1760, in *ColRG*, 28.1:249; and Piker, *Okfuskee*, 53.

19. Ellis to Board of Trade, 20 October 1760, in *ColRG*, 28.1:288–290. See also Cashin, *Governor Henry Ellis*, chap. 6; and *RG*, chap. 3.

20. Ellis to Board of Trade, 25 November 1759 and 13 May 1760, in *ColRG*, 28.1:218–219, 249.

21. Lyttelton to Ellis, 19 August 1759, in LP. Also see 13 May 1760, in *Acts of the Privy Council of England, Colonial Series*, ed. James Munro and Almeric Fitzroy (London, 1966), 5:397–398.

22. Knox to Lyttelton, 5 March 1760, in William Knox and Howard Vicenté Knox, *Manuscripts of Captain H. V. Knox* (Boston, 1972), 82–83. Knox had been appointed acting provost marshal. The climate proved especially problematic for him, as he "was struck by lightning on the crown of my head, but providence gave the shaft an oblique direction which saved me" (Knox to Robert Knox, 28 June 1761, in Knox and Knox, *Manuscripts*, 85–86).

23. Ellis to W. H. Lyttelton, 7 March 1760, in Ed Cashin Papers, Reese Library, Augusta State University, Augusta, Ga.

24. Lyttelton to Ellis, 10 March 1760, and Ellis to Lyttelton, 13 and 14 March 1760, in LP.

25. Ellis to Lyttelton, 13 March 1760, in LP. Ellis clearly struggled with the decision to leave and the consequences of doing so, but he fundamentally admitted that "there is as Shakespeare justly observes, 'a Tide in the Affairs of Men,'" and "my ambition is pretty well abated" (Ellis to Lyttelton, 14 March 1760, in LP). Also see 17 March and 3 April 1760, in *Detailed Report on the Salzburger Emigrants Who Settled in America*, ed. George F. Jones (Athens, 1993), 17:140–141, 151–152.

26. For Wright's appointment, see 13 May 1760, in *Board of Trade Journal*, 11:91–101; 13 May 1760, in *ColRG*, 28.1:249; and 13 May 1760, in *ColRG*, 34:363–364.

27. Stephen Berry, *A Path in the Mighty Waters: Shipboard Life and Atlantic Crossings to the New World* (New Haven, 2015), 41.

28. Elizabeth had been born in London and christened at St. James's Piccadilly, Westminster, on 25 June 1760. "England, Select Births and Christenings, 1538–1975," database, Ancestry.com, accessed 12 May 2020. She was buried on 12 September 1760. A. S. Salley Jr., ed., *Register of St. Philip's Parish . . . 1754–1810* (Charleston, 1927), 296. Also see *SCG*, 13 September 1760; and "Collection of Pedigree and Genealogical Memoranda of the Family of Wright," in Davy's Suffolk Collections, vol. 80, British Library. The family sailed from London in July, according to Abercromby to Fauquier, 1 October 1760, in *The Letter Book of James Abercromby, Colonial Agent, 1751–1773*, ed. John C. Van Horne and George Reese (Richmond, 1991), 365–367. Sadly, the Wrights' niece, Gibbon Wright, died five days later, aged thirty-one. See Salley, *Register of St. Philip's*, 296. St. Michael's Church currently stands on that spot.

29. *SCG*, 11 October 1760.

30. *SCG*, 18 October 1760; journal entry, 16 and 26 September 1760, in Jones, *Detailed Report*, 17:245, 248–249. Reverend Urlsperger noted on the sixteenth that "our new governor, Mr. *William* Wright, has landed in Charleston."

31. 5 November 1760, in Jones, *Detailed Report*, 17:260. For the celebration, see *GG*, 20 February 1761. Also see a string of notations in the Salzburger journal dating from 5 August to 5 November 1760, in Jones, *Detailed Report*, 17:227–270.

32. Ellis to Board of Trade, 20 October 1760, in *ColRG*, 28.1:288–290.

33. *SCG*, 22 November and 6 November 1760, in *ColRG*, 13:439–440.

34. *SCG*, 15 November 1760.

35. 24 April 1760, in *ColRG*, 18:388–392. Wright would be horrified that his home lay at Telfair Square, named after Edward Telfair, whom Wright loathed. At the conclusion of the war, Samuel Elbert purchased Wright's Ogeechee River plantation. See Clay Ouzts, *Samuel Elbert and the Age of Revolution in Georgia, 1740–1788* (Macon, 2022), 322–323.

36. John Corry, *The Colonial Houses of Georgia* (Savannah, 1930), 195; and Hoke Kimball and Bruce Henson, *Governor's Houses and State Houses of British Colonial America, 1607–1783* (Jefferson, 2017), 367–379.

37. For the establishment of civil government in Georgia, see 8 March 1754, in *ColRG*, 26:439–443. For the appointment of Georgia's first governor, John Reynolds, see 6 August 1754, in *ColRG*, 26:459. For the inauguration of royal government under Reynolds, see 31 October 1754, in *ColRG*, 7:10–15.

38. In succession, Georgia's colonial governors were John Reynolds (1754–1757), Henry Ellis (1757–1760), and James Wright (1760–1783).

39. James Wright, Loyalist claim, in *BGLC*.

40. Francis Bernard to Lord Halifax, 9 November 1764, in Bernard Bailyn, *The Ordeal of Thomas Hutchinson* (Cambridge, 1974), 180–181. Concerning the waning of patronage toward the end of the colonial era, see Bailyn, *The Ideological Origins of the American Revolution* (Cambridge, 1967), chap. 2. His analysis applies less to Georgia but is still relevant.

41. Jonathan Boucher, *A View of the Causes and Consequences of the American Revolution* (London, 1797), 218; and William H. Nelson, *The American Tory* (Westport, 1961), 3.

42. Coleman, *Colonial Georgia*, chap. 10. For the importance of patronage, see Peter G. Richards, *Patronage in British Government* (London, 1963), 19–36, 62–88, 247–258.

43. Ellis to Board of Trade, 5 May 1757, in *ColRG*, 28.1:16–27. For the Halifax relation,

see Joseph Reed to Charles Pettit, 11 June 1764, in *The Life and Correspondence of Joseph Reed*, ed. William Reed (Philadelphia, 1847), 1:32–34. Reed, later the military secretary for George Washington, had no respect for Ellis, declaring, "He is a man that makes pretensions . . . without the least foundation" for them.

44. Harold Davis, *The Fledgling Province: Social and Cultural Life in Colonial Georgia, 1733–1776* (Chapel Hill, 1976), 32, 36; and Ellis to William Pitt, 1 August 1757, in *ColRG*, 28.1:43–45.

45. Davis, *Fledgling Province*, 7–9; Coleman, *Colonial Georgia*, chap. 2; and Betty Wood, *Slavery in Colonial Georgia, 1730–1775* (Athens, 1984), 1–23. The quote is from Coleman, *Colonial Georgia*, 17.

46. Davis, *Fledgling Province*, 8–13; and Coleman, *Colonial Georgia*, esp. chap. 2.

47. W. W. Abbot, "A Cursory View of Eighteenth-Century Georgia," *South Atlantic Quarterly* 61, no. 3 (1962): 340.

48. George Whitefield to the Trustees of Georgia, 4 December 1748, in George Whitefield, *The Works of George Whitefield* (Shropshire, 2000), 2:209–210.

49. Paul Pressly, *On the Rim of the Caribbean: Colonial Georgia and the British Atlantic World* (Athens, 2013), 2, 11–49; Coleman, *Colonial Georgia*, chaps. 7 and 10; Wood, *Slavery*, esp. chaps. 5 and 6; and Matthew Mulcahy, *Hubs of Empire: The Southeastern Lowcountry and British Caribbean* (Baltimore, 2014), chaps. 4 and 5.

50. Julie Anne Sweet, *William Stephens: Georgia's Forgotten Founder* (Baton Rouge, 2010).

51. "An Act for the better ordering and governing Negroes . . . ," 25 March 1765, in *ColRG*, 18:649–688. The Board of Trade disallowed this slave code because Georgians defined slaves as chattel rather than real estate. The board's decision left Wright apoplectic. He sent frantic missives to London seeking explanations and solutions. Wood, *Slavery*, 128–129; James Wright to Board of Trade, 8 June 1768, in *ColRG*, 28.2:254–255; and Thomas Statom Jr., "Negro Slavery in Eighteenth-Century Georgia" (PhD diss., University of Alabama, 1982), 69–87.

52. Kenneth Coleman, "Oglethorpe and James Wright: A Georgia Comparison," in *Oglethorpe in Perspective: Georgia's Founder after Two Hundred Years*, ed. Phinizy Spalding and Harvey Jackson (Tuscaloosa, 1989), 122, 126; Coleman, "James Wright," in *Georgians in Profile: Essays in Honor of Ellis Merton Coulter*, ed Horace Montgomery (Athens, 1958), 41–42; Coleman, *Colonial Georgia*, 193; and Coleman, "James Wright and the Origins of the Revolution in Georgia," in *The Human Dimensions of Nation Making: Essays on Colonial and Revolutionary America*, ed. James Kirby Martin (Madison, 1976), 104–106.

53. John Ivey Brown, "Relations between Georgia's Royal Governors and Their Assemblies" (master's thesis, University of Georgia, 1970), 44. Brown was a student of Kenneth Coleman, who knew more about Wright than any other historian of the twentieth century.

54. Robert Calhoon, *The Loyalists in Revolutionary America, 1760–1781* (New York, 1973), 4–6.

55. Randall Miller, *"A Warm & Zealous Spirit": John J. Zubly and the American Revolution* (Macon, 1982), 2.

56. *RG*, 85.

57. Calhoon, *Loyalists*, 13.

58. James Wright to Board of Trade, 23 December 1760, in *ColRG*, 28.1:292–299.

59. Ellis to Board of Trade, 20 October 1760, in *ColRG*, 28.1:288–290.

60. James Wright to Board of Trade, 23 December 1760, in *ColRG*, 28.1:292–299; James Wright to John Stuart, 24 February 1762, in *Amherst Papers, 1756–1763: The Southern Sector*, ed. Edith Mays (Bowie, 1999), 377; and, for some context, Juricek, *Endgame for Empire*, 6. Wright mentioned that the Creeks "seem well disposed, tho straggling villains out of their towns sometimes misbehave."

61. James Wright to Board of Trade, 23 October 1760, in *ColRG*, 28.1:29. Wright also begged for assistance in this regard three months later. James Wright to Board of Trade, 7 January 1761, in CO, 5/391.

62. 21 January 1761, in *ColRG*, 8:465.

63. James Wright to Board of Trade, 23 December 1760, in *ColRG*, 28.1:292–299.

64. James M. Johnston, *Militamen, Rangers, and Redcoats: The Military in Georgia, 1754–1776* (Macon, 1992).

65. James Wright to Jeffery Amherst, 20 February 1762, in Amherst Papers, CL, and in WO, 34/34; and James Wright to Board of Trade, 15 February 1762, in *ColRG*, 28.2:179–194.

66. 7 November 1760, in *ColRG*, 8:414–417; and Michelle LeMaster, *Brothers Born of One Mother: British–Native American Relations in the Colonial Southeast* (Charlottesville, 2012), 81–83.

67. James Wright to Board of Trade, 29 November 1766, in *ColRG*, 28.2:179–194.

68. *SCG*, 15 November 1760. For the presents, see *New-York Mercury*, 1 October 1760.

69. 1 and 20 February, 28 March, and 7 April 1760, in *Board of Trade Journal*, 11:83, 190–191, 100, 123. These journal entries illustrate Wright's presentation of South Carolina's Indian affairs, explanations of intelligence, and descriptions of lobbying efforts.

70. Tortora, *Carolina in Crisis*, 181–182.

71. *SCG*, 16 December 1760.

72. James Wright to Board of Trade, 23 December 1760, in *ColRG*, 28.1:292–299; James Wright to Jeffery Amherst, 2 February 1761, in WO, 34/273; *Boston News-Letter*, 19 February 1761; Corkran, *Creek Frontier*, 230–231; and John Richard Alden, *John Stuart and the Southern Colonial Frontier: A Study of Indian Relations, War, Trade, and Land Problems in the Southern Wilderness, 1754–1775* (New York, 1966), 177.

73. James Wright to Board of Trade, 7 January 1761, in CO, 5/391; and Jeffery Amherst to James Wright, 18 March 1761, in CO, 5/60.

74. Roderick MackIntosh to John Stuart, 16 November 1767, in GP.

75. 7–21 November 1760, 29 January, 4 and 31 March, and 28 July 1761, in *ColRG*, 8:414–433, 469–470, 512, 520–521, 540–546. See also *SCG*, 16 December 1760. This statement refers to his dealings with colonists and Native Americans and not his superiors in London.

76. 7 November 1760, in *ColRG*, 8:414–416. See also Amherst to James Wright, 18 March 1761, in CO, 5/60, in which Amherst suggested that British success against the Cherokees would likely convince the Creeks to maintain their loyalty. For the Anglo-Cherokee War, see Tortora, *Carolina in Crisis*; and Corkran, *Creek Frontier*.

77. 29 January 1761, in *ColRG*, 8:469–470.

78. 25 March 1761, in *SCG*, 4 April 1761. For the refusal to finance defensive fortifi-cations, see "Proceedings," 21 May 1761, in *ColRG*, 13:567–569. It should be noted that Wright began this speech with the announcement that George II had died. In February he learned that his appointment as governor would continue under George III. See "Proceedings," 5 February 1761, in *ColRG*, 8:484–491.

79. James Wright to Board of Trade, 28 February 1761, in Brown, "Relations," 47.

80. 4 August 1761, in *ColRG*, 8:553–557.

81. Creek Leaders to James Wright, 4 August 1761, in *ColRG*, 8:553–555.

82. James Wright to Creek Leaders, 4 August 1761, in *ColRG*, 8:553–555. For a general examination of Native problems with traders, see Kathryn E. Holland Braund, *Deer-skins & Duffels: The Creek Indian Trade with Anglo-America, 1685–1815* (Lincoln, 1993), esp. 103–120.

83. Jill Suzanne Hough, "Fathers and Brothers: Familial Diplomacy of the Creek Indians and Anglo-Americans, 1733 to Removal" (PhD diss., Hope College, 1990), 74.

84. Generally speaking, British officials viewed the traders and squatters as the pri-mary reason for the troubles. Juricek, *Endgame for Empire*, 36.

85. James Wright to Board of Trade, 27 August 1764, in *ColRG*, 28.2:50–52; Milligen quoted in Tortora, *Carolina in Crisis*, 62.

86. Gage to Captain Lewis Fuser, 30 April 1767, in GP.

87. James Wright to Board of Trade, 27 August 1764, in *ColRG*, 28.2:51–52. Superin-tendent John Stuart echoed these sentiments. See Robert Paulett, *An Empire of Small Places: Mapping the Southeastern Anglo-Indian Trade, 1732–1795* (Athens, 2012), 42; James Snapp, *John Stuart and the Struggle for Empire on the Southern Frontier* (Baton Rouge, 1996); and Alden, *John Stuart*.

88. Henry Laurens to John Ettwein, 10 November 1760, in *PHL*, 4:39–43.

89. Newton Mereness, ed., *Travels in the American Colonies* (New York, 1916), 508. The trader was named James Lesslie.

90. George Johnstone to Indian Chiefs, 29–30 May 1765, in Braund, *Deerskins & Duffels*, 103.

91. For Wright's attempts to regulate traders, see 10 March 1761, 19 February, and 5 October 1762, in *ColRG*, 8:514–515, 649, 756. For his assessment of the character of colo-nial traders, see James Wright to Board of Trade, 27 August 1764, in *ColRG*, 28.2:50–52.

92. James Wright to John Stuart, 17 August 1765, in *ColRG*, 28.2:124–125.

93. 3 July 1761 and 7 August 1764, in *ColRG*, 8:522–525, 9:202–204; and James Wright to Board of Trade, 27 August and 11 December 1764, in *ColRG*, 28.2:50–52, 69–70. Also see *RG*, 91.

94. William Knox to Robert Knox, 28 June 1761, in Knox and Knox, *Manuscripts*, 85–86.

95. Alan Gallay, *The Formation of the Planter Elite* (Athens, 2007), xviii.

96. 28 July 1761, in *ColRG*, 8:540–541.

97. 22 April, 25 and 27 May 1762, in *ColRG*, 8:673–675, 687–688, 688–690; *SCG*, 1 Au-gust 1761, which detailed Wright's "sending an express" to Charleston informing the legislature about the privateer; and *SCG*, 8 August 1761, which provided the full account.

98. *New-York Mercury*, 7 September 1761; *Boston Evening Post*, 14 September 1761;

Wright to Board of Trade, 15 September 1761, in *Board of Trade Journal*, 11:244–245; and Soame Jenyns to Lord Egremont, 21 January 1762, in *ColRG*, 37:3.

99. James Wright to Board of Trade, 15 September 1761, 20 February and 10 June 1762, in *Board of Trade Journal*, 11:244–245, 275, 303.

100. 4 January 1763, in *ColRG*, 9:12–17.

101. James Wright to Board of Trade, 22 February 1763, in Juricek, *Endgame for Empire*, 7.

102. 11 November 1761, in *ColRG*, 13:586–588.

103. Samuel Sandys to James Wright, 3 June 1762, in *ColRG*, 34:519–520. Sandys was the king's personal secretary. Also see Sandys to Wright, 20 December 1762, in *ColRG*, 34:524–527.

104. James Wright to John Stuart, in Mays, *Amherst Papers*, 377; Juricek, *Endgame for Empire*, 37–38; and Colin G. Calloway, *The Scratch of a Pen: 1763 and the Transformation of North America* (Oxford, 2006), 101. For Wright's quote, see James Wright to Board of Trade, 22 February 1763, in *ColRG*, 28.1:405–406.

105. "Proceedings," 4 January 1763, in *ColRG*, 9:12–17, quote on 16. Also see Hahn, *Invention*, 266–267; and Corkran, *Creek Frontier*, 232.

106. Stuart to Amherst, 15 March 1763, in Juricek, *Endgame for Empire*, 45; and Gage to James Wright, 28 September 1764, in GP.

107. 14 July 1763, in *ColRG*, 9:70–77; Saunt, *New Order*, 46–48; Juricek, *Endgame for Empire*, 39–42.

108. James Wright to Lord Egremont, 15 March 1763, in *ColRG*, 37:35; and *GG*, 7 April 1763. For the founding of the *Georgia Gazette*, see Alexander Lawrence, *James Johnston: Georgia's First Printer* (Savannah, 1956).

109. *GG*, 5 May 1763.

110. *GG*, 26 May 1763.

111. *GG*, 2 June 1763; and James Wright to Board of Trade, 10 June 1763, in *ColRG*, 28.1:445–447.

112. Coleman, "James Wright and the Origins," 109; Snapp, *John Stuart*, 180; Coleman, "Oglethorpe and James Wright," 127; Coleman, "James Wright," 41–42; *RG*, 86; Calhoon, *Loyalists*, 4. For the intimate connection between mercantilism and the founding of Georgia, see Kenneth Coleman, "The Founding of Georgia," in *Forty Years of Diversity: Essays on Colonial Georgia*, ed. Harvey H. Jackson and Phinizy Spalding (Athens, 1984), 4–24; Jack Greene, "Travails of an Infant Colony: The Search for Viability, Coherence, and Identity in Colonial Georgia," in Jackson and Spalding, *Forty Years*, 275–310; Coleman, *Colonial Georgia*, 142–143; Davis, *Fledgling Province*, 95–97; Trevor Reese, *Colonial Georgia: A Study in British Imperial Policy in the Eighteenth Century* (Athens, 1963), 14, 121–122; Sweet, *William Stephens*, 11–12, 127; and James Bonner, *A History of Georgia Agriculture, 1732–1860* (Athens, 1964).

113. Coleman, "James Wright and the Origins," 105. Prior to myself, no one has studied the life of Wright as much as Coleman has. He seriously contemplated writing a biography in the 1950s but believed the lack of personal correspondence to be prohibitive.

114. Corkran, *Creek Frontier*, 234–237; and Juricek, *Endgame for Empire*, 45.

115. For news of the peace treaty, see James Wright to Earl of Egremont, 15 March

and 7 September 1763, in *ColRG*, 37:35, 61. For the Proclamation of 1763, see Coleman, *Colonial Georgia*, chap. 13; Davis, *Fledgling Province*, 247–248; Jack P. Greene, ed., *Colonies to Nation, 1763–1789: A Documentary History of the American Revolution* (New York, 1975), 16–18; and Nelson, *American Tory*, 5.

116. Woody Holton, *Liberty Is Sweet: The Hidden History of the American Revolution* (New York, 2021), chap. 1; James Wright to Egremont, 10 June 1763, in *ColRG*, 37:50–53; James Wright to Board of Trade, 22 June and 23 November 1763, in *ColRG*, 28.1:447, 453–454. Also see Hahn, *Invention*, 266. For an overview of the Congress at Augusta, see Alden, *John Stuart*, chap. 11.

117. James Wright to Stuart, 5 January 1767, in *ColRG*, 37:164–165. Wright very directly chastised Stuart for issuing directives that contradicted his own instructions. Also see Stuart to Gage, 21 July 1767, in GP; and Snapp, *John Stuart*, 74, 139.

118. Snapp, *John Stuart*, 55–59, quote on 57; Alden, *John Stuart*, introduction, 135–136, 170, 311–312; and Dennis, *Patriots & Indians*, 66.

119. Ellis to Egremont, 15 December 1762, in Cashin, *Governor Henry Ellis*, 170–171; Alden, *John Stuart*, 181; Cashin, *Lachlan McGillivray*, 215; and Tortora, *Carolina in Crisis*, 183. For the quote, see Benjamin Hawkins to Henry Dearborn, 1 June 1801, in Saunt, *A New Order*, 1.

120. James Wright to Board of Trade, 10 and 22 June 1763, in *ColRG*, 28.1:445–447; James Wright to Lord Egremont, 10 June 1763, in *ColRG*, 37:50–53; and James Wright to Lord Egremont, 14 July 1763, in *ColRG*, 9:70–79. Also see Juricek, *Endgame for Empire*, 36; Braund, *Deerskins & Duffels*, 100–111; Corkran, *Creek Frontier*, 229–252; Hahn, *Invention*, 264; Cashin, *Lachlan McGillivray*, 213–214; and Calloway, *Scratch*, 101–102.

121. Guyasuta speech, 10 May 1765, in Holton, *Liberty Is Sweet*, 24.

122. James Wright to Board of Trade, 7 September 1763, in *ColRG*, 28.1:450–451; and Juricek, *Endgame for Empire*, 45.

123. James Wright to the Earl of Egremont, 10 June 1763, in *ColRG*, 37:50–53.

124. The entire proceedings of the congress at Augusta can be found in "Minutes of the Southern Congress at Augusta, Georgia . . . October 01, 1763–November 21, 1763," in *Colonial Records of the State of North Carolina*, 11:156–207, in CRNC, https://docsouth .unc.edu/csr/index.php/document/csr11-0084 (hereafter cited as "Minutes"). Also see "Journal of the Southern Congress at Augusta in Georgia, 1763," in *ColRG*, 39:293–394.

125. For example, see "Journal of the Southern Congress." For Wright's sense of urgency, see James Wright to Lord Egremont, 10 June 1763, in *ColRG*, 37:50–53; and James Wright to Francis Fauquier, 22 June 1763, in *ColRG*, 37:57–60.

126. James Wright to Fauquier, 22 June 1763, in *Official Papers of Francis Fauquier*, ed. George Reese (Charlottesville, 1980–1983), 2:983–985; and James Wright to Fauquier, 22 June 1763, in *ColRG*, 37:57–60. Also see Cashin, *Lachlan McGillivray*, 218–219; and Corkran, *Creek Frontier*, 237–238.

127. James Wright to Boone, Dobbs, Fauquier, and Stuart, 8 October 1763, in "Minutes," 158–159. For the smallpox, see Paul Kelton, "Not All Disappeared: Disease and Southeastern Indian Survival, 1500–1800" (PhD diss., University of Oklahoma, 1998), 377, 254, and chap. 3; and Elizabeth A. Fenn, *Pox Americana: The Great Smallpox Epidemic of 1775–1782* (New York, 2001), chap. 1.

128. James Wright to Boone, Dobbs, Fauquier, and Stuart, 8 October 1763, in "Minutes," 159. For the earthquake, see *Annual Register . . . for the Year 1763* (London, 1764), 96.

129. Fauquier to James Wright, 27 May 1763, in Reese, *Official Papers*, 2:956; Tortora, *Carolina in Crisis*, 183; and Cashin, *Lachlan McGillivray*, 215.

130. Boone, Dobbs, Fauquier, Stuart to James Wright, 4 October 1763, in "Minutes," 157–158.

131. James Wright to Boone, Dobbs, Fauquier, Stuart, 8 October 1763, in "Minutes," 159–160; and Cashin, *Lachlan McGillivray*, 218–219.

132. Corkran, *Creek Frontier*, 238.

133. Juricek, *Endgame for Empire*, 48–49; and Daniel Troy, "Ruining the King's Cause: The Defeat of the Loyalists in the Revolutionary South, 1774–1781" (PhD diss., Ohio State University, 2015), 290–291.

134. Hahn, *Invention*, 266–267; and Corkran, *Creek Frontier*, 229–231.

135. Laurens to John Ettwein, 10 November 1760, in *PHL*, 4:39–43, quote on 41; and James Wright to Jeffrey Amherst, 2 February 1761, in CO, 5/60.

136. Boone, Dobbs, Fauquier to James Wright, 14 October 1763, in "Minutes," 160–161.

137. James Wright to Boone, Dobbs, Fauquier, and Stuart, 11 October 1763, in "Minutes," 161–163; and *RG*, 93.

138. *GG*, 27 October 1763; 11 October 1763, in *ColRG*, 9:97–99; and Cashin, *Lachlan McGillivray*, 217–219.

139. Boone, Dobbs, Fauquier to Stuart, 15 October 1763, in "Minutes," 164–165; and Nathan Whiting to Jared Ingersoll, 22 September 1763, in Franklin Dexter, *Jared Ingersoll Papers* (New Haven, 1918), 301–304. For the rejection of Dorchester, see Stuart to Boone, Dobbs, and Fauquier, 23 October 1763, in "Minutes," 176–177.

140. *RG*, 93. Interestingly, Wright shamed his counterparts, arguing that his personal comfort would not factor into the equation when considering "his majesty's service." See Juricek, *Endgame for Empire*, 47.

141. Edward J. Cashin, *Guardians of the Valley: Chickasaws in Colonial South Carolina and Georgia* (Columbia, 2009), 127.

142. Stuart to Boone, Dobbs, Fauquier, 15 October 1763, in "Minutes," 165–168. For the hunting season, which was March to October, see James Wright to Stuart, 22 February 1764, in Piker, *Okfuskee*, 81. Piker suggests that the date range for the hunting season is somewhat flexible based on the age of the hunters and the current diplomatic situation. For the fear of war, see Stuart to Boone, 14 October 1763, in Juricek, *Endgame for Empire*, 48.

143. Boone, Dobbs, Fauquier to Stuart, 18 October 1763, in "Minutes," 170–172; and Boone, Dobbs, Fauquier to James Wright, 18 October 1763, in "Minutes," 172.

144. James Wright to Boone, Dobbs, Fauquier, 18 October 1763, in "Minutes," 174.

145. Stuart to Boone, Dobbs, Fauquier, 23 October 1763, in "Minutes," 176–177; Alden, *John Stuart*, 177, 182; Corkran, *Creek Frontier*, 234–239; Cashin, *Lachlan McGillivray*, 215–217; and Juricek, *Endgame for Empire*, 49.

146. For "gifts" and "benefit," see Juricek, *Endgame for Empire*, 50. For gaining influence, see Knox to ——, 20 May 1760, in Knox and Knox, *Manuscripts*, 83–85. For Native American attendance at the congress, see Juricek, *Endgame for Empire*, 49–50.

147. For Stuart's opening remarks, see 5 November 1763, in "Minutes," 180–183; Alden, *John Stuart*, 181; Corkran, *Creek Frontier*, 237–239.

148. Juricek, *Endgame for Empire*, 39 and chap. 2; Hahn, *Invention*, 267; and Calloway, *Scratch*, 100–102.

149. Juricek, *Endgame for Empire*, chap. 2; Hahn, *Invention*, 267; and Calloway, *Scratch*, 100–102.

150. "Talks of the Chickesaw, Upper & Lower Creeks[,] Chactaw[,] Cherokee & Catawba Indians" to Wright, Dobbs, Boone, Fauquier, and Stuart, 7–8 November 1763, in "Minutes," see nn. 125183–125187; Juricek, *Endgame for Empire*, 1; and Corkran, *Creek Frontier*, 231–232.

151. "Tribal Response," 188–190. The Mortar, among others, had also complained of this earlier that spring, saying that "their buffalo, deer and bear [have been] drove off the land and killed" by squatters. Juricek, *Endgame for Empire*, 41.

152. "Talks of the Chickesaw," in "Minutes," 188–190.

153. Hahn, *Invention*, 266–268; Cashin, *Lachlan McGillivray*, 216–217; Calloway, *Scratch*, 102–103; and Juricek, *Endgame for Empire*, 44–45.

154. "Talks of the Chickesaw," in "Minutes," 190–191.

155. Governors to various Indian leaders, 9 November 1763, in "Minutes," 192–200.

156. James Wright to Jeffrey Amherst, 10 November 1763, in Amherst Papers. For the value, see Alden, *John Stuart*, 181; and Cashin, *Lachlan McGillivray*, 215. Historian Louis DeVorsey Jr. has argued that obtaining the agreement from so many tribesmen "was to complicate and add greatly to the expense" of the Indian congresses (*Indian Boundary*, 19).

157. Tortora, *Carolina in Crisis*, 184. Tortora notes that "despite earlier promises, Indian lands *were* taken." Superintendent Stuart suggested that it was Captain Allick who had "voluntarily proposed enlarging the bounds of Georgia" (Juricek, *Endgame for Empire*, 53–55).

158. Board of Trade to James Wright, 27 February 1761, in *ColRG*, 34:374–382. The board encouraged Wright to seek a session, but Wright understood that he was in no position yet to obtain such an agreement. He bided his time until the opportunity arose.

159. James Wright to Lord Halifax, 23 December 1763, in *ColRG*, 37:69–72; and Davis, *Fledgling Province*, 29.

160. Cashin, *Lachlan McGillivray*, 213–214, 219–222; Bryan C. Rindfleisch, *George Galphin's Intimate Empire: The Creek Indians, Family, and Colonialism in Early America* (Tuscaloosa, 2019), 49–50, 124, 142; Michael P. Morris, *George Galphin and the Transformation of the Georgia–South Carolina Backcountry* (Lanham, 2015), 1–5; and Calloway, *Scratch*, 103. Cashin even argued that "the essential business of the Augusta Congress was accomplished" in the homes of McGillivray and Galphin before Wright and the other governors arrived. Although this is possible, there is no ironclad proof to support this thesis.

161. Corkran, *Creek Frontier*, 239; and Cashin, *Lachlan McGillivray*, 222.

162. "A Treaty for the Preservation and Continuance of a Firm and Perfect Peace and Friendship . . . ," 10 November 1763, in "Minutes," 200–204; and James Wright

to Board of Trade, 10 November 1763, in *ColRG*, 37:62–65. Also see De Vorsey, *Indian Boundary*, 149–157; Cashin, *Lachlan McGillivray*, 220–221.

163. Coleman, "James Wright and the Origins," 112.

164. James Wright to Lord Halifax, 10 November 1763, in CO, 323/17; and Juricek, *Endgame for Empire*, 37. Wright and Stuart both blamed the traders for the ill will on the frontier.

165. Davis, *Fledgling Province*, 27, 65; and David Hackett Fischer, *African Founders: How Enslaved People Expanded American Ideals* (New York, 2022), 395–396.

166. James Wright to Lord Halifax, 23 December 1763, in *ColRG*, 37:69–72.

167. James Habersham to William Russell, 10 October 1764, in *GHS Coll*, 6:26–27.

168. James Wright to Jeffery Amherst, 10 November 1763, in Amherst Papers.

169. Thomas Gage to Earl of Halifax, 7 January 1764, in GP. For the "cautious" quote, see Thomas Gage to Earl of Halifax, 21 January 1764, in GP.

170. Stuart to Egremont, 5 December 1763, in Juricek, *Endgame for Empire*, 65.

171. Juricek, *Endgame for Empire*, 56.

172. See *GG*, 12 March 1764, for Wright's proclamation concerning the ceded lands.

173. Gallay, *Formation*, 110; and Gage to Hillsborough, 10 November 1770, in CO, 5/83.

174. Cashin, *Lachlan McGillivray*, 213, 223; Edward J. Cashin, "Sowing the Wind: Governor Wright and the Georgia Backcountry on the Eve of the Revolution," in *Forty Years of Diversity: Essays on Colonial Georgia*, ed. Harvey H. Jackson and Phinizy Spalding (Athens, 1984), 234; James Wright to Dartmouth, 20 September 1773, *GGCJ*, 1773, 156–162; and William Mylne to Ann Mylne, 4 January 1775, in *Travels in the Colonies in 1773–1775: Described in the Letters of John Mylne*, ed. Ted Ruddock (Athens, 1993), 54–58.

## Chapter 3. A Governor in Crisis

1. Daniel Allen Butler, *The Other Side of the Night: The* Carpathia, *the* Californian, *and the Night the* Titanic *Was Lost* (Philadelphia, 2009), 13.

2. Al-Mas'udi quoted in Wim Klooster, introduction to *The Atlantic World: Essays on Slavery, Migration, and Imagination*, ed. Wim Klooster and Alfred Padula (Upper Saddle River, 2000), 1. For oceanic travel in the eighteenth century, see Stephen R. Berry, *A Path in the Mighty Waters: Shipboard Life and Atlantic Crossings to the New World* (New Haven, 2015).

3. Quoted in William L. Sachse, *The Colonial American in Britain* (Westport, 1978), 7.

4. Robert was admitted on 24 January 1764 and matriculated in 1765. J. A. Venn, ed., *Admissions to Trinity College, Cambridge* (London, 1911–1916), 3:204; and *GG*, 15 and 22 March 1764.

5. *Pennsylvania Gazette*, 28 April 1763. "A letter since received gives some hopes that she may still be saved" (*New York Gazette*, 2 May 1763).

6. *London Evening Post*, 9 July 1763. By 8 March Captain Blake had reported that the vessel had received new masts and rigging and would be ready to sail within a week. *GG*, 8 March 1764; and *SCG*, 17 March 1764.

7. Leland Bellot, *William Knox: The Life & Thought of an Eighteenth-Century Im-*

*perialist* (Austin, 1977), 73; and James Habersham to Sarah Wright, 31 March 1764, in James Habersham Papers, GHS. Habersham asked Lady Wright to give his best to "Miss Sarah, who I hope will not be so much taken up with her new acquaintance as to forget her old friends." For the will, see Will of Sir James Wright, late Governor of the Province of Georgia of Westminster, Middlesex, 22 April 1786, catalog reference B 11/41, TNA.

8. Habersham to Sarah Wright, 31 March 1764, emphasis added, in Habersham Papers. For an example of their close relationship, see Habersham to William Knox, 17 July 1765, in *GHS Coll*, 6:38–40.

9. Habersham to Knox, 31 March 1764, Habersham Papers; Bellot, *William Knox*, 73.

10. David McCullough, *John Adams* (New York, 2001), 205; and Simon Schama, *Rough Crossings: The Slaves, the British, and the American Revolution* (London, 2009), 322–323.

11. *St. James's Chronicle*, 21 July 1764; and *Lloyd's Evening Post* (London), 23 July 1764.

12. *St. James's Chronicle*, 24 July 1764; and *St. James's Chronicle or the British Evening Post*, 26 July 1764.

13. *London Evening Post*, 8 and 11 September 1764.

14. *Lloyd's Evening Post*, 14 November 1764.

15. Jacob Lobb to Archibald Kennedy, 24 October 1764, in the *Pennsylvania Gazette*, 29 November 1764. See also *Boston Evening Post*, 3 December 1764; and *Public Advertiser*, 17 January 1765. Lobb was wounded the following March in a duel with Captain Thomas Simpson. See *GG*, 9 May 1765.

16. Wright to Board of Trade, 26 September 1764, in *ColRG*, 28.2:54–55. Wright also mentioned a communication sent via the *Epreuve* (Wright to Edward Sedgwick, 30 August 1764). Regarding the travel time, see Rick Atkinson, *The British Are Coming: The War for America, Lexington to Princeton, 1775–1777* (New York, 2019), 179; and Harold E. Davis, *The Fledgling Province: Social and Cultural Life in Colonial Georgia, 1733–1776* (Chapel Hill, 2011), 24. Davis suggested a time frame of two to four months, but on at least one instance, instructions from London had been mailed at the end of August 1767 and did not arrive in Georgia until March of the following year.

17. Wright to the Board of Trade, 26 September 1764, in *ColRG*, 28.2:54–55; Habersham to William Russell, 10 October 1764, in *GHS Coll*, 6:26–27; Jacob Lobb to Archibald Kennedy, 24 October 1764, in the *Pennsylvania Gazette*, 29 November 1764; and Bartholomew Zouberbuhler to the Society for Propagating Christian Knowledge, 31 December 1764, in "Collections of the Georgia Historical Society, Other Documents and Notes, Part II," ed. Albert Britt and Lilla Hawes, *GHQ* 57, no. 1 (Spring 1973): 137.

18. Habersham to William Russell, 10 October 1764, in *GHS Coll*, 6:26–27.

19. Zouberbuhler to the Society for Propagating Christian Knowledge, 31 December 1764. For a brief character sketch, see Edgar Legare Pennington, "The Reverend Bartholomew Zouberbuhler," *GHQ* 18, no. 4 (December 1934): 354–363.

20. Habersham to William Russell, 10 October 1764, in *GHS Coll*, 6:26–27.

21. *RG*, 110. Abbot cites Habersham's letter to William Knox (29 January 1766). Although this letter mentions his decision to move into Wright's home, he did so for fear of his personal safety and not because, as Abbot suggested, the two had become

so close and mutually supportive in grief counseling. In discussing moving into Governor Wright's home, Habersham wrote: "How dreadful it is to have one's person and property under the Dominion of a Mob?"

22. Lyttelton to Knox, 20 October 1765, in William Knox and Howard Vicenté Knox, *Manuscripts of Captain H. V. Knox* (Boston, 1972), 91–92.

23. "The Mourning," *GG*, 21 March 1765.

24. Lyttelton to Knox, 10 January, 14 July, and 20 October 1765, in Bellot, *William Knox*, 73.

25. *GG*, 7 July 1763.

26. *GG*, 25 April and 2 May 1765; and Paul Pressly, *On the Rim of the Caribbean: Colonial Georgia and the British Atlantic World* (Athens, 2013), 108. The act passed on 15 February and was signed on 22 March 1765.

27. For the Stamp Act in Georgia, see Trevor Richard Reese, *Colonial Georgia* (Athens, 1963), 245–252; Kenneth Coleman, *American Revolution in Georgia, 1763–1789* (Athens, 1958), 16–24; *RG*, chap. 5; Charles Risher Jr., "Propaganda, Dissension, and Defeat: Loyalist Sentiment in Georgia, 1763–1783" (PhD diss., Mississippi State University, 1976), chap. 2; Carl Garrigus, "Profit and the Press: Georgia Newspapers from the Stamp Act to Nullification" (PhD diss., Georgia State University, 1997); S. F. Roach, "The Georgia Gazette and Stamp Act: A Reconsideration," *GHQ* 55, no. 4 (Winter 1971): 471–491; Ashley Ellefson, "The Stamp Act in Georgia," *GHQ* 46, no. 1 (March 1962): 1–19; Randall Miller, "The Stamp Act in Colonial Georgia," *GHQ* 56, no. 3 (Fall 1972): 318–331; Percy S. Flippin, "The Royal Government in Georgia, 1752–1776," *GHQ* 8, no. 1 (March 1924): 1–37; and Flippin, "The Royal Government in Georgia, 1752–1776 (Continued)," *GHQ* 8, no. 2 (June 1924): 81–120; Carol R. Cunningham, *The Southern Royal Governors and the Coming of the American Revolution* (New York, 1984), 93–106; John Ivey Brown, "Relations between Georgia's Royal Governors" (MA thesis, University of Georgia, 1970), 62–100; Andrea Lynn Williams, "Sir James Wright in Georgia: Local and Imperial Conflict in the American Revolution" (honors thesis, College of William and Mary, 2012), 16–32; Hugh Atkinson, "Georgia and the Stamp Act Crisis" (MA thesis, Georgia State University, 1965); and William Tolleson, "Governor James Wright, 1760–1776" (MA thesis, University of Georgia, 1938).

28. John Bartram, *Diary of a Journey through the Carolinas, Georgia and Florida: From July 1, 1765, to April 10, 1766* (Philadelphia, 1942), 29.

29. Assembly to Wright, 21 February 1764, in *ColRG*, 14:125–129; and Speaker Lewis Johnson to Wright, 24 November 1763, in *ColRG*, 14:69–71. Lord Adam Gordon even observed the harmonious relationship between Wright and the Assembly. See "Journal of Lord Adam Gordon," in *Narratives of Colonial America, 1704–1765*, ed. Howard Peckham (Chicago, 1971), 239–240.

30. *GG*, 15 August 1765; Edmund Morgan and Helen Morgan, *The Stamp Act Crisis: Prologue to Revolution* (New York, 1963), 107.

31. "Proceedings," 25 March 1765, in *ColRG*, 14:252–253, 17:199–200; and James Habersham, Noble Jones, and James Edward Powell to William Knox, 15 April 1765, in *GHS Coll*, 6:30–33. Knox and Wright were "on the best of terms." See Bellot, *William Knox*, 37, and for Knox's career as colonial agent, see 61–80.

32. Habersham, Jones, and Powell to Knox, 15 April 1765, in *GHS Coll*, 6:30–33; and

Habersham to Knox, 28 October 1765, in *GHS Coll*, 6:44–46. Habersham wrote, "It appears to me an insult on the most common understanding to talk of our being virtually represented."

33. Habersham, Jones, Powell, Lewis Johnson, Noble W. Jones, Joseph Ottolenghi, and Pat Houstoun to Knox, 18 July 1765, in *GHS Coll*, 6:40–41.

34. Wright to Dartmouth, 24 April 1775, in *ColRG*, 38.1:424–429. Other Loyalists expressed similar sentiments. For example, see Carol Berkin, *Jonathan Sewell: Odyssey of an American Loyalist* (New York, 1974), 37–42; 8 August 1774, in *Diary and Letters of His Excellency Thomas Hutchinson*, ed. Peter Hutchinson (Boston, 1884), 216; Bernard Bailyn, *The Ordeal of Thomas Hutchinson* (Cambridge, 1976), e.g., 232; and Thomas Walmsley, *Thomas Hutchinson and the Origins of the American Revolution* (New York, 1998), e.g., 141.

35. King George III to Lord North, 5 July 1775, in W. Bodham Donne, *The Correspondence of King George the Third with Lord North from 1768 to 1783* (London, 1867), 253.

36. Morgan and Morgan, *The Stamp Act Crisis*, 108.

37. "Proceedings," 29 October 1765, in *ColRG*, 14:269–274.

38. Lyttelton to Knox, 20 October 1765, in Knox and Knox, *Manuscripts*, 91–92. He wrote: "I do not see how the Mother Country can hope for the future that her laws will be obeyed in such distant dominions."

39. Most Americans opposed the Stamp Act, including royal officials. William H. Nelson, *The American Tory* (Lebanon, 1992), 5.

40. *GG*, 8 August 1765.

41. *RG*, 104. For more on this, see Habersham to Knox, 18 July, 28 and 30 October 1765, in *GHS Coll*, 6:40–41, 44–46, 46–49. Also see *GG*, 1 August 1765.

42. William Knox, *The Claim of the Colonies to an Exemption from Internal Taxes Imposed by Authority of Parliament Examined* (London, 1765); and Bellot, *William Knox*, chap. 4. For the Assembly's instructions, see Assembly to Knox, 15 April and 18 July 1765, in "Letters to the Georgia Colonial Agent, July, 1762 to January, 1771," ed. Lila Hawes, *GHQ* 36, no. 3 (September 1952): 268–270, 273. For the parliamentary perspective, see John Bullian, *A Great and Necessary Measure: George Grenville and the Genesis of the Stamp Act, 1763–1765* (Columbia, 1982), esp. 90–163; and H. T. Dickinson, "Britain's Imperial Sovereignty: The Ideological Case against the American Colonists," in *Britain and the American Revolution*, ed. H. T. Dickinson (New York, 1998), 64–96.

43. Habersham to Knox, 17 July 1765, in *GHS Coll*, 6:38–40.

44. Habersham to Knox, 28 October 1765, in *GHS Coll*, 6:44–46. Knox would serve as one of Wright's executors following the governor's death. James Wright, Loyalist claim, in *BGLC*.

45. Bellot, *William Knox*, 65–67.

46. Wright to Halifax, 24 August and 20 September 1765, in *ColRG*, 37:99, 100–101.

47. *GG*, 3 and 10 October 1765; and Bailyn, *Ordeal of Thomas Hutchinson*, 113–172.

48. For the Liberty Boys, see *GG*, 7 November 1765; *RRSG*, 106; and Coleman, *American Revolution*, 20.

49. Vincent Caretta, "'I Began to Feel the Happiness of Liberty, of Which I Knew Nothing Before': Eighteenth-Century Black Accounts of the Lowcountry," in *African*

*American Life in the Georgia Lowcountry: The Atlantic World and the Gullah Geechee Culture*, ed. Philip Morgan (Athens, 2011), 77–102.

50. 15 November 1765, in *ColRG*, 12:292–293; Sylvia Frey, *Water from the Rock: Black Resistance in a Revolutionary Age* (Princeton, 1991), 51–52; and Gary Nash, *The Unknown American Revolution: The Unruly Birth of Democracy and the Struggle to Create America* (New York, 2006), 61.

51. Peter Wood, "'Liberty Is Sweet': African-American Freedom Struggles in the Years before White Independence," in *Beyond the American Revolution: Explorations in the History of American Radicalism*, ed. Alfred Young (Dekalb, 1993), 156–159; and Donald Wright, *African Americans in the Colonial Era: From African Origins through the American Revolution* (Wheeling, 1990), 150–151.

52. *GG*, 31 October 1765; and Wright to Conway, 31 January 1766, in *ColRG*, 37:103–109.

53. *GG*, 7 November 1765.

54. *GG*, 7 November 1765.

55. Wright to Board of Trade, 9 November 1765, in *ColRG*, 28.2:129–130; and *GG*, 8 August 1765.

56. Wright to Conway, 15 March 1766, in *ColRG*, 37:123. For a global discussion of the radical reaction of the Sons of Liberty, see Justin du Rivage, *Revolution against Empire: Taxes, Politics, and the Origins of American Independence* (New Haven, 2017), 178–204.

57. *GG*, 31 October and 14 November 1765.

58. George Baillie, Loyalist claim, and John Baillie, Loyalist claim, both in *BGLC*.

59. Assembly to Wright, 31 October 1765, in *ColRG*, 14:276–280.

60. *RG*, 112.

61. Morgan and Morgan, *The Stamp Act Crisis*, 107–121; "Proceedings," 29 October 1765, in *ColRG*, 14:269–274; and *GG*, 31 October 1765.

62. 25 and 29 November and 2–14 December 1765, in *ColRG*, 14:299–317.

63. For a full accounting of the petitions and declarations of the Stamp Act Congress, see Morgan and Morgan, *The Stamp Act Crisis*, 110–116, quote on 111.

64. *RG*, 111.

65. *GG*, 7 November 1765.

66. Wright to Henry S. Conway, 31 January 1766, in *ColRG*, 37:103–109. This first meeting of the Liberty Boys was held on Monday, 28 October, at Machenry's Tavern. Also see Philip Davidson, *Propaganda and the American Revolution, 1763–1783* (Chapel Hill, 1941), 67–68.

67. *GG*, 7 November 1765.

68. Wright to Board of Trade, 9 November 1765, in *ColRG*, 28.2:129–130; and Wright to Gage, 1 February 1766, in GP. For a closer look at Charleston's Sons of Liberty, see Rosemary Niner Estes, "Charles Town's Sons of Liberty: A Closer Look" (PhD diss., University of North Carolina, Chapel Hill, 2005); and Robert M. Weir, "'Liberty and Property, and No Stamps': South Carolina and the Stamp Act Crisis" (PhD diss., Case Western Reserve University, 1964).

69. *GG*, 14 November 1765.

70. 12 November 1765, in *ColRG*, 9:439; and *RG*, 107, 112.

71. Habersham to Knox, 17 July 1765, in *GHS Coll*, 6:38–40.

72. Wright to Conway, 24 June 1766, in *ColRG*, 37:97–98.

73. For the Assembly's discussion concerning the removal of Knox, see, for example, 28 October, 15 November, 14 and 16 December 1765, in *ColRG*, 14:266–268, 292–294, 315–317, 317–322.

74. Wright to Assembly, 19 December 1765, in *ColRG*, 14:327, 503–504.

75. Habersham to Knox, 29 January 1766, in *GHS Coll*, 6:56.

76. Knox to the Georgia Committee of Correspondence, 20 May 1766, in *ColRG*, 17:375.

77. 14 December 1765, in *ColRG*, 14:315–317. Garth had been named James Wright's successor as South Carolina's agent. For more on his career as colonial agent, see Joseph Barnwell, "Charles Garth, M.P., the Last Colonial Agent of South Carolina in England, and Some of His Work," *SCHGM* 26, no. 2 (April 1925): 67–92; L. B. Namier, "Charles Garth and His Connexions," *English Historical Review* 54 (July 1939): 443–470; and Namier, "Charles Garth, Agent for South Carolina," *English Historical Review* 54 (October 1939): 632–652.

78. 14 and 21 January 1766, in *ColRG*, 14:328–329, 335–336, for example. Historian Kenneth Coleman asserted that Garth voted in favor of the act. See Coleman, *Colonial Georgia: A History* (Millwood, 1989), 251. This claim, however, is refuted by Lewis Namier, who stated that Garth "was one of the minority of 49 who voted against the stamp act" on 6 February 1765 ("Charles Garth, Agent," 644).

79. Bellot, *William Knox*, 64.

80. Knox, *Claim of the Colonies*, 32.

81. Wright to Conway, 31 January 1766, in *ColRG*, 37:103–109.

82. Wright to Board of Trade, 15 January 1766, in *ColRG*, 28.2:132–134.

83. Habersham to Knox, 29 January 1766, in *ColRG*, 9:56.

84. Wright to Board of Trade, 2 December 1765, in *ColRG*, 28.2:130–132; and 22 November 1765, in *ColRG*, 9:437–440.

85. Wright to Conway, 2 December 1765, in *ColRG*, 37:102; and 22 November 1765, in *ColRG*, 9:437–440.

86. 16 December 1765, in *ColRG*, 9:454–458.

87. Habersham to Knox, 4 December 1765, in *GHS Coll*, 6:49–50, emphasis added.

88. Knox, *Claim of the Colonies*, 2.

89. Wright to Board of Trade, 2 December 1765, in *ColRG*, 28.2:130–132; and 15 January 1766, in *ColRG*, 132–134.

90. Daniel Spindel, "The Stamp Act Riots" (PhD diss., Duke University, 1975), 211.

91. Alexander Lawrence, *James Johnston: Georgia's First Printer* (Savannah, 1956), 9.

92. Roach, "The Georgia Gazette."

93. *RG*, 112–113.

94. *RG*, 112–113; and 18 December 1765, in *ColRG*, 9:459–460.

95. *Pennsylvania Gazette*, 13 February 1766.

96. Morgan and Morgan, *The Stamp Act Crisis*, 172.

97. Daniel McDonough, *Christopher Gadsden and Henry Laurens: The Parallel Lives of Two American Patriots* (Selinsgrove, 2000), 74.

98. Habersham to Daniel Roubadeau, 17 December 1765, in *GHS Coll*, 6:57–58.

99. 6 December 1765, in *ColRG*, 9:453–454.

100. Wright to Conway, 31 January 1766, in *ColRG*, 37:103–109.

101. Wright to Conway, 2 January 1766, in *ColRG*, 37:110–112; and *Pennsylvania Gazette*, 13 February 1766.

102. Wright to Henry Seymour Conway, 31 January 1766, in *ColRG*, 37:103–109.

103. For "friend to liberty," see *Pennsylvania Gazette*, 13 February 1766; Wright to Board of Trade, 15 January 1766; for "confident," see Flippin, "Royal Government (Continued)," 92; *SCG*, 21 January 1766; and Kenneth Coleman, "James Wright and the Origins of the Revolution in Georgia," in *The Human Dimensions of Nation Making: Essays on Colonial and Revolutionary America*, ed. James Kirby Martin (Madison, 1976), 113–115.

104. Wright to the Board of Trade, 15 January 1766, in Flippin, "Royal Government (Continued)," 92.

105. Wright to Conway, 31 January 1766, in *ColRG*, 37:103–109; *GG*, 31 October and 7 and 14 November 1765; Coleman, *Colonial Georgia*, 248; and Coleman, *American Revolution*, 21–22.

106. Wright to Gage, 20 January 1766, in GP; and Jonathan Mercantini, *Who Shall Rule? The Evolution of South Carolina Political Culture, 1748–1776* (Columbia, 2007), 215. Wright constituted Sunbury as a port of entry in September 1762. See John Wright Boyd, *Wright-Lewis-Moore and Connected Families: Early Settlers, Greene County, Georgia* (Atlanta, 1968), 6.

107. *Pennsylvania Journal and Weekly Advertiser*, 13 February 1766, in Miller, "The Stamp Act," 327.

108. *South-Carolina Gazette; and Country Journal*, 21 January 1766; and *RRSG*, 116.

109. Wright to Conway, 31 January 1766, in *ColRG*, 37:103–109; and Wright to Board of Trade, 1 February 1766, in *ColRG*, 28.2:135–136.

110. Wright to Gage, 26 April 1766, in Jonathan Mercantini, "Colony in Conflict: South Carolina, 1748–1766" (PhD diss., Emory University, 2000), 366.

111. Knox to Lyttelton, 5 March 1760, in Knox and Knox, *Manuscripts*, 82–83.

112. Wright to Conway, 31 January 1766, in *ColRG*, 37:103–109.

113. Wright to Conway, 10 March 1766, in *ColRG*, 37:116–118.

114. Wright to Board of Trade, 15 January 1766, in *ColRG*, 28.2:132–134; Wright to Conway, 10 March 1766, in *ColRG*, 37:116–122; Wright to Board of Trade, 7 February 1766, in *ColRG*, 28.2:136–137; Wright to Conway, 7 February 1766, in *ColRG*, 37:110–111; Wright to Board of Trade, 10 February 1766, in *ColRG*, 28.2:137–138; and *RG*, 120.

115. Wright to Gage, 1 February 1766, in Mercantini, "Colony in Conflict," 366. In March he again complained of the effects of the "rebellious spirits in South Carolina" (Wright to Gage, 15 March 1766, in Mercantini, "Colony in Conflict," 366).

116. Habersham to George Whitefield, 27 January 1766, in *GHS Coll*, 6:54–56.

117. Habersham to Knox, 29 January 1766, in *GHS Coll*, 6:56.

118. For "knot," see Wright to Conway, 31 January 1766, in *ColRG*, 37:103–109; and Habersham to Whitefield, 27 January 1766, in Habersham Papers. Also see Jac Wellar, "The Irregular War in the South," *Military Affairs* 24, no. 3 (Autumn 1960): 126. For the remaining quotes, see Wright to Board of Trade, 1 February 1766, in *ColRG*, 28.2:135–136; Wright to Conway, 10 March 1766, in *ColRG*, 37:116–118; Wright to Gage,

1 February 1766, in GP; Wright to Conway, 31 January 1766, in *ColRG*, 37:103–109; Wright to Conway, 7 February 1766, in *ColRG*, 37:110–111; and Wright to Board of Trade, 7 February 1766, in *ColRG*, 28.2:136–137.

119. Wright to Board of Trade, 1 February 1766, in *ColRG*, 28.2:135–136.

120. Wright to Board of Trade, 7 February 1766, in *ColRG*, 28.2:136–137.

121. His name was Charles Webb. Robert Barnwell, "Loyalism in South Carolina, 1765–1785" (PhD diss., Duke University, 1941), 61–62; and John Drayton, *Memoirs of the American Revolution as Relating to the State of South Carolina* (New York, 1969), 1:314. Also see John R. Alden, "John Stuart Accuses William Bull," *WMQ* 2, no. 3 (July 1945): 315–320.

122. Wright to Conway, 12 February 1766, in *ColRG*, 37:112–115.

123. The Stamp Act was repealed on 18 March 1766, but it took two months for the news to arrive in Savannah. For the Stamp Act and its repeal, see in a global perspective du Rivage, *Revolution against Empire*, 101–146.

124. Wright to Conway, 24 June 1766, in *ColRG*, 37:97–98. Thomas Hutchinson of Massachusetts felt the same way, complaining that "all the present disorder in the Colonies" was the result of British neglect. See Hutchinson, *Diary*, 1:116; and Hutchinson to Gage, 13 April 1770, in Bailyn, *Ordeal of Thomas Hutchinson*, 187, 66–69. Also see Walmsley, *Thomas Hutchinson*, chap. 3.

125. Ellefson, "Stamp Act," 15–16; and Wright to Conway, 23 July 1766, in *ColRG*, 37:129–130.

126. Shelburne to Wright, 22 September 1766, in *ColRG*, 37:126–127.

127. *Lloyd's Evening Post and British Chronicle*, 5 June 1766.

128. Earl of Shelburne to Wright, 22 September 1766, in *ColRG*, 37:126–127.

129. William Samuel Johnson to Jared Ingersoll, 16 May 1767, in Morgan and Morgan, *The Stamp Act Crisis*, 308.

130. Wright to Board of Trade, 10 March 1766; and Wright to Conway, 10 March 1766, both in *RRSG*, 108.

131. For example, see Samuel Sandys to Wright, 20 February 1762, in *ColRG*, 34:524–527. Also see Wright to Shelburne, 5 January 1767, in *ColRG*, 37:174–17, quote on 175.

132. Shelburne to Wright, 22 September 1766, in *ColRG*, 37:126–127.

133. Wright to Shelburne, 23 July 1766, in SP. Also see Wright to Duke of Richmond, 28 October 1766, in SP. Richmond was His Majesty's principal secretary of state for the Southern Department.

134. Wright to Conway, 23 July 1766, in *ColRG*, 37:129–130.

135. Bailyn, *Ordeal of Thomas Hutchinson*, 81.

136. Bartram, *Diary*, 29; Wright to Bartram, 22 August 1762, in *Correspondence of John Bartram, 1734–1777*, ed. Edmund Berkely (Gainesville, 1992), 568–569.

137. For "firmness," see Habersham to Whitefield, 2 February 1766, in Habersham Papers. For "servant," see Habersham to Whitefield, 27 January 1766, in Habersham Papers.

138. Wright to Conway, 10 March 1766, in *ColRG*, 37:116–122, emphasis added.

139. Pauline Maier, *From Resistance to Revolution: Colonial Radicals and the Development of American Opposition to Britain, 1765–1776* (New York, 1991), 84.

140. *RG*, 122.

141. Wright to Dartmouth, 24 April 1775, in *ColRG*, 38.1:424–429. Other Loyalists expressed similar sentiments. For example, see Berkin, *Jonathan Sewell*, 37–42; 8 August 1774, in Peter Hutchinson, *Diary and Letters of His Excellency Thomas Hutchinson* (Boston, 1884), 216; Bailyn, *Thomas Hutchinson*, 232; and Walmsley, *Thomas Hutchinson*, 141.

142. During the crisis, the *Georgia Gazette* published sixteen issues that discussed the Stamp Act. Of these, fifteen were decidedly against the act. See Garrigus, "Profit and the Press," 18; and Lawrence, *James Johnston*. For the quote, see Gage to Wright, 26 April and [?] 1766, in GP. Also see *South-Carolina Gazette; and Country Journal*, 21 January 1766.

143. Jack P. Greene, *The Quest for Power: The Lower Houses of Assembly in the Southern Royal Colonies 1689–1776* (Chapel Hill, 2012), 46–47. The Assembly's power, however, began to grow quite swiftly in the ensuing years.

144. James Wright, Loyalist claim, in *BGLC*.

145. Wright to Conway, 24 June 1766, in *ColRG*, 37:97–98. Also see Clay Ouzts, *Samuel Elbert and the Age of Revolution in Georgia, 1740–1788* (Macon, 2022), chap. 2.

147. Wright to Conway, 23 July 1766, quoted in *RG*, 123. Historian Trevor Reese commented on this character trait of Wright's, deeming him to be "a man of ability and fortitude" (Reese, *Colonial Georgia*, 24).

## Chapter 4. A Governor and Colony on the Move

1. Wright to Shelburne, 18 November 1766, in *ColRG*, 37:141–145.

2. Wright to Shelburne, 18 November 1766, in *ColRG*, 37:141–145.

3. "Necessary," "apprehensive," "over stock't," "worst kind," "insolence," and "irregularities" in Wright to Shelburne, 29 November 1766, in *ColRG*, 37:146–149; "great confusion" in Wright to Board of Trade, 27 August 1764, in CO, 5/649; "white Indians" in Mart A. Stewart, "'Whether Wast, Deodand, or Stray': Cattle, Culture, and the Environment in Early Georgia," *Agricultural History* 65, no. 3 (Summer 1991): 25; and "remonstrate" in "Proceedings," 7 August 1764, in *ColRG*, 9:202–203. In fact, Wright issued a proclamation in 1768 forbidding trading with Native Americans without a license. See *GG*, 11 January 1769. Also see Shelburne to John Stuart, 11 December 1766, GP.

4. Habersham to Wright, 20 August 1772, in *GHS Coll*, 6:203–207.

5. Edward J. Cashin, "Sowing the Wind: Governor Wright and the Georgia Backcountry on the Eve of the Revolution," in *Forty Years of Diversity: Essays on Colonial Georgia*, ed. Harvey H. Jackson and Phinizy Spalding (Athens, 1984), 233–239.

6. Alan Gallay, *The Formation of the Planter Elite: Jonathan Bryan and the Southern Colonial Frontier* (Athens, 2007), 111.

7. Shelburne to Wright, 19 February 1767, in SP.

8. Backcountry Settlers to Wright, 29 July and 4 August 1767, in *ColRG*, 10:245–249, 249–280. See also Stuart to Gage, 17 August 1767, in GP.

9. Augusta Magistrates to Gage, 30 July 1767, in GP.

10. "Proceedings," 4 August 1767, in *ColRG*, 10:249–280. Wright's talk to the Creek Nation can be found on pages 275–278. See also Louis de Vorsey Jr., *Indian Boundary in the Southern Colonies, 1763–1775* (Chapel Hill, 1966), 153–155; and John T. Juricek, ed., *Georgia Treaties, 1733–1763* (Frederick, 1989), 11:348–361.

11. Daniel H. Unser Jr., *Indians, Settlers, and Slaves in a Frontier Exchange Economy: The Lower Mississippi Valley before 1783* (Chapel Hill, 1992).

12. Joshua Piker, "Colonists and Creeks: Rethinking the Pre-revolutionary Southern Backcountry," *Journal of Southern History* 70, no. 3 (2004): 505–509, 540.

13. James Wright, Loyalist claim, in *BGLC*; and Betty Wood, *Slavery in Colonial Georgia, 1730–1775* (Athens, 2007), 108. For Georgia's growth in relation to plantation slavery, see Julia Floyd Smith, *Slavery and Rice Culture in Low Country Georgia, 1750–1860* (Knoxville, 1991), chap. 1; and Wood, *Slavery*.

14. Habersham to Wright, 22 August 1772, in *GHS Coll*, 6:203.

15. Wright to Hillsborough, 27 December 1771, in *Board of Trade Journal*, 13:287–294; Wright to Hillsborough, 12 December 1771, in *DAR*, 3:269–275; and for the quote, see Wright to Shelburne, 15 May 1767, in *ColRG*, 37:206–212.

16. Wright to Board of Trade, 23 December 1763, in *ColRG*, 28.1:454–456; Wright to Board of Trade, 5 July 1764, in *CO*, 5/649. For Wright's proclamation following the cession, see *GGCJ*, 1772–1773, 142–143. Also see, Wright to Dartmouth, 12 January 1773, in *GGCJ*, 1772–1773, 151.

17. Wright to Hillsborough, 12 December 1771, in *ColRG*, 28.2:350–377; and Wright to Hillsborough, 31 May 1768, in *ColRG*, 37:311–313.

18. Wright to Hillsborough, 12 December 1771, in *ColRG*, 28.2:350–376. The New Purchase is also known as the New Acquisition or, simply, the Ceded Lands. For the surveying and settlement of the land, see Wright to Dartmouth, 17 June, 10 August, and 20 September 1773, in *GGCJ*, 1772–1773, 152–154, 156–162.

19. Newton Dennison Mereness, *Travels in the American Colonies* (Carlisle, 2007), 396. Also see "Journal of Lord Adam Gordon," in Peckham, *Narratives*, 237–239.

20. Pressly, *On the Rim*, 69.

21. Wright to Board of Trade, 23 December 1763, in *ColRG*, 28.1:454–456; and Wright to Board of Trade, 4 February 1764, in *ColRG*, 28.2:6–10. For an overview of this growing conflict on Georgia's frontier, see, for example, de Vorsey, *Indian Boundary*, 149–180; Cashin, "Sowing the Wind," 233–250; David H. Corkran, *The Creek Frontier, 1540–1783* (Norman, 2016), 253–273; Kathryn E. Holland Braund, *Deerskins & Duffels: The Creek Indian Trade with Anglo-America, 1685–1815* (Lincoln, 1993), 139–163; Jack Sosin, *The Revolutionary Frontier, 1763–1783* (New York, 1967), 61–81; Edward J. Cashin, *William Bartram and the American Revolution on the Southern Frontier* (Columbia, 2000), 38–75; Cashin, *Lachlan McGillivray, Indian Trader: The Shaping of the Southern Colonial Frontier* (Athens, 2012), 231–251; and Gallay, *Formation*, 127–152.

22. Corkran, *Creek Frontier*, 229–239. Also see Tugulki (Young Twin) to Wright and Stuart, 16 January 1764, in John Juricek, *Georgia and Florida Treaties, 1763–1776* (Frederick, 1989), 12:8. Young Twin blamed the murders on "seven [traders] that ha[d] been among the Cherokees these four or five years."

23. Wright to Board of Trade, 17 January 1764, in *CO*, 5/648; Wright to Thomas Gage, 4 January 1764, in *GP*.

24. Gage to Wright, 20 March 1764, in *GP*. Lord Hillsborough used the same phrase in a letter to Wright. See Hillsborough to Wright, 12 July 1764, in *ColRG*, 34:548–550.

25. Gage to Shelburne, 3 April 1764, in *GP*.

26. Wright to Board of Trade, 27 March 1764, in GP. Also see Gage to Wright, 20 March 1764, in GP; and Habersham to Knox, 13 March 1764, in *GHS Coll*, 6:18–20.

27. Stuart to Tugulki and the Creeks, 13 January 1764, Coweta Headmen to Stuart, 6 February 1764, Lower Creeks to Stuart, 6 March 1764, and Upper Creeks to Stuart, ca. mid-February 1764, all in Juricek, *Georgia and Florida Treaties*, 12:9, 10–12.

28. Wright to Stuart, 23 February 1764, in GP.

29. Thomas Boone to Wright, 7 March 1764, in GP.

30. Wright to Halifax, 10 November 1764, in CO, 323/17.

31. Wright to Boone, 21 March 1764, and William Bull to Gage, 11 April 1764, in GP. Gage later applauded Wright's judgment in this instance. "It gives me great satisfaction that my sentiments on the situation of the Indian affairs coincided so entirely with your own, and it appears already that by not being too hasty and precipitate, you have avoided an Indian war." See Gage to Wright, 11 August 1764, in GP; and Gage to Shelburne, 27 May 1767, in CO, 5/83.

32. Gage to Wright, 2 May and 20 March 1764, in GP. For Gage's suggestion, see Gage to Wright, 2 May 1764, and Gage to Stuart, 1 May 1764, in GP. Gage then informed Lord Halifax in London that he desired Wright that "all means should be used to avoid a war with the Creeks, but if it is unavoidable, it behoves us to protract it, till we are better prepared." Gage to Halifax, 12 May 1764, in GP.

33. Gage to Wright, 2 May 1764, in GP.

34. Wright to Board of Trade, 26 May 1764, in *ColRG*, 28.2:28–32.

35. "Talks at a meeting between traders and Headmen of the Creek Indians," 10 April 1764, in CO, 5/649; and Wright to Gage, 16 April 1764, in GP.

36. Wright to Board of Trade, 23 July and 6 August 1764, in CO, 5/649.

37. Gage to Wright, 11 August, 20 and 24 June 1764, in GP.

38. Wright to Board of Trade, 27 August 1764, in CO, 5/649, emphasis added.

39. Wright to Gage, 6 June 1764, Gage to Halifax, 10 August 1764, Gage to Wright, 11 August 1764, Shelburne to Gage, 14 November 1767, Gage to Lord Barrington, 22 February 1767, Gage to Captain Fuser, 30 April 1767, Wright to Gage, 25 February 1767, Gage to Wright, 27 February 1767, Gage to Shelburne, 3 April 1767, Gage to Wright, 30 April 1767, Gage to Captain Ralph Phillips, 8 May 1767, and Wright to Gage, 16 May 1767, all in GP; and Wright to Shelburne, 6 April 1767, in *ColRG*, 28.2:213. Also see Gage to Wright, 16 May 1767, in GP, in which Gage stated: "Am sorry that the reduction of the troops of Rangers should give you so much uneasiness."

40. Wright to Board of Trade, 27 August 1764, in CO, 5/649.

41. The Mortar's talk was delivered on 13 August. Wright to Board of Trade, 27 August 1764, in CO, 5/649.

42. Governor Wright's reply to the Mortar was delivered on 24 August. The Mortar to Wright, 24 August 1764, in Juricek, *Georgia and Florida Treaties*, 12:15–16. For more on the Mortar's relationship with the French during the war, see Corkran, *Creek Frontier*, 183–192. Also see the Mortar to Wright, 23 August 1764, in James Snapp, *John Stuart and the Struggle for Empire on the Southern Frontier* (Baton Rouge, 1996), 92.

43. Gage to Wright, 28 August 1764, and Wright to Gage, 28 August 1764, in GP.

44. Wright to Board of Trade, 14 December 1764, in CO, 5/649.

45. Wright to Board of Trade, 29 December 1764, in CO, 323/20. For the quote, see

Wright to Board of Trade, August 19, 1765, in *ColRG*, 28.2:110–111. During the mid- to late 1760s, Superintendent Stuart often butted heads with Wright and the other southern governors over this issue. See, for example, Stuart to Gage, July 21, 1767, in GP.

46. Hillsborough to Wright, 24 December 1764, in *ColRG*, 34:555–558.

47. Wright to Stuart, 26 September 1768, in Helen Shaw, "British Administration of the Southern Indians, 1756–1783" (PhD diss., Bryn Mawr, 1931), 43.

48. Robert Watkins and George Watkins, eds., *A Digest of Laws of the State of Georgia* (Philadelphia, 1800), 1:125.

49. De Vorsey, *Indian Boundary*, 159–160; Cashin, *Lachlan McGillivray*, 235; Ralph C. Scott Jr., "The Quaker Settlement of Wrightsborough, Georgia," *GHQ* 56, no. 2 (1972): 210–223; "Proceedings," 6 March 1766, in *ColRG*, 17:271; Robert S. Davis, "Children of Dissent and Revolution: Joseph Maddock and the Wrightsborough, Georgia, Quaker Community," *Quaker History* 99, no. 1 (Spring 2010): 1–14; Robert Scott Davis, *Quaker Records in Georgia: Wrightsborough, 1772–1793* (Augusta, 1986); CRNC, 7:250–251, 761–766.

50. Francis Harper, ed., *The Travels of William Bartram* (New Haven, 1958), 23–24.

51. Wright to Board of Trade, 10 February 1769, in *ColRG*, 28.2:323–327. Also see *GGCJ*, 1768–1771, 230–236, for primary documents relating to the recruitment of settlers.

52. George Galphin to Stuart, 2 June 1768, in GP. For an overview of the Queensborough settlement, see E. R. R. Green, "Queensborough Township: Scotch-Irish Emigration and the Expansion of Georgia, 1763–1776," *GHQ* 17, no. 2 (April 1960): 183–199; and Dan Elliott and Rita Elliott, "Life in the Queensborough Township: Data Recovery at Hannah's Quarter, Jefferson County, Georgia," 5 January 2023, https://danelliott.files.wordpress.com/2013/01/life-in-the-queensborough-township.pdf.

53. Kenneth Coleman, *Colonial Georgia: A History* (Millwood, 1989), 228.

54. Wright to Board of Trade, 8 June 1768, in *ColRG*, 28.1:251–259.

55. Cashin, "Sowing the Wind," 237.

56. Gavin Cochrane to Board of Trade, 10 June–14 November 1766, in Cashin, *Setting Out*, 139–142; and Cochrane to Dartmouth, 27 June 1766, in *Manuscripts of the Earl of Dartmouth*, ed. William Hewlett (Ontario, 2013), 2:45.

57. Washington to Richard [no last name], 1749–1750, in FO.

58. Delma Presley, "The Crackers of Georgia," *GHQ* 60, no. 2 (1976): 105.

59. Edward J. Cashin, "But Brothers, It Is Our Land We Are Talking About: Winners and Losers in the Georgia Backcountry," in *An Uncivil War: The Southern Backcountry during the American Revolution*, ed. Ronald Hoffman, Thad Tate, and Peter Albert (Charlottesville, 1985), 244.

60. Wright to Board of Trade, 15 August 1767, in *ColRG*, 28.2:235–236.

61. Gage to Fuser, 30 April 1767, in GP.

62. Gage to Stuart, 1 September 1768, in GP.

63. Anthony Stokes, *A View of the Constitution of the British Colonies* (London, 1783), 140–141; Habersham to Hillsborough, 12 August 1772, in *GHS Coll*, 6:199–200; Habersham to Wright, 12 August 1772, in *GHS Coll*, 6:200–202. Habersham referred to the Virginians and North Carolinians as "great villains [and] horse stealers," many of whom "were amongst the North Carolina Regulators."

64. Grant to Gage, 29 August 1767, and Stuart to Gage, 26 September 1767, in GP.

65. Gage to Shelburne, 10 October 1767, in CO, 5/83. Also see *GG*, 7 November 1760; and Gage to Fuser, 19 September 1767, in GP. Gage informed Fuser that Wright "is not well pleased" with the garrisoning of Georgia's forts.

66. Wright to Shelburne, 15 August 1767, in *ColRG*, 37.1:240–242; and John Richard Alden, *John Stuart and the Southern Colonial Frontier: A Study of Indian Relations, War, Trade, and Land Problems in the Southern Wilderness, 1754–1775* (Ann Arbor, 1944), 296.

67. Stuart to John Pownall, 24 August 1765, quoted in Jeff W. Dennis, *Patriots & Indians: Shaping Identity in Eighteenth-Century South Carolina* (Columbia, 2017), 51.

68. For the Creek request, see Stuart to Gage, 26 September 1767, in GP. For the reply, see Gage to Stuart, 14 November 1767, in GP. Also see Gage to Hillsborough, 10 November 1770, in CO, 5/83.

69. Wright to Gage, 1 December 1767, quoted in Alden, *John Stuart*, 233.

70. Quoted in Jessica Yirush Stearn, *The Lives in Objects: Native Americans, British Colonists, and Cultures of Labor and Exchange in the Southeast* (Chapel Hill, 2017), 114.

71. Wright to Gage, 25 August 1768, in GP; and Wright to Hillsborough, 5 August 1768, in *ColRG*, 37:334–341. Wright and Stuart complained of the British decision to withdraw all commissaries from the Indian nations.

72. Gage to Wright, 25 December 1768, in GP.

73. Wright to Stuart, 10 July 1766, in CO, 5/67; and Stuart to Gage, 27 November 1767, and Captain Fuser to Gage, 18 May 1768, in GP.

74. Quoted in de Vorsey, *Indian Boundary*, 160–161; and Piker, "Colonists and Creeks," 535. Also see Gage to Stuart, 16 May 1767, in GP.

75. "Answer from the headmen of the Lower Creek Nation to John Stuart," 19 September 1767, in CO, 5/59.

76. Patrick Griffin, *American Leviathan: Empire, Nation, and the Revolutionary Frontier* (New York, 2007), 80; and Corkran, *Creek Frontier*, 262–263.

77. Gage to Stuart, 26 January 1768, 16 May 1767, in GP. Gage advised Stuart to make an example of traders who refused to abide by the law.

78. Wright to Board of Trade, 12 February 1767, in CO, 5/649.

79. Wright to Board of Trade, 24 November 1768, in *ColRG*, 28.2:309. It should be noted that Wright held a small congress in Augusta on 12 November to finalize the demarcation line following the 1763 congress. See de Vorsey, *Indian Boundary*, 156–157.

80. *SCG*, 13 April 1769; *GG*, 19 April 1769; and diary entry, 1 April 1769, in "Extracts from the Journal of Mrs. Ann Manigault: 1754–1781," ed. Mabel Weber, *SCHGM* 20, no. 1 (1919): 13. The paper reported her worth at £30,000 sterling. The couple honeymooned in the summer resort town of Newport, Rhode Island. See Carl Bridenbaugh, "Colonial Newport as a Summer Resort," in *Collections of the Rhode Island Historical Society*, 26:1–23. Their voyage from Charleston took twelve days. A few years later, the young couple purchased Richmond Grove plantation for nearly £11,000, "the highest price on record for a plantation in this parish." See Mary Granger, *Savannah River Plantations* (Savannah, 1997), 118.

81. Wright to Hillsborough, 3 July 1769, in *ColRG*, 37:405–407. Wright submitted his request for leave nearly a year in advance of his desired departure because, in his words, "I have purchased lands of considerable value in this province, and have brought in a great number of slaves and settled several plantations," which would require months to put "in proper order."

82. James Wright, Loyalist claim, in *BGLC.*

83. Habersham to Wright, 30 May 1772, in *GHS Coll*, 6:180–182.

84. Gage to Hillsborough, 7 July 1770, in *GP*. For the massacre, see *GG*, 11 April 1770. This tragic event failed to cause a great stir among Georgians.

85. Wright to Hillsborough, 20 July 1770, in *DAR*, 1:150. Wright later wrote directly to Stuart, warning him that "making peace between the Creeks and the Choctaws is making war between the Indians and us." See Wright to Hillsborough, 8 December 1770, in *DAR*, 1:225; and Wright to Hillsborough, 18 January 1771, in *ColRG*, 37:512–515.

86. Wright to the Assembly, 24 October 1770, in *ColRG*, 17:598–600.

87. Assembly to Wright, 24 October 1770, in *ColRG*, 17:602–604.

88. Wright to Hillsborough, 15 November 1770, in *ColRG*, 37:478–479.

89. Wright to Hillsborough, 12 December 1771, in *ColRG*, 28.2:350–376; and *ColRG*, 38.1:15–26.

90. Wright to the Lieutenant of the Cowetas, 2 October 1770, and Samuel Thomas to Stuart, 5 October 1770, in *DAR*, 2:225, 216–218. Also see Wright to Hillsborough, 8 October 1770, in *ColRG*, 37:483–485.

91. Wright to Hillsborough, 12 December 1771, in *ColRG*, 28.2:350–376.

92. "The Talk of [Emistisiguo] one of the principal Head Men of the Creek Country," 3–6 September 1768, *GGCJ*, 1768–1771, 24–30, quote on 29.

93. Wright to Hillsborough, 8 December 1770, in *ColRG*, 37:489–492; and *ColRG*, 38.1:15–26. Also see Lower Creeks to Wright, in *ColRG*, 38.1:15–26; and Gage to Hillsborough, 16 January 1771, in *GP*. Gage described the violence as reciprocal. See also Stuart to Hillsborough, 5 March 1771, in *DAR*, 1:278–279. Stuart said: "The murders lately committed near Augusta show there are still madmen among you." Regarding the friendship between Wright and Hillsborough, see *Public Advertiser* (London), 5 March 1773.

94. Hillsborough to Wright, 11 February 1771, in *ColRG*, 37:507–508. Natives had gone into great debt by purchasing European goods on credit.

95. De Vorsey, *Indian Boundary*, 162.

96. Juricek, *Georgia and Florida Treaties*, 12:80–81. For the best examination of the treaty, see de Vorsey, *Indian Boundary*, 161–172; Alden, *John Stuart*, 300–301; Archie V. Huff, *Greenville: The History of the City and County in the South Carolina Piedmont* (Columbia, 1995), 16–17; William Anderson, *Guide to Cherokee Documents in Foreign Archives* (Metuchen, 1983), 141–143; and "Envisaging the West: Thomas Jefferson and the Roots of Lewis and Clark," University of Nebraska, http://jeffersonswest.unl.edu/archive/view_doc.php?id=jef.00091.

97. "Proceedings," 15 February 1758, in *ColRG*, 18:247–249. An Act to Prevent Private Persons from Purchasing Lands from the Indians, and for Preventing Persons Trading with Them without License was amended on 6 December 1759. See *ColRG*, 18:359–361. Also see 25 March 1765, in *ColRG*, 18:703–705; and 11 April 1768, in Watkins and Watkins, *Digest*, 1:162. (The act was amended after this date also.) Also see de Vorsey, *Indian Boundary*, 161–162; Alden, *John Stuart*, 300–301; and Snapp, *John Stuart*, 116–118.

98. *ColRG*, 38.1:15–26. Wright had "long had it in view to obtain an extension of the Indian boundary," and this scheme literally fell into his lap. Superintendent Stuart vehemently opposed the cession not only because the merchants and traders cir-

cumvented his authority but also because these private individuals had usurped political authority from its rightful holders. Stuart to Hillsborough, 23 September 1771,
in Snapp, *John Stuart*, 121–122, 124–125. Also see B. D. Bargar, *Lord Dartmouth and the
American Revolution* (Columbia, 1965), chap. 7.

99. Augusta Merchants to Habersham, 16 April 1772, in Juricek, *Georgia and Florida
Treaties*, 12:80.

100. Speeches of Judd's Friend and Oconostota to the Traders, 8 June 1771, in
Juricek, *Georgia and Florida Treaties*, 12:101–102. He stated that "the first talk came
from the traders and we all liked it."

101. Stuart to Hillsborough, 12 June 1772, in *DAR*, 5:113–118; and Snapp, *John Stuart*, 117.

102. "Memorial of James Wright to the Earl of Hillsborough, Dec. 12, 1771," in
*ColRG*, 28.2:250–278.

103. "Memorial." Also see Wright to Board of Trade, 10 November 1764, in CO, 323.

104. "Memorial." Wright's estimation of the quality of this land came directly from
a memorial presented to him by the merchants: "three millions of acres of as fine lands
& as fit for the culture of indico, tobacco, hemp, flax, wheat."

105. "Memorial."

106. Dartmouth to Wright, 2 March 1774, in *ColRG*, 38.1:162.

107. "Memorial."

108. "Memorial."

109. "Memorial." Note: I included the traders' talk to Wright in the eighth enclosure
even though it was not officially designated so in the *ColRG*. The editors, however, believed it had to have been included in the enclosures even though it was not properly
labeled in the British Archives.

110. "Deed from the Overhill Cherokees to their Traders," 22 February 1771, in
Juricek, *Georgia and Florida Treaties*, 12:95–96; and "Talk of Cherokees to Governor
Wright," 3 May 1771, in "Memorial."

111. Stuart to Hillsborough, n.d., quoted in de Vorsey, *Indian Boundary*, 163.

112. "Judd's friend's talk," 7 March 1771, in "Memorial."

113. "Talk of Cherokees to Governor Wright," 3 May 1771, in "Memorial."

114. "James Wright's talk to the Cherokees," 23 May 1771, in "Memorial."

115. Quoted in Snapp, *John Stuart*, 126.

116. "Proceedings," 12–13 March 1773, in *ColRG*, 15:419–426; and Alden, *John Stuart*,
302–303.

117. *South-Carolina Gazette; and Country Journal*, 3 July 1771. For Wright's departure,
see 13 July 1771, *GGCJ*, 1768–1771, 188–189.

118. Habersham to Hillsborough, 3 August 1771, in James Habersham Papers, GHS.
See also a separate letter from Habersham to Hillsborough, 3 August 1771, in *ColRG*,
37:548–551. Habersham also looked after Wright's plantations during the governor's
absence. See Frank Lambert, *James Habersham: Loyalty, Politics, and Commerce in Colonial Georgia* (Athens, 2012), 152–153. Moreover, Habersham noted that a mutual friend
had journeyed to Charleston to purchase thirty slaves for Wright. See Habersham to
Wright, 4 December 1772, in *GHS Coll*, 6:216.

119. Habersham to Wright, 30 November 1771, in *GHS Coll*, 6:155–158.

120. *SCG*, 18 July 1771. There are no extant issues of the *Georgia Gazette* after 23 May

1770, though the *Royal Georgia Gazette* is available from 4 January 1781 to 27 December 1781.

121. William Goolsey to Thomas Adams, 1 March 1772, in William L. Sachse, *The Colonial American in Britain* (Westport, 1978), 7.

122. Wright arrived from Georgia on 18 August. See *South-Carolina Gazette; and Country Journal*, 15 October 1771. For the final leg of his journey, see *Bingley's Journal* (London), 17–24 August 1771; *Middlesex Journal or Chronicle of Liberty* (London), 20 August 1771; *London Evening Post*, 22–24 August 1771; and *General Evening Post* (London), 22 August 1771. For Wright's zeal in acquiring royal approbation for the cession, see Laurens to Habersham, 20 December 1771, and Laurens to Lachlan McIntosh, 24 December 1771, in *PHL*, 8:105–108, 114–116. The *Governor Wright* was a 140-ton ship built in Bristol in 1768. It was captained by Thomas Hall and co-owned by Charleston merchant George Abbott Hall and Bristol merchant Nathaniel Wraxall. See R. Nicholas Olsberg, "Ship Registers in the South Carolina Archives, 1734–1780," *SCHM* 74, no. 4 (October 1973): 230.

123. *Public Advertiser*, 30 August 1771.

124. "Memorial."

125. *Public Advertiser*, 28 November 1771.

126. Laurens to Lachlan McIntosh, 24 December 1771, in *PHL*, 8:114–116.

127. Benjamin Franklin to Noble Wimberly Jones, 2 April 1772, in FO; and David T. Morgan, "A New Look at Benjamin Franklin as Georgia's Colonial Agent," *GHQ* 68, no. 2 (Summer 1984): 221–232.

128. Habersham to Wright, 12 March 1772, in *GHS Coll*, 6:168–171; Habersham to Hillsborough, 24 April 1772, in *GHS Coll*, 6:171–174; Habersham to Wright, 13 June 1772, in *GHS Coll*, 6:184–186; and Habersham to Hillsborough, 15 June 1772, in *GHS Coll*, 6:188–189.

129. *Daily Advertiser*, 15 December 1772.

130. Laurens to Habersham, 20 December 1771, and Laurens to McIntosh, 24 December 1771, in *PHL*, 8:105–108, 114–116.

131. Habersham to Wright, 16 July 1772, in *GHS Coll*, 6:190–192.

132. Habersham to Wright, 30 May 1772, *GHS Coll*, 6:180–182.

133. Habersham to Wright, 12 March 1772, in *GHS Coll*, 6:168–171.

134. 12 and 18 December 1771, in *Board of Trade Journal*, 13:269–277.

135. 25 March 1772, in *Board of Trade Journal*, 13:287–294.

136. *South-Carolina Gazette; and Country Journal*, 30 June 1772. This information had likely been communicated by Henry Laurens.

137. Habersham to Wright, 6 June 1772, in *GHS Coll*, 6:183–186.

138. Habersham to Wright, 31 July 1772, in *GHS Coll*, 6:196.

139. Habersham to Wright Jr., 13 September 1772, in *GHS Coll*, 6:210–211.

140. *General Evening Post*, 30 July 1772; *Boston Post Boy*, 28 September 1772; *Virginia Gazette*, 15 October 1772; *South Carolina and American General Gazette*, 5 October 1772; and diary entry, 18 March 1774, in *The Journal of the Reverend John Joachim Zubly*, ed. Lilla Hawes (Savannah, 1989), 31.

141. Hawes, *Journal*, 31. Several years later, as the imperial crisis unfolded, Georgia's provincial (rebel) congress deemed Reverend Smith to be "unfriendly to Amer-

ica" in 1775, and he was forced to leave the province. "Proceedings," 17 July 1775, in *AA*, 2:1554–1555.

142. Dartmouth to King George III, 9 November 1772, in *ColRG*, 38.1:15–31; Dartmouth to Wright, 12 December 1772, in *ColRG*, 38.1:31–35; 2 and 9 November 1772, in *Board of Trade Journal*, 13:316–326; and B. D. Bargar, *Lord Dartmouth and the American Revolution* (Columbia, 1965), 59.

143. *Middlesex Journal or Universal Evening Post*, 5–8 December 1772; *Morning Chronicle and London Advertiser*, 7 December 1772; and *South-Carolina Gazette; and Country Journal*, 9 February 1773.

144. See the introduction.

145. "Proceedings," 2 March 1773, in *ColRG*, 15:393–394; and 21 June 1773, in *ColRG*, 17:706–707.

146. 9 February 1773, in *ColRG*, 15:379–381. Wright arrived in Charleston on 3 February 1773 and departed for Savannah via land two weeks later. See *South-Carolina Gazette; and Country Journal*, 16 February 1773. For the legislative vote, see 11 February 1772, in *ColRG*, 15:384–386.

147. Journal entry, 13 February 1772, in *The Journal of Joseph Pilmore*, ed. Frederick Maser (Philadelphia, 1969), 182. Church services were canceled that week because the "town was in confusion" on account of Wright's arrival. Wright arrived in Charleston on 9 February and in Georgia by the end of the month. He was disappointed upon his arrival to Savannah to be greeted by Samuel Elbert's "Georgia Grenadiers," a militia company Wright had not yet authorized. See Gordon B. Smith, "The Georgia Grenadiers," *GHQ* 64, no. 4 (Winter 1980); and Clay Ouzts, *Samuel Elbert and the Age of Revolution in Georgia, 1740–1788* (Macon, 2022), 62–64.

148. "Proceedings," 16 June 1773 and 21 June 1773, in *ColRG*, 17:704, 706–707. Wright responded to the legislative praise on the 22nd. See 22 June 1773, in *ColRG*, 17:708. Also see 28 June and 30 June 1773, in *ColRG*, 15:438–439, 442.

149. Harper, *Travels*, 33; and, regarding rum, Mereness, *Travels*, 504–505.

150. *GG*, 2 February 1774; Wright to Dartmouth, 31 January 1774, in *ColRG*, 38.1:163–164; and Dartmouth to Wright, 2 March 1774, in *ColRG*, 38.1:162. For additional frontier violence related to the New Purchase, see Habersham to Mary Bagwith, 3 February 1774, in *GHS Coll*, 6:233–235; Ted Ruddock, ed., *Travels in the Colonies in 1773–1775* (Athens, 1993), 51–53; and 9 March 1774, in *ColRG*, 17:769–770, in which the Governor's Council implored King George III to provide military aid because the province remained "in a very defenceless state."

151. Cashin, "Sowing the Wind," 233–234.

152. Cashin, "Sowing the Wind," 234–241. Also see, for example, *GG*, 16 March 1774; and Wright to Dartmouth, 12 and 14 March 1774, in *ColRG*, 38.1:185, 230. These are two of the numerous communications regarding violence on the New Purchase lands.

## Chapter 5. A Governor's Authority Questioned

1. Kenneth Coleman, *Colonial Georgia: A History* (Millwood, 1989); Coleman, *The American Revolution in Georgia, 1763–1789* (Athens, 1958); William W. Abbot, *The Royal Governors of Georgia, 1754–1775* (Chapel Hill, 1959); Robert Calhoon, *The Loyalists in*

*Revolutionary America, 1760–1781* (New York, 1973); and Edward Cashin, "Sowing the Wind: Governor Wright and the Georgia Backcountry on the Eve of the Revolution," in *Forty Years of Diversity: Essays on Colonial Georgia*, ed. Harvey H. Jackson and Phinizy Spalding (Athens, 1984), 233–250.

2. *RG*; Cashin, "Sowing the Wind"; and Alan Gallay, *The Formation of a Planter Elite: Jonathan Bryan and the Southern Colonial Frontier* (Athens, 2007).

3. On the eve of the revolution, Wright's estate was valued at £80,000, making him the wealthiest man in Georgia. See *RG*, 84. For his plantation and slave holdings, see James Wright, Loyalist claim, in *BGLC*.

4. *Columbian Herald*, 27 February 1786; Kenneth Coleman, "James Wright," in *Georgians in Profile: Essays in Honor of Ellis Merton Coulter*, ed. Horace Montgomery (Athens, 1958); *RG*, 86.

5. Gordon S. Wood, *The Radicalism of the American Revolution* (New York, 1992), 87–88; Bernard Bailyn, *The Ideological Origins of the American Revolution* (Cambridge, 1967), chap. 3; *RG*, 83; Calhoon, *Loyalists in Revolutionary America*, 21; Robert G. Killion and Charles T. Waller, *Georgia and the Revolution* (Atlanta, 1975), 6; and Paul Pressly, *On the Rim of the Caribbean: Colonial Georgia and the British Atlantic World* (Athens, 2013). For Governor Wright's appraisal of this growth, see Wright to Board of Trade, 15 February 1762, in "Southeastern Native American Documents, 1730–1842," Document JWR001, Galilleo, 3 January 2023, www.galilleo.com; and Wright to Dartmouth, 20 December 1773, in *GHS Coll*, 3:157–179. This letter includes "Report of Sir James Wright to Lord Dartmouth on the Condition of the Province of Georgia, September 20, 1773."

6. Marjorline Kars, *Breaking Loose Together: The Regulator Rebellion in Prerevolutionary North Carolina* (Chapel Hill, 2002), chap. 10.

7. Thomas Hallock, *From the Fallen Tree: Frontier Narratives, Environmental Politics, and the Roots of a National Pastoral, 1749–1826* (Chapel Hill, 2003), 2–3; Robert Porter, "The Noblest Offspring: Concerning the British Origins of the Eighteenth-Century Colony of Georgia" (master's thesis, Armstrong Atlantic University, 2005), 105; 1, 5, and 24 February 1768, in *ColRG*, 14:524, 527–528, 545–546; Wright to Board of Trade, 27 December 1771, in *ColRG*, 28.2:379; and Colin Calloway, *The Scratch of a Pen: 1763 and the Transformation of North America* (Oxford, 2006).

8. Pressly, *On the Rim*, 110–111.

9. Bernard Bailyn, *The Ordeal of Thomas Hutchinson* (Cambridge, 1974), 25, 170.

10. Wright to Dartmouth, 8 July 1775, in *GHS Coll*, 3:191–192; and Wood, *Radicalism*, 214.

11. Wright to Upper House of Assembly in reply to address of congratulations upon return to Georgia from England, 15 February 1773, in *ColRG*, 17:688–690.

12. "Proceedings," 2 March 1773, in *ColRG*, 15:393–394.

13. Wright to General Assembly, 18 January 1775, in *AA*, 1:1152–1153; and Kenneth Coleman, "James Wright and the Origins of the Revolution in Georgia," in *The Human Dimensions of Nation Making: Essays on Colonial and Revolutionary America*, ed. James Kirby Martin (Madison, 1976), 105.

14. Henry Melchior Muhlenberg, 24 November 1777, in *The Journals of Henry*

*Melchior Muhlenberg*, trans. Theodore Tappert and John Doberstein (Philadelphia, 1958), 3:107.

15. Pressly, *On the Rim*; and Barratt Wilkins, "A View of Savannah on the Eve of the Revolution," *GHQ* 54, no. 4 (Winter 1970): 577–584.

16. Wright to Board of Trade, 8 June 1768, in CO, 5/650.

17. *RG*, 133.

18. Anthony Stokes, A *View of the Constitution of the British Colonies* (London, 1783), 115–116.

19. Dartmouth to Wright, 6 July 1774, in *ColRG*, 38.1:273–274. Discord, however, would increase in the ensuing years, and the promise of Wright's New Purchase never fully materialized because the revolution unfolded in force.

20. Edward Cashin, *Governor Henry Ellis and the Transformation of British North America* (Athens, 1994), chap. 5.

21. James F. Shepherd and Gary M. Walton, *Shipping, Maritime Trade, and the Economic Development of Colonial North America* (New York, 1972).

22. Pressly, *On the Rim*, 9, 211.

23. Jack Greene, "Travails of an Infant Colony: The Search for Viability, Coherences, and Identity in Colonial Georgia," in Jackson and Spalding, *Forty Years*, 301–303.

24. Greene, "Travails," 275–310; and Pressly, *On the Rim*, chaps. 6 and 7 and the table on 114.

25. R. Nicholas Olsberg, "Ship Registers in the South Carolina Archives, 1734–1780," *SCHM* 74, no. 4 (October 1973): 230. Thomas Hall was the master; George Abbott Hall (Charleston merchant) and Nathaniel Wraxall (Bristol merchant) were the identified owners. Wright also cosigned on a request for specific slave cargo in 1775. The memorialist stressed the desire for "Windward Coast Negroes . . . [because they] will afford the best prices." See Pressly, *On the Rim*, 119, 124. West Africans' knowledge of rice cultivation was incredibly desired in the Lowcountry. See Judith Carney, *Black Rice: The African Origins of Rice Cultivation in the Americas* (Cambridge, 2001), chap. 3; and Darold Wax, "New Negroes Are Always in Demand," *GHQ* 68, no. 2 (1984): 193–220. Wright was also the co-owner of a ten-ton schooner named *The Esther*. This schooner engaged in human trafficking. See "A List of All Ships and Vessels which have entered Inwards in the Port of Savannah, 5 April–5 July, 1766," in *GHS Coll*, 8:appendix.

26. Robert Scott Davis, "Free but Not Freed: Stephen Deane's African Family in Early Georgia," *GHQ* 97, no. 1 (Spring 2013): 63.

27. Martha Condray Searcy, "The Introduction of African Slavery into the Creek Nation," *GHQ* 66, no. 1 (Spring 1982): 23.

28. Betty Wood, *Slavery in Colonial Georgia, 1730–1775* (Athens, 2007), 173–180; and Benjamin Quarles, *The Negro in the American Revolution* (Chapel Hill, 1961).

29. "Proceedings," 5 July 1776, in *AA*, 5th series, 1:7–9.

30. John Richardson to John Porteous, 15 March 1779, in "A British Privateer in the American Revolution," ed. Henry Howland, *American Historical Review* 7 (1902): 293–294. Also see Capt. Gavin Cochrane to Lord Dartmouth, 10 June 1766, in Edward J. Cashin, *Setting Out to Begin a New World, Colonial Georgia: A Documentary History* (Savannah, 1995), 139–142.

31. Paul M. Pressly, *On the Rim of the Caribbean: Colonial Georgia* (Athens, 2013), 70, table 7 on p. 77 and chap. 4 in general. Pressly's study is the single best economic study of Georgia available.

32. James Bain Jr., ed., "The Siege of Charleston: Journal of Captain Peter Russell, December 25, 1779, to May 2, 1780," *American Historical Review* 4 (1889): 482.

33. Mary Benjamin, ed., "Memoirs of a Revolutionary Soldier," *The Collector* 63 (October–December 1950): 198–201.

34. "Journal of Lord Adam Gordon: How Our Cities Looked, 1765," in *Narratives of Colonial America, 1704–1765*, ed. Howard H. Peckham (Chicago, 1971), 238–240.

35. Ray W. Pettengill, trans., *Letters from America, 1776–1779, Being Letters of Brunswick, Hessian, and Waldeck Officers with the British Armies during the Revolution* (Boston, 1924), 202.

36. Alexander A. Lawrence, *Storm over Savannah: The Story of Count d'Estaing and the Siege of the Town in 1779* (Savannah, 1979), 1; and Pressly, *On the Rim*, 81–82.

37. Barratt Wilkins, "A View of Savannah on the Eve of the Revolution," *GHQ* 54, no. 4 (1970): 577–584.

38. Admiralty to Vice Admiral Graves, 28 January 1775, in *Naval Documents of the American Revolution*, ed. William Bell Clark (Washington, D.C., 1964), 1:385–389; Dartmouth to Gage, 28 January 1775, in GP; 18 January 1775, in *ColRG*, 38.1:375–379; *RG*, 162–164; Wright to Dartmouth, 1 February 1775 and 16 September 1775, in *GGCJ*, 1774–1775, 90–91, 110–111; and Governor Patrick Tonyn to Gage, 14 September 1775, in Clark, *Naval Documents*, 2:104.

39. Marion Eugene Sirmans, *Colonial South Carolina: A Political History, 1663–1763* (Chapel Hill, 2012), 19–103; and Robert Weir, *Colonial South Carolina: A History* (Columbia, 1997), 65–69.

40. *RG*, 129–132. Abbot gives the examples of Edward Telfair, who ultimately sided with the rebels after seesawing in the early years of the crisis, and Robert Baillie, who was at the forefront of the Liberty Party in the 1760s before aligning himself with Governor Wright in the 1770s. Historian Wallace Brown agreed, declaring that Wright's "ability strengthened Loyalism" in Georgia. Wallace Brown, *The Good Americans: The Loyalists in the American Revolution* (New York, 1969), 81. Also see William Nelson, *The American Tory* (Boston, 1961), chap. 5.

41. Wright to Shelburne, 5 January and 6 April 1767, in *ColRG*, 37:154–156, 177–190.

42. Julie Anne Sweet, "Oglethorpe on America: Georgia's Founder's Thoughts on Independence," *GHQ* 95, no. 1 (Spring 2011): 6.

43. Wright to Shelburne, 6 April 1767, in *ColRG*, 37:177–190.

44. Wright to Shelburne, 6 April 1767, in *ColRG*, 37:177–190; and Wright to Conway, 15 March 1766, in *ColRG*, 37:123.

45. Jack Greene, *The Quest for Power: The Lower Houses of Assembly in the Southern Royal Colonies, 1689–1776* (Chapel Hill, 1963), 440.

46. Wright to Shelburne, 6 April 1767, in *ColRG*, 37:177–190; and *RG*, 127.

47. Ellis to Knox, 22 March 1774, in KP.

48. Greene, *Quest for Power*, 368–385, 424.

49. Wright to Shelburne, 15 June and 15 August 1767, in *ColRG*, 37:215–227, 240–252; *RG*, 132–140; Wright to Dartmouth, 20 June 1775, in Clark, *Naval Documents*, 1:730–731.

"Assembly" and "checked" are in the 15 June letter; "rather hard" is in the 15 August letter. Also see E. Stanly Godbold Jr. and Robert E. Woody, *Christopher Gadsden and the American Revolution* (Knoxville, 1982), 134–177; and Frances Harrold, "Colonial Siblings: Georgia's Relationship with South Carolina during the Pre-revolutionary Period," *GHQ* 73, no. 4 (Winter 1989): 707–744.

50. Wright to Hillsborough, 23 May 1768, in *ColRG*, 37:274–292.

51. Wright to Shelburne, 6 April 1767, in *ColRG*, 37:177–190; and Harold Davis, "The Scissors Thesis, or Frustrated Expectations as a Cause of the Revolution in Georgia," *GHQ* 61, no. 3 (Fall 1977): 246–257.

52. 29 January 1768, in *ColRG*, 14:509–512. Again, Abbot masterfully tells the story of this struggle for power in Georgia. See *RG*, chap. 6.

53. John Derry, "Government Policy and the American Crisis," in *Britain and the American Revolution*, ed. H. T. Dickinson (London, 1998), 49; Patrick Griffin, *The Townshend Moment: The Making of Empire and Revolution in the Eighteenth Century* (New Haven, 2017), 123–124; and B. D. Bargar, *Lord Dartmouth and the American Revolution* (Columbia, 1965), 105, 113.

54. Wright to Hillsborough, 8 June and 30 May 1768, in *ColRG*, 37:318–322, 305–307. John Dickinson was the "Pennsylvania Farmer" whose series of letters were published in every newspaper in America between 27 January and 27 April 1768. See *GG*, 20 April 1768.

55. *RG*, 136–137.

56. Assembly to Wright, 29 January 1768, quoted in Percy S. Flippin, "The Royal Government in Georgia, 1752–1776: The Commons House of Assembly," *GHQ* 8, no. 4 (December 1924): 243–291, 286.

57. 25 March 1768, in *ColRG*, 14:575–576; 11 April 1768, in *ColRG*, 19.1:11–14; David Morgan, "A New Look at Benjamin Franklin as Georgia's Colonial Agent," *GHQ* 68, no. 2 (1984): 221–232; Morgan, *The Devious Dr. Franklin, Colonial Agent: Benjamin Franklin's Years in London* (Macon, 1996), 136, 154–155; and *RG*, chap. 6. A few years later, Franklin lost Wright's support as agent. See Morgan, *Devious Dr. Franklin*, 207–209.

58. Jack P. Greene, "The Georgia Commons House of Assembly and the Power to Appoint Executive Offices, 1765–1775," *GHQ* 46, no. 2 (June 1962): 152–158.

59. *GG*, 27 April 1768.

60. *GG*, 6 July 1768; Wright to Hillsborough, 23 May 1768, in *ColRG*, 37:274–292; Griffin, *Townshend Moment*, 142–150; Hutchinson to Francis Bernard, 30 March 1770, in Bailyn, *Ordeal of Thomas Hutchinson*, 162.

61. *GG*, 14 October 1767.

62. Kenneth Coleman, *American Revolution in Georgia, 1763–1789* (Athens, 1958), 28–32; and Griffin, *Townshend Moment*, 148–150.

63. Wright to Hillsborough, 24 December 1768, in *ColRG*, 37:380–381; Griffin, *Townshend Moment*, 142–150.64. *RG*, 135.

65. *RG*, 134–135; James Glen to Board of Trade, 10 October 1748, in Greene, "Georgia Commons House," 152; Greene, *Quest for Power*.

66. 24 December 1768, in *ColRG*, 14:644–645, emphasis added.

67. *RG*, 149.

68. *London Chronicle*, 28 February 1769, quoting details from Georgia dated 24 December 1768; Wright to Hillsborough, 24 December 1768, in *ColRG*, 37:380–381; *GG*, 28 December 1768; and Charles Colcock Jones Jr., *The History of Georgia* (Boston, 1883; Charleston, 2017), 2:107.

69. Wright to Hillsborough, 15 August 1769, in Jones, *History of Georgia*, 2:109–112.

70. Wright to Hillsborough, 15 August 1769, in Jones, *History of Georgia*, 2:109–112; and in *ColRG*, 37:309–313. Also see *RG*, 149–151.

71. Wright to Board of Trade, 8 June 1768, in *ColRG*, 28.2:253–255.

72. Wright to Hillsborough, 20 September 1769, in *ColRG*, 28.2:333; and 19 September 1769, in *HCG*, 42–44.

73. Wright to Hillsborough, 10 and 11 May 1770, in *ColRG*, 37:440–442, 450–451; James K. Hosmer, *The Life of Thomas Hutchinson* (Boston, 1896), 143–144, 251–252; and *GG*, 25 October 1769.

74. 14 March 1770, in *ColRG*, 15:152.

75. *RG*, 153–154.

76. Wright to Hillsborough, 28 February 1771, in *ColRG*, 37:520–528.

77. Wright to Hillsborough, 30 April 1771, in *ColRG*, 37:535–538.

78. Hutchinson to John Pownall, 21 March 1770, and Hutchinson to Francis Bernard, 30 March 1770, both in Bailyn, *Ordeal of Thomas Hutchinson*, 137, 162.

79. 26 April 1771, in *ColRG*, 11:335–336. Also see Habersham to Wright, 17 February 1772, in *GHS Coll*, 6:166.

80. 25 April 1771, in *ColRG*, 15:312; and Wright to Hillsborough, 30 April 1770, in *ColRG*, 37:535–538. Wright departed for Great Britain on 10 July 1771. See Habersham to John Pownall, 3 July 1771, and Habersham to Hillsborough, 10 August 1771, in *ColRG*, 37:547, 551–554. Also see *South-Carolina Gazette; and Country Journal*, 23 July 1771.

81. Wright to Dartmouth, 24 March 1773, in *ColRG*, 38.1:42–45.

82. Gregory Waselkov and Kathryn Holland Braund, "William Bartram and Southeastern Indians: An Introduction," in *William Bartram on the Southeastern Indians*, ed. Gregory Waselkov and Kathryn Holland Braund (Lincoln, 1995), 12–13. The treaty was concluded on 1 June 1773. See Edward J. Cashin and Heard Robertson, *Augusta and the American Revolution: Events in the Georgia Back Country, 1773–1783* (Darien, 1975), 2–3. Wright issued a proclamation announcing the sale of the land ten days later. See Thomas Brown, Loyalist claim, in *BGLC*; and Thomas Waters, Loyalist claim, in *BGLC*.

83. Wright to Dartmouth, 30 September 1773, in *ColRG*, 38.1:96; and Dartmouth to Wright, 8 January 1774, in *ColRG*, 38.1:97. For the cession, see various correspondence in *ColRG*, 38.1:46–95.

84. Griffin, *Townshend Moment*, 142–150; Mark Puls, *Samuel Adams: Father of the American Revolution* (New York, 2006), 140–147; Benjamin Woods Labaree, *The Boston Tea Party* (London, 1966), chaps. 2, 7; Alfred Young, *The Shoemaker and the Tea Party* (Boston, 1999), chap. 6; Benjamin Carp, *Defiance of the Patriots: The Boston Tea Party and the Making of America* (New Haven, 2011), chaps. 5–6.

85. Ellis to Knox, 15 July 1774, in William Knox and Howard Vicenté Knox, *Manuscripts of Captain H. V. Knox* (Boston, 1972), 111–112.

86. Georgia Council to George III, 9 March 1774, in CO, 5/663. The Governor's Council sought protection "against the outrages of our savage enemies."

87. For Native concerns, see, for example, Wright to Dartmouth, 31 January 1774, in *ColRG*, 38.1:163–171; and "Proceedings," 17 July 1775, in *ColRG*, 38.1:516–523, quote on 517. Also see Michael Cecere, *March to Independence: The Revolutionary War in the Southern Colonies, 1775–1776* (Yardley, 2021), 29–34.

88. Peter Dean, Loyalist claim, in *BGLC*.

89. Joseph Clay to Bright and Pechin, 10 June 1775, in MS 0153, vol. 2, Joseph Clay and Company Papers, GHS; Clay to James Thomson Jr., 24 April 1790, in *GHS Coll*, 8:223–228.

90. Wright to Dartmouth, 25 July 1774, in *AA*, 1:633–634; and *RRSG*, 1:11.

91. Charles Colcock Jones, *History of Savannah* (Syracuse, 1890), 212.

92. Wright to Dartmouth, 25 July 1774, in *AA*, 1:633–634; and, for example, *GG*, 24 August 1774.

93. Wright to Dartmouth, 25 July 1774, in *ColRG*, 38.1:292–294; and Wright to Dartmouth, 24 August 1774, in *GGCJ*, 1774–1777, 20–21.

94. *GG*, 20 July 1774, 27 July 1774, and 3 August 1774; 5 August 1774, in *ColRG*, 38.1:299–300; Wright to Dartmouth, 25 July 1774, in *ColRG*, 38.1:292–294; and Mary Beth Norton, *1774: The Long Year of Revolution* (New York, 2020), 156–158.

95. 10 August 1774, in *AA*, 1:700–701.

96. 10 August 1774, in *RRSG*, 1:15–17; *GG*, 17 August 1774; Wright to Dartmouth, 13 August 1774, in *ColRG*, 38.1:298–300; and Wright to Dartmouth, 24 August 1774, in *GHS Coll*, 3:180–182.

97. Gage to Frederick Haldimand, 18 August 1774, and Gage to Wright, 18 August 1774, both in GP.

98. *GG*, 19 October 1774; 24 October and 11 November 1774, in *AA*, 1:889–891, 974; 4 November 1774, in Tappert and Doberstein, *Journals of Henry M. Muhlenberg*, 2:603–604; Cashin and Robertson, *Augusta*, 7; and John Richard Alden, *John Stuart and the Southern Colonial Frontier: A Study of Indian Relations, War, Trade, and Land Problems in the Southern Wilderness, 1754–1775* (Ann Arbor, 1944), 311.

99. *GG*, 7 September 1774, in Norton, *1774*, 157. For the derivation and usage of the term "Loyalist" or "loyalism," see Norton, *1774*, xv; and Mary Beth Norton, *The British-Americans: The Loyalist Exiles in England, 1774–1789* (Boston, 1972), 3–7. Also see Haddon Smith, Loyalist claim, in *BGLC*.

100. Maya Jasanoff, *Liberty's Exiles: American Loyalists in the Revolutionary South* (New York, 2011), 8; also see Nelson, *American Tory*, chap. 5; Catherine Crary, *Price of Loyalty: Tory Writings from the Revolutionary War* (New York, 1973), 3–4; Ruma Chopra, *Unnatural Rebellion: Loyalists in New York City during the Revolution* (Charlottesville, 2011), 65–67; Robert Calhoon, Timothy Barnes, and Robert Davis, eds., *Tory Insurgents: The Loyalist Perception and Other Essays* (Columbia, 2010), 216–227, 375–385; and Holger Hoock, *Scars of Independence: America's Violent Birth* (New York, 2017), 30–31.

101. Wright to Dartmouth, 13 August, 24 August, and 13 October 1774, in *ColRG*, 38.1:298, 302–306, 333.

102. *GG*, 30 August 1774; and Norton, *1774*, 157.

103. Coleman, *American Revolution*, 39–54; and *GG*, 3 August 1774.

104. 27 July 1774, in *AA*, 1:638–639; and Wright to Dartmouth, 24 April 1775, in *ColRG*, 38.1:424–429.

105. Bailyn, *Ordeal of Thomas Hutchinson*, 91.

106. 1 August 1774, in *AA*, 1:699–700.

107. Wright to Dartmouth, 24 August 1774, in CO, 5/663.

108. Hutchinson to John Pownall, 28 June 1773, in Bailyn, *Ordeal of Thomas Hutchinson*, 268–269.

109. Wright to Germain, 12 February 1777, in Robert G. Mitchell, "Sir James Wright Looks at the American Revolution," *GHQ* 53 (Winter 1969): 514; Richard Beeman, *Our Lives, Our Fortune and Our Sacred Honor: The Forging of American Independence, 1774–1776* (New York, 2013), chaps. 12–13; James Wright Memorial, 8 October 1777, in *ColRG*, 39:4–9; Wright to Germain, 8 October 1777, in *GHS Coll*, 3:245–248.

110. 27 July and 5 August 1774, in *RRSG*, 1:12–13, 14–15.

111. Wright to Dartmouth, 8 July 1775, in *ColRG*, 38.1:480–502; Coleman, *American Revolution*, 40–41; 10 August 1774, in *RRSG*, 1:15–17; and *GG*, 17 August 1774. An unidentified letter from St. John's Parish suggested that the meeting had been taken over by some Savannahians sympathetic to Britain. The veracity of this letter is questioned by historian Kenneth Coleman, who edited most volumes of the *ColRG* and *RRSG*. See 2 September 1774, in *AA*, 1:766–767.

112. Wright to Dartmouth, 13 August 1774, in *AA*, 1:708; Wright to Dartmouth, 24 August 1774, in *GHS Coll*, 3:180–182; Wright to Gage, 19 August 1774, in GP; and Wright to Dartmouth, 23 August 1774, in *GHS Coll*, 3:180.

113. Coleman, *American Revolution*, 42–43.

114. Hall later attended. See 15 May 1775, in *JCC*.

115. Coleman, *American Revolution*, 43–44; *GG*, 14 July 1774; *RRSG*, 1:11–12; Wright to Dartmouth, 25 July 1774, in *AA*, 1:633–634; and John Glen to [?], 27 July 1774, in *RRSG*, 1:12–14.

116. Wright to Gage, 4 November 1774, in GP; and Wright to Gage, 13 December 1774, in *ColRG*, 38.1:361–362.

117. *GG*, 16 November 1774; and Wright to Dartmouth, 13 December 1774, in *ColRG*, 38.1:361–362. Also see Wright to Dartmouth, 20 December 1774, in *ColRG*, 38.1:367–368.

118. "Darien Committee Resolutions," 12 January 1775, in *HCG*, 554–556.

119. Wright to Dartmouth, 20 December 1774, in *ColRG*, 38.1:367–368; Wright to Dartmouth, 13 December 1774, in *AA*, 1:1040.

120. Wright to Dartmouth, 1 February 1775, in *ColRG*, 38.1:371–374; and Coleman, *American Revolution*, 46–47. Also see Clay Ouzts, *Samuel Elbert and the Age of Revolution in Georgia, 1740–1788* (Macon, 2022), 99.

121. Wright to Dartmouth, 13 December 1774, in *ColRG*, 38.1:361; and Wright to Dartmouth, 17 July 1775, in *GGCJ*, 1774–1777, 81–82.

122. "Letter from Savannah to a Gentleman in Philadelphia," 9 December 1774, in *AA*, 1:1033–1034; and *GG*, 14 December 1774. The election took place on 8 December.

123. Wright to Dartmouth, 1 February 1775, in *ColRG*, 38.1:371–389.

124. Wright to Hillsborough, 20 September 1769, in *ColRG*, 37:417–419.

125. Wright to Shelburne, 15 June 1767, in SP; and Wright to Board of Trade, 15 June 1767, in *ColRG*, 37:215–227.

126. Wright to Dartmouth, 1 February 1775, in *ColRG*, 38.1:371–374.

127. William Foster, "James Jackson in the American Revolution," *GHQ* 31, no. 4 (December 1947): 276; Alexander A. Lawrence, "James Jackson: Passionate Patriot," *GHQ* 34, no. 2 (June 1950): 75–86; and William Foster, *James Jackson: Duelist and Militant Statesman, 1757–1806* (Athens, 2009), 21.

128. James Wright, Loyalist claim, in *BGLC*. The rebels burned such barns and buildings on various Wright plantations in both 1776 and in the years following the siege of Savannah. James Wright, Loyalist claim, in *BGLC*.

129. Wright to Dartmouth, 1 February 1775, in *ColRG*, 38.1:371–374. In 1991 Bull biographer Kinloch Bull wrote that Wright always seemed "alert to opportunities to report [the] failings of William Bull" (*The Oligarchs in Colonial and Revolutionary Charleston: Lieutenant Governor William Bull II and His Family* [Columbia, 1991], quote at 146, and see also 164).

130. *RG*, 164–166; and Wright to Dartmouth, 1 February 1775, in *ColRG*, 38.1:371–374. Also see Wright to Dartmouth, 13 February 1775, *GGCJ*, 1774–1777, 91. In this letter, Wright mentioned that the radicals seemed determined in "their right to resist what they call unconstitutional laws."

131. Wright Address to Assembly, 18 January 1775, in *ColRG*, 38.1:375–379. This address is enclosed in Wright to Dartmouth, 1 February 1775, in *ColRG*, 38.1:371–374.

132. Bailyn, *Ordeal of Thomas Hutchinson*, 39.

133. Thomas Wooldridge to Dartmouth, 8 May 1772, in *The Manuscripts of the Earl of Dartmouth* (London, 1887), 2:83.

134. Wright to Hillsborough, 15 August 1769, in *ColRG*, 37:309–313; *RG*, 159–161; and Harvey H. Jackson, "Consensus and Conflict: Factional Politics in Revolutionary Georgia, 1774–1777," *GHQ* 59, no. 4 (Winter 1975): 388–401. Also see Thomas L. Stokes, *The Savannah* (Athens, 1982), 129–130.

135. 18 January 1775, in *RRSG*, 1:43–48; and *HCG*, 58–61.

136. Jones, Bulloch, and Houstoun to the Continental Congress, 6 April 1775, in *RRSG*, 1:63–66; and Coleman, *American Revolution*, 46–47.

137. Wright to Dartmouth, 13 February 1775, in *ColRG*, 38.1:392–393.

138. Wright to Dartmouth, [?] December 1774, in James Wright, Loyalist claim, in *BGLC*.

139. Wright to Dartmouth, 13 February 1775, in *ColRG*, 38.1:392–393.

140. Wright to Dartmouth, 24 April 1775, in *ColRG*, 38.1:424–429.

141. Henry Laurens to William Manning, 22 May 1775, in Clark, *Naval Documents*, 1:507–509.

142. Wright to Dartmouth, 24 April 1775, *GGCJ*, 1774–1777, 96–97; and Wright to Dartmouth, 25 May 1775, George Bancroft Collection, Manuscripts and Archives Division, New York Public Library, New York.

143. Wright to Dartmouth, 1 February 1775, in *ColRG*, 38.1:371–389.

144. Gage to Wright, 6 March 1775, in GP. Gage said that the new Parliament was determined "to enforce its laws" at all costs.

145. Habersham to Clark and Milligan, 17 April 1775, in *AA*, 2:337.

146. Gage to Wright, 16 April 1775, in *ColRG*, 38.1:473; and Gage to Lord Barrington, 13 May 1775, in GP.

147. *RG*, 168; Wright to Dartmouth, 1 February 1775, in *ColRG*, 38.1:371–374; Joseph Clay to Benjamin Stead, 13 May 1775, in Pressly, *On the Rim*, 218; Wright to Board of Trade, 5 August 1776, in AO, 13/37/104; Coleman, *American Revolution*, 68–69.

148. Elizabeth Lichtenstein Johnston, *Recollections of a Georgia Loyalist* (New York, 1901), 45.

149. "Letter from the Georgia Delegates to the Continental Congress," 6 April 1775, in *HCG*, 61–63. The delegates were Noble Wimberly Jones, Archibald Bulloch, and John Houstoun.

150. Norton, *1774*, 267; and Andrew Elton Wells to Samuel Adams, 18 March 1775, in Coleman, *American Revolution*, 49.

151. Wright to Dartmouth, 18 July 1775, in *GHS Coll*, 3:196–199; and Wright to Dartmouth, 18 July 1775, in *ColRG*, 38.1:511–522. Also see Daniel Troy, "Ruining the King's Cause: The Defeat of the Loyalists in the Revolutionary South, 1774–1781" (PhD diss., Ohio State University, 2015), 122–124; and Jackson, "Consensus and Conflict," 393.

152. "Letter from the Georgia Delegates to the Continental Congress," 6 April 1775, in *HCG*, 61–63.

153. Norton, *1774*, 267–268.

154. *RG*, 167–169.

155. *GG*, 7 September 1774; and Robert S. Davis, *Georgia Citizens and Soldiers of the American Revolution* (Greenville, 1999), 11–18.

156. Dartmouth to Wright, 3 May 1775, in *ColRG*, 38.1:423.

157. Dartmouth to Wright, 3 May 1775, in *ColRG*, 38.1:423; *RG*, 171; Wright to Dartmouth, 1 May and 2 May 1775, in *ColRG*, 38.1:431–432, 434–435, 437.

158. Wright to Gage, 27 June 1775, in *ColRG*, 38.2:26–28.

159. Wright to Dartmouth, 25 May 1775, in Bancroft Collection; Robert Olwell, "'Domestic Enemies': Slavery and Political Independence in South Carolina, May 1775–March 1776," *Journal of Southern History* 55, no. 1 (February 1989): 36.

160. Lorenzo Sabine, *Sketches of Loyalists of the American Revolution* (Boston, 1864), 2:466–468; Eunice Ross Perkins, "John Joachim Zubly: Georgia's Conscientious Objector," *GHQ* 14, no. 4 (December 1931): 313–323; and Marjorie Daniel, "John Joachim Zubly: Georgia Pamphleteer of the Revolution," *GHQ* 19, no. 1 (March 1935): 1–16. Daniel makes a convincing argument as to the value of Zubly's revolutionary ideology in the early days of the crisis.

161. Joseph W. Barnwell, "Barnard Elliott's Recruiting Journal," *South Carolina Historical Magazine* 17, no. 3 (July 1916): 97.

162. Loyalist Samuel Curwen acknowledged his concern that, "like, Cain, I had not a discouraging mark upon me, or a strong feature of Toryism" (4 May 1775, in *The Journal and Letters of Samuel Curwen*, ed. George Ward [Boston, 1864], 25–26).

163. *GG*, 17 May 1775.

164. Quoted in Kevin Phillips, *1775: A Good Year for Revolution* (New York, 2012), 229.

165. Charles Risher Jr., "Propaganda, Dissension, and Defeat: Loyalist Sentiment in Georgia, 1763–1783" (PhD diss., Mississippi State University, 1976), 13. Rebel propa-

ganda in Georgia may not have "overwhelmed the whole province" or "subdued Loyalist sentiment," but it "did abet and hasten such an end."

166. Noble W. Jones to Benjamin Franklin, 16 May 1775, in FO.

167. *RG*, 170–171; Wright to Dartmouth, 12 May 1775, in *ColRG*, 38.1:439; and 6 June 1775, in *GGCJ*, 1774–1777, 79–80.

168. Wright to Dartmouth, 7 August 1775, in *ColRG*, 38.1:541–543.

169. Wright to Dartmouth, 12 May 1775, in *ColRG*, 38.1:439; Wright to Graves, 27 June 1775, in Clark, *Naval Documents*, 1:764–765; and Patrick Tonyn to Dartmouth, 1 July 1775, in Clark, *Naval Documents*, 1:802–803, in which Wright informed Governor Tonyn that "things are taking a wrong turn."

170. Wright to Dartmouth, 25 May 1775, in Bancroft Collection.

171. Wright to Dartmouth, 25 May 1775, in Bancroft Collection; Leslie Hall, *Land and Allegiance in Revolutionary Georgia* (Athens, 2001); and Sylvia Frey, *Water from the Rock: Black Resistance in a Revolutionary Age* (Princeton, 1992).

172. James Corbett David, *Dunmore's New World: The Extraordinary Life of a Royal Governor in Revolutionary America—with Jacobites, Counterfeiters, Land Schemes, Shipwrecks, Scalping, Indian Politics, Runaway Slaves, and Two Illegal Royal Weddings* (Charlottesville, 2013), 101–104; and Quarles, *Negro*, 19–32.

173. 29 March 1779, in *JCC*, 13:387–388; and Quarles, *Negro*, 60.

174. Patricia Bradley, *Slavery, Propaganda, and the American Revolution* (Jackson, 1998), 133.

175. *GG*, 7 December 1774.

176. Frey, *Water*, 53–54; Wood, *Slavery*, 201–203; Gary Nash, *The Unknown American Revolution: The Unruly Birth of Democracy and the Struggle to Create America* (New York, 2006), 159.

177. Ralph Izard to a friend in Bath, 27 October 1775, in Ralph Izard, *Correspondence of Mr. Ralph Izard of South Carolina from the Year 1774 to 1804* (New York, 1844), 1:135–136.

178. For example, Sidney Kaplan, "The 'Domestic Insurrections' of the Declaration of Independence," *Journal of Negro History* 61, no. 3 (July 1976): 243–255.

179. South Carolina Council of Safety to Stephen Bull, 16 March 1776, in *PHL*, 11:172; and William Ryan, *The World of Thomas Jeremiah: Charles Town on the Eve of the American Revolution* (Oxford, 2010).

180. Jim Piecuch, *Three Peoples, One King: Loyalists, Indians, and Slaves in the Revolutionary South* (Columbia, 2008), introduction; Frey, *Water*, chap. 2; and Randall Miller, "A Backcountry Loyalist Plan to Retake Georgia and the Carolinas, 1778," *SCHM* 75 (1974): 207–214. This plan advocated British utilization of the enslaved as soldiers.

181. Wright to Dartmouth, 9 June 1775, in *ColRG*, 38.1:446–449.

182. Wright to Dartmouth, 9 June 1775, in *ColRG*, 38.1:446–449.

183. "Letter from Charleston," 10 June 1775, in *AA*, 2:953; and 4 July 1775, in Keith Krawczynski, *William Henry Drayton: South Carolina Revolutionary Patriot* (Baton Rouge, 2001), 129.

184. Walter Edgar, ed., *The South Carolina Encyclopedia Guide to the American Revolution in South Carolina* (Columbia, 2012), kindle edition.

185. Wright to Dartmouth, 17 June and 17 June 1775, in *ColRG*, 38.1:466–470, 474.

186. Wright to Dartmouth, 17 June, 1 November, and 11 December 1775, all in *GHS Coll*, 3:183–185, 218–220, 226–227. It was in this last letter that Wright learned that the king had granted his request. For prisoners, see Wright to Dartmouth, 16 November 1775, in *GGCJ*, 1774–1777, 115–116.

187. William Grant to Samuel Graves, 18 June 1775, in Clark, *Naval Documents*, 1:716–717.

188. Wright to Dartmouth, 10 July 1775, in *GHS Coll*, 3:195.

189. Frederick Haldimand to Thomas Gage, 6 April and 6 August 1774, and Gage to Haldimand, 18 August 1774, in GP. Also see Laurens to John Laurens, 8 April 1774, and Laurens to John Lewis Gervais, 9 April 1774, in *PHL*, 9:379–382, 389–398.

190. 4 July 1775, in *GGCJ*, 1774–1777, 81–82. "There was," they said, "nothing they could do . . . to stop . . . lawless proceedings."

191. 6 June and 4, 7, and 17 July, in *GGCJ*, 1774–1777, 79–82.

192. William Campbell to Thomas Gage, 29 July 1775, in GP.

193. For Laurens's work with Alexander Wright, see Laurens to Wright, 7 August 1768, in *PHL*, 6:51–54. Laurens proved a strict taskmaster, but he offered his services free of charge, "having no other views in taking upon me this charge than the . . . honour of being serviceable to a gentleman of your Excellency's rank & merit." As it turned out, Alexander Wright was not the most focused student, and Laurens canceled the apprenticeship. For Laurens's comment regarding Wright and the Assembly, see Laurens to John Laurens, 3 May 1774, in *PHL*, 9:422–425. Also see Laurens to William Manning, 22 May 1775, in Clark, *Naval Documents*, 1:507–509.

194. Laurens to Alexander Wright, 30 July 1778, in *PHL*, 14:98–99. Laurens wrote: "I am prompted by friendship and regard to request you will let me know by the earliest opportunity if by any means I can contribute to your happiness. . . . If on your return to South Carolina you shall take this city in your way, I beg you will do me the favor to call first at my house on Chesnut Street."

195. Wright to Dartmouth, 10 July 1775, in *GHS Coll*, 3:195; and Wright to Dartmouth, 16 November 1775, in *ColRG*, 38.2:22–35.

196. *GG*, 25 October 1775; and Wright to Dartmouth, in *GGCJ*, 1774–1777, 113–115; Wright to Dartmouth, 1 November 1775, in *ColRG*, 38.2:13–16. Habersham died on 28 August in Brunswick, New Jersey. The same issue of the *Gazette* announced the death of Peter Tondee, whose "Long Room" was a home of Georgia's earliest rebellious moments. See Carl Solana Weeks, *Savannah in the Time of Peter Tondee: The Road to Revolution in Colonial Georgia* (Columbia, 1997).

197. Troy, "Ruining the King's Cause," 185–195.

198. Wright to William Campbell, 27 June 1775, in Clark, *Naval Documents*, 1:766; and John Pownall to Wright, 4 October 1775, in *ColRG*, 38.1:508–510. Pownall informed Wright that the inability to safely deliver mail had necessitated the discontinuance of the typical mail packets.

199. Wright to Gage, 27 June 1775, in *ColRG*, 38.2:26–30; and Wright to Dartmouth, 10 July 1775, in *ColRG*, 38.1:503–505.

200. Tonyn to Dartmouth, 1 July 1775, in Clark, *Naval Documents*, 1:802–803.

201. Graves to Philip Stephens, 29 July 1775, in Clark, *Naval Documents*, 1:1001–1002.

202. William Henry Drayton, *Memoirs of the American Revolution* (Charleston, 1821), 348.

203. Wright to Gage, 27 June 1775, in Drayton, *Memoirs*, 346–348.

204. The forged letter is "Wright to Gage," 27 June 1775, in *ColRG*, 38.2:26–30. For South Carolina, see Stan Deaton, "Revolutionary Charleston, 1765–1800" (PhD diss., University of Florida, 1997).

205. Wright to Graves, 27 June 1775, in *ColRG*, 38.2:30–31; 15 July 1775, in *JCC*, 2:185; and 15 July 1775, in *AA*, 2:1884.

206. John J. Zubly, "The Law of Liberty," in *AA*, 2:1557–1569.

207. Haddon Smith, Loyalist claim, in *BGLC*; 17 July 1775, in *RRSG*, 1:258; Wright to Dartmouth, *ColRG*, 38.1:523–525; and 17 July 1775, in *AA*, 2:1554–1555.

208. 6 July 1775, in *RRSG*, 1:235–239; Benjamin Harrison to George Washington, 24 July 1775, in FO; William Campbell to Gage, 29 July 1775, in GP; and William Campbell to Dartmouth, 19 July 1775, in *Manuscripts of the Earl of Dartmouth*, ed. William Hewlett (Ontario, 2013), 2:331–332.

209. 14 July 1775, in *RRSG*, 1:263–267; Georgia Committee of Intelligence to George Johnston, two letters dated 14 July 1775, in *AA*, 2:1555–1556, 1556–1557.

210. 10 July 1775, in *RRSG*, 1:244–248.

211. 11 July 1775, in *RRSG*, 1:248–251; and Wright to Dartmouth, 11 July 1775, in *ColRG*, 38.1:506–507. Also see Harvey H. Jackson, *Lachlan McIntosh and the Politics of Revolutionary Georgia* (Athens, 1979); Gallay, *Formation*; and Ouzts, *Samuel Elbert*.

212. 17 July 1775, in *RRSG*, 1:258–259; and Coleman, *American Revolution*, 57–61.

213. Wright to Dartmouth, 7 August 1775, in *GHS Coll*, 3:204–205; Wright to Dartmouth, 7 August and 17 August 1775, in *ColRG*, 38.1:541–561, 562–583; and 6 October 1775, in *RRSG*, 1:93.

214. Campbell to Gage, 29 July and 30 June 1775, in Clark, *Naval Documents*, 1:1007–1008, 792.

215. Laurens to William Henry Drayton, 15 September 1775, and Laurens to Committee for Saxe Gotha Township, 19 September 1775, in "Papers of the First Council of Safety of the Revolutionary Party in South Carolina, June–November 1775," *SCHGM* 1 (1900): 279–310.

216. Ralph Izard to George Dempster, 25 June 1775, in Izard, *Correspondence*, 1:93–95. Also see Peter Manigault to Miles Brewton, 1 July 1768, in "Letterbook of Peter Manigault," ed. Maurice Crouse, *SCHM* 70, no. 2 (April 1969): 95–96.

217. Wright to Dartmouth, 16 September 1775, in *AA*, 11:114; Wright to Dartmouth, 14 October 1775 and 9 December 1775, in *GHS Coll*, 3:215–217, 223–225. For an excellent analysis of Georgia's final descent into the rebel camp, see *RG*, chap. 8. Concerning the militia, see, for example, Thomas Netherclift to Wright, August 19, 1775, in *GHS Coll*, 10:44–45; and James Robertson to Wright, 14 August 1775, in *GHS Coll*, 10:45–46.

218. Wright to Dartmouth, 17 August 1775, in CO, 5/664.

219. 15 July 1775, in *AA*, 2:1553; and Coleman, *American Revolution*, 63.

220. Wright to Germain, 8 October 1777, in CO, 5/665.

221. Wright to Dartmouth, 29 July 1775, in CO, 5/664; and Wright to Dartmouth, 17 August 1775, *GGCJ*, 1774–1777, 109–110. Also see John Hopkins, Loyalist claim, in

*BGLC*; Haddon Smith, Loyalist claim, in *BGLC*; John Hopkins testimony, 29 July 1775, in Edward J. Cashin, *Setting Out to Begin a New World, Colonial Georgia: A Documentary History* (Savannah, 1995), 157–158; and Ouzts, *Samuel Elbert*, 102–103.

222. 17 July 1775, in *AA*, 2:1554–1555; and Hadden Smith memorial, 29 July 1775, in Cashin, *Setting Out*, 158–159. Also see Haddon Smith, Loyalist claim, in *BGLC*.

223. Wright to Dartmouth, 23 September 1775, in *GHS Coll*, 3:212–214; and 15 August 1775, in *GGCJ*, 1774–1777, 82–84.

224. Wright to Dartmouth, 23 September 1775, in *GHS Coll*, 3:212–213. Also see Wright to Dartmouth, 16 September 1775, *GGCJ*, 1774–1777, 110–111.

225. *Pennsylvania Journal*, 11 October 1775, in Clark, *Naval Documents*, 2:405–407.

226. Wright to David Taitt, 6 July 1775, in CO, 5/76.

227. Governor Wright's speech to the General Assembly, 18 January 1775, in *AA*, 1:1152–1153.

228. Wright to Dartmouth, 17 August 1775, in CO, 5/664.

229. Thomas Brown, Loyalist claim, in *BGLC*; Thomas Brown to Jonas Brown, 10 November 1775, in Cashin, *Setting Out*, 160–164; and Edward Cashin, *The King's Ranger: Thomas Brown and the American Revolution on the Southern Frontier* (New York, 1999), 27–29.

230. Cashin, *King's Ranger*; Gary Olson, "Thomas Brown, Loyalist Partisan, and the Revolutionary War in Georgia, 1777–1782, Part I," *GHQ* 54, no. 1 (Spring 1970): 1–19; and Olson, "Thomas Brown, Loyalist Partisan, and the Revolutionary War in Georgia, 1777–1782, Part II," *GHQ* 54, no. 2 (Summer 1970): 183–208.

231. Brown to David Ramsay, 25 December 1786, in *HCG*, 614–619.

232. Thomas Birkia to Harvey Birkia, 30 December 1775, in Heard Robertson, Loyalist Research Papers, Reese Library, Augusta State University, Augusta, Ga.

233. Wright to Dartmouth, 9 December 1775, in *ColRG*, 38.2:36–50.

234. Wright to Dartmouth, 23 September 1775, in *ColRG*, 38.1:600–627; and Peter Taarling to John Houstoun, 24 October 1775, in MS 397, John Houstoun Papers, GHS. Taarling was a delegate to Georgia's provincial congress from St. Andrew's Parish.

235. John Pownall to Wright, 7 November 1775, in *ColRG*, 38.1:594.

236. Wright to Dartmouth, 11 December 1775, in *ColRG*, 38.2:51–52.

237. Reply of Wright to Assembly, in *ColRG*, 17:688–690.

238. Wright to the Loyalist Commission, 8 September 1783, in James Wright, Loyalist claim, in *BGLC*.

## Chapter 6. A Governor Arrested

1. Wright to Dartmouth, 3 January 1776, 16 November 1775, in CO, 5/665. Also see Wright to Dartmouth, 19 December 1775, in *ColRG*, 38.2:53–55; and Bernard Bailyn, *The Ordeal of Thomas Hutchinson* (Cambridge, 1974), 71.

2. Wright to Dartmouth, 3 January 1776, and 16 November 1775, in CO, 5/665. Also see Wright to Dartmouth, 19 December 1775, in *GHS Coll*, 3:228; Wright to Dartmouth, 3 January 1776, in CO, 5/665.

3. *Middlesex Journal and Evening Advertiser*, 26 December 1775.

4. Thomas Taylor to Mr. Morrison of Birtley White House, 16 December 1775, in

Robert Scott Davis, "A Georgia Loyalist's Perspective on the American Revolution: The Letters of Dr. Thomas Taylor," *GHQ* 81, no. 1 (Spring 1997): 125.

5. James Rogers, Loyalist claim, in *BGLC*.

6. James Wright, Loyalist claim, in *BGLC*.

7. *GG*, 10 January 1776.

8. "Proceedings," 2 January 1776, in *RRSG*, 1:83–85. My discussion of the Battle of the Rice Boats is drawn largely from Harvey H. Jackson, "The Battle of the Riceboats: Georgia Joins the Revolution," *GHQ* 58, no. 2 (Summer 1974): 229–243; Robert S. Davis, "The Battle of the Riceboats: British Views of Georgia's First Battle of the American Revolution," paper delivered to the Georgia Historical Association, 1983; James M. Johnson, *Militiamen, Rangers, and Redcoats* (Macon, 1992), chap. 6; McIntosh to George Washington, 8 March 1776, in *GHS Coll*, 12:1–4; journal of H.M. Sloop *Tamar*, 25 March 1776, in Clark, *Naval Documents*, 4:515–516; and William Ewan to the South Carolina Council of Safety, 4 March 1776, in *HCG*, 88–89.

9. 7 and 8 January 1776, in *RRSG*, 1:86–92.

10. 12, 13, and 16 January 1776, in *RRSG*, 1:95–100.

11. 13 January 1776, in *RRSG*, 1:97–98; and Wright to the "Town of Savannah," 18 January 1776, in Clark, *Naval Documents*, 3:852. Also see Michael Cecere, *March to Independence: The Revolutionary War in the Southern Colonies, 1775–1776* (Yardley, 2021), 136–139.

12. Sarah Gober Temple and Kenneth Coleman, *Georgia Journeys: Being an Account of the Lives of Georgia's Original Settlers and Many Other Early Settlers from the Founding of the Colony until the Institution of Royal Government in 1754* (Athens, 1961), 291; and E. Merton Coulter, *Wormsloe: Two Centuries of a Georgia Family* (Athens, 1955), 82–107.

13. "At a special meeting of the Council of Safety, Jan. 18th, 1776, p.m.," in *RRSG*, 1:100–103. For a reasonably detailed and similar examination of the arrest of Wright, see Robert G. Mitchell, "Loyalist Georgia" (PhD diss., Tulane University, 1965), 35, 38, 46, 56, 64–72; Charles Risher Jr., "Propaganda, Dissension, and Defeat: Loyalist Sentiment in Georgia, 1763–1783" (PhD diss., Mississippi State University, 1976), 110–117; Kenneth Coleman, *The American Revolution in Georgia, 1763–1789* (Athens, 1958).

14. Laurens to John Laurens, 23 June 1775, in *PHL*, 10:186–196.

15. One George Kincaid wrote after the war that he and "a number of Loyalists" sped toward Wright's home in Savannah to protect him once they heard that Wright might be imprisoned. George Kincaid, Loyalist claim, in *BGLC*.

16. 20 December 1779, in *The Diary and Letters of His Excellency Thomas Hutchinson, Esq.*, ed. Peter Orlando Hutchinson (London, 1883), 2:312–313.

17. "At a special meeting of the Council of Safety, Jan. 18th, at 11 o'clock at night, 1776," in *RRSG*, 1:102. Also see John Mehane, "Joseph Habersham in the Revolutionary War," *GHQ* 47, no. 1 (1963): 80–81; Charles Colcock Jones, *The History of Georgia* (Boston, 1883), 2:211–212. Interestingly, Jones cites McCall's *History of Georgia* as the source of the quotation, but that quote is not found in McCall's history of Georgia. See Hugh McCall, *History of Georgia* (Atlanta, 1909), a one-volume edition of McCall's two-volume history, which was originally published in 1811 and 1816.

18. For further details concerning Wright's property, see James Wright, Loyal-

ist claim, in *BGLC*. In the 107-page typed transcript of his claim, there is no mention of Wright's arrest, only a reference to his escape. Also see "At a special meeting of the Council of Safety, Jan. 18th, at 11 o'clock at night, 1776," in *RRSG*, 1:102; Jones, *History of Georgia*, 2:211–212; Martin Jollie to Patrick Tonyn, February 13, 1776, in Mitchell, "Loyalist Georgia," 65. Wright later wrote of Jollie that "I conceive him to be a person worthy of the humanity & assistance of Government" (Wright's testimony in Martin Jollie, Loyalist claim, in *BGLC*; and for the butler, see John Martindale, Loyalist claim, in *BGLC*).

19. James Edward Powell, Loyalist claim, in *BGLC*.

20. Basil Cowper, Loyalist claim, in *BGLC*. Cowper claimed that "he continued with [the rebels] till the Governor and Council were made prisoners when [I] quitted them." Also see "At a meeting of the Council of Safety, Jan. 19th, 1776," in *RRSG*, 1:103–104.

21. Gage to Lord Barrington, 12 November 1770, in GP.

22. Oliver Hart diary entry, 11 August 1775, in *Three Peoples, One King: Loyalists, Indians, and Slaves in the Revolutionary South*, by Jim Piecuch (Columbia, 2008), 51; Egerton Leigh, *The Man Unmasked: or, The World Undeceived* (Charles Town, 1769), 27; Robert Calhoon and Robert Weir, "The Scandalous History of Sir Egerton Leigh," *WMQ* 26, no. 1 (1969): 57; Gordon S. Wood, *The Radicalism of the American Revolution* (New York, 1992), 214; and Chaim Rosenberg, *The Loyalist Conscience: Principled Opposition to the American Revolution* (Jefferson, 2018), 1. For the war as a civil war, see Holger Hoock, *Scars of Independence: America's Violent Birth* (New York, 2017), 4–82, 122, 295, 299–301, 304–305; John Pancake, *This Destructive War: The British Campaign in the Carolinas, 1780–1782* (Tuscaloosa, 1985), esp. 36–55, 108–121; and Jerome Nadelhaft, *The Disorders of War: The Revolution in South Carolina* (Orono, 1981), chaps. 4, 7.

23. Otho Holland Williams to Elie Williams, 12 June 1781, in Otho Holland Williams Papers, Maryland Center for History and Culture, Baltimore. Also see Philip Moore, Loyalist claim, in *BGLC*; and George d'Erbage, Loyalist claim, in *BGLC*.

24. Anthony Stokes affidavit, in Alexander Thomas, Loyalist claim, in *BGLC*. Many of the Georgia Loyalists who filed Loyalist claims referred to the war as a civil war, including in Stokes's own claim.

25. Georgia Congress to the Inhabitants of Georgia, 25 July 1775, in *AA*, 2:1554–1555.

26. William Howe to Germain, 7 May 1776, in Clark, *Naval Documents*, 4:1435–1438.

27. Frederick J. E. Woodbridge, ed., *The Philosophy of Hobbes* (Minneapolis, 1903), 8.

28. Thomas Brown to David Ramsay, 25 December 1786, in *HCG*, 614–619.

29. John Ferling, *Almost a Miracle: The American Victory in the War of Independence* (Oxford, 2007), 15.

30. Wright to Noble W. Jones, 18 and 22 January 1776, in *AA*, 4:799; unknown to J. Morrison of Birtley White House, 22 March 1776, in *Newcastle Courant*; and 17 August 1776 and Committee of Congress to Commodore Eseck Hopkins, 18 January 1776, in *AA*, 4:763–764.

31. 18 January 1776, in *RRSG*, 1:100–103. Also see Clay Ouzts, *Samuel Elbert and the Age of Revolution in Georgia, 1740–1788* (Macon, 2022), 120.

32. *Newcastle Journal and General Advertiser*, 17 February 1776, from a Georgia letter dated 7 October 1775.

33. Jackson, "Battle of the Riceboats," 232–233; Coleman, *American Revolution*, 87–88; Charles Francis Jenkins, *Button Gwinnett: Signer of the Declaration of Independence* (Garden City, 1926), 55–80, quote on 186; and Harvey Jackson, *Lachlan McIntosh and the Politics of Revolutionary Georgia* (Athens, 1979), 20–50.

34. 19 January 1776, in *RRSG*, 1:104.

35. Anthony Stokes, *Desultory Observations, on the Situation, Extent, Climate, Population, Manners, Customs, Commerce, Constitution, Government, Religion, &c. of Great Britain* (London, 1792), 26.

36. John Graham, Loyalist claim, in *BGLC*.

37. The *Scarborough* had been ordered to Savannah to obtain rice. See Howe to Dartmouth, 19 December 1775, and Samuel Graves to Andrew Barkley, 26 December 1775, in Clark, *Naval Documents*, 3:166–167, 255–257.

38. Wright to Germain, 23 September 1775, in *GHS Coll*, 3:212–214, quote on 213.

39. Josiah Tattnall, Loyalist claim, in *BGLC*; Jones, *History of Georgia*, 2:212; and "At a Council of Safety at Mrs. Tondee's, January 16th, 1776," in *RRSG*, 1:98–100. The veracity of the account concerning shots fired into Wright's home cannot be conclusively affirmed or refuted, but shots were fired into his home during the Stamp Act crisis, making it a real probability that it happened again. Josiah Tattnall mentioned in his claim that Wright had been continually harassed and "insulted." Also see Wright to Dartmouth, September 23, 1775, in *GHS Coll*, 3:212–213.

40. 14 July 1775, *RRSG*, 1:269.

41. Hugh McCall asserted that Wright escaped through his back door and "went down the river about five miles by land to Bonaventure, where Mullryne lived, and where a boat and crew were waiting for him." Though Mullryne was twice banished from Georgia by the rebels, he did *not* file a Loyalist claim, and this part of the story cannot be verified. His death shortly after the war may be the cause of his failure to file a claim. See McCall, *History of Georgia*, 300. Also see Wright to Germain, 12 February 1776, in James Wright, Loyalist claim, in *BGLC*; Coleman, *American Revolution*, 68–69; Kenneth Coleman, "James Wright," in *Georgians in Profile: Essays in Honor of Ellis Merton Coulter*, ed. Horace Montgomery (Athens, 1958), 54. Wright made his escape on 11 February 1776. For his explanation of breaking parole, see Wright to His Council, 18 February 1776, in *Georgia and the Revolution*, ed. Ronald Killian and Charles Waller (Atlanta, 1975), 162–163. For his arrival, see "Captain's Log, H.M.S. *Scarborough*, 10 February 1776," in AO, 5/657, 51/867; n.d., *RRSG*, 1:269; James Wright, Loyalist claim, in *BGLC*; Martin Jollie to Patrick Tonyn, 13 February 1776, Andrew Barkley to Clinton, 23 February 1776, and Wright to Clinton, 21 February 1776, all in CP; journal of H.M.S. *Scarborough*, 12 February 1776, in Clark, *Naval Documents*, 3:1239–1242; and Laurens to John Laurens, 28 February 1776, in Clark, *Naval Documents*, 4:113–115. Laurens's is the only account to mention Wright's son Charles as the male child to escape with his father. The *South-Carolina and American General Gazette* (9–16 February 1776) stated that Wright and "his two daughters" made their way to the *Scarborough*.

42. Tattnall's assistance is mentioned in Josiah Tattnall, Loyalist claim, in *BGLC*. Lieutenant Governor John Graham confirmed this in his testimony of Tattnall's claim. Also see *General Gazette*, 9–16 February 1776.

43. James Wright, Loyalist claim, in *BGLC*.

44. James Wright, Loyalist claim, in *BGLC*. See also Coleman, *American Revolution*, 68–69; Coleman, "James Wright," 54.

45. Howe to Germain, 7 May 1776, in Clark, *Naval Documents*, 4:1435–1438. Laurens "blushed for Governor Wright's perfidy." See Laurens to Georgia Provincial Council, 16 February 1776, in "Letters from Hon. Henry Laurens to His Son, John, 1773–1776," *SCHGM* 4, no. 2 (April 1903): 92–93.

46. Journal of the H.M.S. *Scarborough*, 12 February 1776, in Clark, *Naval Documents*, 3:1239–1241.

47. Wright to Council of Safety, 13 February 1776, in *RRSG*, 1:269–272.

48. Wright to Council, 13 February 1776, in Keith Read Collection, Hargrett Library, University of Georgia, Athens; and Wright to Henry Clinton, in CP.

49. McIntosh to George Washington, 8 March 1776, in *GHS Coll*, 12:1–4.

50. Barkley to J. E. Powell, 19 February 1776, in *RRSG*, 1:107.

51. Jackson, "Battle of the Riceboats," 235–236; and "Captain's Log of the Ship Scarborough," in *GGCJ*, 1774–1777, 154. Harvey Jackson apparently named the battle. See Johnson, *Militiamen*, 151n. For Wright's brief account, see Wright to Dartmouth, 10 March 1776, *GGCJ*, 1774–1777, 144–145. Also see Jacob Fletcher, Loyalist claim, in *BGLC*.

52. Wright to Clinton, 10 March 1776, and Clinton to Wright, 20 March 1776, both in Clark, *Naval Documents*, 4:293–294, 428.

53. Wright to Dartmouth, 10 March 1776, in *GHS Coll*, 3:233–235.

54. *Purdie's Virginia Gazette*, 5 April 1776.

55. James Wright, Loyalist claim, in *BGLC*.

56. James Wright, Loyalist claim, in *BGLC*.

57. Wright to Germain, 12 February 1776, in James Wright, Loyalist claim, in *BGLC*; Coleman, *American Revolution*, 68–69; Coleman, "James Wright," 54; and Barkley to Admiral Clark Gayton, 21 March 1776, in Clark, *Naval Documents*, 4:443–444.

58. Wright to George Germain, 26 April 1776, in *GGCJ*, 1774–1777, 151–152.

59. McIntosh to George Washington, 8 March 1776, in *GHS Coll*, 12:1–4.

60. McIntosh to Washington, 8 March 1776, in *GHS Coll*, 12:1–4; Barkley to Lachlan McIntosh, 6 March 1776, in *AA*, 5:601; and William Henry Drayton to Georgia Council of Safety, 6 March 1776, in *AA*, 5:588.

61. "Transactions of the Society," 6 March 1776, in *The Published Records of Midway Church* (Newnan, 1951), 1:30; and Allen Tankersley, "Midway District: A Study of Puritanism in Colonial Georgia," *GHQ* 32, no. 3 (September 1948): 149–157.

62. McIntosh to Washington, 8 March 1776, in *GHS Coll*, 12:1–4; and William H. Mathers, pension application S4846, Southern Campaigns American Revolution Pension Statements & Rosters, http://revwarapps.org/s45846.pdf.

63. 2 March 1776, in *RRSG*, 1:110–111, 272–273.

64. William Ewan to the South Carolina Council of Safety, 4 March 1776, in *HCG*, 88–89; Johnson, *Militiamen*, 145–146; Raymond Demere to McIntosh, 4 March 1776, Council of Safety to Barkley, and Council of Safety to South Carolina Council of Safety, in *AA*, 5:599–600, 602.

65. Wright to Germain, 20 March 1776, in *GHS Coll*, 3:239–241; Barkley to Stokes,

14 March 1776, and Georgia Council of Safety to Barkley, 16 March 1776, in *AA*, 5:602–603.

66. Unknown to S. Morrison, 22 March 1776, in Heard Robertson, Loyalist Research Papers, Augusta State University, Augusta, Ga.

67. William Ewan to the South Carolina Council of Safety, 4 March 1776, in *HCG*, 88–89.

68. McIntosh to Washington, 8 March 1776, in *GHS Coll*, 12:1–4; and McIntosh to Barkley, 5 March 1776, in *AA*, 5:601.

69. Jackson, "Battle of the Riceboats," 238–239.

70. Barkley to Mr. Mackenzie, 2 February 1789, in Jacob Fletcher, Loyalist claim, in *BGLC*.

71. McIntosh to Washington, 8 March 1776, in *GHS Coll*, 12:1–4. It is likely that all burned vessels unleashed upon the British were owned by Loyalists, including at least one owned by Lachlan McGillivray. See *GGCJ*, 1774–1777, 158.

72. McIntosh to Washington, 8 March 1776, in *GHS Coll*, 12:1–4; and "Governor Wright's Narrative," in *GGCJ*, 1774–1777, 157.

73. "Receipt for rice seized on the Savannah River," in *GGCJ*, 1774–1777, 159.

74. McIntosh to Washington, 8 March 1776, in *GHS Coll*, 12:1–4. Some Creek Indians had come to the aid of the rebels after the British attacked Jonathan Bryan's plantation. See "Extract of a letter from Charlestown," 4 July 1776, in *The Remembrancer or Impartial Repository of the Public Events for the Year 1776* 3 (1777): 333–334.

75. Jackson, "Battle of the Riceboats," 240–243; and Coleman, *American Revolution*, 70.

76. Wright to Dartmouth, 10 March 1776, and Wright to Germain, 13 March and 14 March 1776, all in *GHS Coll*, 3:233–234, 235–236, 236–237, 238. For information concerning his private business, see James Wright, Loyalist claim, in *BGLC*. From the *Scarborough*, Wright sent detailed instructions to his plantation managers, seeking, among other things, rice for the British ships.

77. Wright to Germain, 20 March 1776, in *GHS Coll*, 3:239–241. This letter includes Wright's letters of 13, 14, and 26 March.

78. Wright to Germain, 20 March 1776, and Wright to Clinton, 2 April 1776, in *GGCJ*, 1774–1777, 146–147, 151–152.

79. Wright to Clinton, 21 February 1776, in CP. For the usual reasons behind a person's early loyalty, see Ruma Chopra, *Choosing Sides: Loyalists in Revolutionary America* (Lanham, 2013), chap. 1; Chopra, *Unnatural Rebellion: Loyalists in New York City during the Revolution* (Charlottesville, 2011), chap. 2; Chaim Rosenberg, *The Loyalist Conscience: Principled Opposition to the American Revolution* (Jefferson, 2018), chap. 6; Robert Calhoon, *The Loyalists in Revolutionary America, 1760–1781* (New York, 1973); Henry Lawrence Gipson, *American Loyalist: Jared Ingersoll* (New Haven, 1971), chap. 12; Hoock, *Scars of Independence*, chap. 1; Wallace Brown, *The Good Americans: The Loyalists in the American Revolution* (New York, 1969), chaps. 3, 5; and William Nelson, *The American Tory* (Boston, 1961), chap. 4.

80. *Middlesex Journal and Evening Advertiser*, 21–23 May 1776. This published extract from a letter from Kirkwell, Orkney, dated 4 May, noted that Wright arrived at that place with his secretary and "domesticks." The *St. James's Chronicle or the British Eve-*

*ning Post* of 21–23 May 1776 mentioned that Wright was in Boston prior to his arrival in Kirkwell. The *Public Advertiser* mentioned the same details on 23 May 1776. Wright to Council, February 13, 1776, in Read Collection. Also see Wright to Clinton, 2 April 1776, in CP; and Laurens to John Laurens, 14 March 1776, in Clark, *Naval Documents*, 4:343.

81. Hutchinson to Bernard, 9 March 1774, in Hutchinson, *Diary and Letters*, 130–132.

82. Stephen R. Berry, *A Path in the Mighty Waters: Shipboard Life and Atlantic Crossings to the New World* (New Haven, 2015), 44–45.

83. Hutchinson to Bernard, 9 March 1774, in Hutchinson, *Diary and Letters*, 2:130–132; and, in part, Bailyn, *Ordeal of Thomas Hutchinson*, 270. Also see Bernard Bailyn, *Faces of Revolution: Personalities and Themes in the Struggle for American Independence* (New York, 1990), chap. 3.

84. William Fielding to Basil Fielding, 28 April 1776, in *Lost War: Letters from British Officers during the American Revolution*, ed. Marion Balderston (New York, 1975), 76–79; *Pennsylvania Evening Post*, 23 April 1776; and *Constitutional Gazette*, 24 April 1776.

85. Wright to Germain, 26 April 1776, in *GHS Coll*, 3:243–244; *Pennsylvania Evening Post*, 23 April 1776; Hutchinson, *Diary and Letters*, 2:61–62; Captain Francis Hutcheson to Major General Frederick Haldimand, 24 April 1776, and Vice Admiral Molyneux Shuldham to Philip Stephens, 24 April 1776, both in Clark, *Naval Documents*, 4:1220–1222, 1223–1224.

86. Bob Rupert, "The Great Hurricane(s) of 1780," *Journal of the American Revolution*, https://allthingsliberty.com/2022/07/the- great-hurricanes-of-1780/.

87. Hutchinson, *Diary and Letters*, 2:61–62; and *American Gazette*, 25 June 1776, which stated that Wright departed on 5 May.

88. 19 June 1776, in Hutchinson, *Diary and Letters*, 2:72.

89. Leland Bellot, *William Knox: The Life & Thought of an Eighteenth-Century Imperialist* (Austin, 1977), 145–146.

90. James Wright, Loyalist claim, in *BGLC*, 5/657; Coleman, *American Revolution*, 72–73; *RG*, 151; and Calhoon, *Loyalists*, 13–15.

91. James Wright, Loyalist claim, in *BGLC*.

92. Wright to Commissioners of Loyalist Claims, 8 September 1783, in James Wright, Loyalist claim, in *BGLC*.

93. Charles Deshler, "How the Declaration Was Received in the Old Thirteen," *Harper's New Monthly* 85 (July 1892): 187.

94. Diary entries of 17, 19, and 21 June 1776, 15 January, 1 February, 19 July, 29 September, 7 December 1777, 2 March, and 11 August 1778, in Hutchinson, *Diary and Letters*, 2:70, 72, 152, 158, 170, 189, 212–213.

95. Hutchinson, *Diary and Letters*, 2:170; Germain to Knox, 19 October 1776, in William Knox and Howard Vicenté Knox, *Manuscripts of Captain H. V. Knox* (Boston, 1972), 6:126. For the role of exiles in the creation of the southern strategy, see, for but a few examples, Paul Smith, *Loyalists and Redcoats: A Study in British Revolutionary Policy* (Chapel Hill, 1964), 79–98, esp. 86–87, 98, 175–177; John Shy, "British Strategy for Pacifying the Southern Colonies, 1778–1781," in *The Southern Experience in the American Revolution*, ed. J. J. Crow and L. E. Tise (Chapel Hill, 1978), esp. 157–159; Piecuch,

*Three Peoples*, 2–6, 11, 127–129; David K. Wilson, *The Southern Strategy: Britain's Conquest of South Carolina and Georgia, 1775–1780* (Columbia, 2005), 63–64; Ira Gruber, "Britain's Southern Strategy," in *The Revolutionary War in the South: Power, Conflict, and Leadership; Essays in Honor of John Richard Alden*, ed. W. Robert Higgins (Durham, 1979), 218; Christopher Hibbert, *Redcoats & Rebels: The American Revolution through British Eyes* (New York, 1990), 235; Henry Clinton, *The American Rebellion: Sir Henry Clinton's Narrative of His Campaigns, 1775–1782*, ed. William B. Willcox (New Haven, 1954), 27, 109, 149–156; Robert G. Mitchell, "Sir James Wright Looks at the American Revolution," *GHQ* 53 (Winter 1969): 509–518; Bellot, *William Knox*, 39–40, 143–144, 155–157, 163–165; Robert S. Davis, "Loyalism and Patriotism at Askance: Community, Conspiracy, and Conflict on the Southern Frontier," in *Tory Insurgents: The Loyalist Perception and Other Essays*, ed. Robert Calhoon, Timothy Barnes, and Robert Davis (Columbia, 2010); John Buchanan, *The Road to Guilford Courthouse: The American Revolution in the Carolinas* (New York, 1997), 26; North Callahan, *Royal Raiders: The Tories of the American Revolution* (Indianapolis, 1963), 37; and Don Cook, *The Long Fuse: How England Lost the American Colonies, 1760–1785* (New York, 1995), chap. 18; Wright to Hutchinson, 27 February 1779, quoted in Patrick Furlong, "Civilian-Military Conflict and the Restoration of the Royal Province of Georgia, 1778–1782," *Journal of Southern History* 38 (August 1972): 422; and Wright to John Robinson, 11 March 1779, in AO, 13/37.

96. Piecuch, *Three Peoples*, 6, 11.

97. Wright to Hutchinson, 27 February 1779, in Furlong, "Civilian-Military Conflict," 422; and Wright to John Robinson, 11 March 1779, in AO, 13/37.

98. Gruber, "Britain's Southern Strategy," 218.

99. Wright to Germain, 13 February 1777, in George Sackville-Germain Papers, vol. 5, CL. At different times, Wright noted that he had 522, 523, 525, or 526 slaves.

100. James Wright, Loyalist claim, in *BGLC*.

101. Thomas Brown to Patrick Tonyn, 6 April 1778, in *RAM*, 1:224–225.

102. For Loyalist confiscation of the enslaved, see Clay to Laurens, 9 September 1778, in *GHS Coll*, 8:106.

103. Germain to Wright, 27 October 1779, in *ColRG*, 38.2:204–205.

104. James Wright, Loyalist claim, in *BGLC*. It should be noted that later in his testament, Wright mentioned that 522 slaves were confiscated in January 1777. He said he owned 526 slaves, worth £27,787, in February 1776, of which 522 were taken in January 1777. Upon his return to power in 1779, he claimed to have reclaimed only 323 of these slaves. He purchased an additional thirty-seven and witnessed the birth of forty-eight more between 1779 and the end of the war. The rebels utilized many of Wright's slaves in the defense of Savannah in 1778. Also see Thomas Brown to Patrick Tonyn, 6 April 1778, in *RAM*, 1:224–225. "The [rebel] gallies are laying manned entirely with Governor Wright's Negroes." Wright to Germain, 12 February 1777, in Mitchell, "Sir James Wright," 511–514.

105. For the Carlisle Commission, see Gerald Brown, *American Secretary: The Colonial Policy of Lord George Germain, 1775–1778* (Ann Arbor, 1963), 139–147; Weldon Brown, *Empire or Independence: A Study in the Failure of Reconciliation, 1774–1783* (Baton Rouge, 1941), 241–292; Andrew Jackson O'Shaughnessy, *The Men Who Lost America: British Leadership, the American Revolution, and the Fate of the Empire* (New Haven,

2013), 61–64; Smith, *Loyalists and Redcoats*, chap. 6 and 113–115; and Jerome Reich, *British Friends of the American Revolution* (Hoboken, 2015), 121. The commission, according to Brown, was "futile" largely because Americans now believed independence was possible. Germain advised against granting amnesty to insurgents for fear of alienating Loyalists. See Hoock, *Scars of Independence*, 123; and Alan S. Brown, "William Eden and the American Revolution" (PhD diss., University of Michigan, 1953), chap. 5.

106. Memorial, 29 August 1777, in *ColRG*, 39:4–9. See also Gruber, "Britain's Southern Strategy." The *Georgia Gazette* published many issues that identified prominent persons opposed to revolutionary ideals. See all issues of the *Gazette* from September through November 1774. British historian Piers Mackesy stated that Knox sought to preserve the South "even at the cost of throwing off" the northern colonies. He also noted that there is no definitive proof of the extent of Knox's influence but that his opinion likely mattered. Piers Mackesy, *The War for America, 1775–1783* (Lincoln, 1993), 44.

107. Margaret Marion Spector, *The American Department of the British Government, 1768–1782* (New York, 1940), 119. Also see Ellis to Knox, 13 August 1777, in KP. Ellis asked Knox to give his compliments to "Gov. Wright & his family."

108. Memorial of Lord William Campbell, Sir James Wright, William Bull, and John Graham, 29 August 1777, in *ColRG*, 39:4–9. Interestingly and incorrectly, opponents of Lord North claimed that he had falsely claimed that large numbers of Loyalists existed in the southern colonies. See Smith, *Loyalists and Redcoats*, 97.

109. Simpson to Germain, 28 August 1779, in "James Simpson's Reports on the Carolina Loyalists, 1779–1780," ed. Alan S. Brown, *JSH* 21, no. 4 (November 1955): 514–517; Piecuch, *Three Peoples*, 125–132; Alan Valentine, *Lord George Germain* (Oxford, 1962), 334–335; O'Shaughnessy, *The Men Who Lost America*, 188–190; and Smith, *Loyalists and Redcoats*, 122. Smith asserted that Simpson's influence "has been overrated."

110. See the appropriate disqualifying acts in *RRSG*, 1:374–387, 348–356. Also see Piecuch, *Three Peoples*, 2–6.

111. Smith, *Loyalists and Redcoats*, 79.

112. Memorial of Lord William Campbell, Sir James Wright, William Bull, and John Graham, 29 August 1777, in *ColRG*, 39:4–9.

113. Piecuch, *Three Peoples*, 6, 37–38; Smith, *Loyalists and Redcoats*, 29–31, 121–125, 168–169; and O'Shaughnessy, *The Men Who Lost America*, 188–190.

114. Memorial of Wright and John Graham to Germain, 17 July 1778, in *ColRG*, 39:10–15. Also see Memorial of Lord William Campbell, Sir James Wright, William Bull, and John Graham, 29 August 1777, in *ColRG*, 39:4–9.

115. Memorial, 8 October 1777, in *ColRG*, 39:4–9; Jenkins, *Button Gwinnett*, 153; and Wright to Germain, 8 October 1777, in CO, 5/664. Wright also mentioned that Georgians "may be disposed to return to their allegiance." Gwinnett and McIntosh had been political rivals since the earliest days of the revolutionary movement. The nature of their rivalry was both personal and professional, culminating with the death of Gwinnett on 19 May 1777. See Jackson, *Lachlan McIntosh*, 64–66; and Jenkins, *Button Gwinnett*, 150–157.

116. Wright to Germain, 8 October 1777, in *GHS Coll*, 3:245–248.

117. Diary entry, 7 December 1777, in Hutchinson, *Diary and Letters*, 2:170.

118. *Public Advertiser*, 3 March 1778; and diary entry, 1 July 1774, in Hutchinson, *Diary and Letters*, 1:157–174.

119. Wright to Germain, 8 October 1777, in *GHS*, 3:245–248. Not all agreed with the ministry's new plans or with the promised support of southern Loyalists. See Smith, *Loyalists and Redcoats*, chap. 6; diary entry, 7 December 1777, in Hutchinson, *Diary and Letters*, 2:170. For the southern strategy, see Greg Brooking, "'Of Material Importance': Governor James Wright and the Siege of Savannah," *GHQ* 98, no. 4 (Winter 2014): 251–299; Gruber, "Britain's Southern Strategy," 205–238; Germain to Clinton, 8 March 1778, in *Manuscripts of Stopford-Sackville*, ed. William Hewlett (London, 1884), 94–99; Smith, *Loyalists and Redcoats*, 82–125, 170–173; Shy, "British Strategy," 155–173; Piecuch, *Three Peoples*, chap. 4; Mackesy, *War for America*, 251–259; Smith, *Loyalists and Redcoats*, chap. 6; John Buchanan, *Road to Guilford Courthouse: The American Revolution in the Carolinas* (New York, 1997), 25–33; Pancake, *This Destructive War*, 20–35; Stanley Carpenter, *Southern Gambit: Cornwallis and the British March to Yorktown* (Norman, 2019), 41–44; and Wilson, *Southern Strategy*, esp. 159–164.

120. "The Organization of the British Army in the American Revolution," American Revolution.org, 5 January 2023, https://www.americanrevolution.org/britisharmy7a.php.

121. Wright to Lord North, 16 December 1777, in AO, 13/37. For the purchase of the commission, see A. P. C. Bruce, *The Purchase System in the British Army, 1660–1871* (London, 1980), 33. By the end of 1777, Charles Wright had been promoted to lieutenant in the Fifty-Second Foot and, later, to captain of the Sixty-Fourth. See Worthington Chauncey Ford, *British Officers Serving in the American Revolution, 1774–1783* (Brooklyn, 1897), 186; and Charles Wright affidavit, in AO, 13/37. Wright gave two plantations (Mulberry Hill and Sedgefield) to his son James. He also gave his Orange Grove plantation to his son-in-law Sir James Wallace and the Knowle to another son-in-law, Major Thomas Barrow. See AO, 12/4.

122. Wright to North, 23 February 1778, in AO, 13/37.

123. Clinton to Germain, 5 March 1779, in *DAR*, 15:132–133.

124. Clinton to Germain, 5 March 1779, in *DAR*, 15:132–133; and Germain to Clinton, 8 March 1779, in *FM*, no. 1062. Also see Clinton, *American Rebellion*, chap. 6; Smith, *Loyalists and Redcoats*, 86–88; Mackesy, *War for America*, 154–159; William B. Willcox, "British Strategy in America, 1778," *Journal of Modern History* 19 (June 1947): 97–102; Willcox, *Portrait of a General: Sir Henry Clinton in the War of Independence* (New York, 1964), chaps. 6 and 7; Ira Gruber, *The Howe Brothers and the American Revolution* (New York, 1972), 300–302; Clinton, *American Rebellion*, 86; Valentine, *Lord George Germain*, chap. 22; O'Shaughnessy, *Men Who Lost America*, chap. 5; and Mark E. Lender and Gary W. Stone, *Fatal Sunday: George Washington, the Monmouth Campaign, and the Politics of Battle* (Norman, 2016), 15.

125. For the reconquest of Georgia, I primarily rely upon Colin Campbell, ed., *Journal of an Expedition* (Augusta, 1981); Wilson, *Southern Strategy*, chap. 6; Joshua B. Howard, "Things Here Wear a Melancholy Experience: The American Defeat at Briar Creek," *GHQ* 88, no. 4 (Winter 2004): 477–497; Kenneth Coleman, "Restored Colonial Georgia, 1779–1782," *GHQ* 40, no. 1 (March 1956): 1–20; Wilson, *Southern Strategy*, chaps. 1, 5, and 6; Furlong, "Civilian-Military Conflict," 415–442; K. G. Davies, "The

Restoration of Civil Government by the British in the War of Independence," in *Red, White & True Blue: The Loyalists in the Revolution*, ed. Esmond Wright (New York, 1976), 111–133; and Clinton Memorandum, 11 October 1778, in CP.

126. Clinton to Germain, 27 July 1778, Clinton to Newcastle, 11 July 1778, and Clinton to Drummond, 22 October 1778, in CP; Valentine, *Lord George Germain*, 334–338; Germain to Clinton, March 8, 1778, quoted in Smith, *Loyalists and Redcoats*, 83, 90–92; Gruber, *Howe Brothers*, 306–307; and Willcox, "British Strategy," 102–106. Also see Germain's instructions to Clinton on 21 March 1778, in Clinton, *American Rebellion*, 87; Clinton Memorandum, 6 June 1778, in Smith, *Loyalists and Redcoats*, 92. Concerning his doubts, see, for example, Clinton to Germain, 27 July 1778, and Clinton Memorandum, 11 October 1778, in Smith, *Loyalists and Redcoats*, 91–92, 93. Clinton finally determined that if he failed to move, the administration would never formulate any "solid plan." See Clinton to Newcastle, 22 October 1778, in Smith, *Loyalists and Redcoats*, 93. Regarding his support, see, for example, Henry Clinton to John Pownall, 3 May 1776, quoted in Smith, *Loyalists and Redcoats*, 88. See also Willcox, *Portrait of a General*, 223, 261, 271, 283, 293–299; O'Shaughnessy, *Men Who Lost America*, chap. 6; and Clinton, *American Rebellion*, esp. 140–161.

127. Nelson, *American Tory*, 143; and Paul David Nelson, *Sir Charles Grey, First Earl Grey: Royal Soldiers, Family Patriarch* (Madison, 1996), 115.

128. Campbell, *Journal*, 4; and Campbell to Germain, 20 January 1779, in Campbell, *Journal*, 44. For Clinton's lack of enthusiasm, see Duncan Drummond to Clinton, 29 November 1778, and Clinton to William Eden, 24 December 1778, in Willcox, *Portrait of a General*, 262, 266. In the first letter, Drummond relayed communication with Lord Germain, who complained of Clinton's attitude. "Good God, M[r.] Drummond," Germain shrieked, "is it possible that Sir Henry Clinton can think of desiring to come home at this critical time, when . . . this country looks upon him as the only chance we have of saving America."

129. Alexander A. Lawrence, *Storm over Savannah: The Story of Count d'Estaing and the Siege of the Town in 1779* (Savannah, 1979), 41.

130. Campbell to William Eden, 19 January 1779, in *FM*, no. 1252.

131. Lawrence, *Storm over Savannah*, 26–27.

132. Coleman, "Restored Colonial Georgia," 3–5, 17; Captain Hyde Parker to Philip Stephens, 14–15 January 1779, in *FM*, no. 1246; Campbell to Germain, 16 January 1779, in *FM*, no. 1247; and Campbell to Germain, 22–26 December, in *RRSG*, 2:121–125, 127–129. For Campbell's account of his time in Georgia, see Campbell, *Journal*. For General Howe, see Alexander Lawrence, "General Robert Howe and the British Capture of Savannah in 1778," *GHQ* 36, no. 4 (December 1952): 303–327; Carpenter, *Southern Gambit*, 51–56; and L. Van Loan Naisawald, "Major General Robert Howe's Activities in South Carolina and Georgia, 1776–1779," *GHQ* 35, no. 1 (March 1951): 23–30.

133. Mary A. Benjamin, ed., "Memoirs of a Revolutionary Soldier," *Collector: A Monthly Magazine for Autograph and Historical Collectors* 63 (October–December 1950): 198–201, 223–225, 247–249; 64 (January 1951): 2–5.

134. Coleman, *American Revolution*, 120; and letter of S. D. H———n, 16 January 1779, in *Letters from America, 1776–1779*, trans. Ray Pettengill (New York, 1924), 199.

135. Wilson, *Southern Strategy*, 72; and Barratt Wilkins, "A View of Savannah on the Eve of the Revolution," *GHQ* 54, no. 4 (Winter 1970): 579.

136. Campbell, *Journal*, 24. Also see Robert Scott Davis, "The British Invasion of Georgia in 1778," *Atlanta Historical Journal* 24 (1980): 5–26.

137. Campbell, *Journal*, 24.

138. Campbell, *Journal*, 26; and Lawrence, *Storm over Savannah*, 3. Although Wright detailed by name, age, gender, and occupation hundreds of slaves, there is no record of either a Quamino or a Quash Dolly in James Wright's personal papers. There are, however, three Quashes in the papers of Georgia Loyalists. The first, valued at £150, belonged to Elizabeth and Thomas Young and resided at their Southampton plantation; the second, owned by James Hume (a Wright in-law), lived on his Cypress Grove plantation and was valued at £65; the third, a gardener valued at £40, was owned by Lieutenant Governor John Graham (a good friend of Wright) and lived on his Mulberry Grove plantation. See Thomas Young, Loyalist claim, in *BGLC*; James Hume, Loyalist claim, in *BGLC*; and John Graham, Loyalist claim, in *BGLC*. Also see Thomas Hamilton, pension application S30470, Southern Campaigns American Revolution Pension Statements & Rosters, http://revwarapps.org/s30470.pdf.

139. Campbell, *Journal*, 27.

140. Wilson, *Southern Strategy*, 74–76; and L. Carroll Judson, *A Biography of the Signers of the Declaration of Independence* (Philadelphia, 1853), 2:145.

141. *HCG*, 340–342.

142. Wright to Germain, 9 March 1781, in *GHS Coll*, 3:340–342. Also see Arthur Hertzberg, *The Jews in America: Four Centuries of an Uneasy Encounter* (New York, 1997), 51; and David T. Morgan, "The Sheftalls of Savannah," *American Jewish Historical Quarterly* 62, no. 4 (June 1973): 354.

143. Campbell to Germain, 16 January 1779, in *FM*, 17:33–38 and 39–42 and no. 113. Also see Campbell, *Journal*, 25.

144. Jacob Bühler, Loyalist claim, in *BGLC*. Bühler was later captured during the siege by Count Pulaski's Legion, by whom he "received very severe usage" and, later, "his wife & children was treated exceedingly ill," leading to the death of two of his children.

145. Archibald Campbell's Proclamation, 8 January 1779, in Campbell, *Journal*, 38–39.

146. Campbell to Earl of Carlisle, 19 January 1779, in *FM*, no. 113; Campbell, *Journal*, 43; and Piecuch, *Three Peoples*, chap. 4.

147. Campbell, *Journal*, 29.

148. Henry C. Van Schaack, *The Life of Peter Van Schaack* (New York, 1842), 247.

149. John Jervis to Clinton, 4 March 1779, in "Letters of Captain Sir John Jervis," ed. Marie Hatch, *American Neptune* 7 (1947): 98–99.

150. Edmund Jennings to John Adams, 10 March 1779, in FO.

151. McIntosh to Washington, 12 March 1779, in FO.

152. General Clinton was stunned and upset by Prévost's attempts into the interior with such a small force. Clinton to Prévost, 10 August 1779, in Smith, *Loyalists and Redcoats*, 104.

153. Doyce Nunis Jr., ed., "Colonel Archibald Campbell's March from Savannah to

Augusta, 1779," *GHQ* 45, no. 3 (September 1961): 275–286; and John Wilson, *Encounters on a March through Georgia in 1779: The Maps and Memorandums of Lt. John Wilson, 71st Highlanders* (Sylvania, 1986).

154. Howard, "Things Here Wear," 484.

155. Campbell to Clinton, 4 March 1779, *GGCJ*, 1778–1779, 80–82.

156. Wright to Dartmouth, 20 June 1775, in *ColRG*, 38.1:475–478; John Stuart to Committee of Intelligence, 18 July 1775, in *AA*, 2:1681–1682; and Philip M. Hamer, "John Stuart's Indian Policy during the Early Months of the American Revolution," *Mississippi Valley Historical Review*, no. 17 (December 1930): 351–366.

157. James Snapp, *John Stuart and the Struggle for Empire on the Southern Frontier* (Baton Rouge, 1996), 160.

158. Stuart to "Gentlemen," 18 July 1775, in William Henry Drayton, *Memoirs of the American Revolution* (Charleston, 1821), 292–296; and James Habersham to Philotheos Chiffelle, 16 June 1775, in *AA*, 2:1007–1008.

159. Patrick Tonyn to Dartmouth, 1 July 1775, in Clark, *Naval Documents*, 1:802–803.

160. Campbell to Germain, 16 January 1779, in *FM*, no. 1247; Coleman, "Restored Colonial Georgia," 3–8; and Piecuch, *Three Peoples*, introduction and chap. 4 (esp. 128).

161. Campbell to Germain, 16 January 1779, in *FM*, no. 1247.

162. Leslie Hall, *Land and Allegiance in Revolutionary Georgia* (Athens, 2001), xi–xiv; and Alan Gallay, The *Formation of a Planter Elite: Jonathan Bryan and the Southern Colonial Frontier* (Athens, 2007), chap. 4.

163. William Moultrie to Charles Pinckney, 10 February 1779, in *Memoirs of the American Revolution*, by William Moultrie (New York, 1802), 309–310; and Ronald Hoffman, "The 'Disaffected' in the Revolutionary South," in *The American Revolution: Exploration in the History of American Radicalism*, ed. Alfred Young (DeKalb, 1976), 296–298.

164. Cornwallis to Turnbull, 5 October 1780, and Cornwallis to Alexander Leslie, 12 November 1780, in Franklin Wickwire and Mary Wickwire, *Cornwallis and the War of Independence* (London, 1971), 221.

165. Wickwire and Wickwire, *Cornwallis*, 186; Cornwallis to Brown and Wright, 21 July 1780, and Wright to Cornwallis, 20 August 1780, in *The Cornwallis Papers: The Campaigns of 1780 and 1781 in the Southern Theatre of the American Revolutionary War*, ed. Ian Saberton (Uckfield, 2010), 1:282, 2:300–302. Also see Robert Scott Davis, "Lord Montagu's Mission to South Carolina in 1781: American POWs for the King's Service in Jamaica," *SCHM* 84, no. 2 (April 1983): 92. Wright earlier received permission from Colonel Jacques Mark Prévost to augment his meager forces with fifty Georgians from the Continental prisons in Savannah. Fifteen of these deserted, contrary to Cornwallis's belief that they all had.

166. Ian Saberton, *The American Revolutionary War in the South: A Re-evaluation from a British Perspective in the Light of "The Cornwallis Papers"* (Tolworth, 2018), 2. Also see Robert Gray, "Col. Robert Gray's Observations on the War in Carolina," *SCGHM* 11 (July 1910): 139–159. Gray maintained that Loyalists comprised half the population of the southern backcountry.

167. O'Shaugnessy, *Men Who Lost America*, 189.

168. Robert Scott Davis, "1778: Loyalism and the Failure of the British Military

in the Southern Colonies," in *Proceedings of the South Carolina Historical Association* (2018), 65–78.

169. Cadwallader Colden to Dr. Myles Cooper or Isaac Wilkins, 4 September 1775, in Hoock, *Scars of Independence*, 434.

170. James Butler, Loyalist claim, in *BGLC*.

171. Clyde R. Ferguson, "Carolina and Georgia Patriot and Loyalist Militia in Action, 1778–1783," in Crow and Tise, *Southern Experience*, 180.

172. Pancake, *This Destructive War*, xiv.

173. Moultrie, *Memoirs*, 2:336; and Dr. Thomas Taylor to Rev. John Wesley, 28 February 1782, in SP.

174. John Dooly to General Samuel Elbert, 15 February 1779, in Coleman, "Restored Colonial Georgia," 7; Robert Scott Davis, "A Frontier for Pioneer Revolutionaries: John Dooly and the Beginnings of Popular Democracy in Original Wilkes County," *GHQ* 90, no. 3 (Fall 2006): 315–349; and Davis, "Civil War in the Midst of Revolution: Community Divisions and the Battle of Brier Creek, 1779," *GHQ* 100, no. 2 (2016): 136–159. Davis provides a thorough social history of the battle and its aftermath.

175. Prévost to Lincoln, 28 March 1779, in Piecuch, *Three Peoples*, 141.

176. Quoted in Howard, "Things Here Wear," 485.

177. Martha Condray Searcy, "1779: The First Year of the British Occupation of Georgia," *GHQ* 67 (Summer 1983): 168, 174, 188; Piecuch, *Three Peoples*, 6, 37–38; Smith, *Loyalists and Redcoats*, 29–31, 121–125, 168–169; and O'Shaughnessy, *Men Who Lost America*, 188–190.

178. Otis Ashmore and Charles Olmstead, "The Battles of Kettle Creek and Brier Creek," *GHQ* 10, no. 2 (June 1926): 85–125; Howard, "Things Here Wear," 484; and Robert Scott Davis, "Augusta in the Center: The Revolutionary War Battles of Kettle Creek and Shell Bluff," *Augusta Richmond County History* 49, no. 1 (Spring 2018): 17–29.

179. Smith, *Loyalists and Redcoats*, 102–113; and Ashmore and Olmstead, "Battles," 85–125.

180. Clinton to William Eden, 8 August 1779, in CP.

181. Howard, "Things Here Wear," 488.

182. Augustine Prévost to George Germain, 5 March 1779, in *GGCJ*, 1778–1779, 84–86.

183. Howard, "Things Here Wear," 495.

184. John Ashe to Richard Caswell, 3 April 1779, in Howard, "Things Here Wear," 496; and Ouzts, *Samuel Elbert*, esp. chaps. 2–3.

185. Wilson, *Southern Strategy*, 81–99. Wilson claims British casualties to be five killed and eleven wounded; Prévost reported an excess of 150 rebel deaths on the battlefield and untold scores drowned. The British took 227 prisoners (Wilson, *Southern Strategy*, 96).

186. *General Advertiser and Morning Intelligencer*, 3 July 1778; *St. James Chronicle*, 11 July 1778; see diary entry, 11 August 1778, in Hutchinson, *Diary and Letters*, 2:212–213; and *London Evening News*, 13 October 1778.

187. Memorial of Wright and John Graham to Germain, 17 July 1778, *ColRG*, 39:10–15. Also see Archibald Campbell to Germain, 16 January 1779, in *DAR*, 17:33–38.

188. Germain to Clinton, 27 September 1779, in Robert Barnwell, "Loyalism in South Carolina, 1765–1785" (PhD diss., Duke University, 1941), 157.

189. Wright to Germain, 6 January 1779, in *DAR*, 16:16. Also see 26 July 1779, in *GGCJ*, 1778–1779, 93–96.

190. Benjamin Quarles, *The Negro in the American Revolution* (Chapel Hill, 1961), 132. Also see John Bird, pension application S10372, Southern Campaigns American Revolution Pension Statements & Rosters, http://revwarapps.org/s10372.pdf.

191. Campbell to Germain, January 16, 1779, in *DAR*, 17:39–42. Campbell argued that maintaining military control of the government would be counterproductive to Britain's interests, as it would raise the ire of rebels and perhaps even Loyalists. See also Germain to Campbell, March 13, 1779, in Campbell, *Journal*, 80–81.

192. Wright to Hutchinson, 27 February 1779, in Furlong, "Civilian-Military Conflict," 422; Wright to Germain, 6 January 1779, in *DAR*, 16:16; *GGCJ*, 1778–1779, 44–45; Campbell to Germain, 16 January 1779, in *DAR*, 17:39–42.

193. Wright to Hutchinson, 27 February 1779, in Furlong, "Civilian-Military Conflict," 422; Mitchell, "Sir James Wright," 511; Germain to Wright, 8 March 1779, in *DAR*, 16:50. For the marriage of Wallace to Anne Wright, see *Pennsylvania Evening Post*, 21 August 1779. Germain informed Campbell that Wright had received orders to immediately prepare to return to Georgia. See Germain to Campbell, 13 March 1779, in Campbell, *Journal*, 81. In one letter, Wright wrote that he expected to sail for America aboard H.M.S. *Seymour*, commanded by Wallace. Wright to John Robinson, 11 March 1779, in AO, 13/37.

194. George Washington to Nicholas Cooke, 6 January 1776, in FO.

195. Germain to Knox, 12 March 1779, in Mitchell, "Sir James Wright," 511.

196. Mercy Otis Warren, *The History of the Rise, Progress, and Termination of the American Revolution* (Boston, 1805), 1:205; Wilson, *Southern Strategy*, 63–64; and Smith, *Loyalists and Redcoats*, 89–90.

197. Germain to Augustine Prévost, 13 March 1779, in *DAR*, 16:54; Germain to Commissioners for Quieting Disorders, 16 March 1779, in *DAR*, 16:55; Germain to Lords of the Admiralty, 18 March 1779, in *DAR*, 16:57; and Germain to Knox, 22 March 1779, in *DAR*, 16:61.

198. Wright to John Robinson, 2 March 1779, in James Wright, Loyalist claim, in *BGLC*.

199. Wright to Germain, fall 1782, in James Wright, Loyalist claim, in *BGLC*.

200. Germain to Wright, 31 March 1779, in *ColRG*, 38.2:155–159.

201. Wright to Hutchinson, 27 February 1779, in Furlong, "Civilian-Military Conflict," 422. Wright also wrote to Lord Germain on this same date and failed to mention his return. Also see Germain to Knox, 12 March 1779, in Mitchell, "James Wright," 511; Germain to Wright, 8 March 1779, in *DAR*, 16:50; Germain to Wright, 31 March 1779, in *DAR*, 17:90–92; Franklin to Charles-Guillaume-Frédéric Dumas, 26 July 1780, in FO. Franklin could speak with some confidence, as he had recently heard that the British forces in Georgia had been confined to Savannah. See Thomas Digges to Franklin, 11 June 1779, in FO. Also see James Madison to William Bradford, from Williamsburg, 5 November 1779, in FO. For the marriage of Wallace to Anne Wright, see *GGCJ*, 1778–1779; James Wright, Loyalist claim, in *BGLC*; *Rivington's Royal Gazette*, 18 August 1779; Germain to Wright, 31 March 1779, in *DAR*, 17:90–92.

202. Germain to Wright, 31 March 1779, in *DAR*, 17:90–92. See also James Wright to George Germain, February 12, 1777, in Mitchell, "Sir James Wright," 512–518.

203. Wright departed Portsmouth on 1 May. See *Morning Chronicle* (London), 4 May 1779.

## Chapter 7. A Governor Redeemed?

1. *London Monthly Magazine*, 1 January 1818.

2. Leslie Hall, *Land & Allegiance in Revolutionary Georgia* (Athens, 2001), xiii. Another historian has focused on the inherent problems facing an occupying force amid the turmoil of a civil war. See Martha Condray Searcy, "1779: The First Year of the British Occupation of Georgia," *GHQ* 67, no. 2 (1983): 168–188. She argued that if the British "had done in 1776 what they proposed to do in 1778, they might very well have succeeded" (80).

3. Wright to Germain, 9 August 1779, in *ColRG*, 38.2:197–199; and Kenneth Coleman, *The American Revolution in Georgia, 1763–1789* (Athens, 1958), 125.

4. Robert Scott Davis, "A Georgia Loyalist's Perspective on the American Revolution: The Letters of Dr. Thomas Taylor," *GHQ* 81, no. 1 (Spring 1997): 123.

5. Wright to Germain, 31 July 1779, in *ColRG*, 38.2:168–179. For Germain's reply, see Germain to Wright, 27 October 1779, in *ColRG*, 38.2:204–205. Germain wrote that his joy upon learning of Wright's safe arrival "was much lessened" by the "distressed state" of affairs in Georgia.

6. For Wright's return, see Wright to Germain, 31 July 1779, *DAR*, 17:171; and Wright to Germain, 1 August 1779, in *GGCJ*, 1778–1779, 110–111. Also see, for example, James Marcus Prévost to Germain, 14 April 1779, in *DAR*, 16:80, in which Prévost stated that the rebels were in control of the backcountry. Major General Prévost concurred. See A. Prévost to Clinton, 14 July 1779, in *DAR*, 16:134; Brigadier General Augustine Prévost to Clinton, 30 July 1779, in *Report on American Manuscripts in the Royal Institution of Great Britain* (Dublin, 1899–1906), 1:483. Prévost also notified Clinton that Wright had arrived and complained of his own "ill health" and "wish[ed] the management [of the province] in hands more equal to it" than his own. See Wright to Clinton, 30 July 1779, in *DAR*, 16:163; Wright to Clinton, 30 July 1779, in *DAR*, 1:483; Wright to Germain, 31 July 1779, in *DAR*, 17:171; George Killian and Charles Waller, *Georgia and the Revolution* (Atlanta, 1975), 192–193; Wright to Clinton, 7 August 1779, in *DAR*, 16:163; Clinton to Germain, 21 August 1779, in *DAR*, 17:189–191; and Wright to Germain, 9 August 1779, in *DAR*, 17:185–186.

7. Thomas Pinckney to William Johnson, 27 July 1822, in Thomas Pinckney, "IV—General Gate's Southern Campaign," *Historical Magazine* 10 (August 1866): 244–253. Pinckney also claimed that d'Estaing had "no other qualifications for command" (252).

8. D'Estaing to M. de Sartine, n.d., quoted in Alexander A. Lawrence, *Storm over Savannah: The Story of Count d'Estaing and the Siege of the Town in 1779* (Savannah, 1979), 14. Also see Charles Moran, "D'Estaing, an Early Exponent of Amphibious Warfare," *Military Affairs* 9, no. 4 (1945): 314–332.

9. George P. Clark, "The Role of the Haitian Volunteers at Savannah in 1779: An Attempt at an Objective View," *Phylon* 41 (December 1980): 360; Benjamin Lincoln to d'Estaing, 1 September 1779, in Gregory Massey, *John Laurens and the American Revolution* (Columbia, 2000), 50; "Journal of Major General Lincoln from September 3 to October 19, 1779," in Kennedy, *Muskets*, 121–127; Wright to Germain, 5 November 1779,

in *GHS Coll*, 3:262–268 (hereafter "Wright's Diary"); Captain John Henry's account of the siege is in Killian and Waller, *Georgia and the Revolution*, 209; and the *London Gazette*, 21 December 1779. There are many primary accounts of the siege of Savannah, including a variety of French, Loyalist, and rebel entries in Kennedy, *Muskets*; "An English Journal of the Siege of Savannah in 1779," *Historical Magazine* 8 (1864): 12–16; "Papers Relating to the Allied Attack on Savannah in 1779," *Historical Magazine* 8 (September 1864): 290–297; "The Siege of Savannah 1779, as Related by Colonel John Harris Cruger," *Magazine of American History* 2 (August 1878): 489–492; Henry Steele Commager and Richard B. Morris, *Spirit of Seventy-Six: The Story of the American Revolution as Told by Participants* (New York, 1968), 1090–1097; and "Account of the Siege of Savannah, from a British Source," in *GHS Coll*, 5.1:129–139. These accounts are in essential agreement concerning dates and basic facts, although the dates in Cruger's account are typically a day or two off. Although specific citations from these accounts would be applicable henceforth, I have decided, for the sake of brevity, against such an application, and I refer the reader to the "Account of the Siege of Savannah, from a British Source." In addition to these print collections, also see "The Siege of Savannah, 1779," and "The Siege of Savannah," Lincoln Papers, Emmet Collection, New York Public Library; and Benjamin Lincoln's diary of the siege, in MS 3478, Kenneth Coleman Papers, Hargrett Library, University of Georgia, Athens. For the best historical treatment of the siege of Savannah, see Lawrence, *Storm*. Also see Benjamin Franklin Hough, *Siege of Savannah, by the Combined American and French Forces, under the Command of Gen. Lincoln and the Count d'Estaing, in the Autumn of 1779* (Spartanburg, 1975); Ronald Freeman, *Savannah under Siege* (Savannah, 2002); and "Prévost's Journal of the Siege of Savannah," Prévost to Germain, 1 November 1779, in Kennedy, *Muskets*, 93.

10. Clinton to Prévost, 9 September 1779, in Lawrence, *Storm*, 18; and from a letter dated 8 November 1779 by a Scottish merchant then garrisoned at Savannah, also in Lawrence, *Storm*, 18.

11. Moultrie to Benjamin Lincoln, 26 September 1779, in William Moultrie, *Memoirs of the American Revolution* (New York, 1802), 2:33–35.

12. Jim Piecuch, *Three Peoples, One King: Loyalists, Indians, and Slaves in the Revolutionary South* (Columbia, 2008), 146–148; and Chief Justice Anthony Stokes to his wife, 9 November 1779, in Kennedy, *Muskets*, 108–116. D'Estaing's arrival also caused much angst in the Board of Trade; many observers believed the board would have fallen if the siege had been successful. See Herbert Butterfield, *George III, Lord North, and the People* (New York, 1968), chap. 4.

13. George Walton to John Houstoun, 30 September 1779, in *GGCJ*, 1778–1779, 164.

14. William Bingham to Benjamin Franklin, 28 August 1779, in FO. Bingham assured Franklin of d'Estaing's readiness to aid the rebels. In his personal correspondence with him, Bingham wrote, "He always expressed an eager desire of rendering us" great assistance. Also see Madison to Bradford, 5 November 1779, in National Archives and Records Administration, FO.

15. Coleman, *American Revolution*, 129; "Proceedings," 20 October 1779, in *JCC*, 15:1191–1193; Laurens to Washington, 24 October 1779, in *PHL*, 15:195–198; "Chaplain Waldeck's account," 11 October 1779, in *Enemy Views: The American Revolutionary War*

*as Recorded by the Hessian Participants*, ed. Bruce Burgoyne (Bowie, 1996), 312. At the time, Waldeck was stationed in Pensacola (the capital of British West Florida) with the Third Waldeck Regiment.

16. See Lawrence, *Storm*, 59–60; and Moran, "D'Estaing."

17. Louis-Antoine de Bougainville's journal, in Lawrence, *Storm*, 58.

18. "Chaplain Waldeck's account," 312; "Summons," 6 September 1779, in *GHS Coll*, 10:49–50; Wright to Germain, 5 November 1779, in *DAR*, 17:252–253; Wright to Tonyn, 11 September 1779, in CP. One account, however, states the number to be about half the number Wright mentioned. See *Rivington's Royal Gazette*, 11 December 1779. Some enslavers failed to send the requested slaves. For those on Hutchinson Island, see Lawrence, *Storm*, 53. Historian Peter Voelz noted that the employment of Blacks in the raising of military fortifications was quite rare in British North America during the seventeenth century. Voelz, *Slave and Soldier: The Military Impact of Blacks in the Colonial Americas* (New York, 1993), 66–67. Also see Benjamin Quarles, *The Negro in the American Revolution* (Chapel Hill, 1961), 135 (for the figure of one thousand), 142–146; Piecuch, *Three Peoples*, 169; Sylvia Frey, *Water from the Rock: Black Resistance in a Revolutionary Age* (Princeton, 1992), 96–98; Philip D. Morgan, "Lowcountry Georgia and the Early Modern Atlantic World, 1733–1820," in *African American Life in the Georgia Lowcountry: The Atlantic World and the Gullah Geechee*, ed. Philip D. Morgan (Athens, 2010), 36; and Cassandra Pybus, *Epic Journeys of Freedom: Runaway Slaves of the American Revolution and Their Global Quest for Liberty* (Boston, 2006), 37–38. For a brief character sketch of Handley, see Pybus, *Epic Journeys*, 211–212. For more on Handley's regiment, see A. B. Ellis, *History of the First West India Regiment* (London, 1885), chap. 1.

19. While prospects for the enslaved were better under the British banner, it must be noted that the prospects for some, if not many, were still quite bleak. The British offered land and human property as an enticement for would-be Loyalists and as thanks to Loyalists and militia officers, and they even sold the enslaved, using the proceeds to purchase supplies. Clinton's Philipsburg Proclamation is in *Proceedings of the Massachusetts Historical Society* 6 (1863): 219. Also see Frey, *Water*, 130–131; Leslie Hall, *Land and Allegiance* (Athens, 2001); Don Higginbotham, *War of American Independence: Military Attitudes, Policies, and Practice, 1763–1789* (Boston, 1971), 354–357; Piecuch, *Three Peoples*, 220; Ricardo A. Herrera, "The King's Friends: Loyalists in British Strategy," in *Strategy in the American War of Independence: A Global Approach*, ed. Donald Stoker, Kenneth Hagan, and Michael McMaster (Routledge, 2010), 101–119; Andrew Jackson O'Shaughnessy, *The Men Who Lost America: British Leadership, the American Revolution, and the Fate of the Empire* (New Haven, 2013), 263–263; Gary Nash, *The Unknown American Revolution: The Unruly Birth of Democracy and the Struggle to Create America* (New York, 2006), 329–331; and Holger Hoock, *Scars of Independence: America's Violent Birth* (New York, 2017), 300.

20. Clyde R. Ferguson, "General Andrew Pickens" (PhD diss., Duke University, 1960), 93–94; and Wright to Germain, 4 April 1780, in *GHS Coll*, 3:281.

21. Alan Gilbert, *Black Patriots and Loyalists: Fighting for Emancipation in the War for Independence* (Chicago, 2012), 152, 179. Also see Judith L. Van Buskirk, *Standing in Their Own Light: African American Patriots in the American Revolution* (Norman, 2017);

and Douglas R. Egerton, *Death or Liberty: African Americans and Revolutionary America* (New York, 2009).

22. "Council held at His Excellency's House," 23 October 1779, and "Council held at His Excellency's House," 28 December 1779, in *GHS Coll*, 10:53–55, 74–75.

23. 26 July 1779, in *GGCJ, 1778–1779*, 93. Historian Donnie Bellamy has argued that free Blacks never constituted more than 1 percent of Georgia's population. Donnie Bellamy, "The Legal Status of Black Georgians during the Colonial and Revolutionary Years," *Journal of Negro History* 74, no. 1–4 (Winter–Fall 1989): 1.

24. Olaudah Equiano, *The Interesting Narrative of the Life of Olaudah Equiano* (London, 1794), 165, 232.

25. Nash, *Unknown American Revolution*, 330–335; and Quarles, *Negro*, chap. 7.

26. Bernard Uhlendorf, trans. and ed., *The Siege of Charleston: Capts. Johann Ewald, Johann Hinrichs, and Maj. Gen. Christoph von Huyn* (New York, 1968), 183–186. Wright recorded the number as "400 to 500" ("Wright's Diary," 262). Also see J. J. Zubly to Wright, 30 November 1779, in Lilla Hawes, *The Journal of the Reverend John Joachim Zubly, A.M., D.D., March 5, 1770 through June 22, 1781* (Savannah, 1989), 108–109. Zubly also outlined the great loss of his personal property during the siege and noted that "our place of worship which we had but just repaired at considerable expense was made use of during the siege as a magazine which brought it upon heavy fire from the enemy." Additionally, Zubly mentioned that his brick home, "one of the best in the place, had for near twelve months been made use of [as] an hospital & is almost totally ruined." In both instances, Zubly filed petitions for their "restoration and repair" (108).

27. Egerton, *Death or Liberty*, 152; Piecuch, *Three Peoples*, 9.

28. William Prince, Loyalist claim, in *BGLC*.

29. Frey, *Water*, 45–46.

30. Nash, *Race and Revolution* (Madison, 1990), 57; Maya Jasanoff, *Liberty's Exiles: American Loyalists in the Revolutionary World* (New York, 2012), 70; Frey, *Water*, 86, 51. She credits Henry Laurens with this estimate. See also Quarles, *Negro*; and Benjamin Quarles, "The Revolutionary War as a Black Declaration of Independence," in *Slavery and Freedom in the Age of the American Revolution*, ed. Ira Berlin and Ronald Hoffman (Urbana, 1986), 283–304; Morgan, "Lowcountry Georgia," 5; Ellen Gibson Wilson, *The Loyal Blacks* (New York, 1976), 3; Peter Wood, "Dream Deferred," in *In Resistance: Studies in African, Caribbean, and Afro-American History*, ed. Gary Okihiro (Amherst, 1986), 173; and Lathan Windley, *Runaway Slave Advertisements: A Documentary History from the 1730s to 1790* (Westport, 1983).

31. Ira Berlin, *Many Thousands Gone: The First Two Centuries of Slavery in North America* (Cambridge, 2000), 11–12, 217–357 (for slave agency); Andrew Billingsley, *Mighty Like a River: The Black Church and Social Reform* (New York, 1999), 14–16; Frey, *Water*; Quarles, *Negro*; and Quarles, "The Revolutionary War"; W. E. B. Du Bois, *Black Reconstruction: An Essay toward a History of the Part in Which Black Folk Played in the Attempt to Reconstruct Democracy in America, 1860–1880* (New York, 1935). Temporally distant from these events, Du Bois's work is appropriate in this context. For the opposite argument, see Stanley Elkins, *Slavery: A Problem in American Institutional and Intellectual Life* (Chicago, 1968). Elkins believed that the trauma associated with slavery resulted in a psychological helplessness, rendering slaves unable to rebel. Also see

Ira Berlin, introduction to Berlin and Hoffman, *Slavery and Freedom*, xv. Berlin also rightly observed that the revolution "gave rise to a new slave order on the frontier" (xxii). Also see Duncan MacLeod, *Slavery, Race, and the American Revolution* (New York, 1974), 8; MacLeod, "Toward Caste," in Berlin and Hoffman, *Slavery and Freedom*, 217–236; Philip D. Morgan, "Black Society in the Lowcountry, 1760–1810," in Berlin and Hoffman, *Slavery and Freedom*, 83–142.

32. Wright to Germain, July 31, 1779, in *ColRG*, 38.2:180–195. Wright also made note of perhaps as many as two hundred slaves from South Carolina who had been brought to Savannah by the Creeks. Also see Frey, *Water*, 94–95; Piecuch, *Three Peoples*, 167–168; and "Proceedings," 26 July 1779, in *ColRG*, 12:443–449.

33. "Proceedings," 26 July 1779, in *ColRG*, 12:443–449.

34. A. Prévost to Clinton, 9 September 1779, in *GGCJ*, 1779–1779, 89.

35. Lawrence, *Storm*, 31; "Journal of the Siege of Savannah," Francis Rush Clark Papers, Sol Feinstone Collection, DLAR (hereafter cited as "Clark's Journal"). Also see "An English Journal," 12; *Rivington's Royal Gazette*, 15 December 1779; Hough, *Siege of Savannah*, 59; "Wright's Diary," 262–263; Wright to Patrick Tonyn, 11 September 1779, in CP.

36. Robert Baillie, Loyalist claim, in *BGLC*. George Baillie had also been captured by the French "and underwent a most disagreeable confinement" (George Baille, Loyalist claim, in *BGLC*).

37. Lawrence, *Storm*, 57. Governor Wright previously noted that the weather at this time of year was "generally very pleasant." See Wright to Dartmouth, 20 September 1773, in *GGCJ*, 1772–1773, 156–162.

38. Coleman, *American Revolution*, 136–137.

39. Translation of the German text quoted in Lawrence, *Storm*, 17.

40. Rodney Atwood, *The Hessians: Mercenaries from Hesse-Kassel in the American Revolution* (New York, 1980), 168–169; and Joseph Tustin, trans., *Diary of the American War: A Hessian Journal* (New Haven, 1979), 183–186. Wright's account of the preparation for the assault is in full accord with Ewald's. See "Wright's Diary," 262–263.

41. Ricardo Herrera, email communication, 1 February 2022.

42. Prévost to Clinton, 9 September 1779, in *ColRG*, 39:254–255.

43. Wright to Tonyn, 11 September 1779, in CP.

44. "Address of the Judges & Inhabitants of Georgia," 20 May 1780, in *GHS Coll*, 3:300–301.

45. John Harris Cruger, "The Siege of Savannah 1779, as Related by Colonel John Harris Cruger," *Magazine of American History* 2 (August 1878): 489–492.

46. "Proceedings," 11 July 1780, in *GHS Coll*, 10:112–113.

47. Affidavit of John Murray, 7 June 1780, in Lawrence, *Storm*, 26.

48. Prévost to Admiral John Byron, 9 September 1779, in CO, 5/131.

49. Augustine Prévost to Germain, 14 April 1779, in *GGCJ*, 1778–1779, 86–88. Prévost reiterated the concern later in the letter. Tybee Island also housed the Lazaretto, a two-story house used to quarantine the recently arrived enslaved. See Darold Wax, "New Negroes Are Always in Demand," *GHQ* 68, no. 2 (1984): 204.

50. See, for example, John Rutledge to d'Estaing, 12 October 1779, in Lawrence, *Storm*, 90.

51. "Prévost's Journal," 94. See also Comte d'Estaing, "Journal of the Siege of Savannah, with some observations by M. le comte d'Estaing," in Kennedy, *Muskets*, 47 (hereafter cited as "D'Estaing's Journal"); and A. Prévost to Germain, 10 September 1779, in *DAR*, 17:242–243. This letter, along with a lengthy daily journal of the siege, is also in "Prévost's Journal," 92–105. Also see Francis Henry Harris to Benjamin Lincoln, from Charleston, 1 November 1779, Miscellaneous MSS, EM 20130, Lincoln Papers. This letter details Wright's 1776 parole violation and the hopes that the "British commander will render him up."

52. Casimir Pulaski to Congress, 19 August 1779, in *The Executive Documents of the Senate of the United States* (Washington, D.C., 1887), 1:27–30.

53. *South Carolina and American General Gazette*, 17 September 1779.

54. Rutledge and Lincoln to d'Estaing, 5 September 1779, in Lawrence, *Storm*, 31.

55. Lawrence, *Storm*, 31–32.

56. Clay to John Lewis Gervais, 22 September 1779, in *GHS Coll*, 8:142–145.

57. D'Estaing to M. de Sartine, 5 December 1779, in Lawrence, *Storm*, 42.

58. Joseph Habersham to Isabella Rae Habersham, 28 September 1779, in Lawrence, *Storm*, 42.

59. Clay to William Palfrey, 27 September 1779, in *GHS Coll*, 8:142–144; and Clay to John Lewis Gervais, 28 September and 1 October 1779, in *GHS Coll*, 8:145–147, 147–148.

60. Information given by Two Merchants, September 1779, in *FM*, no. 2013.

61. "Count d'Estaing's Notes on O'Connor's Journal of the Siege of Savannah," in Lawrence, *Storm*, 21.

62. All quotes in Lawrence, *Storm*, 38.

63. Alexander Garden, *Anecdotes of the American Revolution* (Charleston, 1828), 108.

64. Prévost to L. V. Fuser, 11 September 1779, in Lawrence, *Storm*, 25.

65. "Journal of an anonymous French naval officer," in Commager and Morris, *Spirit*, 1091–1093; "Journal of Major General Lincoln," 122–123; "Wright's Diary," 263–264; Lawrence, *Storm*, 21–22; Charles Colcock Jones, *The Siege of Savannah in 1779* (Albany, 1874), 58–60; and *South Carolina & American General Gazette*, 17 September 1779.

66. Count d'Estaing to Prévost, 16 September 1779, in *Georgia and the Revolution*, by Ronald Killion and Charles Waller (Atlanta, 1975), 194–195; "D'Estaing's Journal," 49. General Lincoln remonstrated with d'Estaing for demanding that the British surrender to the king of France. "Journal of Major General Lincoln," 123; and "D'Estaing's Journal," 50–51. Also see "Wright's Diary," 263. For d'Estaing's actual summons and the negotiations, see "Papers Relating," 294. Lieutenant Colonel John Harris Cruger added that d'Estaing also placed the blame for any future loss of life and property squarely on Prévost's shoulders. Prévost to d'Estaing, 16 September 1779, and D'Estaing to Prévost, 16 September 1779, in Killion and Waller, *Georgia*, 195–196. For the junction between the allied armies, see Lincoln to Major Everard Meade, 1 November 1779, in Lincoln Papers.

67. "Chaplain Waldeck's account," 29 October 1779, in Burgoyne, *Enemy Views*, 316.

68. Samuel Douglass, Loyalist claim, in *BGLC*.

69. Lawrence, *Storm*, 33.

70. Prévost to d'Estaing, 16 September 1779, in Killion and Waller, *Georgia*, 196; "Cruger's Siege," 490; *Boston Gazette*, 15 November 1779; Samuel Douglas, Loyalist

claim, in *BGLC*; and Lawrence, *Storm*, 20. See David K. Wilson, *The Southern Strategy: Britain's Conquest of South Carolina and Georgia, 1775–1780* (Columbia, 2005), 180, concerning the size of Maitland's force. For the invaluable aid provided by the Gullah fisherman, see Quarles, *Negro*, 145. Also see "Notes from the Observations of Count d'Estaing on M. O'Conner's Journal of the Siege of Savannah," in *FM*, 519–523, no. 2018. Regarding the discord between the rebels and the French concerning the failure to stop Maitland, see Lawrence, *Storm*, 46–53.

71. D'Estaing to Chevalier Durumain, 20 September 1779, in Lawrence, *Storm*, 34.

72. Jean-Denis G. G. Lepage, *French Fortifications, 1715–1815: An Illustrated History* (Jefferson, 2010), 82. The author states: "Standard protocol dictated that the attackers demand the surrender . . . , but it was expected that this would be rejected for reason of honor," if only temporarily. Moreover, the "formalized 'rules' of siege warfare [maintained that] a garrison should be allowed to surrender with honor." Also see Jones, *Siege of Savannah*, 58–60; Commager and Morris, *Spirit*, 1091–1093; Richard Cole, "The Siege of Savannah and the British Press, 1779–1780," *GHQ* 65, no. 3 (Fall 1981): 195; and Wright to Germain, 5 November 1779, in *GHS Coll*, 3:260–262.

73. "James Wright's Journal," in *GHS Coll*, 5.1:132; Elizabeth Lichtenstein Johnston, *Recollections of a Georgia Loyalist* (New York, 1901), 16; Major T. W. Moore to unknown, 4 November 1779, in Hough, *Siege of Savannah*, 82–85.

74. Garden, *Anecdotes*, 109.

75. John Graham affidavit, AO, 12/4. Graham was the provincial lieutenant governor before and after independence had been declared. He returned with Wright in July 1779 at the urging of Wright, who deemed "his personal presence in Georgia . . . essential to the King's Service." The quote comes from Graham's Loyalist claim, in *BGLC*. For "unanimous," see "Wright's Diary," 264. For the importance of Wright's opinion, see Lorenzo Sabine, *Biographical Sketches of Loyalists of the American Revolution* (Boston, 1864), 2:458.

76. Wright to Germain, 4 November 1779, in *GHS Coll*, 3:287–288; and Colonel James Moncrief's evidence for James Wright's Loyalist claim, in *BGLC*. See also Moncrief's evidence for John Graham's Loyalist claim, in *BGLC*.

77. *RGG*, 18 November 1779; Elizabeth Lichtenstein Johnston for John Graham's Loyalty claim, in *BGLC*; Prévost to d'Estaing, 17 September 1779, in Killion and Waller, *Georgia*, 197; and Charles Colcock Jones Jr., *The History of Georgia* (Boston, 1883), 2:379–383.

78. Wright to Germain, 5 November 1779, *GHS Coll*, 3:260–262.

79. Henry Lee, *Memoirs of the War in the Southern Department of the United States* (Washington, D.C., 1827), 54.

80. Lawrence, *Storm*, 38.

81. Ron Chernow, *George Washington: A Life* (New York, 2010), 348.

82. Lawrence, *Storm*, 40; "Cruger's Journal," 2:490. It should be noted that Cruger's account was written on 8 November 1779. Also see "D'Estaing's Journal," 50; D'Estaing to Lincoln, September 17, 1779, "Journal of Major General Lincoln"; "Clark's Journal," 123–124; and Henry Lumpkin, *From Savannah to Yorktown: The American Revolution in the South* (Columbia, 1981), 33.

83. "Chaplain Waldeck's account," October 29, 1779, in Burgoyne, *Enemy Views*, 316.

84. Stokes to his wife, 9 November 1779, in Kennedy, *Muskets*, 108–116; and "Wright's Diary," 264. Although historians have generally lambasted the admiral's indecision, two of the most well versed historians on the subject of the siege, Alexander Lawrence and David Wilson, stand staunchly in his corner. See Lawrence, *Storm*, 87–93; and Wilson, *Southern Strategy*, esp. 139. Also see A. Prévost to Germain, 1 November 1779, in "Papers Relating," 292. The French losses were not quite as substantial as Wright had heard. The actual tally included twelve officers and eighty-five men killed and wounded. See "Wright's Diary," 264; and *RGG*, 18 November 1779.

85. Clark, "Role," 356–366; Quarles, *The Negro*, 143–150; Robert Scott Davis, "Black Haitian Soldiers at the Siege of Savannah," *Journal of the American Revolution*, https://allthingsliberty.com/2021/02/black-haitian-soldiers-at-the-siege-of-savannah/. See also Patricia Bradley, *Slavery, Propaganda, and the American Revolution* (Jackson, 1998), 23.

86. *Rivington's Royal Gazette*, 11 August 1781 and 20 December 1779, in *The Diary and Letters of His Excellency Thomas Hutchinson, Esq.*, ed. Peter Orlando Hutchinson (London, 1883), 2:313.

87. D'Estaing informed General Lincoln that the capture of the *Experiment* would "prevent assistance from reaching the garrison at Savannah" (September [no exact date] 1779, in Lincoln Papers). Also see Henry Remsem to Governor [George?], from Morristown, 28 October 1779, in Booth's History of New York, EM 10851, Lincoln Papers; *Morning Post and Daily Advertiser*, 1 March 1780. D'Estaing noted that Wallace was captured with "30,000 pounds sterling in piasters" and some twenty-two hundred barrels of foodstuffs. See "D'Estaing's Journal," 60. Also see Anthony Stokes to his wife, 9 November 1779, in Kennedy, *Muskets*, 114–115; "Chaplain Waldeck's account," 29 October 1779, in Burgoyne, *Enemy Views*, 316; *Morning Chronicle and London Advertiser*, 14 February 1780. Surely, then, Wright would have known by this date. See also *GGJC*, 1780, 144.

88. Phillipe Séguier de Terson, "Journal of the events and proceedings, in the campaign of M. le comte d'Estaing, I myself on board the *Robuste*, commanded by M. de Grasse, commodore," in Kennedy, *Muskets*, 17. Also see "D'Estaing's Journal," 56–57.

89. For McIntosh, see *Storm over Savannah*, 159; Johnston, *Recollections*, 60.

90. "The Siege of Savannah 1779, as Related by Colonel John Harris Cruger," *Magazine of American History* 2 (August 1878): 490–491; "Wright's Diary," 265; Stokes to his wife, 1 November 1779, in Kennedy, *Muskets*, 108–116. This letter is also contained in *Diary of the American Revolution*, ed. Frank Moore (New York, 1969), 2:224–228. For the pen, see Paul Pressly, *On the Rim of the Caribbean: Colonial Georgia and the British Atlantic World* (Athens, 2013), 127.

91. Augustine Prévost, journal entry, 4 October 1779, in *DAR*, 17:246.

92. Samuel Douglass, John Fox, James Wright Jr., and James Graham, among many others, Loyalist claims, all in *BGLC*.

93. "Wright's Diary," 265.

94. George Washington to the New York Convention, 17 August 1776, in *FO*.

95. "Cruger's Siege," 491; Johnston, *Recollections*, 58–59; John Graham, Loyalist claim, in *BGLC*. Also see A. Prévost, journal entry, 4 October 1779, in *DAR*, 17:246; "Wright's Diary," 265; Lawrence, *Storm*, 51; and Moses Buffington to Peter Buffington, 8 December 1779, in "Moses Buffington Revolutionary War letter," GHS 0101, GHS. Repairing

the damage from the attack on the town occupied Wright's energies throughout the remainder of the war. See 29 June and 28 August 1780, *GGCJ*, 1780, 22, 26.

96. T. W. Moore to his wife, 4 November 1779, in Hough, *Siege of Savannah*, 84.

97. Anthony Stokes to his wife, 9 November 1779, in Moore, *Diary*, 749–757. In addition, Stokes "lost eight negroes." Anthony Stokes, Loyalist claim, *BGLC*.

98. Lawrence, *Storm*, 50.

99. Anthony Stokes to his wife, 9 November 1779, in Moore, *Diary*, 749–757.

100. John Jones to Mary Jones, 3 October 1779, in *HCG*, 535. These were the grandparents of planter and historian Charles Colcock Jones, who wrote numerous books about Savannah and Georgia, including one about the siege of Savannah. He is a central character in Erskine Clarke, *Dwelling Place: A Plantation Epic* (New Haven, 2005); and Manson Myers, *Children of Pride: A True Story of Georgia and the Civil War* (New Haven, 1972).

101. John Jones to Mary Jones, 4 October 1779, in *HCG*, 535–536.

102. John Jones to Mary Jones, 7 October 1779, in *HCG*, 536. Major Moore confirmed this: "The town was torn to pieces. . . . [N]othing but shrieks from women and children [could] be heard" (Lawrence, *Storm*, 52).

103. Mary Jones to John Jones, n.d., in *HCG*, 537.

104. Petition of Catherine Eirick to A. Prévost, 12 January 1780, in Georgia Loyalist Supporters of the King's Cause, CL. This letter was furnished by historian Robert Scott Davis.

105. Johnston, *Recollections*, 52, 58.

106. "Wright's Diary," 265. Nineteenth-century historian Charles Colcock Jones Jr. wrote: "In order to avoid the projectiles," Wright and Lieutenant Governor John Graham "moved out of the town and occupied a tent next to Maitland's" (*Siege of Savannah*, 25).

107. Lawrence, *Storm*, 60.

108. *Monthly Magazine* (London), 1 January 1818. No extant Wright correspondence can verify the veracity of this account.

109. *Royal Georgia Gazette*, 18 November 1779; and "Wright's Diary," 265. Two more men were killed, and nine additional men received wounds of varying degrees.

110. Lawrence, *Storm*, 51.

111. A. Prévost to Germain, November 1, 1779, in "Papers Relating," 293.

112. A. Prévost to Germain, 1 November 1779, in "Papers Relating," 296; and Benjamin Lincoln and Count d'Estaing to Major General Prévost, 6 October 1779, in *HGC*, 351–352.

113. *RGG*, 18 November 1779; and "Wright's Diary," 265. Two more men were killed; nine additional men received wounds of varying degrees. See Lawrence, *Storm*, 51–52. Also see Anthony Stokes, *A Narrative of the Official Conduct of Anthony Stokes* (London, 1784), 50.

114. "Wright's Diary," 265.

115. Alured Clarke to Loyalist Commission, 27 May 1787, in James Wright Jr., Loyalist claim, in *BGLC*.

116. "Wright's Diary," 265; and "Clark's Journal." The 12 December 1779 edition of *Rivington's Royal Gazette* erroneously reported Captain Simpson's death as having oc-

curred on 18 October 1779. In August Major Wright placed an ad for "all spirited young men" who sought "an opportunity of distinguishing themselves." A five-guinea bounty was offered. See *RGG*, 5 August 1779. Wright "expended several hundred pounds in raising men" for this regiment. See Wright Jr. to George Street, 19 February 1789, in James Wright Jr., Loyalist claim, in *BGLC*.

117. D'Estaing to Chevalier Durumain, 20 September 1779, in Lawrence, *Storm*, 60. Writing weeks before the final battle, he predicted how it must end.

118. David Hopkins to Charles Sims, 8 October 1779, in Laura Hopkins, *Lower Richland Planters: Hopkins, Adams, Weston, and Related Families of South Carolina* (Charlottesville, 1976), 105.

119. For d'Estaing's general orders for 8 and 9 October, see Lincoln Papers. For the specific plan of operations for the attack, see Benjamin Lincoln and Count d'Estaing, document, October 1779, in Lincoln Papers. Also see "Wright's Diary," 266; "D'Estaing's Journal," 65; Augustine Prévost to Germain, 1 November 1779, in "Papers Relating," 292. Philip Mazzei later informed Thomas Jefferson that the "villainy of one of our officers from New-England ... deserted and informed the enemy" of d'Estaing's plans. Mazzei to Jefferson, 18 December 1779, and Mazzei to Jefferson, 8 January 1780, in FO.

120. All quotes in Lawrence, *Storm*, 69–70.

121. For the weather, see "Wright's Diary," 266. Also see Lawrence, *Storm*, 80–81.

122. Atwood, *Hessians*, 243. Wright later expressed doubts about the "foreigner" von Porbeck's ability to command the British soldiers in Savannah. See Lt. Col. Alured Clarke to Charles Cornwallis, 6 April 1781, and Wright to Cornwallis, 2 April 1781, in *The Cornwallis Papers: The Campaigns of 1780 and 1781 in the Southern Theatre of the American Revolutionary War*, ed. Ian Saberton (East Sussex, 2010), 5:334–335. Also see L'Enfant to George Washington, 18 February 1782, in FO. L'Enfant had been wounded at Savannah. See Elizabeth Kite, *Brigadier-General Louis Lebègue Duportail, Commandant of Engineers in the Continental Army, 1777–1783* (Baltimore, 1933), 250.

123. "Wright's Diary," 266. For the laudatory comment regarding the Loyalists, see "Case of Sir James Wright," MS 884, Sir James Wright Papers, GHS. Also see Wright to Germain, 5 November 1779, in "Wright's Diary," 261; "Wright's Diary," 267; and "Clark's Journal." Pulaski died at sea on 11 October en route to Charleston. See *South Carolina and American General Gazette*, 29 October 1779. Historian Charles Royster believed Pulaski's desire for battlefield glory compelled him to recklessly pursue an ill-advised attack on that fateful day. See Royster, *A Revolutionary People at War: The Continental Army and American Character, 1775–1783* (Chapel Hill, 1979), 206. For more concerning d'Estaing's wound, see Mazzei to Jefferson, 9 January 1780, in FO. Mazzei wrote that d'Estaing could not yet "stand without crutches" and had received a "joyous reception" in France. See "D'Estaing's Journal," 72; and Sylvia Frey, "The British and the Black: A New Perspective," *The Historian* 38, no. 2 (1976): 230.

124. *RGG*, 12 October 1779.

125. *GHS Coll*, 11:13.

126. Lawrence, *Storm*, 79.

127. Wright to Germain, 5 November 1779, in *GHS Coll*, 3:262–268.

128. L. V. Fuser to Clinton, 30 October 1779, in Lawrence, *Storm*, 71.

129. Lawrence, *Storm*, 81. Also see Wilson, *Southern Strategy*, 181–182. These totals reflect the casualties for 9 October alone. For the entire siege, the allies suffered about 941, compared to 103 for the British and Loyalists. See also Howard Peckham, ed., *The Toll of Independence: Engagements & Battle Casualties of the American Revolution* (Chicago, 1974), 65. Peckham determined that the British lost forty killed, sixty-two wounded, and forty-eight deserted. "The most reliable figures seem to be 183 killed and 454 wounded among the French. There is also great variation in the American count, but a total of 457 killed and wounded seems authentic."

130. Lawrence, *Storm*, 80, 87.

131. John Ferling, *John Adams: A Life* (New York, 2010), 224.

132. Lawrence, *Storm*, 69.

133. A. Prévost to Germain, 1 November 1779, in "Papers Relating," 293; "Cruger's Journal," 491; "Wright's Diary," 267. Also see Lawrence, *Storm*, 69; and "Clark's Journal." For the debate relative to the French and rebel retreat, see Benjamin Lincoln and Count d'Estaing, document from Thunderbolt Bluff, 13 October 1779, in Lincoln Papers.

134. Pybus, *Epic Journeys*, 37–40; Alexander A. Lawrence, "General Robert Howe and the British Capture of Savannah in 1778," *GHQ* 36 (1932): 317; and Lawrence, *Storm*, 18, 43, 81; "Return of Loyal Refugees who have come into Georgia for Protection and Assistance," Savannah, 15 April 1780, in CP; Michael L. Lanning, *Defenders of Liberty: African Americans in the Revolutionary War* (New York, 2000), 123–125; and Janice L. Sumter-Edmond, "Free Black Life in Savannah," in *Slavery and Freedom in Savannah*, ed. Leslie M. Harris and Diana Ramey Berry (Athens, 2014), 128. Also see Stuart J. McCulloch, *A Scion of Heroes: The World of Captain James Murray* (Leicestershire, 2005).

135. Gilbert, *Black Patriots*, 124, 133; Gordon Smith, *Morningstars of Liberty* (Milledgeville, 2006), 1:53–57; and Smith, *History of the Georgia Militia, 1783–1861*, 4 vols. (Milledgeville, 2001), 3:128–29; Coleman, *American Revolution*, 183, 265–266; Timothy Lockley, "'The King of England's Soldiers': Armed Blacks in Savannah and Its Hinterlands during the Revolutionary War Era, 1778–1787," in Harris and Berry, *Slavery and Freedom*, 26–41.

136. Clark, "Role," 361; and *RGG*, 18 November 1779. This is likely the plantation of Sophia McGillivray Durant, daughter of Scottish trader Lachlan McGillvray. See J. Norman Heard, ed., *Handbook of the American Frontier: Four Centuries of Indian-White Relationships* (Metuchen, 1987–1998), 4:141. Also see "Wright's Diary," 268; "An English Journal," 15–16. The rebel militia evacuated Savannah's environs on 15 October. Both Lincoln's and d'Estaing's forces began their withdrawal on 18 October.

137. Lawrence, *Storm*, 36–37.

138. "Wright's Diary," 268.

139. Clinton to Germain, 10 November 1779, in CP.

140. Charles Grey to Clinton, 8 November 1779, and William Eden to Clinton, 4 December 1779, in Paul Smith, *Loyalists and Redcoats: A Study in British Revolutionary Policy* (Chapel Hill, 1964), 123, 80.

141. Wright to Germain, 9 November 1779, in *GHS Coll*, 3:270–271.

142. *RGG*, 18 November 1779; "List of Passengers on the vessels of Count D'Es-

taing's Squadron, bound for France, after the Siege of Savannah," dated "end of October 1779," in *FM*, no. 2019; and Wright to Messrs. Clark & Milligan, 4 November 1779, EM 20300, Lincoln Papers.

143. Wright to Germain, 6 November and 9 November 1779, in *GHS Coll*, 3:268–270, 270–271. See also John Ferling, *Winning Independence: The Decisive Years of the Revolutionary War, 1778–1781* (New York, 2021), chap. 11; and Ferling, *Almost a Miracle: The American Victory in the War of Independence* (Oxford, 2007), chap. 16.

144. Wright to Thomas Townshend, 3 September 1782, in CO, 5/116.

145. *Boston Gazette*, 1 November 1779; James Madison to William Bradford, 5 November 1779, John Bondfield to Benjamin Franklin, 3 December 1779, Jonathan Williams Jr. to Franklin, 1 December 1779, and Thomas Digges to Franklin, 4 December 1779, all in FO. For information about Bondfield, see the footnote in John Bondfield to the American Commissioners, 10 August 1777, Benjamin Franklin Papers, FO. Also see Adams to Franklin, 8 December 1779, in FO.

146. Horace Walpole to the Countess of Ossory, 21 December 1779, in *The Letters of Horace Walpole, Earl of Orford*, ed. Peter Cunningham (London, 1857), 7:294–295.

147. Abigail Adams to John Adams, 10 December 1779, diary entry, diary of John Quincy Adams, 24 December 1779, John Adams to Samuel Huntington from Paris, 20 February 1780, Bondfield to Franklin, 13 December 1779, and Adams to Samuel Huntington from Paris, 20 February 1780, all in FO. See also John Laurens to Henry Laurens, Charleston, 23 October 1779, in Lincoln Papers.

148. Wright to Germain, 5 November 1779, in *ColRG*, 38.2:206–209. We are fortunate that Wright chronicled the siege of Savannah. At least two handwritten copies were made, one of which he sent to his London agents; he wished for them to "communicate [it] to my city friends." Wright to Messrs. Clarke & Milligan, 4 November 1779, in *GHS Coll*, 3:286–288; and "Wright's Diary." In this letter, to which the journal was attached, Wright assured Germain that his diary "is as just & true an account of the whole matter as will be transmitted from any hand whatever." For Moncrief's quote, see James Moncrief testimony, 17 November 1783, in James Wright, Loyalist claim, *BGLC*.

149. Stokes, *A Narrative*, 73.

150. 22 October 1779, in *ColRG*, 12:449–450; *RGG*, 23 December 1779; *Rivington's Royal Gazette*, 6 November 1779, quoted in Cole, "Siege of Savannah," 198. Also see Clinton to Newcastle, 19 November 1779, in Papers of Henry Fiennes Pelham-Clinton, 2nd Duke of Newcastle under Lynne (1720–1794), in the Newcastle (Clumber) Collection, University of Nottingham. And see "Chaplain Waldeck's account," 15 November 1779, in Burgoyne, *Enemy Views*, 316–317.

151. *London Gazette*, 20 December 1779; Cole, "Siege of Savannah," 190–198; King George III, 1 November 1780, in *The Parliamentary History of England, 1066–1803*, by William Cobbett (New York, 1966), 21:809. Also see A. Barrister, ed., *The Speeches of the Right Honourable Charles James Fox in the House of Commons* (London, 1853), 2:65; and *The New Annual Register . . . for the Year 1781* (London, 1782), 112.

152. *Caledonian Mercury*, 25 December 1779, quoted in Cole, "Siege of Savannah," 192.

153. *Lloyd's Evening Post*, 26–28 January 1780, quoted in Cole, "Siege of Savannah," 195.

154. *Public Advertiser*, 2 December 1779.

155. *St. James's Chronicle*, 21 December 1779. Also see James Gaston, *London Poets and the American Revolution* (New York, 1979), 215–216. For additional poems of this nature, see Cole, "Siege of Savannah," 191–194.

156. Germain to Wright, 19 January 1780, in *ColRG*, 38.2:247–253; Mansfield to Wright, 19 January 1780, in James Wright, Loyalist claim, in *BGLC*; and A. Prévost, journal entry, 4 October 1779, in *DAR*, 17:246.

157. William Johnson, *Sketches of the Life and Correspondence of Nathanael Greene* (Charleston, 1822), 1:272.

158. Clark, "Role," 361; Tustin, *Diary*, 186; Jones, *Siege of Savannah*, 58–60; Commager and Morris, *Spirit*, 1091–1093; and Lawrence, *Storm*, 92–93.

159. Marquis de Lafayette to the comte de Maurepas, 25 January 1780, in *Lafayette in the Age of the American Revolution: Selected Letters and Papers, 1776–1790*, ed. Stanley Idzerda et al. (Ithaca, 1979), 2:345–349, quote on 346.

160. Adams to Huntington from Paris, 18 April 1780, in FO; *Rivington's Royal Gazette*, 8 December 1779; François Louis Teissedre de Fleury to John Adams, 1 May 1780, in FO. Fleury admitted that the French feared any "rash" endeavors lest "we may find an other Savannah."

161. Lawrence, *Storm*, 73.

162. Cole, "Siege of Savannah," 192. For an example of the role of the rebel militia, see Philip Mazzei to Thomas Jefferson, 18 December 1779, in FO. Mazzei wrote: "We hear that it was the militia who did not keep their ground." He also noted in a letter dated 9 January 1780 that a newspaper in Nantes "takes notice of the great harmony which subsisted between the French and Americans." Dubious, Mazzei added that he hoped such was the case. Also see Chevalier de Kéralio to William Temple Franklin, 8 January 1780, in FO.

163. Wright to Germain, 21 December 1779, in *GHS Coll*, 3:329.

164. Wright to Germain, 4 November 1779, contained in Wright to Germain, 6 April 1780, in *GHS Coll*, 3:286–288. Wright also mentioned the difficulty of operating as a royal governor without any real power of patronage. Also see Peter Richards, *Patronage in British Government* (Toronto, 1963), 247–258.

165. Lawrence, *Storm*, x–xi, 91; Barnet Schecter, *The Battle for New York: The City in the Heart of the American Revolution* (New York, 2002), 330; Jonathan T. Engel, "The Force of Nature: The Impact of Weather during the American War of Independence, 1775–1781" (PhD diss., Florida State university, 2011), 37, 52–55; George Daughan, *Revolution on the Hudson: New York City and the Hudson River Valley in the American War of Independence* (New York, 2016), 233.

### Chapter 8. A Governor Evacuated

1. Wright to Townshend, 3 September 1782, in CO, 5/657. Townshend was the 1st Viscount Sydney. Wright opened this letter: "When I last had the honor to wait on your excellency I mentioned that with your leave, I would lay before you a short sketch of the situation of affairs in the province of Georgia." The Palace of Whitehall is several blocks to the northeast of Downing Street.

2. For the first such instance of this complaint, see Wright to Board of Trade,

13 May 1760, in *Journals of the Board of Trade and Plantations*, ed. K. H. Ledward (London, 1935), 11:154–161; and Wright to Board of Trade, 23 October 1760, in *ColRG*, 28.1:291.

3. Wright to Germain, 20 January 1780, in CO, 5/665. Regarding Wright's departure from London, see Germain to Wright, 8 March 1779, in *DAR*, 16:50; Germain to Wright, 31 March 1779, in *ColRG*, 38.2:155–159; and *Lloyd's Evening Post* (London), 24–26 March 1779: "On Tuesday last Sir James Wright, Governor of Georgia, had the honour to kiss his Majesty's hand, on taking leave previous to his return to the government of that province."

4. John Joachim Zubly to Wright, 30 November 1779, in *GHS Coll*, 21:108–109. For Zubly's loyalties, see, for example, Kenneth Coleman, *The American Revolution in Georgia, 1763–1789* (Athens, 1958), 58 (delegate to the Continental Congress) and 66 (condemned as a Tory).

5. "Proceedings," 5, 10, 19, 25 January and 4 February 1780, *GGCJ*, 1780, 9–12. The quote is from 25 January. Also see Elizabeth Fenn, *Pox Americana: The Great Smallpox Epidemic of 1775–1782* (New York, 2001); John Walker pension, w9875, http://revwarapps.org/w9875.pdf; and James Nelson pension, w9588, http://revwarapps.org/w9588.pdf.

6. "Proceedings," 28 January 1780, in *GGCJ*, 1780, 10–11.

7. Benjamin Quarles, *The Negro in the American Revolution* (Chapel Hill, 1961), 132–133.

8. Wright to Germain, 6 November 1779, in *GHS Coll*, 3:268–270; and Wright to Townshend, 3 September 1782, in CO, 5/176.

9. The quote is in Ruth Holmes Whitehead, *Black Loyalists: Southern Settlers of Nova Scotia's First Free Black Communities* (Halifax, 2013), 112–113, 127–128. Also see *DAR*, 21:140; and Joseph Barnwell, "The Evacuation of Charleston by the British in 1782," *SCHGM* 11, no. 1 (January 1910): 26.

10. Coleman, *American Revolution*, 131.

11. Journal entry, 19 April 1781, in *William Smith's Historical Memoirs*, ed. William Sabine (New York, 1969), 3:400–401. For Arbuthnot's fiery personality, see Andrew Jackson O'Shaughnessy, *The Men Who Lost America: British Leadership, the American Revolution, and the Fate of the Empire* (New Haven, 2013), 8–9, 231–232.

12. Balfour to Cornwallis, 5 November 1780, in *The Cornwallis Papers: The Campaigns of 1780 and 1781 in the Southern Theatre of the American Revolutionary War*, ed. Ian Saberton (Uckfield, 2010), 3:63–68.

13. Wright to William Knox, 16 February 1782, in *GHS Coll*, 3:371–372.

14. See Henry Clinton, *The American Rebellion: Sir Henry Clinton's Narrative of His Campaigns, 1775–1782*, ed. William B. Willcox (New Haven, 1954); and William B. Willcox, *Portrait of a General: Sir Henry Clinton in the War of Independence* (New York, 1964).

15. Germain to Clinton, 8 March 1778, in CP. For analysis of the strategy, see, for example, Paul Smith, *Loyalists and Redcoats: A Study in British Revolutionary Policy* (Chapel Hill, 1964), 82–125, 170–173; Ira Gruber, "Britain's Southern Strategy," in *The Revolutionary War in the South: Power, Conflict, and Leadership; Essays in Honor of John Richard Alden*, ed. W. Robert Higgins (Durham, 1979), 205–238; John Shy, "Brit-

ish Strategy for Pacifying the Southern Colonies, 1778–1781," in *The Southern Experience in the American Revolution*, ed. J. J. Crow and L. E. Tise (Chapel Hill, 1978), 155–173; Jim Piecuch, *Three Peoples: Loyalists, Indians, and Slaves in the Revolutionary South, 1775–1782* (Columbia, 2008), chap. 4; and David K. Wilson, *The Southern Strategy: Britain's Conquest of South Carolina and Georgia, 1775–1780* (Columbia, 2005), 159–164.

16. Shy, "British Strategy," 158–159. For the importance of the potential utility of Native Americans, see Piecuch, *Three Peoples*. For a similar view of African Americans, see Piecuch, *Three Peoples*; and Sylvia Frey, *Water from the Rock: Black Resistance in a Revolutionary Age* (Princeton, 1992).

17. Piecuch, *Three Peoples*, esp. 328–335. Historian Andrew Jackson O'Shaughnessy has claimed that while enlistments of Loyalists increased after 1778, they "barely replaced casualties and desertions" by 1780–1781. O'Shaughnessy, *Men Who Lost America*, 192. Also see Stephen Brumwell, *Redcoats: The British Soldier and War in the Americas, 1755–1763* (Cambridge, 2002), 117; Fred Anderson, *A People's Army: Massachusetts Soldiers and Society in the Seven Years' War* (Chapel Hill, 1984), 111–142; Smith, *Loyalists and Redcoats*, 74–78 (see n14); William H. Nelson, *The American Tory* (Westport, 1980), 143–144; and John Shy, *A People Armed and Numerous: Reflections on the Military Struggle for American Independence* (Ann Arbor, 1990), 130.

18. Clinton to Wright, 20 March 1776, in Clark, *Naval Documents*, 4:428 and n2; and Josiah Martin to Clinton, 20 March 1776, in Clark, *Naval Documents*, 4:429–430.

19. Clinton to Germain, 21 August 1779, in *DAR*, 17:189; and Clinton, *American Rebellion*, 418–419.

20. Wright to Henry Clinton, 29 December 1779, in *RAM*, 2:77.

21. Wright to Clinton, 20 January 1780, in CP. Also see Wright to Germain, 10 February 1780, in *GGCJ*, 1782, 36.

22. Benjamin Lincoln to Thomas Jefferson, 24 January 1780, in FO.

23. Lincoln to Jefferson, 30 January 1780, in FO.

24. Wright to Germain, 18 February 1780, in *GGCJ*, 1780, 13–14, 37. Wright worried that Clinton had given the rebels too much time to prepare their defenses: "I fear many brave men may fall." Also see Clinton to Augustin Prévost, 18 February 1780, Prévost to Clinton, 2 March 1780, and Wright to Germain, 3 February 1780, all in *GGCJ*, 1780, 38–40; and Wright to Clinton, 18 March 1780, in *RAM*, 2:91–92, 96, 103–104. Also see Coleman, *American Revolution*, 130.

25. Wright to Thomas Townshend, 3 September 1782, in CO, 5/116.

26. "Proceedings," 8 March 1780, in *GGCJ*, 1780, 14; and Prévost to Clinton, 13 and 17 February 1780, in *RAM*, 2:89, 91.

27. Wright to Clinton, 3 February 1780, in *GGCJ*, 1780, 38–40, and CP.

28. McKeen Greene pension, w7561, http://revwarapps.org/w7561.pdf; George Gresham pension, w2933, http://revwarapps.org/w2933.pdf; and James McCaw pension, s18117, http://revwarapps.org/s18117.pdf.

29. Clarke to Balfour, 24 January 1781, and Balfour to Clinton, 2 February 1781, in *GGCJ*, 1781, 38. Balfour told Clinton he was unable to meet Wright's and Clarke's request. Balfour wanted to help: Balfour to Wright, 4 and 21 May, in EM 15515 and 15519, Thomas Addis Emmet Collection, New York Public Library.

30. Prévost to Clinton, 2 March 1780, in *RAM*, 2:96.

31. Clinton to Prévost, 8 March 1780, in *RAM*, 2:99.

32. Clinton, *American Rebellion*, 159–160, 162–164 (see n14). Clinton's successor, General Cornwallis, assured Colonel Cruger that "I will give you every assistance in my power . . . [but there is a] great want of men elsewhere" (Cornwallis to Cruger, 23 September 1780, in Saberton, *Cornwallis Papers*, 191–192).

33. Clinton to Wright, 25 March 1780, in CP.

34. Wright to Charles Cornwallis, 3 July 1780, in Saberton, *Cornwallis Papers*, 1:344–345.

35. Wright to Germain, 3 February 1780, in *GGCJ*, 1780, 38–40.

36. Wright to Clinton, 6 April 1780, in CO, 30/15.

37. "Sir Henry Clinton's Manifesto and Proclamation," 3 March 1778, www.digital history/uh.edu.

38. Wright to Clinton, 28 March 1780, in CP.

39. Wright to Germain, 24 March 1780, in CO, 5/665. In this letter, Wright stated his "fear that every Rebel who has fled this province and committed crimes of the blackest dye may come back and claim pardon and protection." Also see Wright to Germain, 20 December 1780, in CO, 5/176; and Wright to Germain, 3 February 1780, in *GGCJ*, 1780, 38–40.

40. Wright to Germain, 4 April 1780, in CO, 5/665.

41. Alured Clarke to Cornwallis, 10 July 1780, in Saberton, *Cornwallis Papers*, 1:339–340; and Cornwallis to Clinton, 6 August 1780, in Coleman, *American Revolution*, 137.

42. 1 February 1780, in *RS*, 2:207–209; and Wright to Germain, 9 June 1780, in *GHS Coll*, 3:305–306.

43. Wright to Germain, 4 April 1780, and Wright to Clinton, 6 April 1780, in CO, 5/665, 30/15.

44. For the best modern study of the siege, see Carl Borick, *A Gallant Defense: The Siege of Charleston, 1780* (Columbia, 2012). Also see Clinton, *American Rebellion*, chap. 11; and Piecuch, *Three Peoples*, chap. 5. For the surrender, see Clinton to Lincoln, 12 May 1780, in Benjamin Lincoln Papers—Siege of Charleston, in Emmet Collection. For the reports of the commanding officers, see Clinton to Germain, 13 May 1780, in CP; and Lincoln to Continental Congress, 24 May 1780, in Benjamin Hough, *The Siege of Charleston* (Albany, 1867), 173–174. Wright first wrote of the successful siege at the end of May. Wright to Germain, 25 May 1780, in *GGCJ*, 1780, 53–54.

45. Wright to Germain, 17 May 1780, in *GGCJ*, 1780, 44–45.

46. Wright to Germain, 20 May 1780, in CO, 5/66; and Wright to Germain, 25 May 1780, in *GGCJ*, 1780, 53–54. In May the districts of Ebenezer and St. Matthew's elected Wright's son Alexander as their representative. See May 1780, in *GGCJ*, 1780, 19; and Wright to Germain, 20 January 1780, in CO, 5/665.

47. Wright to Clinton, 3 June 1780, in *GGCJ*, 1780, 54. This was Wright's way of emphasizing that his promises of support were correct, but Loyalist loyalties depended upon protection. Otherwise, the need for physical safety might necessitate other decisions.

48. Wright to Germain, 9 June 1780, in *GHS Coll*, 3:305–306; and Brown to Cornwallis, 18 and 28 June 1780, in Coleman, *American Revolution*, 131.

49. Robert S. Davis, "A Frontier for Pioneer Revolutionaries: John Dooly and the

Beginnings of Popular Democracy in Original Wilkes County," *GHQ* 90, no. 3 (Fall 2006): 315–349.

50. Wright to Germain, 22 September 1780, in *GHS Coll*, 3:320.

51. Hugh McCall, *History of Georgia* (Atlanta, 1909), 2:326–327.

52. Wright to Germain, 27 October 1780, in *GHS Coll*, 3:321–322; and Wright to Germain, 22 September and 27 October 1780, in *ColRG*, 38.2:435–436, 439–440.

53. Brown to David Ramsay, 25 December 1786, in *HGC*, 614–619.

54. Edward J. Cashin, *The King's Ranger: Thomas Brown and America's Revolution on the Southern Frontier* (New York, 1999), 118.

55. For Kings Mountain, see Robert Dunkerly, *The Battle of Kings Mountain: Eyewitness Accounts* (Charleston, 2012); Lyman Draper, *King's Mountain and Its Heroes* (Baltimore, 1967); Philip Thomas Tucker, *Kings Mountain: America's Most Forgotten Battle That Changed the Course of the American Revolution* (New York, 2021); J. David Dameon, *King's Mountain: The Defeat of the Loyalists, October 7, 1780* (Cambridge, 2003); John Pancake, *This Destructive War: The British Campaign in the Carolinas, 1780–1782* (Tuscaloosa, 1985), 108–121; and John Buchanan, *The Road to Guilford Courthouse: The American Revolution in the Carolinas* (New York, 1997), 208–241.

56. Wright to Germain, 9 June 1780, in *GGCJ*, 1780, 54–55.

57. Clinton, *American Rebellion*, 188–189; Franklyn Wickwire and Mary Wickwire, *Cornwallis and the War of Independence* (London, 1971), chap. 6; Richard Middleton, *Cornwallis: Soldier and Statesman in a Revolutionary World* (New Haven, 2022), chap. 3, esp. 61; and O'Shaughnessy, *Men Who Lost America*, chap. 6.

58. Henry Clinton, Proclamation, 3 June 1780, in Hough, *Siege of Charleston*, 182–184 (see n43).

59. Charles Stedman, *The History of the Origin, Progress, and Termination of the American Revolution* (London, 1794), 2:198–200. Clinton unconvincingly rationalized the decision in his account of his service in America. See Clinton, *American Rebellion*, 181–182. Clinton's biographer, William Willcox, declared the decision ill-advised. See Willcox, *Portrait of a General*, 321–322.

60. John Glen, Memorial, 12 June 1780, James Robertson (Attorney General) to Wright, 10 June 1780, "Proceedings," 14 June 1780, James Houston to Clarke, 21 June 1780, and Robertson to Wright, 22 June 1780, all in *ColRG*, 12:476–477, 475, 478, 479–480, 480–483. Also see "Proceedings," 9, 10, 12, and 14 June 1780, Wright to Germain, 17 August 1780, and Houstoun to Alured Clarke, 21 June 1780, all in *GGCJ*, 1780, 20, 58–59, 479–483.

61. Cornwallis to Clarke, 4 July 1780, in Saberton, *Cornwallis Papers*, 1:334; and James Simpson to Wright, 6 July 1780, in *ColRG*, 12:484–485.

62. "Proceedings," 10 July 1780, in *GGCJ*, 1780, 22–23. It is, however, important to note that Wright's advice for his council may have come after he received Cornwallis's missive to cease and desist.

63. Wright to Germain, 19 July 1780, in *CO*, 5/665.

64. Cornwallis to Wright, 18 and 24 July 1780, Wright to Cornwallis, 3 and 9 July 1780, and Cornwallis to Clarke, 17 July 1780, all in Saberton, *Cornwallis Papers*, 1:346–347, 350–351, 344–345, 347–350, 275–277.

65. Wright to Cornwallis, 28 July 1780, in Saberton, *Cornwallis Papers*, 1:351–353.

66. Wright to Germain, 1 December 1780, in *GHS Coll*, 322–323; 27 September 1780, in *ColRG*, 15:625–627; and Coleman, *American Revolution*, 139. Also see Leslie Hall, *Land and Allegiance in Revolutionary Georgia* (Athens, 2001), 106–112, 129–130.

67. Franklin to C. W. F. Dumas, 10 August 1781, and Robert Livingston to Franklin, 20 October 1781, both in *The Diplomatic Correspondence of the American Revolution*, ed. Jared Sparks (Boston, 1829), 3:235–236, 238–240.

68. Wright to Balfour, 27 July 1781, in *GGCJ*, 1781, 39. Also see Loyalist Papers, ca. 1782, MS 506, GHS. This document, which identifies the struggles of Georgia Loyalists, states that "upwards of 200 men in this province have within the last 12 months been cruelly murdered in cold blood by their inhuman enemies."

69. Balfour to Wright, 1 August 1781, in *GGCJ*, 1781, 39–40.

70. Wright to Balfour, 16 August 1781, in *GGCJ*, 1781, 40–41.

71. Thomas Brown to David Ramsay, 25 December 1786, in *HCG*, 614–619.

72. Coleman, *American Revolution*, 133.

73. Wickwire and Wickwire, *Cornwallis*, 149–165; Jim Piecuch, *The Battle of Camden: A Documentary History* (Charleston, 2006); and Buchanan, *Road to Guilford Courthouse*, 157–172.

74. Wright to Rogers, 25 May 1781, in Thomas Rogers, Loyalist claim, in *BGLC*; Wright to Germain, 18, 22, 25, and 27 September 1780, in CO, 5/665. Note that there are six 18 September letters. Also see Cashin, *King's Ranger*, 114–120; Coleman, *American Revolution*, 133–135; Pancake, *This Destructive War*, 91–107; Hugh McCall, *History of Georgia* (Savannah, 1816), 2:320–333; and "Proceedings," 18 September 1780, in *GGCJ*, 1780, 28–29. Wright also employed his plantation manager, Nathaniel Hall, "in confidential departments," which he completed with "credit and fidelity." See Nathaniel Hall, Loyalist claim, in *BGLC*.

75. Alexander Wright, Loyalist claim, in *BGLC*. Colonels Alexander Innis and Nisbet Balfour and Generals Alexander Leslie, Henry Clinton, Charles Cornwallis, and Augustine Prévost all praised Wright's services.

76. Washington to the president of Congress, 22 October 1780, in FO; and Samuel Huntington to Greene, 31 October 1780, in *PNG*, 6:450–452. For a modern accounting of Greene's substantial ability as a commander, see Gregory Massey and Jim Piecuch, eds., *General Nathanael Greene and the American Revolution in the South* (Columbia, 2012); and Terry Galway, *Washington's General: Nathanael Greene and the Triumph of the American Revolution* (New York, 2005).

77. Wright to Nisbet Balfour, 18 September 1780, in MS 884, James Wright Papers, GHS. Also see Wright to Germain, 27 October 1780, in CO, 5/176.

78. Wright to Assembly, 27 September 1780, in *ColRG*, 15:625–626.

79. Cornwallis to Cruger, 31 August 1780, in Saberton, *Cornwallis Papers*, 2:174–175.

80. Cornwallis to Cruger, 4 September 1780, in Saberton, *Cornwallis Papers*, 2:177–178.

81. Cruger to Balfour, 19 September 1780, and Cruger to Cornwallis, 28 September 1780, both in CO, 30/11.

82. Lieutenant William Stevenson to Mrs. Susannah Kennedy, 25 September 1780, in Cashin, *King's Ranger*, 118; and Heard Robertson, "The Second British Occupation of Augusta, 1780–1781," *GHQ* 58, no. 4 (1974): 422–446.

83. Wright to Clinton, 16 October 1781, in CP.

84. Burke to Arthur Middleton, 6 July 1782, in "Correspondence of Arthur Middleton, Signer of the Declaration of Independence," ed. Joseph Barnwell, *SCHGM* 26, no. 5 (October 1925): 202–206.

85. Wright to Germain, 22 September 1780, in CO, 5/665; and Wright to Germain, 27 October and 1 December 1780, in CO, 5/176.

86. Wright to Clinton, 18 December 1780, in CP. Wright begged for "immediate relief or the province must fall."

87. Wright to Germain, 21 December 1780, in *GGCJ*, 1780, 69.

88. Greg Brooking, "'I Am an Independent Spirit, and Confide in My Own Resources': Nathanael Greene and His Continental Subordinates, 1780–1781," in Massey and Piecuch, *General Nathanael Greene*, 85–118.

89. Banastre Tarleton, *A History of the Campaigns of 1780 and 1781, in the Southern Province of North America* (London, 1787), 215–222; Don Higginbotham, *Daniel Morgan: Revolutionary Rifleman* (Chapel Hill, 1961), 135–155; Larry Babits, *A Devil of a Whipping: The Battle of Cowpens* (Chapel Hill, 1998); Anthony Scotti, *Brutal Virtue: The Myth and Reality of Banastre Tarleton* (Bowie, 2002); John Knight, *War at Saber Point: Banastre Tarleton and the British Legion* (Yardley, 2020); Jim Piecuch, *The Blood Be upon Your Head: Tarleton and the Myth of Buford's Massacre, the Battle of the Waxhaw's, May 29, 1780* (Charleston, 2010); and Buchanan, *Road to Guilford Courthouse*, 296–332.

90. James Grant, *John Adams: Party of One* (New York, 2005), 265.

91. General Orders, 14 February 1781, in FO.

92. *RGG*, 18 January 1781.

93. Wright to Germain, 26 January and 5 March 1781, in *GGCJ*, 1781, 14–17.

94. Wright to Cornwallis, 23 April 1781, in *ColRG*, 38.2:505–508; and Wright to Germain, 5 March 1781, in CO, 5/176. Also see Wright to Cornwallis, 23 April 1781, in Saberton, *Cornwallis Papers*, 5:326–328.

95. Coleman, *American Revolution*, 133–135; and Wright to Cornwallis, 23 April 1781, in Saberton, *Cornwallis Papers*, 5:326–328.

96. Wright to Germain, 24 April 1781, in *ColRG*, 38.2:503–504.

97. Wright to Cornwallis, 23 April 1781, in *ColRG*, 38.2:505–508.

98. Wright to Germain and Cornwallis, 2 April 1781, in *ColRG*, 38.2:494–496; Lawrence Babits and Joshua Howard, *Long, Obstinate, and Bloody: The Battle of Guilford Courthouse* (Chapel Hill, 2009); Buchanan, *Road to Guilford Courthouse*, 372–383; and Pancake, *This Destructive War*, 172–186.

99. Henry Steele Commager and Richard B. Morris, *The Spirit of 'Seventy-Six: The Story of the American Revolution as Told by Participants* (New York, 1968), 1160.

100. Thomas Taylor to the Reverend John Wesley, 28 February 1782, in *GGCJ*, 1781, 144–146.

101. Wright to Germain, 5 and 25 May and 12 June 1781, in *GGCJ*, 1781, 26–29.

102. Wright to Germain, 24 April and 9 March 1781, and Wright to Cornwallis, 23 April 1781, all in *GGCJ*, 1781, 20–24, 24–25, 65–66.

103. Ian Saberton, *The American Revolutionary War in the South: Further Reflections from a British Perspective in the Light of the Cornwallis Papers* (Surrey, 2022), 12–13.

104. Wright to Cornwallis, 23 April 1781, in Saberton, *Cornwallis Papers*, 5:326–328;

Wright to Germain, 1 May and 25 May 1781, both in CO, 5/176. Also see Wright to Germain, 2 April 1781, in which Wright cries that these times "are very distressing & discouraging" (*GGCJ*, 1781, 22).

105. Wright to Germain and Cornwallis, 2 April 1781, in *ColRG*, 38.2:494–496. Wright complained that command of the military now "devolves on a . . . foreigner."

106. For example, see the petition of Valentine Clem, 12 September 1781, in *GGCJ*, 1781, 128; and the petition of John Stirk, 6 April 1782, in *GGCJ*, 1782, 21–22. Also see, for example, *RGG*, 5 January, 14 March, and 23 May 1782. For militia pay, see Thomas Rogers, Loyalist claim, in *BGLC*.

107. "Address of the Upper and Commons House of Assembly to Wright," 27 February 1781, and Wright to Germain, April 2, 1781, both in *GGCJ*, 1781, 19–20, 22.

108. James Grierson to Wright, 4 March 1781, in *GGCJ*, 1781, 19.

109. *RGG*, 26 April 1781.

110. Wright to Germain, 24 April 1781, in *ColRG*, 38.2:503–504.

111. Wright to Germain, 5 May 1781, in *ColRG*, 38.2:518–521.

112. Wright to Germain, 23 April, 1 May, and 5 May 1781, all in *ColRG*, 38.2:505–508, 514, 518–521.

113. Wright to Germain, 25 May 1781, in *ColRG*, 38.2:522–531.

114. Thomas Taylor to the Reverend John Wesley, 28 February 1782, in *GGCJ*, 1781, 144–146.

115. Wright to Germain, 5 May 1781, in MS 884, Wright Papers; and "Proceedings," 8 and 25 May 1781, in *GGCJ*, 1781, 4–6, 27–28.

116. Balfour to Wright, 21 May 1781, in General Leslie's Letter book, EM 15519, Emmet Collection. The British ultimately held the fort at Ninety-Six. Balfour to Wright, 1 August 1781, in EM 15525; and *RGG*, 5 and 12 July 1781.

117. Nathaniel Pendleton to Dr. William Read, 21 May 1781, in *PNG*, 8:291.

118. Wright to Balfour, 11 June 1781, in *GGCJ*, 1781, 29. Wright discussed Grierson's death in this letter and in Wright to Germain, 11 June 1781, in *GGCJ*, 1781, 28. "Poor Grierson was basely murdered after the capitulation & laying down his arms." Also see Wright to Thomas Rogers, 10 June 1781, in Thomas Rogers, Loyalist claim, in *BGLC*; James Grierson's Heirs, Loyalist claim, in *BGLC*; Charles Colcock Jones Jr., *The History of Georgia* (Boston, 1883), 2:477–495; and *HCG*, 611–614.

119. 11 June 1781, in *GGCJ*, 1781, 6–7.

120. Brooking, "'I Am an Independent Spirit,'" 101–103; Cashin, *The King's Ranger*, chap. 7; Wright to Balfour, 11 June 1781, and Wright to Germain, 12 June 1781, both in *ColRG*, 38.2:536–537, 532.

121. Heirs of James Grierson, Loyalist claim, in *BGLC*.

122. Wright to Germain, 14 June 1781, in *GGCJ*, 1781, 30–31.

123. Rawdon to Cornwallis, 5 June 1781, in *GGCJ*, 1781, 115.

124. Germain to Wright, 2 August 1781, in James Wright, Loyalist claim, in *BGLC*.

125. *RGG*, 27 December 1781. Also see Stanley D. M. Carpenter, *Southern Gambit: Cornwallis and the British March to Yorktown* (Norman, 2019), 167–255.

126. Greene to Robert Livingston, 13 December 1781, in Sparks, *Diplomatic Correspondence*, 11:210.

127. *Salem Gazette*, 28 March 1782; and Wright to Germain, 18 December 1781, in *HCG*, 3:360–361 (this volume is in the GHS).

128. N. William Rexall, *Historical Memoirs of My Own Time* (London, 1818), 2:435.

129. Wright to Germain, 18 December 1781, in CO, 5/176. Lafayette never made it to Georgia during the war. In Wright to Germain, 23 April 1781, in *GGCJ*, 1781, 24–25, Wright identified the threats closing in on Savannah from multiple positions.

130. Thomas Taylor to the Reverend John Wesley, 28 February 1782, in *GGCJ*, 1781, 144–146.

131. Wright to Clinton, 18 December 1781, in *GGCJ*, 1781, 171.

132. Wright to Knox, 23 February 1782, in *GHS Coll*, 3:374. For Wayne's "Savannah Campaign," see John Buchanan, *The Road to Charleston: Nathanael Greene and the American Revolution* (Charlottesville, 2019), 311–314; and Paul David Nelson, *Anthony Wayne: Soldier of the Early Republic* (Bloomington, 1985), 163–185. For the destruction, see James Butler, Loyalist claim, in *BGLC*; and Samuel Douglass, Loyalist claim, in *BGLC*.

133. Nelson, *Anthony Wayne*, 94.

134. Coleman, *American Revolution*, 140–142; Greene to Wayne, 9 January 1782, in *PNG*, 10:175–176; John Graham to Germain, 31 January 1782, in *ColRG*, 38.2:568–569; and January 1782 statement, in Mark King Papers, GHS.

135. Wright to Germain, 18 January 1782, in CO, 5/176. Wright informed Germain that a "party of Continental horse" had been edging closer and closer to Savannah in the past "2 or 3 days."

136. Coleman, *American Revolution*, 142.

137. Wright to Germain, 23 January 1782, in CO, 5/176.

138. Wright to Germain, 26 January 1782, in CO, 5/657.

139. Anthony Wayne to Greene, 17 and 26 January 1781, in *PNG*, 10:215, 267–268; Wright to Germain, 18 and 23 January 1782, in *GHS Coll*, 3:362–363, 364; Wayne to Greene, 25 January and 1 February 1782, in Nathanael Greene Papers, CL; Greene to Washington, 12 March 1782, in *PNG*, 10:517–521.

140. Wayne to Greene, 23 January and 28 February 1782, in *PNG*, 10:247; John Graham to Germain, 25 February 1782, in *GGCJ*, 1782, 11–12.

141. Wright to Knox, 12 February 1782, in CO, 5/176.

142. Wright to Knox, 16 February 1782, in *GHS Coll*, 3:271–372.

143. Wright to Germain, 15 February 1782, and Wright to William Knox, 16 February 1782, in CO, 5/176.

144. Wright to Germain, 15 February 1782, and Wright to Knox, 16 February 1782, in CO, 5/176. Also see Saberton, *American Revolutionary War*, 1–21.

145. Wright to Cornwallis, 3 and 28 July 1780, in Saberton, *Cornwallis Papers*, 344–345, 351–353.

146. Wright to Germain, 16 February 1782, in CO, 5/176.

147. Wright to Knox, 23 February 1782, in CO, 5/176. The rebels had also burned no fewer than ten of Wright's barns. "Fine ample protection of government," he sarcastically wrote.

148. For desertion, see Wright to Knox, 23 February 1782, in CO, 5/176. Rebel state governor John Martin issued a proclamation encouraging Hessians to desert. See Coleman, *American Revolution*, 142–143. Also see journal entry, 28 April 1782, in *Revolutionary Journal of Baron Ludwig von Closen*, ed. Evelyn Acomb (Chapel Hill, 1958), 194–195.

149. Eldon Lewis Jones, "Guy Carleton and the Close of the American Revolution, 1782–1783" (PhD diss., Duke University, 1968), iii; and Carleton to Shelburne, 15 August 1782, in *GGCJ*, 1782, 32–33. Also see diary entry, 16 June 1782, in "Diary of Henry Nase, King's American Regiment," transcribed by Todd Braisted, Nase Family Papers, New Brunswick Museum, Saint John, New Brunswick, Canada.

150. Wright to Alexander Leslie, 15 May 1782, in General Leslie's Letter book, Emmet Collection.

151. Wright to Thomas Townshend, 3 September 1782, in CO, 5/116.

152. Wright to Knox, 16 February and 3 March 1782, in CO, 5/176. Also see James Wright, Loyalist claim, in *BGLC*, in which Wright again argued that Georgia would never have entered the revolution had it not been for pressure from the South Carolinians.

153. Coleman, *American Revolution*, 143.

154. Guy Carleton to Leslie, 23 May 1783, in Jones, "Guy Carleton," 178.

155. Leslie to Wright, 4 June 1782, in General Leslie's Letter book, Emmet Collection.

156. Wright to Leslie, 16 June 1782, in *ColRG*, 15:662–663.

157. Leslie to Wright, 20 June 1782, in General Leslie's Letter book, Emmet Collection. For the arrival of the fleet, see Jones, "Guy Carleton," 166–168.

158. Wright to Carleton, 6 July 1782, in *GGCJ*, 1782, 14.

159. Washington to Robert R. Livingston, 14 August 1782, in FO.

160. Wright to Thomas Townshend, 3 September 1782, in CO, 5/116.

161. Robert Lambert, "The Flight of the Georgia Loyalists," *Georgia Review* 17, no. 4 (Winter 1963): 443.

162. Wright to Townshend, 3 September 1782, in CO, 5/116. Also see Francis Dana to Robert Livingston, 29 September 1782, in Sparks, *Diplomatic Correspondence*, 8:373–379.

163. Wright to Townshend, 3 September 1782, in CO, 5/116. This is an incredible letter that fully enumerates the sufferings of Loyalists in Georgia. It is also available in print in *GGCJ*, 1782, 14–17. Also see Anthony Stokes, "Narrative," in *GGCJ*, 1782, 25–26; and Loyalist Papers, ca. 1782, MS 506, GHS.

164. Michael Hattem, *Past and Prologue: Politics and Memory in the American Revolution* (New Haven, 2020), 19–20.

## Epilogue

1. Wright to Guy Carleton, 30 May 1782, film 57, British Headquarters Papers, David Library of the American Revolution (now the David Center for the American Revolution in Philadelphia). For an overview of the Whig confiscation of Loyalist property, see Robert Mitchell, "The Confiscation of Loyalist Property in Georgia, 1782–1786," *WMQ* 20, no. 1 (January 1963): 80–94; and Mitchell, "Loyalist Georgia" (PhD diss., Tulane University, 1964), chaps. 3 and 7. Also see Wright to Germain, 8 October 1777, in CO, 5/665.

2. *Parker's General Advertiser and Morning Intelligencer*, 26 September 1782.

3. Sam Farley (Speaker of the House) to Guy Carleton, 31 May 1782, in *ColRG*, 15:660–661.

4. *Gazette of the State of Georgia*, 4 September 1782, 11 September 1782; *RRSG*, 1:326–347, 373–397. See also James Wright, Loyalist claim, in *BGLC*. Major James Wright would receive half pay for life for his service in the revolution. See "Pensions," in *GGCJ*, 1782, 40–43.

5. Wright to Guy Carleton, 6 July 1782, in *RAM*, 3:11. Also see Wright to Shelburne, 1 September 1782, in Charles Colcock Jones Jr., *The History of Georgia* (Boston, 1883), 2:526. Wright stated that he was "utter[ly] astonished" to receive the order of evacuation from Lieutenant General Alexander Leslie on the fourteenth. See James Wright, Loyalist claim, in *BGLC*.

6. Wright to Townshend, 3 September 1782, in CO, 5/657. For a complete transcription of this lengthy letter, see *GGCJ*, 1782, 14–17.

7. *RGG*, 6 June 1782. The dinner was provided for by a "Mr. Lewis at his own house and Mrs. Tondee's."

8. *Morning Chronicle and London Advertiser*, 24 August 1782. This news appeared in several other London papers as well. See also Eldon Lewis Jones, "Guy Carleton and the Close of the American Revolution, 1782–1783" (PhD diss., Duke University, 1968), 168–169.

9. Lyttelton to Knox, 14 July 1782, in William Knox and Howard Vicenté Knox, *Manuscripts of Captain H. V. Knox* (Boston, 1972), 187–188.

10. Wright to Shelburne, 16 December 1777, James Wright, Loyalist claim, in *BGLC*.

11. *Morning Herald and Daily Advertiser*, 30 August 1782. Wright also attended numerous levees. See *Parker's General Advertiser and Morning Intelligencer* and *Morning Herald and Daily Advertiser*, 12 September 1782; *London Courant and Daily Advertiser*, September 20, 1782; *Parker's General Advertiser and Morning Intelligencer*, 16 October 1782.

12. Samuel Curwen to Judge [Thomas] Sewell, 31 December 1776, in *The Journal and Letters of Samuel Curwen*, ed. George Ward (Boston, 1864), 100–102.

13. John Eardley-Wilmot, *Historical View of the Commission for Enquiring into the Losses, Services, and Claims of the American Loyalists at the Close of the War between Great Britain and her Colonies in 1783* (Boston, 1972), 17–20, 51–55. In March 1784 Colonel Robert Kingston, Colonel Thomas Dundas, and John Marsh were added to the commission (44).

14. See each volume of Mary Bondurant Warren et al., *Georgia Governor and Council Journals*, which span the entirety of Wright's gubernatorial career. Also see *BGLC*.

15. Abigail Adams to Isaac Smith Jr., 30 June 1785, in FO.

16. *London Chronicle*, 15 February 1783. See also *Morning Chronicle and London Advertiser*, 18 April 1783; and *General Evening Post*, 19 April 1783.

17. Eardley-Wilmot, *Historical View*, 46–47.

18. Laurens to Ralph Izard, 23 April 1783, in *PHL*, 16:187–190. Wright's son Alexander had married into the Izard family.

19. *The Case and Claim of the American Loyalists: Impartially Stated and Considered* (London, 1783), 7, 9.

20. *Case and Claim*, 17, 38.

21. "The Particular Case of the Georgia Loyalists: in addition to the General Case and Claim of the American Loyalists," February 1783. See AO, 13/85. The letter is Ger-

main to Wright, 2 August 1781. See also Robert Mitchell, "The Losses and Compensation of Georgia Loyalists," *GHQ* 68, no. 2 (Summer 1984): 233–243.

22. *BGLC*. Also see Mitchell, "Losses and Compensation," 235.

23. Henry Ferguson, Loyalist claim, in *BGLC*.

24. George Johnston, Loyalist claim, in *BGLC*.

25. Samuel Montgomery, Loyalist claim, in *BGLC*.

26. "James Wright Inventory," 3 January 1777 and 1 March 1778, in James Wright, Loyalist claim, in *BGLC*; and 4 May 1782, in CO, 5/657. Also see Wright to Shelburne, 21 November 1782, in AO, 12/4.

27. Mitchell, "Losses and Compensation," 239–240. See also Eardley-Wilmot, *Historical View*, 47. Bear in mind that at the time James Wright arrived in Georgia, the departing governor claimed that the colony could not boast even ten men worth £500 sterling. Ellis to Board of Trade, 11 March 1757, in *ColRG*, 28.1:2–14. Also see James Wright, Loyalist claim, in *BGLC*.

28. Wallace Brown, *King's Friends: The Composition and Motives of the American Loyalist Claimants* (Providence, 1965), 231–246. More recent research has also found that Loyalists came from a wide variety of backgrounds. See, for example, Maya Jasanoff, *Liberty's Exiles: American Loyalists in the Revolutionary World* (New York, 2011); and Holger Hoock, *Scars of Independence: America's Violent Birth* (Cambridge, 2017).

29. Wright to George Rose, 16 February 1785, in James Wright, Loyalist claim, in *BGLC*.

30. Wright's headstone is within a couple of dozen steps from the north entrance but is barely visible. His stone is also omitted from the official Westminster Abbey guide to headstones.

31. *Morning Chronicle and London Advertiser*, 24 November 1785.

32. *Gazette of the State of Georgia*, 23 February 1786.

33. Bernard Bailyn, *The Ordeal of Thomas Hutchinson* (Oxford, 1976), 25. Wright acquired so much land that at some point one must wonder whether he, like his former friend Henry Laurens, came to realize he had spent far too much time in the pursuit, cultivation, and management of land. After the war Laurens examined his "impoverished and almost ruined" estates and lamented that he had "abundantly more land than one man ought to hold." Quoted in S. Max Edelson, *Plantation Enterprise in Colonial South Carolina* (Cambridge, 2011), 1.

34. Wright to Dartmouth, 8 July 1775, in *GHS Coll*, 3:191–192; and Gordon S. Wood, *The Radicalism of the American Revolution* (New York, 1992), 214.

# INDEX

EARLY AMERICAN PLACES

*On Slavery's Border: Missouri's*
*Small Slaveholding Households, 1815–1865*
BY DIANE MUTTI BURKE

*Sounds American: National Identity and the Music Cultures*
*of the Lower Mississippi River Valley, 1800–1860*
BY ANN OSTENDORF

*The Year of the Lash: Free People of Color in Cuba*
*and the Nineteenth–Century Atlantic World*
BY MICHELE REID–VAZQUEZ

*Ordinary Lives in the Early Caribbean:*
*Religion, Colonial Competition, and the Politics of Profit*
BY KIRSTEN BLOCK

*Creolization and Contraband:*
*Curaçao in the Early Modern Atlantic World*
BY LINDA M. RUPERT

*An Empire of Small Places: Mapping the*
*Southeastern Anglo–Indian Trade, 1732–1795*
BY ROBERT PAULETT

*Everyday Life in the Early English Caribbean:*
*Irish, Africas, and the Construction of Difference*
BY JENNY SHAW

*Natchez Country: Indians, Colonists, and the*
*Landscapes of Race in French Louisiana*
BY GEORGE EDWARD MILNE

*Slavery, Childhood, and Abolition in Jamaica, 1788–1838*
BY COLLEEN A. VASCONCELLOS

*Privateers of the Americas: Spanish American Privateering*
*from the United States in the Early Republic*
BY DAVID HEAD

*Charleston and the Emergence of*
*Middle–Class Culture in the Revolutionary Era*
BY JENNIFER L. GOLOBOY

*Anglo–Native Virginia: Trade, Conversion, and*
*Indian Slavery in the Old Dominion, 1646–1722*
BY KRISTALYN MARIE SHEFVELAND

*Slavery on the Periphery: The Kansas–Missouri*
*Border in the Antebellum and Civil War Eras*
BY KRISTEN EPPS

*In the Shadow of Dred Scott: St. Louis Freedom Suits and*
*the Legal Culture of Slavery in Antebellum America*
BY KELLY M. KENNINGTON

Milton Keynes UK
Ingram Content Group UK Ltd.
UKHW011820150724
445436UK00019B/229